Lecture Notes in Computer Science 5299

Commenced Publication in 1973
Founding and Former Series Editors:
Gerhard Goos, Juris Hartmanis, and Jan van Leeuwen

Johannes Buchmann   Jintai Ding (Eds.)

Post-Quantum Cryptography

Second International Workshop, PQCrypto 2008
Cincinnati, OH, USA, October 17-19, 2008
Proceedings

 Springer

Volume Editors

Johannes Buchmann
Technische Universität Darmstadt
Fachbereich Informatik
Hochschulstraße 10, 64289 Darmstadt, Germany
E-mail: buchmann@cdc.informatik.tu-darmstadt.de

Jintai Ding
The University of Cincinnati
Department of Mathematical Sciences
P.O. Box 210025, Cincinnati, OH 45221-0025, USA
E-mail: jintai.ding@uc.edu

Library of Congress Control Number: 2008936091

CR Subject Classification (1998): E.3, D.4.6, K.6.5, F.2.1-2, C.2, H.4.3

LNCS Sublibrary: SL 4 – Security and Cryptology

ISSN   0302-9743
ISBN-10   3-540-88402-5 Springer Berlin Heidelberg New York
ISBN-13   978-3-540-88402-6 Springer Berlin Heidelberg New York

Springer is a part of Springer Science+Business Media

springer.com

© Springer-Verlag Berlin Heidelberg 2008

Typesetting: Camera-ready by author, data conversion by Scientific Publishing Services, Chennai, India
Printed on acid-free paper   SPIN: 12538829   06/3180   5 4 3 2 1 0

Preface

Three decades ago public-key cryptosystems made a revolutionary breakthrough in cryptography. They have developed into an indispensable part of our modern communication system. In practical applications RSA, DSA, ECDSA, and similar public key cryptosystems are commonly used. Their security depends on assumptions about the difficulty of certain problems in number theory, such as the Integer Prime Factorization Problem or the Discrete Logarithm Problem.

However, in 1994 Peter Shor showed that quantum computers could break any public-key cryptosystem based on these hard number theory problems. This means that if a reasonably powerful quantum computer could be built, it would put essentially all modern communication into peril. In 2001, Isaac Chuang and Neil Gershenfeld implemented Shor's algorithm on a 7-qubit quantum computer. In 2007 a 16-qubit quantum computer was demonstrated by a start-up company with the prediction that a 512-qubit or even a 1024-qubit quantum computer would become available in 2008. Some physicists predicted that within the next 10 to 20 years quantum computers will be built that are sufficiently powerful to implement Shor's ideas and to break all existing public key schemes. Thus we need to look ahead to a future of quantum computers, and we need to prepare the cryptographic world for that future.

The research community has put much effort into developing quantum computers and at the same time searching for alternative public-key cryptosystems that could resist these quantum computers. Post-quantum cryptography is a new fast developing area, where public key cryptosystems are studied that could resist these emerging attacks. Currently there are four families of public-key cryptosystems that have the potential to resist quantum computers: the code-based public-key cryptosystems, the hash-based public-key cryptosystems, the lattice-based public-key cryptosystems and the multivariate public-key cryptosystems.

Clearly there is a need to organize an event for researchers working in this area to present their results, to exchange ideas and, most importantly, to allow the world to know what is the state of art of research in this area. In May of 2006, the First International Workshop on Post-Quantum Cryptography was held at the Catholic University of Louven in Belgium with support from the European Network of Excellence for Cryptology (ECRYPT), funded within the Information Societies Technology Programme (IST) of the European Commission's Sixth Framework Programme. This workshop did not have formal proceedings.

PQCrypto 2008, the Second International Workshop on Post-Quantum Cryptography, was held at the University of Cincinnati in Cincinnati, USA, October 17–19. This meeting was sponsored by the University of Cincinnati, the Taft Research Center and FlexSecure®GmbH. This workshop had a devoted international Program Committee, who worked very hard to evaluate and select the high-quality papers for presentations. Each paper was anonymously reviewed by at least three Program Committee members. Revised versions of the accepted papers are published in these proceedings.

We would like to thank all the authors for their support in submitting their papers and the authors of the accepted papers for their efforts in making these proceedings possible on time. We are very grateful to the Program Committee members for devoting for their time and efforts in reviewing and selecting the papers and we are also very grateful to the external reviewers for their efforts.

We would like to thank the efforts of the local Organization Committee, in particular, Timothy Hodges and Dieter Schmidt, without whose support this workshop would not be possible. We would also like to thank Richard Harknett, Chair of the Taft research center, for his support.

We would like to thank the Easychair electronic conference system, which made the handling of the submission and reviewing process easy and efficient. In addition, we would like to thank Daniel Cabarcas for managing all the electronic processes.

We would also like to thank Springer, in particular Alfred Hofmann and Anna Kramer for their support in publishing these proceedings.

August 2008   Johannes Buchmann
                                                 Jintai Ding

Organization

PQCrypto 2008 was organized by the Department of Mathematical Sciences, University of Cincinnati.

Executive Committee

Program Chairs   Johannes Buchmann (Technical University of Darmstadt)
Jintai Ding (University of Cincinnati)
General Chair   Timothy Hodges (University of Cincinnati)
Local Committee   Timothy Hodges (University of Cincinnati)
Jintai Ding (University of Cincinnati)
Dieter Schmidt (University of Cincinnati)

Program Committee

Gernot Albert, Germany
Koichiro Akiyama, Japan
Daniel J. Bernstein, USA
Claude Crepeau, Canada
Cunshen Ding, China
Bao Feng, Singapore
Louis Goubin, France
Tor Helleseth, Norway
Tanja Lange, The Netherlands
Christof Paar, Germany

Louis Salvail, Denmark
Werner Schindler, Germany
Nicolas Sendrier, France
Alice Silverberg, USA
Martijn Stam, Switzerland
Michael Szydlo, USA
Shigeo Tsujii, Japan
Thomas Walther, Germany
Chaoping Xing, Singapore
Bo-yin Yang, Taipei

Referees

G. Albert
K. Akiyama
R. Avanzi
J. Baena
D. Bernstein
J. Buchmann
D. Cabarcas
C. Clough
C. Crepeau
A. Diene
C. Ding

J. Ding
B. Feng
R. Fujita
P. Gaborit
M. Gotaishi
L. Goubin
T. Helleseth
T. Lange
X. Nie
C. Paar
L. Salvail

W. Schindler
N. Sendrier
A. Silverberg
M. Stam
M. Szydlo
K. Tanaka
S. Tsujii
T. Walther
C. Xing
B. Yang

Sponsors

The Taft Research Center at the University of Cincinnati
Department of Mathematical Sciences, University of Cincinnati
FlexSecure®GmbH, Darmstadt, Germany

Table of Contents

A New Efficient Threshold Ring Signature Scheme Based on Coding Theory

Carlos Aguilar Melchor, Pierre-Louis Cayrel, and Philippe Gaborit

Université de Limoges, XLIM-DMI,
123, Av. Albert Thomas 87060 Limoges Cedex, France
{carlos.aguilar,pierre-louis.cayrel,philippe.gaborit}@xlim.fr

Abstract. Ring signatures were introduced by Rivest, Shamir and Tauman in 2001. Bresson, Stern and Szydlo extended the ring signature concept to t-out-of-N threshold ring signatures in 2002. We present in this paper a *generalization* of Stern's code based authentication (and signature) scheme to the case of t-out-of-N threshold ring signature. The size of our signature is in $\mathcal{O}(N)$ and does not depend on t. Our protocol is anonymous and secure in the random oracle model, it has a very short public key and has a complexity in $\mathcal{O}(N)$. This protocol is the first efficient code-based ring signature scheme and the first code-based threshold ring signature scheme. Moreover it has a better complexity than number-theory based schemes which have a complexity in $\mathcal{O}(Nt)$.

Keywords: Threshold ring signature, code-based cryptography, Stern's Scheme,syndrome decoding.

1 Introduction

In 1978, McEliece published a work where he proposed to use the theory of *error correcting codes* for confidentiality purposes. More precisely, he designed an asymmetric encryption algorithm whose principle may be sum up as follows: Alice applies a secret encoding mecanisms to a message and add to it a large number of errors, that can only be corrected by Bob who has information about the secret encoding mechanisms. The *zero-knowledge* authentication scheme proposed by Stern in [24] is based on a well-known error-correcting codes problem usually referred as the *Syndrome Decoding Problem* (*SD* in short). It is therefore considered as a good alternative to the numerous authentication schemes whose security relies on number theory problems, like the factorization and the discrete logarithm problems.

The concept of *ring signature* was introduced by Rivest, Shamir and Tauman [20] (called RST in the following). A ring signature is considered to be a simplified group signature without group managers. Ring signatures are related, but incomparable, to the notion of group signatures in [8]. On one hand, group signatures have the additional feature that the anonymity of a signer can be revoked (i.e. the signer can be traced) by a designated group manager, on the other hand, ring signatures allow greater flexibility: no centralized group

J. Buchmann and J. Ding (Eds.): PQCrypto 2008, LNCS 5299, pp. 1–16, 2008.

manager or coordination among the various users is required (indeed, users may be unaware of each other at the time they generate their public keys). The original motivation was to allow secrets to be leaked anonymously. For example, a high-ranking government official can sign information with respect to the ring of all similarly high-ranking officials, the information can then be verified as coming from someone reputable without exposing the actual signer.

Bresson et al. [5] extended the ring signature scheme into a *threshold ring signature* scheme using the concept of partitioning and combining functions. Assume that t users want to leak some secret information, so that any verifier will be convinced that t users *among a select group* held for its validity. Simply constructing t ring signatures clearly does not prove that the message has been signed by different signers. A *threshold ring signature* scheme effectively proves that a minimum number of users of a certain group must have actually collaborated to produce the signature, while hiding the precise membership of the subgroup (for example the ring of public keys of all members of the President's Cabinet).

Contribution. In this paper, we present a *generalization* of Stern's authentication and signature scheme [24] for ring and threshold ring signature schemes. Our scheme's performance does not depend on the number t of signers in the ring, the overall complexity and length of signatures only depend linearly in the maximum number of signers N. Our protocol also guarantees computational anonymity in the random oracle model. Besides these features and its efficiency, our protocol is also the first non generic coding theory based ring signature (and threshold ring signature) protocol and may constitute an interesting alternative to number theory based protocols. Overall our protocol has a very short public key size, a signature length linear in N and the best known complexity in $\mathcal{O}(N)$ when other number theory based threshold ring signature schemes have a complexity in $\mathcal{O}(Nt)$.

Organization of the paper. The rest of this paper is organized as follows. In Section 2, we give a state of the art of ring signature and threshold ring signature. In Section 3, we describe Stern's authentication and signature scheme and give some backround and notation. In Section 4, we present our new *generalization* of Stern's scheme in a threshold ring signature context. In Section 5, we study the security of the proposed scheme. In Section 6 we consider a variation of the protocol with double circulant matrices. In Section 7 we discuss the signature cost and length. Finally, we conclude in Section 8.

2   Overview of Ring Signatures

2.1   Ring Signature

Following the formalization about ring signatures proposed in [20], we explain in this section the basic definitions and the properties eligible to ring signature schemes. One assumes that each user has received (via a PKI or a certificate) a public key p_{k_i}, for which the corresponding secret key is denoted s_{k_i}. A regular ring signature scheme consists of the following triple (Key-Gen, Sign and Verify):

- **Key-Gen** is a probabilistic polynomial algorithm that takes a security parameter(s) and returns the system, private, and public parameters.
- **Sign** is a probabilistic polynomial algorithm that takes system parameters, a private parameter, a list of public keys $p_{k_1}, , p_{k_N}$ of the ring, and a message M. The output of this algorithm is a ring signature σ for the message M.
- **Verify** is a deterministic algorithm that takes as input a message M, a ring signature σ, and the public keys of all the members of the corresponding ring, then outputs *True* if the ring signature is valid, or *False* otherwise.

Most of the existing ring signature schemes have a signature length linear in N, the size of the ring. Many schemes have been proposed, one can cite the work of Bendery,Katzyz and Morselli in [2] where they present three ring signature schemes which are provably secure in the standard model. Recently, Shacham and Waters [22] proposed a ring signature where for N members the signature consists of $2N + 2$ group elements and requires $2N + 3$ pairings to verify.

A breathrough on the size of ring signature was obtained in [10] in which the authors proposed the first (and unique up to now) constant-size scheme based on accumulator functions and the Fiat-Shamir zero-knowledge identification scheme. However, the signature derived from the Fiat-Shamir scheme has a size of at least 160 kbits. Another construction proposed by Chandran, Groth and Sahai ([7]) has a size in $\mathcal{O}(\sqrt{N})$.

Recently in [32], Zheng, Li and Chen presented a code-based ring signature scheme with a signature length of $144 + 126N$ bits, but this scheme is based on the signature of [9] which remains very slow in comparison with other schemes.

Eventually a generalization of ring signature schemes in mesh signatures was proposed by Boyen in [4].

2.2   Threshold Ring Signature

In [5], Bresson, Stern and Szydlo introduced the notion of threshold ring signature. We explain in this section the basic definitions and the properties of threshold ring signature schemes.

One assumes that each user has created or received a secret key s_{k_i} and that a corresponding public key p_{k_i} is availabe to everyone.

Let $A_1, \ldots, A_N$ be the N potential signers of the ring with their $p_{k_1}, , p_{k_N}$ public keys. Then t of the N members form a group of signers, one of them, L, is the leader on the t-subgroup.

- Setup : initializes the state of the system. On input a security parameter 1^l, create a public database $p_{k_1}, , p_{k_N}$, choose a leader L of the group and generate the system's parameters;
- Make-GPK : the Group Public Key construction algorithm;
- Commitment-Challenge-Answer : an electronic way to temporarily hide a sequence of bits that cannot be changed;
- Verification : takes as input the answers of the challenges and verifies the honestly of the computation, and returns a boolean.

In [5], the size of the signature grows with the number of users N and the number of signers t. More precisely, the size of such t-out-of-N signature is : $2^{\mathcal{O}(t)}\lceil \log_2 N \rceil \times (tl + Nl)$ computations in the easy direction where l is the security parameter.

Later, Liu et al. [15] proposed another threshold ring signature based on Shamir's secret sharing scheme. Their scheme is separable, with a signature length linear in N but a complexity in $\mathcal{O}(N^2)$ for $t \approx N/2$ (the cost of secret sharing scheme). The Mesh signature of [4] can also be used in that case: the signature length is also linear in N but the verification is in Nt bilinear pairings verifications.

A variation for ring signature was introduced in [26], where the author introduced the notion of *linkable ring signature* by which a signer can sign only once being anonymous, since a verifier can link a second signature signed by the same signer. Although this property may have interesting applications (in particular for e-vote) it does not provide full anonymity (in the sense that it cannot be repeated). Later their scheme was extended to threshold ring signature with a complexity in $\mathcal{O}(N)$, but again, only a linkable ring signature which does not correspond to original researched feature of [20] and [5], a fully anonymous scheme.

3   Notation and Backround on Coding Theory and Stern's Signature Scheme

3.1   Permutation Notation

We first introduce two notions of *block permutation* that we will use in our protocol. Consider n and N two integers.

Definition 3.1. *A constant n-block permutation Σ on N blocks is a permutation by block which permutes together N blocks of length n block by block. Each block being treated as a unique position as for usual permutations.*

A more general type of permutation is the n-block permutation Σ on N blocks.

Definition 3.2. *A n-block permutation Σ on N blocks is a permutation which satisfies that the permutation of a block of length n among N blocks is exactly included in a block of length n.*

A constant n-block permutation is a particular n-block permutation in which the blocks are permuted as such. For instance the permutation $(6, 5, 4, 3, 2, 1)$ is 2-block permutation on 3 blocks and the permutation $(3, 4, 5, 6, 1, 2)$ is a constant 2-block permutation on 3 blocks since the order on each block $((1, 2), (3, 4)$ and $(5, 6))$ is preserved in the block permutation.

The notion of product permutation is then straightforward. Let us define σ, a family of N permutations $(\sigma_1, \ldots, \sigma_N)$ of $\{1, \ldots, n\}$ on n positions and Σ a constant n-block permutation on N blocks defined on $\{1, \ldots, N\}$. We consider a vector v of size nN of the form :

$$v = (v_1, v_2, \ldots, v_n, v_{n+1}, \ldots, v_{n+n}, v_{2n+1}, \ldots, v_{nN}),$$

we denote V_1 the first n coordinates of v and V_2 the n following coordinates and so on, to obtain: $v = (V_1, V_2, ..., V_N)$. We can then define a n-block permutation on N blocks, $\Pi = \Sigma \circ \sigma$ as

$$\Pi(w) = \Sigma \circ \sigma(w) = (\sigma_1(W_{\Sigma(1)}), \ldots, \sigma_N(W_{\Sigma(N)})) = \Sigma(\sigma_1(W_1), \cdots, \sigma_N(W_N)).$$

3.2 Difficult Problems in Coding Theory

Let us recall recall that a linear binary code C of length n and dimension k, is a vector subspace of of dimension k of $GF(2)^n$. The weight of an element x of $GF(2)^n$ is the number of non zero coordinates of x. The minimum distance of a linear code is the minimum weight of any non-zero vector of the code. For any code one can define the scalar product $x.y = \sum_{i=1}^{n} x_i y_i$. A generator matrix G of a code is a generator basis of a code, the dual of code C is defined by $C^{perp} = \{y \in GF(2)^n | x.y = 0, \forall x \in C\}$. Usually a generator matrix of the dual of a code C is denoted by H. Remark that $c \in C <=> Hc^t = 0$. For $x \in GF(2)^n$, the value Hx^t is called the syndrome of x for H.

The usual hard problem considered in coding theory is the following Syndrome Decoding (SD) problem, proven NP-complete in [3] in 1978.

Problem:(SD) Syndrome decoding of a random code:

Instance: A $n - k \times n$ random matrix H over $GF(2)$, a non null target vector $y \in GF(2)^{(n-k)}$ and an integer ω.

Question: Is there $x \in GF(2)^n$ of weight $\leq \omega$, such that $Hx^t = y^t$?

This problem was used by Stern for his protocol [24], but in fact a few years later a variation on this problem called the Minimum Distance (MD) problem was also proven NP-complete in [27]:

Problem: (MD) Minimum Distance:
Instance: A binary $n - k \times n$ matrix H and an integer $\omega > 0$.
Question: Is there a non zero $x \in GF(2)^n$ of weight $\leq \omega$, such that $Hx^t = 0$?

It was remarked in [12] that this problem could also be used with Stern's scheme, the proof works exactly the same. Notice that the practical difficulty of both SD and MD problems are the same: the difficulty of finding a word of small weight in a random code. The associated intractable assumptions associated to these problems are denoted by **SD assumption** and **MD assumption**, see [25] for a precise formal definition of the SD assumption related to the SD problem.

3.3 Stern's Authentication Scheme

This scheme was developed in 1993 (see [24]). It provides a zero-knowledge authentication scheme, not based on number theory problems. Let h be a hash function. Given a public random matrix H of size $(n - k) \times n$ over $\mathbb{F}_2$. Each user receives a secret key s of n bits and of weight ω. A user's public identifier is the secret's key syndrome $i_L = Hs^t$. It is calculated once in the lifetime of H. It can thus be used by several future identifications. Let us suppose that L wants to prove to V that he is indeed the person corresponding to the public identifier i_L. L has his own private key s_L such that the public identifier is its syndrome $i_L = Hs_L^t$.

Our two protagonists run the following protocol :

---

1. [Commitment Step] L randomly chooses $y \in \mathbb{F}^n$ and a permutation σ of $\{1, 2, \ldots, n\}$. Then L sends to V the commitments c_1, c_2 and c_3 such that :

$$c_1 = h(\sigma | Hy^t); \quad c_2 = h(\sigma(y)); \quad c_3 = h(\sigma(y \oplus s))$$

   where $h(a|b)$ denotes the hash of the concatenation of the sequences a and b.
2. [Challenge Step] V sends $b \in \{0, 1, 2\}$ to L.
3. [Answer Step] Three possibilities :
   − if $b = 0$: L reveals y and σ.
   − if $b = 1$: L reveals $(y \oplus s)$ and σ.
   − if $b = 2$: L reveals $\sigma(y)$ and $\sigma(s)$.
4. [Verification Step] Three possibilities :
   − if $b = 0$: V verifies that c_1, c_2 have been honestly calculated.
   − if $b = 1$: V verifies that c_1, c_3 have been honestly calculated.
   − if $b = 2$: V verifies that c_2, c_3 have been honestly calculated, and that the weight of $\sigma(s)$ is ω.
5. Iterate the steps 1,2,3,4 until the expected security level is reached.

Fig. 1. Stern's protocol

Remark 1. During the fourth Step, when b equals 1, it can be noticed that Hy^t derives directly from $H(y \oplus s)^t$ since we have:

$$Hy^t = H(y \oplus s)^t \oplus i_A = H(y \oplus s)^t \oplus Hs^t .$$

It is proven in [24] that this scheme is a zero-knowledge Fiat-Shamir like scheme with a probability of cheating in $2/3$ (rather than in $1/2$ for Fiat-Shamir).

Remark 2. In [12] the authors propose a variation on the scheme by taking the secret key to be a small word of the code associated to H. The Minimum Distance problem MD, defined in the previous section. This results in exactly the same protocol except that, as the secret key is a codeword, the public key (i.e. the secret key's syndrome) is not the matrix H and the syndrome but only the matrix H. The protocol remains zero-knowledge with the same feature. The problem of finding a small weight codeword in a code has the same type of complexity that the syndrome decoding problem (and is also NP-complete).

The only drawback of this point of view is that it relates the secret key with the matrix H but in our case we will be able to take advantage of that.

4   Our Threshold Ring Signature Scheme

In this section, we describe a new efficient threshold ring identification scheme based on coding theory. This scheme is a *generalization* of Stern's scheme. Furthermore, by applying the Fiat-Shamir heuristics [11] to our threshold ring identification scheme, we immediately get a t-out-of-N threshold ring signature which size is in $\mathcal{O}(N)$.

4.1   High-Level Overview

Consider a ring of N members $(P_1, \cdots, P_N)$ and among them t users who want to prove that they have been cooperating to produce a ring signature. Each user P_i computes a public matrix H_i of $(n - k) \times n$ bits. A user's public key consists of the public matrix H_i and an integer w (common to all public keys). The associated secret key is s_i a word of weight w of the code C_i associated to the dual of H_i.

The general idea of our protocol is that each of the t signers performs by himself an instance of Stern's scheme using matrix H_i and a null syndrome as parameters (as in the scheme's variation proposed in [12]). The results are collected by a leader L among the signers in order to form, with the addition of the simulation of the $N - t$ non-signers, a new interactive Stern protocol with the verifier V. The master public matrix H is created as the direct sum of the ring members' public matrices. Eventually, the prover P, formed by the set of t

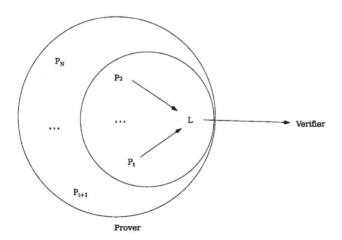

Fig. 2. Threshold ring signature scheme in the case where the t signers are $P_1, \cdots, P_t$ and the leader $L = P_1$, for a group of N members

signers among N (see Fig 2), proves (by a slightly modified Stern's scheme - one adds a condition on the form of the permutation) to the verifier V that he knows a codeword s of weight tw with a particular structure:s has a null syndrome for H and a special form on its N blocks of length n: each block of length has weight 0 or ω. In fact this particular type of word can only be obtained by a cooperation processus between t members of the ring. Eventually the complexity is hence the cost of N times the cost of a Stern authentication for a single prover (the multiplication factor obtained on the length of the matrix H used in the protocol) and this *for any value of t*.

Besides the combination of two Stern protocols (one done individually by each signer P_i with the leader, and one slightly modified done by the leader with the verifier), our scheme relies on the three following main ideas:

1. The master public key H is obtained as the direct sum of all the public matrices H_i of each of the N users.

2. Indistinguashability among the members of the ring is obtained first, by taking a common syndrome value for all the members of the ring: the null syndrome, and second, by taking secret keys s_i with the same weight ω (public value) associated to public matrices H_i.

3. Permutation constraint: a constraint is added in Stern's scheme on the type of permutation used: instead of using a permutation of size Nn we use a n-block permutation on N blocks, which guarantees that the prover knows a word with a special structure, which can only be obtained by the interaction of t signers.

4.2   Setup

The Setup algorithm is run to obtain the values of the parameters l, n, k, t, w. l is the security parameter, n and $n - k$ the matrix parameters, ω the weight of the secret key s_i, t the number of signers. This algorithm also creates a public database $p_{k_1},, p_{k_N}$, (here matrices H_i). remark that parameters:n, k and ω are fixed once for all, and that any new user knowing these public parameters can join the ring. The parameter t has just to be precised at the beginning of the protocol.

The matrices H_i are constructed in the following way: choose s_i a random vector of weight ω, generate $k - 1$ random vectors and consider the code C_i obtained by these k words (the operation can be reiterated until the dimension is exactly k). The matrix H_i is then a $(n - k) \times n$ generator matrix of the dual code of C_i. Remark that this construction lead to a rather large public matrix H_i, we will consider in Section 7, an intersting variation of the construction.

4.3   Make-GPK

Each user owns a $(n - k) \times n$-matrix H_i (public) and a n-vector s_i (secret) of small weight ω (public) such that

$$H_i s_i^t = 0.$$

1. [Commitment Step]
   - Each of the signers chooses $y_i \in \mathbb{F}_2^n$ randomly and a random permutation σ_i of $\{1, 2, \ldots, n\}$ and sends to L the commitments $c_{1,i}, c_{2,i}$ and $c_{3,i}$ such that :

   $$c_{1,i} = h(\sigma_i | H_i y_i^t); \quad c_{2,i} = h(\sigma_i(y_i)); \quad c_{3,i} = h(\sigma_i(y_i \oplus s_i))$$

   where $h(a_1 | \cdots | a_j)$ denotes the hash of the concatenation of the sequence formed by $a_1, \cdots, a_j$.
   - L chooses $N - t$ random $y_i \in \mathbb{F}^n$ and $N - t$ random permutations σ_i of $\{1, 2, \ldots, n\}$
   - L fixes the secret s_i of the $N - t$ missing users at 0 and computes the $N - t$ corresponding commitments by choosing random y_i and σ_i ($t + 1 \leq i \leq N$).
   - L chooses a random constant n-block permutation Σ on N blocks $\{1, \cdots, N\}$ in order to obtain the *master commitments*:

   $$C_1 = h(\Sigma | c_{1,1} | \ldots | c_{1,N}), C_2 = h(\Sigma(c_{2,1}, \ldots, c_{2,N})), C_3 = h(\Sigma(c_{3,1}, \ldots, c_{3,N})).$$

   - L sends C_1, C_2 and C_3 to V.
2. [Challenge Step] V sends a challenge $b \in \{0, 1, 2\}$ to L which sends b to the t signers.
3. [Answer Step] Let P_i be one of the t signers. The first part of the step is between each signer and L.
   - Three possibilities :
     - if $b = 0$: P_i reveals y_i and σ_i.
     - if $b = 1$: P_i reveals $(y_i \oplus s_i)$ (denoted by $(y \oplus s)_i$) and σ_i.
     - if $b = 2$: P_i reveals $\sigma_i(y_i)$ (denoted by $(\sigma(y))_i$) and $\sigma_i(s_i)$ (denoted by $(\sigma(s))_i$).
   - L simulates the $N - t$ others Stern's protocol with $s_i = 0$ and $t + 1 \leq i \leq N$.
   - L computes the answer for V (and sends it) :
     - if $b = 0$: L constructs $y = (y_1, \cdots, y_N)$ and $\Pi = \Sigma \circ \sigma$ (for $\sigma = (\sigma_1, \cdots, \sigma_N)$) and reveals y and Π.
     - if $b = 1$: L constructs $y \oplus s = ((y \oplus s)_1, \cdots, (y \oplus s)_N)$ and reveals $y \oplus s$ and Π.
     - if $b = 2$: L constructs $\Pi(y)$ and $\Pi(s)$ reveals them.
4. [Verification Step] Three possibilities :
   - if $b = 0$: V verifies that $\Pi(s)$ is a n-block permutation and that C_1, C_2 have been honestly calculated.
   - if $b = 1$: V verifies that $\Pi(s)$ is a n-block permutation and that C_1, C_3 have been honestly calculated.
   - if $b = 2$: V verifies that C_2, C_3 have been honestly calculated, and that the weight of $\Pi(s)$ is $t\omega$ and that $\Pi(s)$ is formed of N blocks of length n and of weight ω or 0.
5. Iterate the steps 1,2,3,4 until the expected security level is reached.

Fig. 3. Generalized Stern's protocol

The problem of finding s of weight ω is a MD problem defined earlier. The t signers choose a leader L among them which sends a set of public matrices $H_1, \cdots, H_N$.

Remark: In order to simplify the description of the protocol (and to avoid double indexes), we consider in the following that the t signers correspond to the first t matrices H_i ($1 \leq i \leq t$) (although more generally their order can be considered random in $\{1, .., N\}$ since the order depends of the order of the N matrices sent by the leader.

Construction of a public key for the ring
The RPK (Ring Public Key) is contructed by considering, the matrix H described as follow:

$$H = \begin{pmatrix} H_1 & 0 & 0 & \cdots & 0 \\ 0 & H_2 & 0 & \cdots & 0 \\ \vdots & \vdots & \ddots & \vdots & \vdots \\ \vdots & \vdots & \vdots & \ddots & \vdots \\ 0 & 0 & 0 & \cdots & H_N \end{pmatrix}.$$

H, ω and $H_i, \forall i \in \{1; \ldots; N\}$ are public. The $s_i, \forall i \in \{1; \ldots; N\}$ are private.

4.4   Commitment-Challenge-Answer and Verification Steps

We now describe formally our scheme.

The leader L collects the comitments given from the $t-1$ other signers, simulates the $N-t$ non-signers and chooses a random constant n-block permutation Σ on N blocks. From all these comitments L creates the master comitments C_1, C_2 and C_3 which are sent to the verifier V, who answers by giving a challenge b in $\{0,1,2\}$. Then L sends the challenge to each of the other $t-1$ signers and collects their answers to create a global answer for V. Upon reception of the global answer, V verifies that it is correct by checking the comitments as in the regular Stern's scheme.

All the details of the protocol are given in Fig. 3. *Recall that in the description of the protocol, in order to avoid complex double indexes in the description we considered that the t signers corresponded to the first t matrices H_i.*

5   Security

5.1   Our Security Model

The security of our protocol relies on two notions of unforgeability and anonymity secure under the Mininum Distance problem assumption in the random oracle model.

To prove the first notion we prove that our protocol is an Honest-Verifier Zero-Knowledge (HZVZK) Proof of Knowledge. It has been proven in [11] that every HVZK protocol can be turned into a signature scheme by setting the challenge to the hash value of the comitment together with the message to be signed. Such a scheme has been proven secure against existential forgery under adaptatively chosen message attack in the random oracle model in [19].

The second notion of anonymity for our scheme in a threshold context is defined as follows:

Definition 5.1 (Threshold ring signature anonymity). *Let $R = \{R_k(\cdot, \cdot)\}$ be a family of threshold ring signature schemes.*

We note $SIG \leftarrow S(G, M, R_k)$ a random choice among the signatures of a t user group G concerning a message M using the ring signature scheme R_k.

R is said to be anonymous if for any $c > 0$, there is a K such that for any $k > K$, any two different subgroups G_1, G_2 of t users, any message M and any polynomial-size probabilistic circuit family $C = \{C_k(\cdot, \cdot)\}$,

$$Pr(C_k(SIG, G_1, G_2, \mathcal{P}(k)) = G|SIG \leftarrow S(G, M, R_k))) < 1/2 + k^{-c}$$

G being randomly chosen among $\{G_1, G_2\}$, and $\mathcal{P}(k)$ being the set of all the public information about the ring signature scheme.

5.2   Security of Our Scheme

We first prove that our scheme is HVZK with a probability of cheating of $2/3$. We begin by a simple lemma.

Lemma 1. *Finding a vector v of length nN such that the global weight of v is $t\omega$, the weight of v for each of the N blocks of length n is 0 or ω and such that v has a null syndrome for H, is hard under the MD assumption.*

Proof. The particular structure of H (direct sum of the H_i of same length n) implies that finding such a n-block vector of length nN is exactly equivalent to finding a solution for the local hard problem of finding s_i of weight ω such that $H_i s_i^t = 0$, which is not possible under our assumption.   □

Theorem 1. *Our scheme is a proof of knowledge, with a probability of cheating $2/3$, that the group of signers P knows a vector v of length nN such that the global weight of v is $t\omega$, the weight of v for each of the N blocks of length n is 0 or ω and such that v has a null syndrome for H. The scheme is secure under the MD assumption in the random oracle model.*

Proof. (sketch) We need to prove the usual three properties of completeness, soundness and zero-knowledge. The property of completeness is straightforward since for instance for $b = 0$, the knowledge of y and Π permits to recover Σ, σ_i and the y_i so that it is possible for the verifier to recover all the c_i and hence the master comitment C_1, the same for C_2. The cases $b = 1$ and $b = 2$ works the same. The proof for the soundness and zero-knowledge follow the original proof of Stern in [25] for the problem defined in the previous lemma, by remarking that the structure of our generalized protocol is copied on the original structure of the protocol with Σ in Fig.3 as σ in Fig.1, and with the fact that one checks in the answers $b = 0$ and $b = 1$ in the protocol that the permutation Π is an n-block permutation on N blocks.   □

Remark. It is also not possible to have information leaked between signers during the protocol since each signer only gives information to L (for instance) as in a regular Stern's scheme which is zero-knowledge.

Now we consider anonymity of our protocol, the idea of the proof is that if an adversary has the possibility to get more information on who is a signer among the N potential signers or who is not, it would mean in our case that the adversary is able to know with a better probability than 2/3 that a block s_i of $s = (s_1, \cdots, s_N)$ of size n among the N such blocks associated to the created common secret s is completely zero or not. But since we saw that our protocol was zero-knowledge based on a light modification of the Stern protocol, it would mean that the adversary is able to get information on the secret s during the interaction between L and V, which is not possible since the protocol is zero-knowledge. Formally we obtain:

Theorem 2. *Our protocol satisfies the treshold ring signature anonymity.*

Proof. Suppose that for a given M, a given $c > 0$ and two given subgroups G_1, G_2 of t users there is a family of circuits $C = \{C_k(\cdot, \cdot)\}$ such that for any K there is a $k > K$ such that

$$Pr(C_k(SIG, G_1, G_2, \mathcal{P}(k)) = G | SIG \leftarrow S(G, M, R_k))) > 1/2 + k^{-c}.$$

Consider a user $P_i \in G_1$ such that $U \notin G_2$ (such a user exists as the groups are different), and the following circuit: - Whenever the circuit C_k outputs G_1: output that the i-th (out of N) block of size n of the secret s associated to the matrix H is not null. - Whenever the circuit C_k outputs G_2: output that the i-th (out of N) block of size n of the secret s associated to the matrix H is null. Such a circuit guesses with non-negligible advantage whether a part of the secret s associated to the ring key matrix H is null or not, and therefore breaks the zero-knowledge property of the protocol. the family of circuits $C' = \{C_k(\cdot, \cdot)\}$ □

5.3   Practical Security of Stern's Scheme from [24]

The security of Stern's Scheme relies on three properties of random linear codes:

1. Random linear codes satisfy a Gilbert-Varshamov type lower bound [16],
2. For large n almost all linear codes lie over the Gilbert-Varshamov bound [18],
3. Solving the syndrome decoding problem for random codes is NP-complete [3].

In practice Stern proposed in [24] to use rate 1/2 codes and ω just below the Gilbert-Varshamov bound associated to the code. For such code the exponential cost of the best known attack [6] is in $\approx O(n) \frac{\binom{n}{\omega}}{\binom{n-k}{\omega}}$, which gives a code with today security (2^{80}) of $n = 634$ and rate 1/2 and $\omega = 69$.

6   An Interesting Variation of the Scheme Based on Double-Circulant Matrices

In Section 5 we described a way to create the public matrices H_i, this method as in the original Stern's paper, leads to a large size of the public keys H_i in $n^2/2$ bits. It was recently proposed in [12], to use double-circulant random matrices rather than pure random matrice for such matrices. A double circulant matrix is a matrix of the form $H_i = (I|C)$ for C a random $n/2 \times n/2$ cyclic matrix and I the identity matrix. Following this idea one can construct the matrices H_i as follows: consider $s_i = (a|b)$ where a and b are random vectors of length $n/2$ and weight $\approx \omega/2$, then consider the matrix $(A|B)$ obtained for A and B square $(n/2 \times n/2)$ matrices obtained by the $n/2$ cyclic shifts of a and b (each row of A is a shift of the previous row, begining with first row a or b).

Now consider the code G_i generated by the matrix $(A|B)$, the matrix H_i can then be taken as $H_i = (I|C)$ such that H_i is a dual matrix of G_i and C is cyclic since A and B are cyclic, and hence can be described with only its first row). It is explained in [12] that this construction does not decrease the difficulty of the decoding but clearly decrease dramatically the size of the description of H_i: $n/2$ bits against $n^2/2$.

It is then possible to define a new problem:

Problem: (MD-DC) Minimum Distance of Double circulant codes:
Instance: A binary $n/2 \times n$ double circulant matrix H and an integer $\omega > 0$.
Question: Is there a non zero $x \in GF(2)^n$ of weight $\leq \omega$, such that $Hx^t = 0$?

It is not known whether this problem is NP-complete or not, but the problem is probably as hard as the MD problem, and on practical point of view (see [12] for details) the practical security is almost the same for best known attack that the MD problem. Practicly the author of [12] propose $n = 347$.

Now all the proof of security we considered in this paper can also be adpated to the MD-DC problem, since for the generalized Stern protocol we introduced we can take any kind of H_i with the same type of problem: knowing a small weight vector associated to H_i (in fact only the problem assumption changes).

7 Length and Complexity

In this section examine the complexity of our protocol and compare it to other protocol.

7.1 The Case $t = 1$

This case corresponds to the case of classical ring signature scheme, our scheme is then not so attractive in term of length of signature since we are in $\mathcal{N}$ but more precisely in $\approx 20ko \times N$ (for $20ko$ the cost of one Stern signature), meanwhile since the Stern protocol is fast in term of speed our protocol is faster that all others protocols for $N = 2$ or 3 which may have some applications.

7.2 The General Case

Signature length
It is straight forward to see that the signature length of our protocol is in $\mathcal{O}(N)$, more precisely in $\approx 20ko \times N$, for $20ko$ the length of one signature by the Fiat-Shamir paradigm applied to the Stern scheme (a security of 2^{-80} is obtained

by 140 repetitions od the protocol). For instance consider a particular example with $N = 100$ and $t = 50$, we obtain a $2Mo$ signature length, which is quite large, but still tractable. Of course other number theory based protocols like [4] or [15] have shorter signture lengths (in 8Ko or 25Ko) but are slower.

Public key size
If we use the double-circulant construction described in Section 6, we obtain, a public key size in $347N$ which has a factor 2 or 3 better than [15] and of same order than [4].

Complexity of the protocol
The cost of the protocol is N times the cost of one Stern signature protocol hence in $\mathcal{O}(N)$, (more precisely in $140n^2N$ operations) and this *for any t*. When all other fully anonymous threshold ring signature protocol have a complexity in $\mathcal{O}(tN)$ operations (multiplications or modular exponentiations in large integer rings, or pairings). Hence on that particular point our algorithm is faster than other protocols.

8   Conclusion

In this paper we presented a new (fully anonymous) t-out-of-N threshold ring signature scheme based on coding theory. Our protocol is a very natural general-ization ot the Stern authentication scheme and our proof is based on the original proof of Stern. We showed that the notion of weight of vector particularly went well in the context of ring signature since the notion of ad hoc group corresponds well to the notion of direct sum of generator matrices and is compatible with the notion of sum of vector of small weight. Eventually we obtain a fully anony-mous protocol based on a proof of knowledge in the random oracle model. Our protocol is the first non-generic protocol based on coding theory and (as usual for code based protocol) is very fast compared to other number theory based protocols.

Moreover the protocol we described can also be easily generalized to the case of general access scenario. Eventually the fact that our construction is not based on number theory but on coding theory may represent an interesting alternative. We hope this work will enhance the potential of coding theory in public key cryptography.

References

1. Abe, M., Ohkubo, M., Suzuki, K.: 1-out-of-N signatures from a variety of keys. In: Zheng, Y. (ed.) ASIACRYPT 2002. LNCS, vol. 2501. Springer, Heidelberg (2002)
2. Bender, A., Katz, J., Morselli, R.: Ring Signatures: Stronger Definitions, and Con-structions Without Random Oracles. In: Halevi, S., Rabin, T. (eds.) TCC 2006. LNCS, vol. 3876, pp. 60–79. Springer, Heidelberg (2006)
3. Berlekamp, E., McEliece, R., van Tilborg, H.: On the inherent intractability of cer-tain coding problems. IEEE Transactions on Information Theory IT-24(3) (1978)

4. Boyen, X.: Mesh Signatures. In: Naor, M. (ed.) EUROCRYPT 2007. LNCS, vol. 4515, pp. 210–227. Springer, Heidelberg (2007)
5. Bresson, E., Stern, J., Szydlo, M.: Threshold ring signatures and applications to ad-hoc groups. In: Yung, M. (ed.) CRYPTO 2002. LNCS, vol. 2442. Springer, Heidelberg (2002)
6. Canteaut, A., Chabaud, F.: A new algorithm for finding minimum-weight words in a linear code: application to primitive narrow-sense BCH codes of length 511. IEEE Transactions on Information Theory IT-44, 367–378 (1988)
7. Chandran, N., Groth, J., Sahai, A.: Ring signatures of sub-linear size without random oracles. In: Arge, L., Cachin, C., Jurdziński, T., Tarlecki, A. (eds.) ICALP 2007. LNCS, vol. 4596, pp. 423–434. Springer, Heidelberg (2007)
8. Chaum, D., van Heyst, E.: Group signatures. In: Davies, D.W. (ed.) EUROCRYPT 1991. LNCS, vol. 547, pp. 257–265. Springer, Heidelberg (1991)
9. Courtois, N., Finiasz, M., Sendrier, N.: How to achieve a MCEliece based digital signature scheme. In: Boyd, C. (ed.) ASIACRYPT 2001. LNCS, vol. 2248. Springer, Heidelberg (2001)
10. Dodis, Y., Kiayias, A., Nicolosi, A., Shoup, V.: Anonymous identification in ad-hoc groups. In: Cachin, C., Camenisch, J.L. (eds.) EUROCRYPT 2004. LNCS, vol. 3027. Springer, Heidelberg (2004)
11. Fiat, A., Shamir, A.: How to Prove Yourself: Practical Solutions to Identification and Signature Problems. In: Odlyzko, A.M. (ed.) CRYPTO 1986. LNCS, vol. 263, pp. 186–194. Springer, Heidelberg (1987)
12. Gaborit, P., Girault, M.: Lightweight code-based authentication and signature ISIT 2007 (2007)
13. Herranz, J., Saez, G.: Forking lemmas for ring signature schemes. In: Johansson, T., Maitra, S. (eds.) INDOCRYPT 2003. LNCS, vol. 2904, pp. 266–279. Springer, Heidelberg (2003)
14. Kuwakado, H., Tanaka, H.: Threshold Ring Signature Scheme Based on the Curve. Transactions of Information Processing Society of Japan 44(8), 2146–2154 (2003)
15. Liu, J.K., Wei, V.K., Wong, D.S.: A Separable Threshold Ring Signature Scheme. In: Lim, J.-I., Lee, D.-H. (eds.) ICISC 2003. LNCS, vol. 2971, pp. 352–369. Springer, Heidelberg (2004)
16. MacWilliams, F.J., Sloane, N.J.A.: The Theory of Error Correcting Codes. North-Holland, Amsterdam (1977)
17. Naor, M.: Deniable Ring Authentication. In: Yung, M. (ed.) CRYPTO 2002. LNCS, vol. 2442, pp. 481–498. Springer, Heidelberg (2002)
18. Pierce, J.N.: Limit distributions of the minimum distance of random linear codes. IEEE Trans. Inf. theory IT-13, 595–599 (1967)
19. Pointcheval, D., Stern, J.: Security proofs for signature schemes. In: Maurer, U.M. (ed.) EUROCRYPT 1996. LNCS, vol. 1070, pp. 387–398. Springer, Heidelberg (1996)
20. Rivest, R.L., Shamir, A., Tauman, Y.: How to leak a secret. In: Boyd, C. (ed.) ASIACRYPT 2001. LNCS, vol. 2248, pp. 552–565. Springer, Heidelberg (2001)
21. Sendrier, N.: Cryptosystèmes à clé publique basés sur les codes correcteurs d'erreurs, Mémoire d'habilitation, Inria 2002 (2002), http://www-rocq.inria.fr/codes/Nicolas.Sendrier/pub.html
22. Shacham, H., Waters, B.: Efficient Ring Signatures without Random Oracles. In: Okamoto, T., Wang, X. (eds.) PKC 2007. LNCS, vol. 4450, pp. 166–180. Springer, Heidelberg (2007)
23. Shamir, A.: How to share a secret. Com. of the ACM 22(11), 612–613 (1979)

24. Stern, J.: A new identification scheme based on syndrome decoding. In: Stinson, D.R. (ed.) CRYPTO 1993. LNCS, vol. 773. Springer, Heidelberg (1994)
25. Stern, J.: A new paradigm for public key identification. IEEE Transactions on Information THeory 42(6), 2757–2768 (1996), http://www.di.ens.fr/~stern/publications.html
26. Tsang, P.P., Wei, V.K., Chan, T.K., Au, M.H., Liu, J.K., Wong, D.S.: Separable Linkable Threshold Ring Signatures. In: Canteaut, A., Viswanathan, K. (eds.) INDOCRYPT 2004. LNCS, vol. 3348, pp. 384–398. Springer, Heidelberg (2004)
27. Vardy, A.: The intractability of computing the minimum distance of a code. IEEE Transactions on Information Theory 43(6), 1757–1766 (1997)
28. Véron, P.: A fast identification scheme. In: Proceedings of IEEE International Symposium on Information Theory 1995, Whistler, Canada (Septembre 1995)
29. Wong, D.S., Fung, K., Liu, J.K., Wei, V.K.: On the RSCode Construction of Ring Signature Schemes and a Threshold Setting of RST. In: Qing, S., Gollmann, D., Zhou, J. (eds.) ICICS 2003. LNCS, vol. 2836, pp. 34–46. Springer, Heidelberg (2003)
30. Xu, J., Zhang, Z., Feng, D.: A ring signature scheme using bilinear pairings. In: Lim, C.H., Yung, M. (eds.) WISA 2004. LNCS, vol. 3325. Springer, Heidelberg (2005)
31. Zhang, F., Kim, K.: ID-Based Blind Signature and Ring Signature from Pairings. In: Zheng, Y. (ed.) ASIACRYPT 2002. LNCS, vol. 2501. Springer, Heidelberg (2002)
32. Zheng, D., Li, X., Chen, K.: Code-based Ring Signature Scheme. International Journal of Network Security 5(2), 154–157 (2007), http://ijns.nchu.edu.tw/contents/ijns-v5-n2/ijns-2007-v5-n2-p154-157.pdf

Square-Vinegar Signature Scheme

John Baena[1,2], Crystal Clough[1], and Jintai Ding[1]

[1] Department of Mathematical Sciences,
University of Cincinnati,
Cincinnati, OH, 45220, USA
{baenagjb,cloughcl}@email.uc.edu,ding@math.uc.edu
http://math.uc.edu
[2] Department of Mathematics,
National University of Colombia,
Medellin, Colombia

Abstract. We explore ideas for speeding up HFE-based signature schemes. In particular, we propose an HFEv$^-$ system with odd characteristic and a secret map of degree 2. Changing the characteristic of the system has a profound effect, which we attempt to explain and also demonstrate through experiment. We discuss known attacks which could possibly topple such systems, especially algebraic attacks. After testing the resilience of these schemes against F4, we suggest parameters that yield acceptable security levels.

Keywords: Multivariate Cryptography, HFEv$^-$, Signature Scheme, Odd Characteristic.

1 Introduction

Multivariate public-key cryptosystems (MPKCs) stand among the systems thought to have the potential to resist quantum computer attacks [4]. This is because their main security assumption is based on the problem of solving a system of multivariate polynomial equations, a problem which is still as hard for a quantum computer to solve as a conventional computer [12,22].

The area of multivariate public-key cryptography essentially began in 1988 with an encryption scheme proposed by Matsumoto and Imai [17]. This system has since been broken [19], but has inspired many new encryption and signature schemes. One of these is HFE (Hidden Field Equations), proposed in 1996 by Patarin [20].

An HFE scheme could still be secure, but the parameters required would make it so inefficient as to be practically unusable. Many variants of HFE have been proposed and analyzed, in particular one called HFEv$^-$, a signature scheme which combines HFE with another system called Oil-Vinegar and also uses the "$-$" construction. More about HFEv$^-$ in Sect. 2.2. A recent proposal is Quartz, a signature scheme with HFEv$^-$ at its core. Quartz-7m, with slightly different parameter choices, is believed secure. These schemes have enticingly short signatures.

J. Buchmann and J. Ding (Eds.): PQCrypto 2008, LNCS 5299, pp. 17–30, 2008.

However, the problem with HFE-based signature schemes is that until now, they were quite slow. In this paper, we study how some simple but very surprising changes to existing ideas can yield a system with much faster signing and key generation at the same security levels as other HFE-based signature schemes. In particular, we set out to make an HFEv⁻ system with similarly short signatures *and* greater efficiency in the form of fast signing times.

This paper is organized as follows. In Sect. 2, we discuss relevant background on HFE and Quartz systems. In Sect. 3, we introduce the new variant Square-Vinegar, providing a theoretical overview along with explicit constructions and experimental data. In Sect. 4, known attacks are addressed and more experimental results presented. Additional data can be found in the appendix.

2   Hidden Field Equations and Quartz

2.1   The Basic HFE Scheme

Let k be a finite field of size q and K a degree n extension field of k. In the original design, the characteristic of k is 2. K can be seen as an n-dimensional vector space over k and therefore we can identify K and k^n by the usual isomorphism $\varphi : K \to k^n$ and its inverse. HFE makes use of an internal secret map $F : K \to K$ defined by

$$F(X) = \sum_{\substack{0 \le i < j < n \\ q^i + q^j \le D}} a_{ij} X^{q^i + q^j} + \sum_{\substack{0 \le i < n \\ q^i \le D}} b_i X^{q^i} + c, \tag{1}$$

where the coefficients a_{ij}, b_i, c are randomly chosen from K and D is a fixed positive integer. A map of this form is often referred to as an HFE map.

By composing F with φ and its inverse we obtain the set of n quadratic multivariate polynomials $\tilde{F} = \varphi \circ F \circ \varphi^{-1} : k^n \to k^n$. Then we hide the structure of this map by means of two invertible affine linear transformations $S, T : k^n \to k^n$. The public key is the set of quadratic multivariate polynomials $(g_1, g_2, \ldots, g_n) = T \circ \tilde{F} \circ S$. The private key consists of the map F and the affine linear transformations S and T.

In such a scheme the most delicate matter is the choice of the total degree D of F. D cannot be too large since decryption (or signing) involves solving the equation $F(X) = Y'$ for a given $Y' \in K$ using the Berlekamp algorithm, a process whose complexity is determined by D. However this total degree cannot be too small either to avoid algebraic attacks, like the one developed by Kipnis and Shamir [15] and the Gröbner Bases (GB) Attack [9].

2.2   HFE Variants

There are several variations of this construction intended to enhance the security of HFE, among which we find the HFE⁻ [23] and HFEv [20] signature schemes.

HFE⁻ is the signature scheme obtained from HFE in which we omit r of the polynomials $g_1, g_2, \ldots, g_n$ from the public key. The intent of doing this is to eliminate the possibility of certain attacks, in particular algebraic and Kipnis-Shamir attacks, provided the number r is not too small.

HFEv is a combination of HFE and the Unbalanced Oil & Vinegar scheme [14,21]. The main idea of HFEv is to add a small number v of new variables, referred to as the vinegar variables, to HFE. This makes the system somehow more complicated and changes the structure of the private map. In this case we replace the map F with a more complicated map $G : K \times k^v \to K$.

We can combine HFE$^-$ and HFEv to obtain the so called HFEv$^-$ signature scheme. In this scheme, r polynomials are kept secret and v additional variables are introduced.

Quartz is an HFEv$^-$ signature scheme with a special choice of the parameters, which are $k = \mathbb{F}_2$, $n = 103$, $D = 129$, $r = 3$ and $v = 4$ [24,25]. These parameters of Quartz have been chosen in order to produce very short signatures: only 128 bits. This makes Quartz specially suitable for very specific applications in which short signatures are required, like RFID. Quartz was proposed to NESSIE [18], but it was rejected perhaps due to the fact that its parameters were not chosen conservatively enough. In 2003 Faugère and Joux stated in [9] that the published version of Quartz could be broken using Gröbner bases with slightly fewer than 2^{80} computations.

At present time two modified versions of Quartz are thought to be secure, based on the estimations of [9] on Quartz. The first one, called Quartz-513d, has parameters $k = \mathbb{F}_2$, $n = 103$, $D = 513$, $r = 3$ and $v = 4$. The second version, Quartz-7m, has parameters $k = \mathbb{F}_2$, $n = 103$, $D = 129$, $r = 7$ and $v = 0$. In these versions the high degree D makes the signing process very slow. In fact Quartz-513d was considered impractical for this reason, even as it was proposed.

3 The Square-Vinegar Scheme

We now propose a way to build a fast and highly secure short signature cryptosystem, using the ideas of the HFEv$^-$ signature scheme and the new idea of using finite fields of odd characteristic. With a new choice of parameters we gain computational efficiency without risking the security of the signature scheme. From now on we call these Square-Vinegar schemes. Signatures are still short, which is very convenient to implement in small devices.

3.1 Overview of the New Idea

The set up is basically the same as in the HFEv$^-$ signature scheme. As mentioned above, we replace the map F with the more complicated map $G : K \times k^v \to K$ defined by

$$G(X, X_v) = \sum_{\substack{0 \le i < j < n \\ q^i + q^j \le D}} a_{ij} X^{q^i + q^j} + \sum_{\substack{0 \le i < n \\ q^i \le D}} \beta_i(X_v) X^{q^i} + \gamma(X_v) , \qquad (2)$$

where the coefficients a_{ij} are randomly chosen from K, $\gamma : k^v \to K$ is a randomly chosen quadratic map, $\beta_i : k^v \to K$ are randomly chosen affine linear maps, and

$X_v = (x'_1, \ldots, x'_v)$ represents the new vinegar variables. More precisely the maps β_i and γ are of the form

$$\beta_i(X_v) = \sum_{1 \leq j \leq v} \xi_{i,j} \cdot x'_j + \nu_i \,,$$

$$\gamma(X_v) = \sum_{1 \leq j < l \leq v} \eta_{j,l} \cdot x'_j x'_l + \sum_{1 \leq j \leq v} \sigma_j \cdot x'_j + \tau \,,$$

where $\xi_{i,j}$, ν_i, $\eta_{j,l}$, σ_j and τ are randomly chosen from K. As in HFE, we compose G with φ and its inverse we obtain the set of n quadratic multivariate polynomials. Then we compose with two invertible affine linear transformations $T : k^n \rightarrow k^n$ and $S : k^{n+v} \rightarrow k^{n+v}$, obtaining the polynomials $(g_1, g_2, \ldots, g_n) = T \circ \varphi^{-1} \circ G \circ \varphi \circ S$. Finally, we remove the last r of these polynomials. The public key is the set of quadratic multivariate polynomials $(g_1, g_2, \ldots, g_{n-r}) : k^{n+v} \rightarrow k^{n-r}$. The private key consists of the map G and the affine linear transformations S and T.

While the setup is the same, we make some significant changes. First of all, we will use a field k of odd characteristic. The benefits of working in an odd characteristic are discussed in [5] and will be summarized below in Sect. 4. After making this change, we studied the effect of changing of D and v in order to find the most efficient values. The motivation was that by using the proper number of vinegar variables, we could use a smaller degree D and hence considerably speed up the signing process with the same security level.

With this in mind, we conducted experiments to determine new secure values for D and v. Much to our surprise, in all of our experiments we found that $D = 2$ is sufficiently secure when the field is of odd characteristic, as we will see in Sect. 4. This makes the signature scheme much faster, as we will see in Sect. 3.2.

3.2   The Signing Process

Although HFE is perfectly suitable for encryption and digital signatures, the map F defined by (1) is usually not a surjection. However, in the case of Square-Vinegar schemes, for every different set of vinegar variables we usually obtain a totally different quadratic polynomial in X, which increases the probability of finding a signature for a given document. Actually, in our experiments we were always able to find a signature.

To sign a given document $(\tilde{y}_1, \ldots, \tilde{y}_{n-r}) \in k^{n-r}$, we start by randomly choosing r elements $\tilde{y}_{n-r+1}, \ldots, \tilde{y}_n \in k$ to complete a vector in k^n. Next, we randomly choose values $(w_1, \ldots, w_v) \in k^v$ for the vinegar variables X_v, and then solve for X the equation

$$G(X, (w_1, \ldots, w_v)) = \varphi^{-1}(T^{-1}(\tilde{y}_1, \ldots, \tilde{y}_{n-r}, \tilde{y}_{n-r+1}, \ldots, \tilde{y}_n)). \qquad (3)$$

If this equation has no solutions, a new choice of vinegar variables is made yielding a new equation to be solved. We continue in this manner until we find

Table 1. Number of tries to sign a document

q	D	n	v	r	Average number of trials to sign
2	129	103	4	3	1.74
2	2	103	4	3	2.26
13	2	27	3	0	1.85
13	2	28	3	1	1.80
13	2	36	4	3	1.88
31	2	31	4	3	2.09

Table 2. Signing times for some HFEv⁻ systems

q	D	n	v	r	Number of documents tried	Average time to sign
2	129	103	4	3	100	2.646 s
2	2	103	4	3	100	0.166 s
13	2	27	3	0	100	0.024 s
13	2	28	3	1	100	0.026 s
13	2	36	4	3	100	0.034 s
31	2	31	4	3	100	0.041 s

a choice of vinegar variables whose associated equation in X has a solution. The probability of finding a suitable selection of vinegar variables in a few trials is high. We could confirm this fact with our computer experiments, as evidenced in Table 1 below. We used MAGMA 2.14, the latest version, on a Dell Computer with Windows XP which has an Intel(R) Pentium(R) D CPU 3.00 GHz processor with 2.00 GB of memory installed, to run the computer experiments.

In each case 100 different random documents were signed. We observed that, on average, two tries would be enough to find a solution for that equation. Now suppose that $\tilde{X}$ is a solution of (3), then a signature for the document $(\tilde{y}_1, \ldots, \tilde{y}_{n-r})$ – actually for the whole vector $(\tilde{y}_1, \ldots, \tilde{y}_n)$ – is given by

$$S^{-1}(\varphi(\tilde{X}), w_1, \ldots, w_v) \in k^{n+v}.$$

As mentioned above, with our experiments we found that $D = 2$ suffices as the degree of the secret map G; we will see more about this in Sect. 4. This is undoubtedly a novel and surprising discovery since in the previous versions of HFE and its modifications – all of which are characteristic two – D was always conservatively chosen, usually $D > 128$. These high values of D made the process of signing very slow since solving a univariate equation of such a large degree, even with the fastest algorithms, is not necessarily a fast procedure. On the other hand, when $D = 2$, once the vinegar values have been set, (3) becomes simply a quadratic equation over the field K. Berlekamp's Algorithm can solve a univariate quadratic equation rather quickly, and MAGMA's implementation automatically uses the Berlekamp-Zassenhaus algorithm when appropriate [2]. See Table 2 for signing times for several choices of parameters. Note that signing for the $q = 31$ case shown is 65 times faster than using Quartz parameters.

Another important consequence of the use of $D = 2$ is that generation of the public key for this signature scheme is more efficient. We attribute this to the large number of multiplications that are needed over the field K for $D > 128$. Some results are summarized in Table 3 below.

Table 3. Public key generation times for some HFEv⁻ systems

q	D	n	v	r	Number of trials	Average time
2	129	103	4	3	100	58.066 s
13	2	27	3	0	100	0.780 s
13	2	28	3	1	100	0.830 s
13	2	36	4	3	100	2.019 s
31	2	31	4	3	100	1.271 s

4   Security Analysis

In this section we will consider known attacks against MPKCs (Gröbner Basis, Kipnis-Shamir, and Vinegar attacks) and discuss their effectiveness against our new scheme. This will lead us to suggest parameter values for a viable Square-Vinegar system.

Before considering the aforementioned attacks in detail, let us mention some minor attacks. First, there do not yet seem to be any attacks against MPKCs utilizing knowledge of plaintext-ciphertext (or document-signature) pairs. Secondly, the recent attack on SFlash [8] does not apply here because that attack used hidden symmetry and invariants of the SFlash public key to overcome the omission of certain polynomials from the public key, but our public key does not have such hidden invariants or symmetry due the presence of the vinegar variables. Also, the attacks used against perturbed systems such as IPHFE, [6,7], do not seem directly applicable, especially considering the differences between even and odd characteristic and internal and external perturbation.

4.1   Gröbner Basis Attack

First let us recall what we mean by a Gröbner Basis Attack. Suppose that someone, who does not know the private key, wants to forge a signature for a given document $(\tilde{y}_1, \ldots, \tilde{y}_{n-r}) \in k^{n-r}$. This attacker has access only to the public key $(g_1, g_2, \ldots, g_{n-r}) : k^{n+v} \to k^{n-r}$. In order to find a valid signature for the given document, the attacker has to solve the system of equations

$$g_1(x_1, \ldots, x_n, x'_1, \ldots, x'_v) - \tilde{y}_1 = 0$$
$$g_2(x_1, \ldots, x_n, x'_1, \ldots, x'_v) - \tilde{y}_2 = 0$$
$$\vdots \qquad\qquad (4)$$
$$g_{n-r}(x_1, \ldots, x_n, x'_1, \ldots, x'_v) - \tilde{y}_{n-r} = 0.$$

Solving these equations directly, without the use of the internal structure of the system, is known as the algebraic attack. Currently the most efficient algebraic attacks are the Gröbner basis algorithms F_4 [10] and F_5 [11]. Another algorithm called XL has also been widely discussed but F_4 is seen to be more efficient [1], so we focused our energy on studying algebraic attacks via F_4. Among the best implementations of these algorithms is the F_4 function of MAGMA [2], which represents the state of the art in polynomial solving technology.

In [9], algebraic attacks were used to break HFE. The results in that paper seem to indicate that for any q, an HFE system with small D can be broken in such a way. However, this is not the case and their claims only hold up when working over characteristic 2.

Since the system (4) is underdetermined, we expect to find many solutions for it. In order to forge a signature for the given document, it suffices to find only one such solution. So we can guess values for some of the variables yielding a system with the same number of equations but fewer variables, as was done in [3]. This speeds up the attack significantly. Therefore we randomly guessed $v + r$ of the variables and then used the Gröbner basis attack to solve the resulting system of $n - r$ equations with $n - r$ variables, which is faster to solve than (4).

Based on recent observations about MPKCs over odd characteristic [5], we believe that the choices $q = 13$ or $q = 31$ provide a strong defense against an algebraic attack via Gröbner bases. The key point in the case of odd characteristic is that the field equations $x_i^q - x_i$ for $i = 1, 2, \ldots, n + v$, appear to be less useful to an attacker due to their higher degree. In particular, the efficiency of the Gröbner basis attack seems to rely on small characteristic. It is stated in [5] that this stems from the fact that characteristic 2 field equations $x_i^2 - x_i = 0$ help to keep the degrees of the polynomials used in the Gröbner basis algorithm low whereas, for example, $x_i^{13} - x_i = 0$ or $x_i^{31} - x_i = 0$ are much less useful equations in that regard.

Extensive experiments were run to test this idea on the same computer that was used for the signing experiments. For different sets of the parameters (q, D, n, v and r), we generated HFEv$^-$ systems and used F_4 to solve the system of equations in (4) for different random documents.

We sought the lowest value of D for which F_4 took an acceptably long time. By extrapolating the data we could then determine what values of n and r should be used and see if such values were practical. It turns out that $D = 2$ suffices and we did not have to test higher values of D. Notice also that the choice of odd characteristic is important since for even characteristic $X \mapsto X^2$ over K is just a linear map, which cannot be used as a secret internal map.

Further examination of the data showed that with respect to v the attack time hit a plateau at some point, and further increasing v did not appear to increase resistance to the Gröbner basis attack. This behavior can be seen on Fig. 4 in the Appendix section. By extrapolating the data we think that for our choices of D, q, r and n the plateau should occur before $v = 4$, thus we think the choice of $v = 4$ is optimal in this sense.

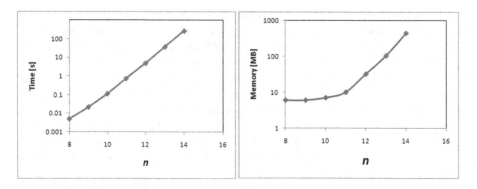

Fig. 1. Running time and required memory under GB Attack for $q = 31$, $v = 4$, $r = 3$ and $D = 2$. No field equations are used in the attack.

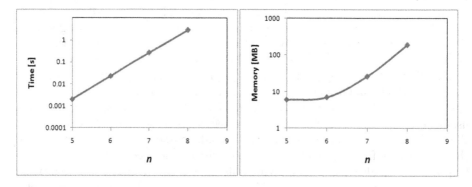

Fig. 2. Running time and required memory under GB attack for $q = 31$, $v = 4$, $r = 3$ and $D = 2$. Including the field equations in the attack.

As mentioned above, for our choice of q – 13 or 31 – the field equations are somehow useless during the Gröbner basis attack. To confirm this, we ran extensive experiments considering this situation, *i.e.*, including and excluding the field equations from the attack. On Figs. 1 and 2 we can see that, in either case, the running time and the required memory under the Gröbner bases attack are exponential in n (similar graphs for $q = 13$ can be seen on Figs. 5 and 6 in the Appendix section).

We can observe that when we include the field equations, the memory used grows much faster than when we do not include them in the attack. This agrees with what we explained above and this is why we say that the field equations are useless for the GB attack. Actually, the field equations not only require more memory but also they slow down the attack for large values of q, for instance $q = 31$. The extrapolations made to suggest parameters in Sect. 4.4 take into account both cases, including and excluding the field equations.

Another important feature that we observed when we excluded the field equations is that, for fixed n, v and r, we did not get any significant change in the

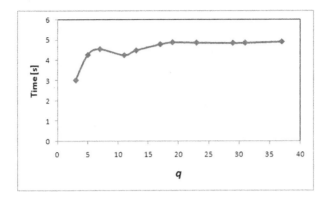

Fig. 3. Running time under GB attack for $n = 9$, $v = 4$, $r = 0$ and $D = 2$, for several values of q. No field equations are used in the attack.

Table 4. Time comparison of some Square-Vinegar systems and random equations under GB attack. $q = 31$, $d = 2$, $v = 4$, and $r = 3$.

n	Our scheme	Random equations
7	0.002 s	0.002 s
8	0.005 s	0.005 s
9	0.022 s	0.022 s
10	0.114 s	0.113 s
11	0.741 s	0.738 s
12	4.921 s	4.755 s
13	37.002 s	37.996 s
14	268.410 s	272.201 s

time required by the GB attack to forge a signature for large values of q, as seen in Fig. 3. This also justifies the choices of $q = 13$ and $q = 31$, since increasing q will not augment the security of the system.

We also constructed random polynomial equations of the same dimensions (same q, n, v and r) and found that the time needed to solve such random equations using Gröbner bases is essentially the same as is needed to break Square-Vinegar with our choices of parameters. Table 4 shows these times for different n.

As observed on the graphs, we could only obtain data for n up to 14, due to memory limitations (any request above 1.2 GB would be immediately rejected by the computer that we used). However, even among the data that we were able to collect, we observed that as n increases, the maximum degree of polynomial used by F4 also increases. Larger scale experiments are being conducted to study systematically how fast this degree increases as n increases; these results will be presented in a future paper.

From the information gathered with our experiments it appears that under our choices of parameters, F4 is no more efficient in solving the public key equations (4) of a Square-Vinegar scheme than a system of random equations.

4.2 Kipnis-Shamir Attack

Kipnis and Shamir developed an attack against HFE [15]. Their original claims were questioned in [13], where it was shown that the Kipnis-Shamir attack was less effective than originally thought and some arguments were made as to why this should be so.

The original attack on HFE was translated to an attack on HFEv in [6]. The resulting attack had a high complexity estimate even though the original, more generous complexity estimates for the HFE attack were used in the computation. Considering [13] and the fact that we are omitting r polynomials from the public key, it seems that a Kipnis-Shamir style attack should not work against Square-Vinegar.

4.3 Vinegar Attack

Since Square-Vinegar utilizes vinegar variables, a priori there is a possibility that it is vulnerable to an attack similar to the one that felled the original Oil-Vinegar scheme.

In the original Oil-Vinegar scheme, the core map $k^n \to k^n$ had a specific shape: each component was a polynomial in which the "oil" variables appeared only linearly, and thus had a quadratic form with a large block of zeros [14,21]. Upon inspection of the attack, we realize that it exploits this property of the quadratic forms [16]. In the Square-Vinegar construction, there are no variables which appear only linearly. The map G ensures that $x_1, \ldots, x_n$ appear quadratically, and the choice of γ ensures that $x'_1, \ldots, x'_v$ appear quadratically.

Once a specific K is fixed (in other words, once a specific irreducible polynomial is chosen to define the extension over k), certain blocks of the quadratic forms of $\varphi \circ G \circ \varphi^{-1}$ are predetermined, but nonzero and not even likely to be sparse. It appears that an attacker would have to find a matrix that simultaneously converts the quadratic forms of all public key polynomials to the prescribed forms. At present time there does not seem to be any method to solve such a problem.

4.4 Parameter Suggestions

Based on the analysis and results obtained throughout Sects. 3 and 4 we are able to suggest new sets of parameters for HFEv⁻, which we call *Square-Vinegar-31* and *Square-Vinegar-13*. Descriptions are as follows:

Square-Vinegar-31

- $q = 31$, $D = 2$, $n = 31$, $v = 4$ and $r = 3$.
- Size of the public key: 12 Kbytes.
- Length of the signature: 175 bits.

- Time needed to sign a message[1]: 0.041 seconds on average.
- Time to verify a signature[1]: less than 1 ms.
- Best known attack: more than 2^{80} computations.

Square-Vinegar-13

- $q = 13$, $D = 2$, $n = 36$, $v = 4$ and $r = 3$.
- Size of the public key: 14 Kbytes.
- Length of the signature: 160 bits.
- Time needed to sign a message[1]: 0.034 seconds on average.
- Time to verify a signature[1]: less than 1 ms.
- Best known attack: more than 2^{80} computations.

We would also like to propose parameters as toy challenges. The first challenge is $q = 13$, $n = 27$, $v = 3$ and $r = 0$. The second challenge is $q = 13$, $n = 28$, $v = 3$ and $r = 1$. We expect that with these parameter choices, an attack may be practically possible.

5   Conclusion

In this paper we analyzed a new HFEv$^-$ system that seems to have great potential. We showed that with relatively short signatures, Square-Vinegar can be used to sign documents very fast. This was accomplished by working in an odd characteristic and using a low-degree polynomial where previously a very high degree was required. We performed computer experiments to test the security of Square-Vinegar. We used algebraic attacks against smaller-scale systems to determine proper q, D, n, r, and v values for plausible schemes. We also examined other MPKC attacks and gave reasons why Square-Vinegar should be resistant to them.

In the future we would like to have a better understanding of the apparent benefit of odd characteristic. We will also, as mentioned above, study the relationship between n and the polynomials used in GB attacks. In addition, we will further study the effectiveness of attacks similar to those against perturbed systems.

References

1. Ars, G., Faugère, J.-C., Imai, H., Kawazoe, M., Sugita, M.: Comparison Between XL and Gröbner Basis Algorithms. In: Lee, P.J. (ed.) ASIACRYPT 2004. LNCS, vol. 3329, pp. 338–353. Springer, Heidelberg (2004)
2. Computational Algebra Group, University of Sydney. The MAGMA computational algebra system for algebra, number theory and geometry (2005), http://magma.maths.usyd.edu.au/magma/
3. Courtois, N., Daum, M., Felke, P.: On the Security of HFE, HFEv- and Quartz. In: Desmedt, Y.G. (ed.) PKC 2003. LNCS, vol. 2567, pp. 337–350. Springer, Heidelberg (2002)

---

[1] On an Intel(R) Pentium(R) D CPU 3.00 GHz.

4. Ding, J., Gower, J.E., Schmidt, D.: Multivariate Public Key Cryptosystems. Springer, Heidelberg (2006)
5. Ding, J., Schmidt, D., Werner, F.: Algebraic Attack on HFE Revisited. In: The 11th Information Security Conference, Taipei, Taiwan (September 2008)
6. Ding, J., Schmidt, D.: Cryptanalysis of HFEv and the Internal Perturbation of HFE cryptosystems. In: Vaudenay, S. (ed.) PKC 2005. LNCS, vol. 3386, pp. 288–301. Springer, Heidelberg (2005)
7. Dubois, V., Granboulan, L., Stern, J.: Cryptanalysis of HFE with Internal Perturbation. In: Okamoto, T., Wang, X. (eds.) PKC 2007. LNCS, vol. 4450, pp. 249–265. Springer, Heidelberg (2007)
8. Dubois, V., Fouque, P.-A., Shamir, A., Stern, J.: Practical Cryptanalysis of SFLASH. In: Menezes, A. (ed.) CRYPTO 2007. LNCS, vol. 4622, pp. 1–12. Springer, Heidelberg (2007)
9. Faugère, J.-C., Joux, A.: Algebraic cryptanalysis of hidden field equation (HFE) cryptosystems using Gröbner bases. In: Boneh, D. (ed.) CRYPTO 2003. LNCS, vol. 2729, pp. 44–60. Springer, Heidelberg (2003)
10. Faugère, J.-C.: A new efficient algorithm for computing Gröbner bases (F_4). Journal of Pure and Applied Algebra 139, 61–88 (1999)
11. Faugère, J.-C.: A new efficient algorithm for computing Gröbner bases without reduction to zero (F_5). In: International Symposium on Symbolic and Algebraic Computation — ISSAC 2002, pp. 75–83. ACM Press, New York (2002)
12. Gray, M.R., Johnson, D.S.: Computers and Intractability – A guide to the Theory of NP-Completeness. W.H. Freeman and Company, New York (1979)
13. Jiang, X., Ding, J., Hu, L.: Kipnis-Shamir's Attack on HFE Revisited. Cryptology ePrint Archive, Report 2007/203, http://eprint.iacr.org/
14. Kipnis, A., Patarin, J., Goubin, L.: Unbalanced oil and vinegar signature schemes. In: Stern, J. (ed.) EUROCRYPT 1999. LNCS, vol. 1592, pp. 206–222. Springer, Heidelberg (1999)
15. Kipnis, A., Shamir, A.: Cryptanalysis of the HFE public key cryptosystem by relinearization. In: Wiener, M. (ed.) CRYPTO 1999. LNCS, vol. 1666, pp. 19–30. Springer, Heidelberg (1999)
16. Kipnis, A., Shamir, A.: Cryptanalysis of the Oil and Vinegar Signature Scheme. In: Krawczyk, H. (ed.) CRYPTO 1998. LNCS, vol. 1462, pp. 257–267. Springer, Heidelberg (1998)
17. Matsumoto, T., Imai, H.: Public quadratic polynomial-tuples for efficient signature verification and message encryption. In: Günther, C.G. (ed.) EUROCRYPT 1988. LNCS, vol. 330, pp. 419–453. Springer, Heidelberg (1988)
18. NESSIE: New European Schemes for Signatures, Integrity, and Encryption. Information Society Technologies Programme of the European Commission (IST-1999-12324), http://www.cryptonessie.org/
19. Patarin, J.: Cryptanalysis of the Matsumoto and Imai public key scheme of Eurocrypt 1988. In: Coppersmith, D. (ed.) CRYPTO 1995. LNCS, vol. 963, pp. 248–261. Springer, Heidelberg (1995)
20. Patarin, J.: Hidden Field Equations (HFE) and Isomorphism of Polynomials (IP): Two new families of asymmetric algorithms. In: Maurer, U. (ed.) EUROCRYPT 1996. LNCS, vol. 1070, pp. 33–48. Springer, Heidelberg (1996); extended Version, http://www.minrank.org/hfe.pdf
21. Patarin, J.: The Oil and Vinegar Signature Scheme. In: Dagstuhl Workshop on Cryptography (September 1997)

22. Patarin, J., Goubin, L.: Trapdoor one-way permutations and multivariate polyno-
    mials. In: Han, Y., Quing, S. (eds.) ICICS 1997. LNCS, vol. 1334, pp. 356–368.
    Springer, Heidelberg (1997); extended Version,
    http://citeseer.nj.nec.com/patarin97trapdoor.html
23. Patarin, J., Goubin, L., Courtois, N.: C^*_{-+} and HM: variations around two schemes
    of T. Matsumoto and H. Imai. In: Ohta, K., Pei, D. (eds.) ASIACRYPT 1998.
    LNCS, vol. 1514, pp. 35–50. Springer, Heidelberg (1998)
24. Patarin, J., Goubin, L., Courtois, N.: Quartz, 128-bit long digital signatures. In:
    Naccache, D. (ed.) CT-RSA 2001. LNCS, vol. 2020, pp. 352–357. Springer, Heidel-
    berg (2001)
25. Patarin, J., Goubin, L., Courtois, N.: Quartz, 128-bit long digital signatures. An
    updated version of Quartz specification, pp. 357-359,
    http://www.cryptosystem.net/quartz/

Appendix: Some Additional Graphs

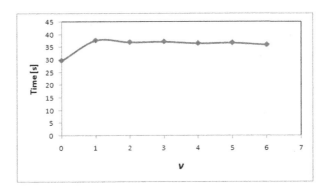

Fig. 4. Running time under GB attack for $n = 13$, $r = 3$ and $D = 2$, for several values
of v. No field equations are used in the attack.

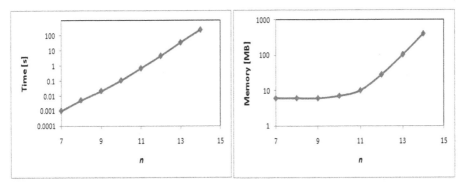

Fig. 5. Running time and required memory under GB attack for $q = 13$, $v = 4$, $r = 3$
and $D = 2$. No field equations are used in the attack.

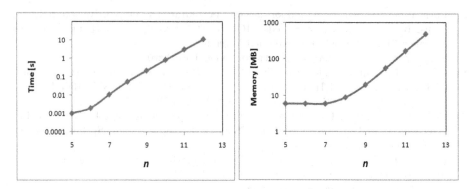

Fig. 6. Running time and required remory under GB attack for $q = 13$, $v = 4$, $r = 3$ and $D = 2$. Including the field equations in the attack.

Attacking and Defending
the McEliece Cryptosystem*

Daniel J. Bernstein[1], Tanja Lange[2], and Christiane Peters[2]

[1] Department of Mathematics, Statistics, and Computer Science (M/C 249)
University of Illinois at Chicago, Chicago, IL 60607–7045, USA
djb@cr.yp.to
[2] Department of Mathematics and Computer Science,
Technische Universiteit Eindhoven, P.O. Box 513, 5600 MB Eindhoven, Netherlands
tanja@hyperelliptic.org, c.p.peters@tue.nl

Abstract. This paper presents several improvements to Stern's attack on the McEliece cryptosystem and achieves results considerably better than Canteaut et al. This paper shows that the system with the originally proposed parameters can be broken in just 1400 days by a single 2.4GHz Core 2 Quad CPU, or 7 days by a cluster of 200 CPUs. This attack has been implemented and is now in progress.

This paper proposes new parameters for the McEliece and Niederreiter cryptosystems achieving standard levels of security against all known attacks. The new parameters take account of the improved attack; the recent introduction of list decoding for binary Goppa codes; and the possibility of choosing code lengths that are not a power of 2. The resulting public-key sizes are considerably smaller than previous parameter choices for the same level of security.

Keywords: McEliece cryptosystem, Stern attack, minimal weight code word, list decoding binary Goppa codes, security analysis.

1 Introduction

The McEliece cryptosystem was proposed by McEliece in 1978 [10] and the original version, using Goppa codes, remains unbroken. Quantum computers do not seem to give any significant improvements in attacking code-based systems, beyond the generic improvements possible with Grover's algorithm, and so the McEliece encryption scheme is one of the interesting candidates for post-quantum cryptography.

A drawback of the system is the comparably large key size — in order to hide the well-structured and efficiently decodable Goppa code in the public key, the full generator matrix of the scrambled code needs to be published. Various attempts to reduce the key size have used other codes, most notably codes over

* Permanent ID of this document: 7868533f20f51f8d769be2aa464647c9. Date of this document: 2008.08.07. This work has been supported in part by the National Science Foundation under grant ITR–0716498.

J. Buchmann and J. Ding (Eds.): PQCrypto 2008, LNCS 5299, pp. 31–46, 2008.

larger fields instead of subfield codes; but breaks of variants of the McEliece system have left essentially only the original system as the strongest candidate.

The fastest known attacks on the original system are based on information set decoding as implemented by Canteaut and Chabaud [4] and analyzed in greater detail by Canteaut and Sendrier [5].

In this paper we reconsider attacks on the McEliece cryptosystem and present improvements to Stern's attack [17] (which predates the Canteaut–Chabaud attack) and demonstrate that our new attack outperforms any previous ones. The result is that an attack on the originally proposed parameters of the McEliece cryptosystem is feasible on a moderate computer cluster. Already Canteaut and Sendrier had pointed out that the system does not hold up to current security standards but no actual attack was done before. We have implemented our new method and expect results soon.

On the defense side our paper proposes new parameters for the McEliece cryptosystem, selected from a much wider range of parameters than have been analyzed before. The codes we suggest are also suitable for the Niederreiter cryptosystem [11], a variant of the McEliece cryptosystem. The new parameters are designed to minimize public-key size while achieving 80-bit, 128-bit, or 256-bit security against known attacks — and in particular our attack. (Of course, by a similar computation, we can find parameters that minimize costs other than key size.) These new parameters exploit the ability to choose code lengths that are not powers of 2. They also exploit a recently introduced list-decoding algorithm for binary Goppa codes — see [2]; list decoding allows senders to introduce more errors into ciphertexts, leading to higher security with the same key size, or alternatively the same security with lower key size.

2   Review of the McEliece Cryptosystem

McEliece in [10] introduced a public-key cryptosystem based on error-correcting codes. The public key is a hidden generator matrix of a binary linear code of length n and dimension k with error-correcting capability t. McEliece suggested using classical binary Goppa codes. We will briefly describe the main properties of these codes before describing the set-up of the cryptosystem.

Linear codes. A *binary* $[n, k]$ *code* is a binary linear code of length n and dimension k, i.e., a k-dimensional subspace of $\mathbf{F}_2^n$. All codes considered in this paper are binary.

The *Hamming weight* of an element $\mathbf{c} \in \mathbf{F}_2^n$ is the number of nonzero entries of $\mathbf{c}$. The *minimum distance* of an $[n, k]$ code C with $k > 0$ is the smallest Hamming weight of any nonzero element of C.

A *generator matrix* of an $[n, k]$ code C is a $k \times n$ matrix G such that $C = \{\mathbf{x}G : \mathbf{x} \in \mathbf{F}_2^k\}$. A *parity-check matrix* of an $[n, k]$ code C is an $(n-k) \times n$ matrix H such that $C = \{\mathbf{c} \in \mathbf{F}_2^n : H\mathbf{c}^T = 0\}$. Here $\mathbf{c}^T$ means the transpose of $\mathbf{c}$; we view elements of $\mathbf{F}_2^n$ as $1 \times n$ matrices, so $\mathbf{c}^T$ is an $n \times 1$ matrix.

A *systematic generator matrix* of an $[n, k]$ code C is a generator matrix of the form $(I_k|Q)$ where I_k is the $k \times k$ identity matrix and Q is a $k \times (n - k)$ matrix.

The matrix $H = (Q^T | I_{n-k})$ is then a parity-check matrix for C. There might not exist a systematic generator matrix for C, but there exists a systematic generator matrix for an equivalent code obtained by permuting columns of C.

The classical decoding problem is to find the closest codeword $\mathbf{x} \in C$ to a given $\mathbf{y} \in \mathbf{F}_2^n$, assuming that there is a unique closest codeword. Here *close* means that the difference has small Hamming weight. Uniqueness is guaranteed if there exists a codeword $\mathbf{x}$ whose distance from $\mathbf{y}$ is less than half the minimum distance of C.

Classical Goppa codes. Fix a finite field $\mathbf{F}_{2^d}$, a basis of $\mathbf{F}_{2^d}$ over $\mathbf{F}_2$, and a set of n distinct elements $\alpha_1, \ldots, \alpha_n$ in $\mathbf{F}_{2^d}$. Fix an irreducible polynomial $g \in \mathbf{F}_{2^d}[x]$ of degree t, where $2 \le t \le (n-1)/d$. Note that, like [15, page 151] and unlike [10], we do not require n to be as large as 2^d.

The Goppa code $\Gamma = \Gamma(\alpha_1, \ldots, \alpha_n, g)$ consists of all elements $\mathbf{c} = (c_1, \ldots, c_n)$ in $\mathbf{F}_2^n$ satisfying

$$\sum_{i=1}^{n} \frac{c_i}{x - \alpha_i} = 0 \qquad \text{in } \mathbf{F}_{2^d}[x]/g.$$

The dimension of Γ is at least $n - td$ and typically is exactly $n - td$. For cryptographic applications one assumes that the dimension is exactly $n - td$. The $td \times n$ matrix

$$H = \begin{pmatrix} 1/g(\alpha_1) & \cdots & 1/g(\alpha_n) \\ \alpha_1/g(\alpha_1) & \cdots & \alpha_n/g(\alpha_n) \\ \vdots & \ddots & \vdots \\ \alpha_1^{t-1}/g(\alpha_1) & \cdots & \alpha_n^{t-1}/g(\alpha_n) \end{pmatrix},$$

where each element of $\mathbf{F}_{2^d}$ is viewed as a column of d elements of $\mathbf{F}_2$ in the specified basis of $\mathbf{F}_{2^d}$, is a parity-check matrix of Γ.

The minimum distance of Γ is at least $2t+1$. Patterson in [13] gave an efficient algorithm to correct t errors.

The McEliece cryptosystem. The *McEliece secret key* consists of an $n \times n$ permutation matrix P; a nonsingular $k \times k$ matrix S; and a generator matrix G for a Goppa code $\Gamma(\alpha_1, \ldots, \alpha_n, g)$ of dimension $k = n - td$. The sizes n, k, t are public system parameters, but $\alpha_1, \ldots, \alpha_n, g, P, S$ are randomly generated secrets. McEliece suggests in his original paper to choose a $[1024, 524]$ classical binary Goppa code Γ with irreducible polynomial g of degree $t = 50$.

The *McEliece public key* is the $k \times n$ matrix SGP.

McEliece encryption of a message $\mathbf{m}$ of length k: Compute $\mathbf{m}SGP$ and add a random error vector $\mathbf{e}$ of weight t and length n. Send $\mathbf{y} = \mathbf{m}SGP + \mathbf{e}$.

McEliece decryption: Compute $\mathbf{y}P^{-1} = \mathbf{m}SG + \mathbf{e}P^{-1}$. Note that $\mathbf{m}SG$ is a codeword in Γ, and that the permuted error vector $\mathbf{e}P^{-1}$ has weight t. Use Patterson's algorithm to find $\mathbf{m}S$ and thereby $\mathbf{m}$.

The Niederreiter cryptosystem. We also consider a variant of the McEliece cryptosystem published by Niederreiter in [11]. Niederreiter's system, with the same Goppa codes used by McEliece, has the same security as McEliece's system, as shown in [9].

Niederreiter's system differs from McEliece's system in public-key structure, encryption mechanism, and decryption mechanism. Beware that the specific system in [11] also used different codes — Goppa codes were replaced by generalized Reed-Solomon codes — but generalized Reed-Solomon codes were broken by Sidelnikov and Shestakov in 1992; see [16].

The *Niederreiter secret key* consists of an $n \times n$ permutation matrix P; a nonsingular $(n-k) \times (n-k)$ matrix S; and a parity-check matrix H for a Goppa code $\Gamma(\alpha_1, \ldots, \alpha_n, g)$ of dimension $k = n - td$. As before, the sizes n, k, t are public system parameters, but $\alpha_1, \ldots, \alpha_n, g, P, S$ are randomly generated secrets.

The *Niederreiter public key* is the $(n - k) \times n$ matrix SHP.

Niederreiter encryption of a message $\mathbf{m}$ of length n and weight t: Compute and send $\mathbf{y} = SHP\mathbf{m}^T$.

Niederreiter decryption: By linear algebra find $\mathbf{z}$ such that $H\mathbf{z}^T = S^{-1}\mathbf{y}$. Then $\mathbf{z} - \mathbf{m}P^T$ is a codeword in Γ. Apply Patterson's algorithm to find the error vector $\mathbf{m}P^T$ and thereby $\mathbf{m}$.

CCA2-secure variants. McEliece's system as described above does not resist chosen-ciphertext attacks; i.e., it does not achieve "IND-CCA2 security." For instance, encryption of the same message twice produces two different ciphertexts which can be compared to find out the original message since it is highly unlikely that errors were added in the same positions.

There are several suggestions to make the system CCA2-secure. Overviews can be found in [6, Chapters 5–6] and [12]. All techniques share the idea of scrambling the message inputs. The aim is to destroy any relations of two dependent messages which an adversary might be able to exploit.

If we secure McEliece encryption against chosen-ciphertext attacks then we can use a *systematic* generator matrix as a public key. This reduces the public-key size from kn bits to $k(n - k)$ bits: it is sufficient to store the $k \times (n - k)$ matrix Q described above. Similarly for Niederreiter's system it suffices to store the non-trivial part of the parity check matrix, reducing the public-key size from $(n - k)n$ bits to $k(n - k)$ bits.

3   Review of the Stern Attack Algorithm

The most effective attack known against the McEliece and Niederreiter cryptosystems is "information-set decoding." There are actually many variants of this attack. A simple form of the attack was introduced by McEliece in [10, Section III]. Subsequent variants were introduced by Leon in [8], by Lee and Brickell in [7], by Stern in [17], by van Tilburg in [18], by Canteaut and Chabanne in [3], by Canteaut and Chabaud in [4], and by Canteaut and Sendrier in [5].

The new attack presented in Section 4 of this paper is most easily understood as a variant of Stern's attack. This section reviews Stern's attack.

How to break McEliece and Niederreiter. Stern actually states an attack on a different problem, namely the problem of finding a low-weight codeword. However, as mentioned by Canteaut and Chabaud in [4, page 368], one can decode a linear code — and thus break the McEliece system — by finding a low-weight codeword in a slightly larger code.

Specifically, if C is a length-n code over $\mathbf{F}_2$, and $\mathbf{y} \in \mathbf{F}_2^n$ has distance w from a codeword $\mathbf{c} \in C$, then $\mathbf{y} - \mathbf{c}$ is a weight-w element of the code $C + \{0, \mathbf{y}\}$. Conversely, if C is a length-n code over $\mathbf{F}_2$ with minimum distance larger than w, then a weight-w element $\mathbf{e} \in C + \{0, \mathbf{y}\}$ cannot be in C, so it must be in $C + \{\mathbf{y}\}$; in other words, $\mathbf{y} - \mathbf{e}$ is an element of C with distance w from $\mathbf{y}$.

Recall that a McEliece ciphertext $\mathbf{y} \in \mathbf{F}_2^n$ is known to have distance t from a unique closest codeword $\mathbf{c}$ in a code C that has minimum distance at least $2t + 1$. The attacker knows the McEliece public key, a generator matrix for C, and can simply append $\mathbf{y}$ to the list of generators to form a generator matrix for $C + \{0, \mathbf{y}\}$. The only weight-t codeword in $C + \{0, \mathbf{y}\}$ is $\mathbf{y} - \mathbf{c}$; by finding this codeword the attacker finds $\mathbf{c}$ and easily solves for the plaintext.

Similar comments apply if the attacker is given a Niederreiter public key, i.e., a parity-check matrix for C. By linear algebra the attacker quickly finds a generator matrix for C; the attacker then proceeds as above. Similar comments also apply if the attacker is given a Niederreiter ciphertext. By linear algebra the attacker finds a word that, when multiplied by the parity-check matrix, produces the specified ciphertext. The bottleneck in all of these attacks is finding the weight-t codeword in $C + \{0, \mathbf{y}\}$.

Beware that there is a slight inefficiency in the reduction from the decoding problem to the problem of finding low-weight codewords: if C has dimension k and $\mathbf{y} \notin C$ then $C + \{0, \mathbf{y}\}$ has slightly larger dimension, namely $k+1$. The user of the low-weight-codeword algorithm knows that the generator $\mathbf{y}$ will participate in the solution, but does not pass this information to the algorithm. In this paper we focus on the low-weight-codeword problem for simplicity.

How to find low-weight words. Stern's attack has two inputs: first, an integer $w \geq 0$; second, an $(n - k) \times n$ parity-check matrix H for an $[n, k]$ code over $\mathbf{F}_2$. Other standard forms of an $[n, k]$ code, such as a $k \times n$ generator matrix, are easily converted to the parity-check form by linear algebra.

Stern randomly selects $n - k$ out of the n columns of H. He selects a random size-ℓ subset Z of those $n-k$ columns; here ℓ is an algorithm parameter optimized later. He partitions the remaining k columns into two sets X and Y by having each column decide independently and uniformly to join X or to join Y.

Stern then searches, in a way discussed below, for codewords that have exactly p nonzero bits in X, exactly p nonzero bits in Y, 0 nonzero bits in Z, and exactly $w - 2p$ nonzero bits in the remaining columns. Here p is another algorithm parameter optimized later. If there are no such codewords, Stern starts with a new selection of columns.

The search has three steps. First, Stern applies elementary row operations to H so that the selected $n - k$ columns become the identity matrix. This fails, forcing the algorithm to restart, if the original $(n - k) \times (n - k)$ submatrix of H is not invertible. Stern guarantees an invertible submatrix, avoiding the cost of a restart, by choosing each column adaptively as a result of pivots in previous columns. (In theory this adaptive choice could bias the choice of (X, Y, Z), as

Stern points out, but the bias does not seem to have a noticeable effect on performance.)

Second, now that this $(n - k) \times (n - k)$ submatrix of H is the identity matrix, each of the selected $n - k$ columns corresponds to a unique row, namely the row where that column has a 1 in the submatrix. In particular, the set Z of ℓ columns corresponds to a set of ℓ rows. For every size-p subset A of X, Stern computes the sum (mod 2) of the columns in A for each of those ℓ rows, obtaining an ℓ-bit vector $\pi(A)$. Similarly, Stern computes $\pi(B)$ for every size-p subset B of Y.

Third, for each collision $\pi(A) = \pi(B)$, Stern computes the sum of the $2p$ columns in $A \cup B$. This sum is an $(n - k)$-bit vector. If the sum has weight $w - 2p$, Stern obtains 0 by adding the corresponding $w - 2p$ columns in the $(n - k) \times (n - k)$ submatrix. Those $w - 2p$ columns, together with A and B, form a codeword of weight w.

4   The New Attack

This section presents our new attack as the culmination of a series of improvements that we have made to Stern's attack. The reader is assumed to be familiar with Stern's algorithm; see the previous section.

As a result of these improvements, our attack speeds are considerably better than the attack speeds reported by Canteaut, Chabaud, and Sendrier in [4] and [5]. See the next two sections for concrete results and comparisons.

Reusing existing pivots. Each iteration of Stern's algorithm selects $n - k$ columns of the parity-check matrix H and applies row operations — Gaussian elimination — to reduce those columns to the $(n - k) \times (n - k)$ identity matrix.

Any parity-check matrix for the same code will produce the same results here. In particular, instead of starting from the originally supplied parity-check matrix, we start from the parity-check matrix produced in the previous iteration — which, by construction, already has an $(n - k) \times (n - k)$ identity submatrix. About $(n - k)^2/n$ of the newly selected columns will match previously selected columns, and are simply permuted into identity form with minimal effort, leaving real work for only about $n - k - (n - k)^2/n = (k/n)(n - k)$ of the columns.

Stern says that reduction involves about $(1/2)(n - k)^3 + k(n - k)^2$ bit operations; for example, $(3/16)n^3$ bit operations for $k = n/2$. To understand this formula, observe that the first column requires $\leq n - k$ reductions, each involving $\leq n - 1$ additions (mod 2); the second column requires $\leq n - k$ reductions, each involving $\leq n - 2$ additions; and so on through the $(n - k)$th column, which requires $\leq n - k$ reductions, each involving $\leq k$ additions; for a total of $(1/2)(n - k)^3 + (k - 1/2)(n - k)^2$.

We improve the bit-operation count to $k^2(n - k)(n - k - 1)(3n - k)/4n^2$: for example, $(5/128)n^2(n - 2)$ for $k = n/2$. Part of the improvement is from eliminating the work for the first $(n - k)^2/n$ columns. The other part is the standard observation that the number of reductions in a typical column is only about $(n - k - 1)/2$.

Forcing more existing pivots. More generally, one can artificially reuse exactly $n - k - c$ column selections, and select the remaining c new columns randomly from among the other k columns, where c is a new algorithm parameter. Then only c columns need to be newly pivoted. Reducing c below $(k/n)(n - k)$ saves time correspondingly.

Beware, however, that smaller values of c introduce a dependence between iterations and require more iterations before the algorithm finds the desired weight-w word. See Section 5 for a detailed discussion of this effect.

The extreme case $c = 1$ has appeared before: it was used by Canteaut et al. in [3, Algorithm 2], [4, Section II.B], and [5, Section 3]. This extreme case minimizes the time for Gaussian elimination but maximizes the number of iterations of the entire algorithm.

Illustrative example from the literature: Canteaut and Sendrier report in [5, Table 2] that they need $9.85 \cdot 10^{11}$ iterations to handle $n = 1024$, $k = 525$, $w = 50$ with their best parameters $(p, \ell) = (2, 18)$. Stern's algorithm, with the same $(p, \ell) = (2, 18)$, needs only $5.78 \cdot 10^{11}$ iterations. Note that these are not the best parameters for Stern's algorithm; the parameters $p = 3$ and $\ell = 28$ are considerably better.

Another illustrative example: Canteaut and Chabaud recommend $(p, \ell) = (2, 20)$ for $n = 2048$, $k = 1025$, $w = 112$ in [4, Table 2]. These parameters use $5.067 \cdot 10^{29}$ iterations, whereas Stern's algorithm with the same parameters uses $3.754 \cdot 10^{29}$ iterations.

Canteaut and Chabaud say that Gaussian elimination is the "most expensive step" in previous attacks, justifying the switch to $c = 1$. We point out, however, that this switch often loses speed compared to Stern's original attack. For example, Stern's original attack (without reuse of existing pivots) uses only $2^{124.06}$ bit operations for $n = 2048$, $k = 1025$, $w = 112$ with $(p, \ell) = (3, 31)$, beating the algorithm by Canteaut et al.; in this case Gaussian elimination is only 22% of the cost of each iteration.

Both $c = 1$, as used by Canteaut et al., and $c = (k/n)(n - k)$, as used (essentially) by Stern, are beaten by intermediate values of c. See Section 5 for some examples of optimized choices of c.

Faster pivoting. Adding the first selected row to various other rows cancels all remaining 1's in the first selected column. Adding the second selected row to various other rows then cancels all remaining 1's in the second selected column.

It has frequently been observed — see, e.g., [1] — that there is an overlap of work in these additions: about 25% of the rows will have *both* the first row and the second row added. One can save half of the work in these rows by simply precomputing the sum of the first row and the second row. The precomputation involves at most one vector addition (and is free if the first selected column originally began $1, 1$).

More generally, suppose that we defer additions of r rows; here r is another algorithm parameter. After precomputing all $2^r - 1$ sums of nonempty subsets of these rows, we can handle each remaining row with, on average, $1 - 1/2^r$ vector additions, rather than $r/2$ vector additions. For example, after precomputing

15 sums of nonempty subsets of 4 rows, we can handle each remaining row with, on average, 0.9375 vector additions, rather than 2 vector additions; the precomputation in this case uses at most 11 vector additions. The optimal choice of r is roughly $\lg(n-k) - \lg\lg(n-k)$ but interacts with the optimal choice of c.

See [14] for a much more thorough optimization of subset-sum computations.

Multiple choices of Z. Recall that Stern's algorithm finds a particular weight-w word if that word has exactly $p, p, 0$ errors in the column sets X, Y, Z respectively. We generalize Stern's algorithm to allow m disjoint sets $Z_1, Z_2, \ldots, Z_m$ with the same X, Y, each of $Z_1, Z_2, \ldots, Z_m$ having cardinality ℓ; here $m \geq 1$ is another algorithm parameter.

The cost of this generalization is an m-fold increase in the time spent in the second and third steps of the algorithm — but the first step, the initial Gaussian elimination, depends only on X, Y and is done only once. The benefit of this generalization is that the chance of finding any particular weight-w word grows by a factor of nearly m.

For example, if $(n, k, w) = (1024, 525, 50)$ and $(p, \ell) = (3, 29)$, then one set Z_1 works with probability approximately 6.336%, while two disjoint sets Z_1, Z_2 work with probability approximately 12.338%. Switching from one set to two produces a 1.947× increase in effectiveness at the expense of replacing steps $1, 2, 3$ by steps $1, 2, 3, 2, 3$. This is worthwhile if step 1, Gaussian elimination, is more than about 5% of the original computation.

Reusing additions of the ℓ-bit vectors. The second step of Stern's algorithm considers all p-element subsets A of X and all p-element subsets B of Y, and computes ℓ-bit sums $\pi(A), \pi(B)$. Stern says that this takes $2\ell p\binom{k/2}{p}$ bit operations for average-size X, Y. Similarly, Canteaut et al. say that there are $\binom{k/2}{p}$ choices of A and $\binom{k/2}{p}$ choices of B, each using $p\ell$ bit operations.

We comment that, although computing $\pi(A)$ means $p - 1$ additions of ℓ-bit vectors, usually $p - 2$ of those additions were carried out before. Simple caching thus reduces the average cost of computing $\pi(A)$ to only marginally more than ℓ bit operations for each A. This improvement becomes increasingly important as p grows.

Faster additions after collisions. The third step of Stern's algorithm, for the pairs (A, B) with $\pi(A) = \pi(B)$, adds all the columns in $A \cup B$.

We point out that, as above, many of these additions overlap. We further point out that it is rarely necessary to compute *all* of the rows of the result. After computing $2(w - 2p + 1)$ rows one already has, on average, $w - 2p + 1$ errors; in general, as soon as the number of errors exceeds $w - 2p$, one can safely abort this pair (A, B).

5   Attack Optimization and Comparison

Canteaut, Chabaud, and Sendrier announced ten years ago that the original parameters for McEliece's cryptosystem were not acceptably secure: specifically, an attacker can decode 50 errors in a $[1024, 524]$ code over $\mathbf{F}_2$ in $2^{64.1}$ bit operations.

Choosing parameters $p = 2$, $m = 2$, $\ell = 20$, $c = 7$, and $r = 7$ in our new attack shows that the same computation can be done in only $2^{60.55}$ bit operations, almost a $12\times$ improvement over Canteaut et al. The number of iterations drops from $9.85 \cdot 10^{11}$ to $4.21 \cdot 10^{11}$, and the number of bit operations per iteration drops from $20 \cdot 10^6$ to $4 \cdot 10^6$. As discussed in Section 6, we have achieved even larger speedups in software.

The rest of this section explains how we computed the number of iterations used by our attack, and then presents similar results for many more sizes $[n, k]$.

Analysis of the number of iterations. Our parameter optimization relies on being able to quickly and accurately compute the average number of iterations required for our attack.

It is easy to understand the success chance of *one* iteration of the attack:

- The probability of a weight-w word having exactly $w - 2p$ errors in a uniform random set of $n - k$ columns is $\binom{w}{2p}\binom{n-w}{k-2p}/\binom{n}{k}$. The actual selection of columns is adaptive and thus not exactly uniform, but as mentioned in Section 3 this bias appears to be negligible; we have tried many attacks with small w and found no significant deviation from uniformity.
- The conditional probability of the $2p$ errors splitting as p, p between X, Y is $\binom{2p}{p}/2^{2p}$. Instead of having each column decide independently whether or not to join X, we actually make a uniform random selection of exactly $\lfloor k/2 \rfloor$ columns for X, replacing $\binom{2p}{p}/2^{2p}$ with $\binom{\lfloor k/2 \rfloor}{p}\binom{\lceil k/2 \rceil}{p}/\binom{k}{2p}$, but this is only a slight change.
- The conditional probability of the remaining $w - 2p$ errors avoiding Z, a uniform random selection of ℓ out of the remaining $n - k$ columns, is $\binom{n-k-(w-2p)}{\ell}/\binom{n-k}{\ell}$. As discussed in Section 4, we increase this chance by allowing disjoint sets $Z_1, Z_2, \ldots, Z_m$; the conditional probability of $w - 2p$ errors avoiding at least one of $Z_1, Z_2, \ldots, Z_m$ is

$$m \frac{\binom{n-k-(w-2p)}{\ell}}{\binom{n-k}{\ell}} - \binom{m}{2} \frac{\binom{n-k-(w-2p)}{2\ell}}{\binom{n-k}{2\ell}} + \binom{m}{3} \frac{\binom{n-k-(w-2p)}{3\ell}}{\binom{n-k}{3\ell}} - \cdots$$

by the inclusion-exclusion principle.

The product of these probabilities is the chance that the *first* iteration succeeds.

If iterations were independent, as in Stern's original attack, then the average number of iterations would be simply the reciprocal of the product of the probabilities. But iterations are not, in fact, independent. The difficulty is that the number of errors in the selected $n - k$ columns is correlated with the number of errors in the columns selected in the next iteration. This is most obvious in the extreme case $c = 1$ considered by Canteaut et al.: swapping one selected column for one deselected column is quite likely to preserve the number of errors in the selected columns. The effect decreases in magnitude as c increases, but iterations also become slower as c increases; optimal selection of c requires understanding how c affects the number of iterations.

To analyze the impact of c we compute a Markov chain for the number of errors, generalizing the analysis of Canteaut et al. from $c = 1$ to arbitrary c. Here are the states of the chain:

- 0: There are 0 errors in the deselected k columns.
- 1: There is 1 error in the deselected k columns.
- ...
- w: There are w errors in the deselected k columns.
- Done: The attack has succeeded.

An iteration of the attack moves between states as follows. Starting from state u, the attack replaces c selected columns, moving to states $u - c, \ldots, u - 2, u - 1, u, u + 1, u + 2, \ldots, u + c$ with various probabilities discussed below. The attack then checks for success, moving from state $2p$ to state Done with probability

$$\beta = \frac{\binom{\lfloor k/2 \rfloor}{p}\binom{\lceil k/2 \rceil}{p}}{\binom{k}{2p}}\left(m\frac{\binom{n-k-(w-2p)}{\ell}}{\binom{n-k}{\ell}} - \binom{m}{2}\frac{\binom{n-k-(w-2p)}{2\ell}}{\binom{n-k}{2\ell}} + \cdots\right)$$

and otherwise staying in the same state.

For $c = 1$, the column-replacement transition probabilities are mentioned by Canteaut et al.:

- state u moves to state $u - 1$ with probability $u(n - k - (w - u))/(k(n - k))$;
- state u moves to state $u + 1$ with probability $(k - u)(w - u)/(k(n - k))$;
- state u stays in state u otherwise.

For $c > 1$, there are at least three different interpretations of "select c new columns":

- "Type 1": Choose a selected column; choose a non-selected column; swap. Continue in this way for a total of c swaps.
- "Type 2": Choose c distinct selected columns. Swap the first of these with a random non-selected column. Swap the second with a random non-selected column. Etc.
- "Type 3": Choose c distinct selected columns and c distinct non-selected columns. Swap the first selected column with the first non-selected column. Swap the second with the second. Etc.

Type 1 is the closest to Canteaut et al.: its transition matrix among states $0, 1, \ldots, w$ is simply the cth power of the matrix for $c = 1$. On the other hand, type 1 has the highest chance of re-selecting a column and thus ending up with fewer than c new columns; this effectively decreases c. Type 2 reduces this chance, and type 3 eliminates this chance.

The type-3 transition matrix has a simple description: state u moves to state $u + d$ with probability

$$\sum_i \binom{w - u}{i}\binom{n - k - w + u}{c - i}\binom{u}{d + i}\binom{k - u}{c - d - i}\Big/\binom{n - k}{c}\binom{k}{c}.$$

For $c = 1$ this matrix matches the Canteaut-et-al. matrix.

We have implemented the type-1 Markov analysis and the type-3 Markov analysis. To save time we use floating-point computations with a few hundred bits of precision rather than exact rational computations. We use the MPFI library (on top of the MPFR library on top of GMP) to compute intervals around each floating-point number, guaranteeing that rounding errors do not affect our final results.

As a check we have also performed millions of type-1, type-2, and type-3 simulations and millions of real experiments decoding small numbers of errors. The simulation results are consistent with the experimental results. The type-1 and type-3 simulation results are consistent with the predictions from our Markov-chain software. Type 1 is slightly slower than type 3, and type 2 is intermediate. Our graphs below use type 3. Our current attack software uses type 2 but we intend to change it to type 3.

Results. For each (n, t) in a wide range, we have explored parameters for our new attack and set new records for the number of bit operations needed to

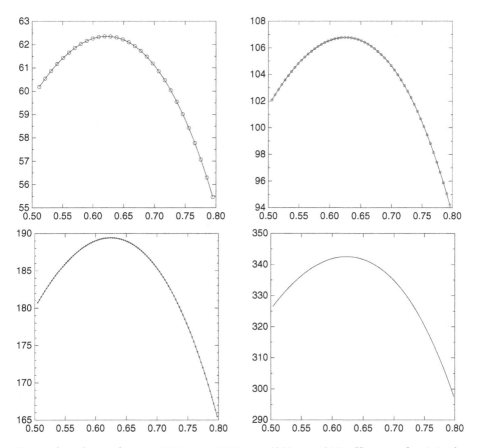

Fig. 1. Attack cost for $n = 1024$, $n = 2048$, $n = 4096$, $n = 8192$. Horizontal axis is the code rate $(n - t \lceil \lg n \rceil)/n$. Vertical axis is $\lg$(bit operations).

decode t errors in an $[n, n - t \lceil \lg n \rceil]$ code. Figure 1 shows our new records. Note that the optimal attack parameters (p, m, ℓ, c, r) depend on n, and depend on t for fixed n.

6 A Successful Attack on the Original McEliece Parameters

We have implemented, and are carrying out, an attack against the cryptosystem parameters originally proposed by McEliece. Our attack software extracts a plaintext from a ciphertext by decoding 50 errors in a $[1024, 524]$ code over $\mathbf{F}_2$.

If we were running our attack software on a single computer with a 2.4GHz Intel Core 2 Quad Q6600 CPU then we would need, on average, approximately 1400 days (2^{58} CPU cycles) to complete the attack. We are actually running our attack software on more machines. Running the software on 200 such computers — a moderate-size cluster costing under \$200000 — would reduce the average time to one week. Note that no communication is needed between the computers.

These attack speeds are much faster than the best speeds reported in the previous literature. Specifically, Canteaut, Chabaud, and Sendrier in [4] and [5] report implementation results for a 433MHz DEC Alpha CPU and conclude that one such computer would need approximately 7400000 days (2^{68} CPU cycles): "decrypting one message out of 10,000 requires 2 months and 14 days with 10 such computers."

Of course, the dramatic reduction from 7400000 days to 1400 days can be partially explained by hardware improvements — the Intel Core 2 Quad runs at 5.54× the clock speed of the Alpha 21164, has four parallel cores (compared to one), and can perform three arithmetic instructions per cycle in each core (compared to two). But these hardware improvements alone would only reduce 7400000 days to 220000 days.

The remaining speedup factor of 150, allowing us to carry out the first successful attack on the original McEliece parameters, comes from our improvements of the attack itself. This section discusses the software performance of our attack in detail. Beware that optimizing CPU cycles is different from, and more difficult than, optimizing the simplified notion of "bit operations" considered in Section 4.

We gratefully acknowledge contributions of CPU time from several sources. At the time of this writing we are carrying out about $3.26 \cdot 10^9$ attack iterations each day:

- about $1.25 \cdot 10^9$ iterations/day from 38 cores of the Coding and Cryptography Computer Cluster (C4) at Technische Universiteit Eindhoven (TU/e)
- about $0.99 \cdot 10^9$ iterations/day from 32 cores in the Department of Electrical Engineering at National Taiwan University;
- about $0.50 \cdot 10^9$ iterations/day from 22 cores in the Courbes, Algèbre, Calculs, Arithmétique des Ordinateurs (CACAO) cluster at Laboratoire Lorrain de Recherche en Informatique et ses Applications (LORIA);

- about $0.26 \cdot 10^9$ iterations/day from 16 cores of the System Architecture and Networking Distributed and Parallel Integrated Terminal (sandpit) at TU/e;
- about $0.13 \cdot 10^9$ iterations/day from 8 cores of the Argo cluster at the Academic Computing and Communications Center at the University of Illinois at Chicago (UIC);
- about $0.13 \cdot 10^9$ iterations/day from 6 cores at the Center for Research and Instruction in Technologies for Electronic Security (RITES) at UIC; and
- about $0.13 \cdot 10^9$ iterations/day from 4 cores owned by D. J. Bernstein and Tanja Lange.

We plan to publish our attack software to allow public verification of our speed results and to allow easy reuse of the same techniques in other decoding problems.

Number of iterations. Recall that the Canteaut-et-al. attack uses $9.85 \cdot 10^{11}$ iterations on average, with (in our notation) $p = 2$, $\ell = 18$, $m = 1$, and $c = 1$.

To avoid excessive time spent handling collisions in the main loop, we increased ℓ from 18 to 20. This increased the number of iterations to $11.14 \cdot 10^{11}$.

We then increased m from 1 to 5: for each selection of column sets X, Y we try five sets Z_1, Z_2, Z_3, Z_4, Z_5. We further increased c from 1 to 32: each iteration replaces 32 columns from the previous iteration. These choices increased various parts of the per-iteration time by factors of 5 and (almost) 32 respectively; but the choices also combined to reduce the number of iterations by a factor of more than 6, down to $1.85 \cdot 10^{11}$.

Further adjustment of the parameters will clearly produce additional improvements, but having reached feasibility we decided to proceed with our attack.

Time for each iteration. Our attack software carries out an attack iteration in 6.38 million CPU cycles on one core of a busy Core 2 Quad. "Busy" means that the other three cores of the Core 2 Quad are also working on the attack; the cycle counts drop slightly, presumably reflecting reduced L2-cache contention, if only one core of the Core 2 Quad is active.

About 6.20 of these 6.38 million CPU cycles are accounted for by the following major components:

- 0.68 million CPU cycles to select new column sets X and Y and to perform Gaussian elimination. We use 32 new columns in each iteration, as mentioned above. Each new column is handled by an independent pivot, modifying a few hundred thousand bits of the matrix; we use standard techniques to combine 64 bit modifications into a small number of CPU instructions, reducing the cost of the pivot to about 20000 CPU cycles. Further improvements are clearly possible with further tuning.
- 0.35 million CPU cycles to precompute $\pi(L)$ for each single column L. There are $m = 5$ choices of π, and $k = 525$ columns L for each π. We handle each $\pi(L)$ computation in a naive way, costing more than 100 CPU cycles; this could be improved but is not a large part of the overall computation.
- 0.36 million CPU cycles to clear hash tables. There are two hash tables, each with $2^\ell = 2^{20}$ bits, and clearing both tables costs about 0.07 million CPU

cycles; this is repeated $m = 5$ times, accounting for the 0.36 million CPU cycles.

- 1.13 million CPU cycles to mark, for each size-p set A, the bit at position $\pi(A)$ in the first hash table. We use $p = 2$, so there are $262 \cdot 261/2 = 34191$ choices of A, and $m = 5$ choices of π, for a total of 0.17 million marks, each costing about 6.6 CPU cycles. Probably the 6.6 could be reduced with further CPU tuning.
- 1.30 million CPU cycles to check, for each set B, whether the bit at position $\pi(B)$ is set in the first hash table, and if so to mark the bit at position $\pi(B)$ in the second hash table while appending B to a list of colliding B's.
- 1.35 million CPU cycles to check, for each set A, whether the bit at position $\pi(A)$ is set in the second hash table, and if so to append A to a list of colliding A's.
- 0.49 million CPU cycles to sort the list of colliding sets A by $\pi(A)$ and to sort the list of colliding sets B by $\pi(B)$. We use a straightforward radix sort.
- 0.54 million CPU cycles to skim through each collision $\pi(A) = \pi(B)$, checking the weight of the sum of the columns in $A \cup B$. There are on average about $5 \cdot 34453 \cdot 34191/2^{20} \approx 5617$ collisions. Without early aborts this step would cost 1.10 million CPU cycles.

For comparison, Canteaut et al. use 260 million cycles on an Alpha 21164 for each of their iterations ("1000 iterations of the optimized algorithm are performed in 10 minutes ... at 433 MHz").

7   Defending the McEliece Cryptosystem

This section proposes new parameters for the McEliece cryptosystem.

Increasing n. The most obvious way to defend McEliece's cryptosystem is to increase n, the length of the code used in the cryptosystem. We comment that allowing values of n between powers of 2 allows considerably better optimization of (e.g.) the McEliece/Niederreiter public-key size. See below for examples. Aside from a mild growth in decoding time, there is no obstacle to the key generator using a Goppa code defined via a field $\mathbf{F}_{2^d}$ of size *much* larger than n.

Using list decoding to increase w. The very recent paper [2] has introduced a list-decoding algorithm for classical irreducible binary Goppa codes, exactly the codes used in McEliece's cryptosystem. This algorithm allows the receiver to efficiently decode approximately $n - \sqrt{n(n - 2t - 2)} \geq t + 1$ errors instead of t errors. The sender, knowing this, can introduce correspondingly more errors; the attacker is then faced with a more difficult problem of decoding the additional errors.

List decoding can, and occasionally does, return more than one codeword within the specified distance. In CCA2-secure variants of McEliece's system there is no difficulty in identifying which codeword is a valid message. Our attack can, in exactly the same way, easily discard codewords that do not correspond to valid messages.

Analysis and optimization of parameters. We now propose concrete parameters $[n, k]$ for various security levels in CCA2-secure variants of the McEliece cryptosystem. Recall that public keys in these variants are systematic generator matrices occupying $k(n - k)$ bits.

For (just barely!) 80-bit security against our attack we propose [1632, 1269] Goppa codes (degree $t = 33$), with 34 errors added by the sender. The public-key size here is $1269(1632 - 1269) = 460647$ bits.

Without list decoding, and with the traditional restriction $n = 2^d$, the best possibility is [2048, 1751] Goppa codes ($t = 27$). The public key here is considerably larger, namely 520047 bits.

For 128-bit security we propose [2960, 2288] Goppa codes ($t = 56$), with 57 errors added by the sender. The public-key size here is 1537536 bits.

For 256-bit security we propose [6624, 5129] Goppa codes ($t = 115$), with 117 errors added by the sender. The public-key size here is 7667855 bits.

For keys limited to $2^{16}, 2^{17}, 2^{18}, 2^{19}, 2^{20}$ bytes, we propose Goppa codes of lengths $1744, 2480, 3408, 4624, 6960$ and degrees $35, 45, 67, 95, 119$ respectively, with $36, 46, 68, 97, 121$ errors added by the sender. These codes achieve security levels $84.88, 107.41, 147.94, 191.18, 266.94$ against our attack. In general, for any particular limit on public-key size, codes of rate approximately 0.75 appear to maximize the difficulty of our attack.

References

1. Bard, G.V.: Accelerating cryptanalysis with the Method of Four Russians. Cryptology ePrint Archive: Report 2006/251 (2006),
   http://eprint.iacr.org/2006/251
2. Bernstein, D.J.: List decoding for binary Goppa codes (2008),
   http://cr.yp.to/papers.html#goppalist
3. Canteaut, A., Chabanne, H.: A further improvement of the work factor in an attempt at breaking McEliece's cryptosystem. In: Charpin, P. (ed.) EUROCODE 1994 (1994), http://www.inria.fr/rrrt/rr-2227.html
4. Canteaut, A., Chabaud, F.: A new algorithm for finding minimum-weight words in a linear code: application to McEliece's cryptosystem and to narrow-sense BCH codes of length 511. IEEE Transactions on Information Theory 44(1), 367–378 (1998)
5. Canteaut, A., Sendrier, N.: Cryptanalysis of the original McEliece cryptosystem. In: Ohta, K., Pei, D. (eds.) ASIACRYPT 1998. LNCS, vol. 1514, pp. 187–199. Springer, Heidelberg (1998)
6. Engelbert, D., Overbeck, R., Schmidt, A.: A summary of McEliece-type cryptosystems and their security. Cryptology ePrint Archive: Report 2006/162 (2006),
   http://eprint.iacr.org/2006/162
7. Lee, P.J., Brickell, E.F.: An observation on the security of McEliece's public-key cryptosystem. In: Günther, C.G. (ed.) EUROCRYPT 1988. LNCS, vol. 330, pp. 275–280. Springer, Heidelberg (1988)
8. Leon, J.S.: A probabilistic algorithm for computing minimum weights of large error-correcting codes. IEEE Transactions on Information Theory 34(5), 1354–1359 (1988)

9. Li, Y.X., Deng, R.H., Wang, X.M.: On the equivalence of McEliece's and Niederreiter's public-key cryptosystems. IEEE Transactions on Information Theory 40(1), 271–273 (1994)
10. McEliece, R.J.: A public-key cryptosystem based on algebraic coding theory, Jet Propulsion Laboratory DSN Progress Report, 42–44 (1978), http://ipnpr.jpl.nasa.gov/progress_report2/42-44/44N.PDF
11. Niederreiter, H.: Knapsack-type cryptosystems and algebraic coding theory. Problems of Control and Information Theory. Problemy Upravlenija i Teorii Informacii 15(2), 159–166 (1986)
12. Overbeck, R., Sendrier, N.: Code-based cryptography. In: Bernstein, D.J., Buchmann, J., Dahmen, E. (eds.) Introduction to post-quantum cryptography. Springer, Berlin (to appear)
13. Patterson, N.J.: The algebraic decoding of Goppa codes. IEEE Transactions on Information Theory IT-21, 203–207 (1975)
14. Pippenger, N.: The minimum number of edges in graphs with prescribed paths. Mathematical Systems Theory 12, 325–346 (1979), http://cr.yp.to/bib/entries.html#1979/pippenger
15. Sendrier, N.: On the security of the McEliece public-key cryptosystem. In: Blaum, M., Farrell, P.G., van Tilborg, H.C.A. (eds.) Information, coding and mathematics. Kluwer International Series in Engineering and Computer Science, vol. 687, pp. 141–163. Kluwer, Dordrecht (2002)
16. Sidelnikov, V.M., Shestakov, S.O.: On insecurity of cryptosystems based on generalized Reed-Solomon codes. Discrete Mathematics and Applications 2, 439–444 (1992)
17. Stern, J.: A method for finding codewords of small weight. In: Cohen, G., Wolfmann, J. (eds.) Coding Theory and Applications 1988. LNCS, vol. 388, pp. 106–113. Springer, Heidelberg (1989)
18. van Tilburg, J.: On the McEliece public-key cryptosystem. In: Goldwasser, S. (ed.) CRYPTO 1988. LNCS, vol. 403, pp. 119–131. Springer, Heidelberg (1990)

McEliece Cryptosystem Implementation: Theory and Practice

Bhaskar Biswas and Nicolas Sendrier

Centre de recherche INRIA Paris - Rocquencourt,
Domaine de Voluceau, Rocquencourt - B.P. 105, 78153 Le Chesnay Cedex, France
{Bhaskar.Biswas,Nicolas.Sendrier}@inria.fr
http://www-rocq.inria.fr/secret/MCE

Abstract. Though it is old and considered fast, the implementation of McEliece public-key encryption scheme has never been thoroughly studied. We consider that problem here and we provide an implementation with a complete description of our algorithmic choices and parameters selection, together with the state of the art in cryptanalysis. This provides a reference for measuring speed and scalability of this cryptosystem. Compared with other, number-theory based, public key scheme, we demonstrate a gain of a factor at least 5 to 10.

Keywords: public-key cryptosystem, McEliece encryption scheme, code-based cryptography, cryptographic implementation.

1 Introduction

McEliece encryption scheme was proposed in 1978 [13]. During the thirty years that have elapsed since, its security, as a one way trapdoor encryption scheme has never been seriously threatened.

Most of the previous works have been devoted to cryptanalysis and to semantic security but fewer attempts have been made to examine implementation issues.

Implementing a (public key) cryptosystem is a tradeoff between security and efficiency. For that reason, cryptanalysis and implementation have to be considered in unison.

Though the public key size is rather large, the McEliece encryption scheme possesses some strong features. It has a good security reduction and low complexity algorithms for encryption and decryption. As a consequence, it is conceivable, compared with number-theory based cryptosystems, to gain an order of magnitude in performance.

In the first part, we will describe a slightly modified version of the scheme (which we call *hybrid*). It has two modifications, the first increases the information rate by putting some data in the error pattern. The second reduces the public key size by making use of a generator matrix in row echelon form. We will show that the same security reduction as for the original system holds. We will then describe the key generation, the encryption and the decryption algorithms and their implementation. Finally we will give some computation time

J. Buchmann and J. Ding (Eds.): PQCrypto 2008, LNCS 5299, pp. 47–62, 2008.

for various parameters, compare them with the best known attacks, and discuss the best tradeoffs.

2 System Description

2.1 McEliece Cryptosystem

Let $\mathcal{F}$ be the family of binary t-error-correcting (n,k) codes. We describe McEliece cryptosystem as[1],

- Public key: a $k \times n$ binary *generator matrix* G of $\mathbf{C} \in \mathcal{F}$.
- Secret key: a decoder $\mathbf{D}$ for $\mathbf{C}$ where $(w_H(e) \leq t) \Rightarrow (\mathbf{D}(xG + e) = x)$.
- Encryption: $x \mapsto xG + e$ where, $w_H(e) \leq t$.
- Decryption: $y \mapsto \mathbf{D}(y)$, *i.e.* decoding.

It was introduced by R. McEliece in 1978 with irreducible binary Goppa codes.

2.2 The *Hybrid* McEliece Scheme

We define an injective mapping $\varphi : \{0,1\}^\ell \to W_{n,t}$ where $W_{n,t}$ denotes the set of words of length n and Hamming weight t. Both φ and φ^{-1} should be easy to compute and the integer ℓ should be close to $\log_2 \binom{n}{t}$. As for the original scheme, we use Goppa codes.

- System parameters: two integers m and t. Let $n = 2^m$ and $k = n - tm$.
- Key generation: let $\Gamma(L,g) \in \mathcal{G}_{m,t}$ (see §A)
  - Public key: a $k \times (n-k)$ binary matrix R such that $(Id \mid R)$ is a generator matrix of $\Gamma(L,g)$
  - Secret key: the pair (L,g), thus the decoder $\Psi_{L,g}$
- Encryption:
$$\begin{array}{ccc} \{0,1\}^k \times \{0,1\}^\ell \to & \{0,1\}^n \\ (x,e) & \mapsto (x \parallel xR) + \varphi(e) \end{array}$$
- Decryption:
$$\begin{array}{ccc} \{0,1\}^n \to \{0,1\}^k \times \{0,1\}^\ell \\ y & \mapsto & (x, \varphi^{-1}(e)) \end{array}$$

  where $e = \Psi_{L,g}(y)$ and $y - e = x \parallel *$.

There are two differences compared with the original system:

- We use the error to encode information bits.
- We use a public key in row echelon form.

Those changes will improve the credentiality of the system and, as we shall see in §3, have no impact on the security of the system.

---

[1] $w_H(\cdot)$ denotes the Hamming weight.

2.3   Choice of Parameters

There are two main approaches for cryptanalysing McEliece system: either decode t errors in a random binary (n, k) code, or construct a fast decoder from a generator matrix. The best known attacks are stated below.

- Decoding attack: a variant of information set decoding proposed by Canteaut and Chabaud in [6].
- Structural attack: enumerate irreducible polynomials g and test the equivalence of $\Gamma(L_0, g)$ with the code defined by the public key. The support L_0 is fixed and equivalence can be tested in polynomial time with the *support splitting algorithm* [16].

Both attacks have an exponential cost. The structural attack is always less efficient. The parameters are thus chosen according to the Canteaut-Chabaud algorithm whose performance is given in Figure 1.

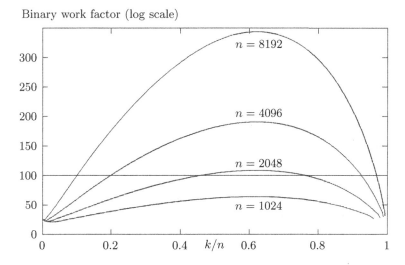

Fig. 1. Work factor of Canteaut-Chabaud algorithm with Goppa parameters

3   Cryptographic Security

The first reductional proof of security for the McEliece encryption scheme was given by Kobara and Imai in [12]. In the same paper, several semantically secure conversions, generic and ad-hoc, are proposed. The purpose of those conversion is to transform a One Way Encryption (OWE) scheme, the weakest notion of security, into a scheme resistant to adaptative chosen ciphertext attack (IND-CCA2), the strongest notion of security.

In this section, we prove that under two algorithmic assumptions (the hardness of decoding and the pseudo-randomness of Goppa codes), the hybrid version of McEliece encryption scheme is one way.

3.1   One Way Encryption Schemes

We consider a public key encryption scheme where the public key is chosen uniformly in the space $\mathcal{K}$. Let $\mathcal{P}$ and $\mathcal{C}$ denote respectively the plaintext and ciphertext spaces. We consider the sample space $\Omega = \mathcal{P} \times \mathcal{K}$ equipped with the uniform distribution P_Ω. An adversary $\mathcal{A}$ for this encryption scheme is a mapping $\mathcal{C} \times \mathcal{K} \to \mathcal{P}$. It is successful for $(x, K) \in \Omega$ if $\mathcal{A}(E_K(x), K) = x$, where $E_K(x)$ denotes the encryption of x with the public key K. The success probability of $\mathcal{A}$ for this cryptosystem is equal to

$$P_\Omega(\mathcal{A}(E_K(x), K) = x).$$

Definition 1 (OWE). *A public key encryption scheme is a* One Way Encryption *scheme if the probability of success of any of its adversary running in polynomial time is negligible.*

In practice, one needs more than just an OWE scheme. For instance, McEliece encryption scheme, though it is OWE, is vulnerable to many attacks [5,7,11,19]. On the other hand, if we admit the existence of perfect hash functions, there are generic conversions (see for instance [2,15]) which, starting from an OWE scheme, provide a scheme resistant against adaptive chosen ciphertext attack.

Those generic conversions as well as other specific ones exist for the original McEliece encryption scheme (see [12]).

3.2   Security Assumptions

Let m and t be two positive integers, let $n = 2^m$ and $k = 2^m - tm$. We denote $\{0,1\}^{k \times n}$ the set of binary $k \times n$ matrices and by $\mathbf{G}_{m,t}$ the subset consisting of all generator matrices of a binary irreducible t-error correcting Goppa code of length n and support $\mathbf{F}_{2^m}$ (up to a permutation). Finally, recall that $W_{n,t}$ denotes the binary words of weight t and length n.

Definition 2. *Let m and t be two positive integers, let $n = 2^m$ and $k = 2^m - tm$. Let P_{Ω_0} be the uniform distribution over the sample space*

$$\Omega_0 = \{0,1\}^k \times W_{n,t} \times \{0,1\}^{k \times n}$$

- *An* adversary *is a procedure* $\mathcal{A} : \{0,1\}^n \times \{0,1\}^{k \times n} \to W_{n,t}$. *We denote* $|\mathcal{A}|$ *its maximal running time.*
- *The* success probability *of an adversary $\mathcal{A}$ is defined as*

$$\mathrm{Succ}(\mathcal{A}) = P_{\Omega_0}\left(\mathcal{A}(xG + e, G) = e\right).$$

- *The* success probability *over $\Omega' \subset \Omega_0$ of an adversary $\mathcal{A}$ is defined as*

$$\mathrm{Succ}(\mathcal{A} \mid \Omega') = P_{\Omega_0}\left(\mathcal{A}(xG + e, G) = e \mid (x, e, G) \in \Omega'\right).$$

- *We call (T, ε)-adversary over Ω' an adversary $\mathcal{A}$ such that $|\mathcal{A}| \leq T$ and* $\mathrm{Succ}(\mathcal{A}, \Omega') \geq \varepsilon$.

- A distinguisher $\mathcal{D}$ *is a mapping* $\{0,1\}^{k \times n} \to \{\text{true}, \text{false}\}$. *We denote* $|\mathcal{D}|$ *its maximal running time.*
- *The* advantage *of a distinguisher* $\mathcal{D}$ *for* $\mathbf{S} \subset \{0,1\}^{k \times n}$ *is defined as*

$$\text{Adv}(\mathcal{D}, \mathbf{S}) = |P_{\Omega_0}(\mathcal{D}(G) \mid G \in \mathbf{S}) - P_{\Omega_0}(\mathcal{D}(G))| \, .$$

- *We call* (T, ε)*-distinguisher over* $\mathbf{S}$ *a distinguisher* $\mathcal{D}$ *such that* $|\mathcal{D}| \leq T$ *and* $\text{Adv}(\mathcal{D}, \mathbf{S}) \geq \varepsilon$.

The first assumption states the difficulty of decoding in the average case in a linear code whose parameters are those of a binary Goppa codes.

Assumption 1. *For all* (T, ε)*-adversary over* Ω_0, *the ratio* T/ε *is not upper bounded by a polymonial in* n.

The worst-case is known to be difficult (the associated decision problem is NP-complete) in the general case [4] (Syndrome Decoding) and in the bounded case [9] (Goppa Parameterized Bounded Decoding). The status of the average case is unknown, but it is believed to be difficult [1].

The second assumption states that there exists no efficient distinguisher for Goppa codes. In other words, the generator matrix of a Goppa code looks random.

Assumption 2. *For all* (T, ε)*-distinguisher over* $\mathbf{G}_{m,t}$, *the ratio* T/ε *is not upper bounded by a polymonial in* n.

There is no formal result to assess this assumption. However, there is no known invariant for linear code, computable in polynomial time, which behave differently for random codes and for binary Goppa codes.

3.3   The Hybrid McEliece Encryption Scheme Is One Way

We use the notations and definitions of the previous section. The public key is a binary $k \times (n - k)$ matrix R. We consider a public injective mapping $\varphi : \{0,1\}^\ell \to W_{n,t}$. The hybrid McEliece encryption is defined as

$$\begin{aligned} \{0,1\}^k \times \{0,1\}^\ell &\longrightarrow \{0,1\}^n \\ (x, e) &\longmapsto (x \parallel xR) + \varphi(e) \end{aligned}$$

Theorem 1. *Under Assumption 1 and Assumption 2, the hybrid McEliece system is a OWE scheme.*

Before proving the theorem, we will prove some intermediate results in the form of three lemmas. We will use the following notations:

- $\mathbf{S}_{k \times n}$ the binary systematic $k \times n$ matrices (*i.e.* of the form $(Id \mid R)$),
- $\mathbf{G}'_{m,t} = \mathbf{G}_{m,t} \cap \mathbf{S}_{k \times n}$ the systematic generator matrices of Goppa codes,
- $\mathcal{E} = \text{Im}(\varphi) \subset W_{n,t}$ the image of $\{0,1\}^\ell$ by φ. In practice $\mathcal{E}$ can be any subset of $W_{n,t}$.

- We consider the three following decreasing subsets of $\Omega_0 = \{0,1\}^k \times W_{n,t} \times \{0,1\}^{k \times n}$

$$\begin{aligned}
\Omega_1 &= \{0,1\}^k \times \mathcal{E} \times \{0,1\}^{k \times n} = \{(x,e,G) \in \Omega_0 \mid e \in \mathcal{E}\} \\
\Omega_2 &= \{0,1\}^k \times \mathcal{E} \times \mathbf{G}_{m,t} = \{(x,e,G) \in \Omega_1 \mid G \in \mathbf{G}_{m,t}\} \\
\Omega_3 &= \{0,1\}^k \times \mathcal{E} \times \mathbf{G}'_{m,t} = \{(x,e,G) \in \Omega_2 \mid G \in \mathbf{S}_{k \times n}\}
\end{aligned}$$

The success probability of an adversary $\mathcal{A}$ for the hybrid McEliece scheme is equal to

$$\mathrm{Succ}(\mathcal{A} \mid \Omega_3) = P_{\Omega_0}\left(\mathcal{A}(xG + e, G) = e \mid G \in \mathbf{G}'_{m,t}, e \in \mathrm{Im}(\varphi)\right).$$

Lemma 1. *Any (T,ε)-adversary over Ω_1 is a $\left(T, \varepsilon|\mathcal{E}|/\binom{n}{t}\right)$-adversary over Ω_0.*

Lemma 2. *If there exists a (T,ε)-adversary over Ω_2 then*

- *either there exists $(T, \varepsilon/2)$-adversary $\mathcal{A}$ over Ω_1,*
- *or there exists $(T + O(n^2), \varepsilon/2)$-distinguisher for $\mathbf{G}_{m,t}$.*

Lemma 3. *If there exists a (T,ε)-adversary over Ω_3 then*

- *either there exists $(T + O(n^3), \lambda\varepsilon/2)$-adversary over Ω_2,*
- *or there a exists $(O(n^3), \lambda/2)$-distinguisher for $\mathbf{G}_{m,t}$,*

where $\lambda \geq 0.288$ is the probability for a binary $k \times k$ matrix to be non-singular.

Proofs of the three lemmas are given in appendix §B.

Proof. (of Theorem 1) A (T,ε)-adversary against the hybrid McEliece scheme is a (T,ε)-adversary over Ω_3 with $\mathcal{E} = \mathrm{Im}(\varphi)$.

If we put together the tree lemmas and the two assumptions, it follows that if the above (T,ε)-adversary exists then

- either there exists a $(T + O(n^3), \lambda\varepsilon 2^{\ell-2}/\binom{n}{t})$-adversary over Ω_0,
- or there a exists a $(T + O(n^3), \lambda\varepsilon/4)$-distinguisher for the Goppa codes,
- or there a exists a $(O(n^3), \lambda/2)$-distinguisher for the Goppa codes.

Provided 2^ℓ is close to $\binom{n}{t}$ (we can reasonably assume, for instance, that the ratio $\binom{n}{t}/2^\ell$ is upper bounded by a small constant, say 4), the existence of an efficient adversary against the hybrid McEliece scheme would contradict one of the two assumptions of the statement.

4   Implementation

4.1   Description

We give in Figure 2 a pseudo-code description of the hybrid McEliece encryption scheme compliant with the description in §2. Algorithms are detailed in the next section.

keygen(m, t)	encrypt(x, e, R)
$\quad L \leftarrow$ rand_permut$(\mathbf{F}_{2^m})$	$\quad$ **return** $(x \parallel x \cdot R) + \varphi(e)$
$\quad g \leftarrow$ rand_irred_poly(t)	
$\quad (R, L') \leftarrow$ get_public_key(L, g)	decrypt(y, L, g)
$\quad SK \leftarrow (L', g)$	$\quad e \leftarrow$ decode(y, L, g)
$\quad PK \leftarrow R$	$\quad$ **return** $(\text{LSB}_k(y - e), \varphi^{-1}(e))$
$\quad$ **return** (PK, SK)	

rand_permut$(\mathbf{F}_{2^m})$ returns the elements of $\mathbf{F}_{2^m}$ in a random order. φ and φ^{-1} are briefly described in §C.

Fig. 2. The hybrid McEliece encryption scheme

rand_irred_poly(t)	is_irred(f)
$\quad$ **do**	$\quad h(z) \leftarrow z$
$\qquad f \leftarrow$ rand_monic_poly(t)	$\quad$ **for** i **from** 1 **to** $\deg(f)/2$ **do**
$\quad$ **while** (is_irred(f) = false)	$\qquad$ **repeat** m **times**
$\quad$ **return** f	$\qquad\quad h(z) \leftarrow h(z)^2 \bmod f(z)$
	$\qquad$ **if** $(\gcd(f(z), h(z) - z) \neq 1)$
	$\qquad\quad$ **return** false
	$\quad$ **return** true

rand_monic_poly(t) returns a random monic polynomial of degree t.

Fig. 3. Generation of irreducible polynomial

4.2 Algorithms

We describe below the main algorithms require for the implementation of the hybrid McEliece encryption scheme. We won't describe the finite field operations, the usual polynomial operations (including the extended Euclidian algorithm for computing the modular inverse) and linear algebra operations (including the Gaussian elimination).

In all the above algorithms, we consider an irreducible binary Goppa code $\Gamma(L, g)$ with $L = (\alpha_1, \ldots, \alpha_n)$ and $g(z) \in \mathbf{F}_{2^m}[z]$ monic irreducible of degree t.

Irreducible polynomial. A given polynomial $f(z) \in \mathbf{F}_{2^m}$ has a factor of degree i if and only if it has a common factor with $z^{2^{im}} - z$. Conversely, if for all $i \leq t/2$ we have $\gcd(f(z), z^{2^{im}} - z) = 1$ then $f(z)$ is irreducible. The polynomial $z^{2^{im}} - z$ has a much too high degree to be handled directly, instead we compute the polynomials $h_j(z) = z^{2^j} \bmod f(z)$ by successive squaring modulo $f(z)$. We have $\gcd(f(z), z^{2^{im}} - z) = \gcd(f(z), h_{im}(z) - z)$ which greatly simplifies the computations. The algorithm given in Figure 3 will produce a random monic irreducible polynomial of degree t.

Building the generator matrix. Let $f_j(z) = (z - \alpha_j)^{-1} \bmod g(z)$ for all $j = 1, \ldots, n$. A word $a = (a_1, \ldots, a_n) \in \mathbf{F}_2^n$ is in $\Gamma(L, g)$ if and only if

$$R_a(z) = \sum_{j=1}^{n} a_j f_j(z) = \sum_{j=1}^{n} \frac{a_j}{z - \alpha_j} \bmod g(z) = 0 \qquad (1)$$

This defines a $t \times m$ parity check matrix over $\mathbf{F}_{2^m}$ whose j-th column is formed by the t coefficients, in $\mathbf{F}_{2^m}$, of the polynomial $f_j(z)$. If we write the field elements of $\mathbf{F}_{2^m}$ in a basis over $\mathbf{F}_2$, each of those columns becomes a binary word of length tm and the n binary column corresponding to the expansions of the $f_j(z)$ form a binary $tm \times n$ parity check matrix H of $\Gamma(L, g)$. We then apply a Gaussian elimination on H, starting with the last columns, to obtain a $k \times (n - k)$ binary matrix R such that $(R^T \mid Id) = UHP$ with U non-singular and P a permutation matrix. The matrix P is the product of a small number (between 0 and a few units) of transpositions. A code with parity check matrix $(R^T \mid Id)$ will admit $G = (Id \mid R)$ as generator matrix, so R is the public key. Figure 4 describes the whole procedure.

Goppa code decoding. Let $b = (b_1, \ldots, b_n)$ be the word to be decoded, we assume that $b = a + e$ with $a\Gamma(L, g)$ and $e \in W_{n,t}$. If $j_1, \ldots, j_t$ are the non zero positions of e, its locator polynomial is defined as $\sigma_e(z) = \prod_{i=1}^{t}(z - \alpha_{j_i})$.

get_public_key(L, g)
    $H \leftarrow$ Goppa_check_matrix(L, g)
    $(R, P) \leftarrow$ gauss_elim(H)
    if $(P \neq Id)$
        $L' \leftarrow$ permute(L, P)
    return (R, L')

Goppa_check_matrix(L, g)
    for j **from** 0 **to** n **do**
        $f_j(z) \leftarrow (z - \alpha_j)^{-1} \bmod g(z)$
        $c_j \leftarrow$ expand(f_j)
    return matrix$(c_1, \ldots, c_n)$

gauss_elim(H) returns a permutation matrix P and a matrix R such
    that $(R^T \mid Id) = UHP$ for some non-singular matrix U.
permute(L, P) adjusts the support L according to the permutation P.
expand(f_j) transforms an element of $\mathbf{F}_{2^m}^t$ into an element of $\mathbf{F}_2^{tm}$.
matrix$(c_1, \ldots, c_n)$ concatenates columns to form a matrix.

Fig. 4. Generation of the parity check matrix

decode(b, L, g)
    $S(z) \leftarrow$ syndrome(b, L, g)
    $\sigma(z) \leftarrow$ solve_key_eq$(S(z), g(z))$
    $(\gamma_1, \ldots, \gamma_t) \leftarrow$ Berlekamp_trace_algorithm(σ)
    $e \leftarrow$ error$((\gamma_1, \ldots, \gamma_t), L)$
    return e

syndrome(b, L, g) returns $R_b(z)$ as in (1).
solve_key_eq$(S(z), g(z))$ applies Patterson algorithm.
Berlekamp_trace_algorithm(σ) is described in §D
error$((\gamma_1, \ldots, \gamma_t), L)$ returns the indexes in L of the γ_i.

Fig. 5. Goppa code decoding

1. Syndrome computation: we compute the syndrome $R_b(z)$ of b as in (1).
2. Key equation solving: the locator polynomial verifies the key equation

$$R_b(z)\sigma_e(z) = \frac{d}{dz}\sigma_e(z) \bmod g(z).$$

   We solve it with Patterson's algorithm [14] (see §E).
3. Roots computation: we compute the roots of σ_e with the Berlekamp trace algorithm [3] (see §D).

5   Simulation Results

We implemented the hybrid version of McEliece encryption scheme in C programming language. In Figures 6 and 7 we plot the running time per plaintext byte versus the logarithm in base 2 of the work factor of the best known attack [6].

Various values of t were tried for an extension degree $11 \leq m \leq 15$. As expected, for a fixed m, the performance gets better for smaller values of t. However, for a fixed security level, the best performance is not obtained for the smallest block size (i.e. extension degree). On the contrary the system works better for higher extension degrees. However, for $m \geq 13$ encryption speed for fixed security becomes steady. See Figure 6 and Figure 7.

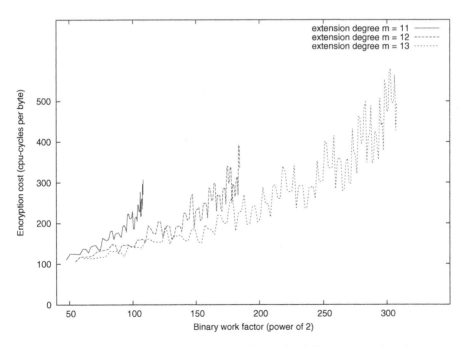

Fig. 6. Encryption cost vs binary work factor for different extension degrees

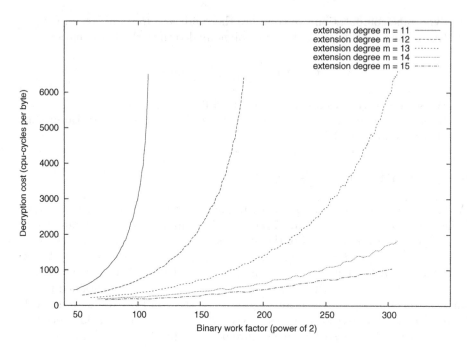

Fig. 7. Decryption cost vs binary work factor for different extension degrees

5.1   Comparison with Other Systems

Our simulations were performed on a machine featuring an Intel Core 2 processor with dual core. It ran on a 32 bits operating system and a single core. The C program was compiled with icc Intel compiler with the options -g -static -O -ipo -xP. Timings are given in Table 1. Compared with the state of the art

Table 1. McEliece: selected parameters at a glance

(m, t)	cycles/byte encrypt	decrypt	key size	security
$(10, 50)$	243	7938	32 kB	60
$(11, 32)$	178	1848	73 kB	88
$(11, 40)$	223	2577	86 kB	96
$(12, 21)$	126	573	118 kB	88
$(12, 41)$	164	1412	212 kB	130
$(13, 18)$	119	312	227 kB	93
$(13, 29)$	149	535	360 kB	129
$(14, 15)$	132	229	415 kB	91
$(15, 13)$	132	186	775 kB	90
$(16, 12)$	132	166	1532 kB	91

Table 2. Performance of some other public key systems (EBATS source)

	cycles/byte	
	encrypt	decrypt
RSA 1024 [1]	800	23100
RSA 2048 [1]	834	55922
NTRU [2]	4753	8445

[1] RSA encryption (with malleability defense) using OpenSSL.

[2] `ntru-enc 1 ees787ep1` NTRU encryption with $N = 787$ and $q = 587$. Software written by Mark Etzel (NTRU Cryptosystem).

implementation of other public key encryption schemes (see Table 2), McEliece encryption gains an order of magnitude for both encryption and decryption.

The source used for Table 2 is an EBATS preliminary report[2] of March 2007.

6   Conclusion

We presented here a new modified version of McEliece cryptosystem and its full implementation. We have shown that code-based public key encryption scheme compares favorably with optimized implementation of number theory based schemes.

The system we have implemented here is very fast and offers much flexibility in the choice of parameters. One of the main observations we made from this implementation work is the fact that increasing the extension degree m seems to offer an interesting trade off. Presently, our program do not allow an extension degree greater than 16.

The source code of the whole implementation is freely avalaible on our website `http://www-rocq.inria.fr/secret/MCE`. The Niederreiter scheme is similar to McEliece's in most aspects. We intend to make it available as well.

References

1. Barg, A.: Complexity issues in coding theory. In: Pless, V.S., Huffman, W.C. (eds.) Handbook of Coding theory, ch. 7, vol. I, pp. 649–754. North-Holland, Amsterdam (1998)
2. Bellare, M., Rogaway, P.: Optimal asymetric encryption. In: De Santis, A. (ed.) EUROCRYPT 1994. LNCS, vol. 950, pp. 92–111. Springer, Heidelberg (1995)
3. Berlekamp, E.R.: Factoring polynomials over large finite fields. Mathematics of Computation 24(111), 713–715 (1970)
4. Berlekamp, E.R., McEliece, R.J., van Tilborg, H.C.: On the inherent intractability of certain coding problems. IEEE Transactions on Information Theory 24(3) (May 1978)
5. Berson, T.: Failure of the McEliece public-key cryptosystem under message-resend and related-message attack. In: Kalisky, B. (ed.) CRYPTO 1997. LNCS, vol. 1294, pp. 213–220. Springer, Heidelberg (1997)

---

[2] `http://www.ecrypt.eu.org/ebats/D.VAM.9-1.1.pdf`

6. Canteaut, A., Chabaud, F.: A new algorithm for finding minimum-weight words in a linear code: Application to McEliece's cryptosystem and to narrow-sense BCH codes of length 511. IEEE Transactions on Information Theory 44(1), 367–378 (1998)
7. Canteaut, A., Sendrier, N.: Cryptanalysis of the original McEliece cryptosystem. In: Ohta, K., Pei, D. (eds.) ASIACRYPT 1998. LNCS, vol. 1514, pp. 187–199. Springer, Heidelberg (1998)
8. Cover, T.: Enumerative source encoding. IEEE Transactions on Information Theory 19(1), 73–77 (1973)
9. Finiasz, M.: Nouvelles constructions utilisant des codes correcteurs d'erreurs en cryptographie à clef publique. Thèse de doctorat, École Polytechnique (October 2004)
10. Ganz, J.: Factoring polynomials using binary representations of finite fields. IEEE Transactions on Information Theory 43(1), 147–153 (1997)
11. Hall, C., Goldberg, I., Schneier, B.: Reaction attacks against several public-key cryptosystems. In: Varadharajan, V., Mu, Y. (eds.) ICICS 1999. LNCS, vol. 1726, pp. 2–12. Springer, Heidelberg (1999)
12. Kobara, K., Imai, H.: Semantically secure McEliece public-key cryptosystems - Conversions for McEliece PKC. In: Kim, K. (ed.) PKC 2001. LNCS, vol. 1992, pp. 19–35. Springer, Heidelberg (2001)
13. McEliece, R.J.: A public-key cryptosystem based on algebraic coding theory. In: DSN Prog. Rep., Jet Prop. Lab., California Inst. Technol., Pasadena, CA, pp. 114–116 (January 1978)
14. Patterson, N.J.: The algebraic decoding of Goppa codes. IEEE Transactions on Information Theory 21(2), 203–207 (1975)
15. Pointcheval, D.: Chosen-ciphertext security for any one-way cryptosystem. In: Imai, H., Zheng, Y. (eds.) PKC 2000. LNCS, vol. 1751, pp. 129–146. Springer, Heidelberg (2000)
16. Sendrier, N.: Finding the permutation between equivalent codes: the support splitting algorithm. IEEE Transactions on Information Theory 46(4), 1193–1203 (2000)
17. Sendrier, N.: Cryptosystèmes à clé publique basés sur les codes correcteurs d'erreurs. Mémoire d'habilitation à diriger des recherches, Université Paris 6 (March 2002)
18. Sendrier, N.: Encoding information into constant weight words. In: IEEE Conference, ISIT 2005, pp. 435–438, Adelaide, Australia (September 2005)
19. Sun, H.M.: Further cryptanalysis of the McEliece public-key cryptosystem. IEEE Trans. on communication letters 4(1), 18–19 (2000)

A   Goppa Code

Let m and t denote two positive integers. We will denote $\mathcal{G}_{m,t}$ the set of all binary irreducible t-error correcting Goppa codes, defined below.

Definition 3. *Let $L = (\alpha_1, \ldots, \alpha_n)$ be a sequence of $n = 2^m$ distinct elements in $\mathbf{F}_{2^m}$ and $g(z) \in \mathbf{F}_{2^m}[z]$ an irreducible monic polynomial of degree t. The binary irreducible Goppa code with support L and generator polynomial $g(z)$, denoted by $\Gamma(L, g)$, is defined as the set of words $(a_1, \ldots, a_n) \in \mathbf{F}_2^n$ such that*

$$R_a(z) = \sum_{j=1}^{n} \frac{a_j}{z - \alpha_j} = 0 \bmod g(z).$$

The Goppa code $\Gamma(L, g)$ has length $n = 2^m$ and dimension[3] $k \geq n - mt$. We can associate to it an efficient (polynomial time) decoding procedure, denoted $\Psi_{L,g}$, which can correct up to t errors. For all $x \in \Gamma(L, g)$ and all $e \in \{0, 1\}^n$, we have $(w_H(e) \leq t) \Rightarrow (\Psi_{L,g}(x + e) = e)$.

B   Additional Proofs

Proof. (of Lemma 1) Let $\mathcal{A}$ denote the (T, ε)-adversary over Ω_1 of the statement. By definition, it is such that

$$\mathrm{Succ}(\mathcal{A} \mid e \in \mathcal{E}) = \mathrm{Succ}(\mathcal{A} \mid \Omega_1) \geq \varepsilon.$$

We have

$$\begin{aligned}
\mathrm{Succ}(\mathcal{A}) = P_{\Omega_0}(\mathcal{A}(xG + e, G) = e) &\geq P_{\Omega_0}(\mathcal{A}(xG + e, G) = e, e \in \mathcal{E}) \\
&\geq P_{\Omega_0}(\mathcal{A}(xG + e, G) = e \mid e \in \mathcal{E})P_{\Omega_0}(e \in \mathcal{E}) \\
&\geq \mathrm{Succ}(\mathcal{A} \mid e \in \mathcal{E})P_{\Omega_0}(e \in \mathcal{E}) \geq \varepsilon\frac{|\mathcal{E}|}{\binom{n}{t}}
\end{aligned}$$

which proves the lemma.

Proof. (of Lemma 2) Let $\mathcal{A}$ denote the (T, ε)-adversary over Ω_2 of the statement. We consider the distinguisher $\mathcal{D}$ defined for all $G \in \{0, 1\}^{k \times n}$ by $\mathcal{D}(G) = (\mathcal{A}(xG+e, G) = e)$ where (x, e) is randomly and uniformly chosen in $\{0, 1\}^k \times \mathcal{E}$. We have

$$\begin{cases} P_{\Omega_0}(\mathcal{D}(G)) & = \mathrm{Succ}(\mathcal{A} \mid e \in \mathcal{E}) \\ P_{\Omega_0}(\mathcal{D}(G) \mid \Omega_2) = \mathrm{Succ}(\mathcal{A} \mid e \in \mathcal{E}, G \in \mathbf{G}_{m,t}) \end{cases}$$

¿From which we easily derive

$$\mathrm{Succ}(\mathcal{A} \mid \Omega_2) \leq \mathrm{Succ}(\mathcal{A} \mid \Omega_1) + \mathrm{Adv}(\mathcal{D}, \mathbf{G}_{m,t}). \tag{2}$$

To run $\mathcal{D}$, one has to compute the ciphertext $xG + e$ which has a cost upper bounded by $O(n^2)$ and to make one call to $\mathcal{A}$. So we have $|\mathcal{D}| \leq T + O(n^2)$. By definition of $\mathcal{A}$, we have $\mathrm{Succ}(\mathcal{A} \mid \Omega_2) \geq \varepsilon$. Thus at least one of the two right-hand side terms of the inequality (2) is greater than $\varepsilon/2$. This implies that either $\mathcal{A}$ verifies

$$\mathrm{Succ}(\mathcal{A} \mid \Omega_1) \geq \frac{\varepsilon}{2}$$

or $\mathcal{D}$ verifies

$$\mathrm{Adv}(\mathcal{D}, \mathbf{G}_{m,t}) \geq \frac{\varepsilon}{2},$$

which proves the lemma.

---

[3] Equality holds in all cases of practical interest.

Proof. (of Lemma 3) We denote $\mathrm{Syst}(G)$ a procedure which returns on any input $G = (U \mid V) \in \{0,1\}^k$ such that U is non-singular the matrix $(Id \mid U^{-1}V) \in \mathbf{S}_{k \times n}$. On other inputs, $\mathrm{Syst}()$ leave G unchanged.

Let $\mathcal{A}$ denote the (T, ε)-adversary over Ω_3 of the statement.

We define the adversary $\mathcal{A}'$ as $\mathcal{A}'(y, G) = \mathcal{A}(y, \mathrm{Syst}(G))$. We define the distinguisher $\mathcal{D}$ which returns true on input G if and only if $\mathrm{Syst}(G) \in \mathbf{S}_{k \times n}$. The running time of $\mathrm{Syst}()$ is upper bounded by $O(n^3)$, thus $|\mathcal{A}'| \leq T + O(n^3)$ and $|\mathcal{D}| = O(n^3)$.

If $\mathcal{A}'$ succeeds with $(x, e, G) \in \Omega_2$ and $\mathrm{Syst}(G) \in \mathbf{S}_{k \times n}$, then $\mathcal{A}$ succeeds with $(x', e, \mathrm{Syst}(G)) \in \Omega_3$ for some x'. We have

$$\mathrm{Succ}(\mathcal{A}' \mid \Omega_2, \mathrm{Syst}(G) \in \mathbf{S}_{k \times n}) \geq \mathrm{Succ}(\mathcal{A} \mid \Omega_3) \geq \varepsilon$$

and (note that the events "$e \in \mathcal{E}$" and "$\mathrm{Syst}(G) \in \mathbf{G}'_{m,t}$" are independent)

$$
\begin{aligned}
\mathrm{Succ}(\mathcal{A} \mid \Omega_3) &\leq \mathrm{Succ}(\mathcal{A}' \mid \Omega_2, \mathrm{Syst}(G) \in \mathbf{S}_{k \times n}) \\
&\leq \mathrm{Succ}(\mathcal{A}' \mid e \in \mathcal{E}, \mathrm{Syst}(G) \in \mathbf{G}'_{m,t}) \\
&\leq \frac{P_{\Omega_0}(\mathcal{A}'(xG + e, G) = e, e \in \mathcal{E}, \mathrm{Syst}(G) \in \mathbf{G}'_{m,t})}{P_{\Omega_0}(e \in \mathcal{E}, \mathrm{Syst}(G) \in \mathbf{G}'_{m,t})} \\
&\leq \frac{P_{\Omega_0}(\mathcal{A}'(xG + e, G) = e, e \in \mathcal{E}, G \in \mathbf{G}_{m,t})}{P_{\Omega_0}(e \in \mathcal{E})P_{\Omega_0}(\mathrm{Syst}(G) \in \mathbf{G}'_{m,t})} \\
&\leq \mathrm{Succ}(\mathcal{A}' \mid e \in \mathcal{E}, G \in \mathbf{G}_{m,t}) \frac{P_{\Omega_0}(G \in \mathbf{G}_{m,t})}{P_{\Omega_0}(\mathrm{Syst}(G) \in \mathbf{G}'_{m,t})} \\
&\leq \frac{\mathrm{Succ}(\mathcal{A}' \mid \Omega_2)}{P_{\Omega_0}(\mathrm{Syst}(G) \in \mathbf{S}_{k \times n} \mid G \in \mathbf{G}_{m,t})}.
\end{aligned}
$$

We consider now the distinguisher $\mathcal{D}$. By definition, we have

$$P_{\Omega_0}(\mathrm{Syst}(G) \in \mathbf{S}_{k \times n} \mid G \in \mathbf{G}_{m,t}) \geq P_{\Omega_0}(\mathrm{Syst}(G) \in \mathbf{S}_{k \times n}) - \mathrm{Adv}(\mathcal{D}, \mathbf{G}_{m,t}).$$

We also have $\lambda = P_{\Omega_0}(\mathrm{Syst}(G) \in \mathbf{S}_{k \times n})$ the proportion of non-singular binary $k \times k$ matrices. Putting everything together, we get

$$\varepsilon \leq \mathrm{Succ}(\mathcal{A} \mid \Omega_3) \leq \frac{\mathrm{Succ}(\mathcal{A}' \mid \Omega_2)}{\lambda - \mathrm{Adv}(\mathcal{D}, \mathbf{G}_{m,t})}$$

and

$$\mathrm{Succ}(\mathcal{A}' \mid \Omega_2) \geq \lambda\varepsilon - \varepsilon\mathrm{Adv}(\mathcal{D}, \mathbf{G}_{m,t}).$$

We easily conclude that, if $\mathcal{D}$ has an advantage smaller than $\lambda/2$ for $\mathbf{G}_{m,t}$ then $\mathcal{A}'$ has a success probability over Ω_2 greater than $\lambda\varepsilon/2$.

C   Constant Weight Encoding

For producing the injective mapping $\varphi : \{0,1\}^\ell \to W_{n,t}$ we need for the hybrid scheme is not an easy task. Existing solutions [8,17,18] are all based on a (source) encoder $W_{n,t} \rightarrow \{0,1\}^*$ whose decoder is used for processing binary data. Unfortunately they all have either a high computation cost, or a variable length encoder.

Here, we use another encoder which uses a new recursive dichotomic model for the constant weight words. Let $x = (x^L \parallel x^R) \in W_{n,t}$, with $n = 2^m$, where x^L and x^R have length $n/2 = 2^{m-1}$ and $i = w_H(x^L)$, we define

$$F_{m,t}(x) = \begin{cases} \mathbf{nil} & \text{if } i \in \{0, 2^m\} \\ i, F_{m-1,i}(x^L), F_{m-1,t-i}(x^R) & \text{else} \end{cases}$$

where $a, \mathbf{nil} = \mathbf{nil}, a = a$. Any element of $W_{n,t}$ is uniquely transformed into a finite sequence of integers. If $x \in W_{n,t}$ is chosen randomly and uniformly then the distribution of the head element i of $F_{m,t}(x)$ is

$$\text{Prob}(i) = \frac{\binom{n/2}{i}\binom{n/2}{t-i}}{\binom{n}{t}}, i \in \{0, 1, 2, \dots, t\}.$$

The sequences of integers produced by $F_{m,t}$ can be modeled by a stochastic process with the above probabilities. We use an adaptative arithmetic source encoder to encode them. This allows us to produce a nearly optimal encoder from which we build a fast and efficient mapping $\varphi : \{0,1\}^\ell \rightarrow W_{n,t}$. For values of (m,t) of practical cryptographic interest we always have $\ell \geq \lfloor \log_2 \binom{n}{t} \rfloor - 1$.

D Berlekamp Trace Algorithm

Berlekamp trace algorithm was originally published in [3]. The following presentation is inspired from [10]. This algorithm is very efficient for finite fields with small characteristic. The trace function $Tr(\cdot)$ of $\mathbf{F}_{2^m}$ over $\mathbf{F}_2$ is defined by

$$Tr(z) = z + z^2 + z^{2^2} + \dots + z^{2^{m-1}},$$

it maps the field $\mathbf{F}_{2^m}$ onto it's ground field $\mathbf{F}_2$. A key property of the trace function is that if $(\beta_1, ..., \beta_m)$ is any basis of $\mathbf{F}_{2^m}$ over $\mathbf{F}_2$, then every element $\alpha \in \mathbf{F}_{2^m}$ is uniquely represented by the binary m-tuple

$$(Tr(\beta_1 \cdot \alpha), ..., Tr(\beta_m \cdot \alpha)).$$

The basic idea of the Berlekamp trace algorithm is that any $f(z) \in \mathbf{F}_{2^m}[z]$, with $f(z) \mid z^{2^m} - z$, splits into two polynomials

$$g(z) = \gcd(f(z), Tr(\beta \cdot z)) \text{ and } h(z) = \gcd(f(z), 1 + Tr(\beta \cdot z)).$$

The above property of the trace ensures that if β iterates through the basis $(\beta_1, ..., \beta_m)$, we can separate all the roots of $f(z)$ (see Figure 8).

$$\begin{array}{l|l}
\text{BTA}(\sigma, i) & \text{Berlekamp\_trace\_algorithm}(\sigma) \\
\quad \textbf{if } \deg(\sigma) \le 1 \textbf{ then} & \quad \textbf{return } \text{BTA}(\sigma, 1) \\
\quad\quad \textbf{return } \text{rootof}(\sigma) & \\
\quad \sigma_0 \leftarrow \gcd(\sigma(z), Tr(\beta_i \cdot z)) & \\
\quad \sigma_1 \leftarrow \gcd(\sigma(z), 1 + Tr(\beta_i \cdot z)) & \\
\quad \textbf{return } \text{BTA}(\sigma_0, i+1), \text{BTA}(\sigma_1, i+1) &
\end{array}$$

Fig. 8. Pseudo code for the Berlekamp trace algorithm

E   Patterson Algorithm

The Patterson algorithm [14] solves the Goppa code key equation: given $R(z)$ and $g(z)$ in $\mathbf{F}_{2^m}[z]$, with $g(z)$ of degree t respectively, find $\sigma(z)$ of degree t such that

$$R(z)\sigma(z) = \frac{d}{dz}\sigma(z) \bmod g(z)$$

We write $\sigma(z) = \sigma_0(z)^2 + z\sigma_1(z)^2$. Since $\dfrac{d}{dz}\sigma(z) = \sigma_1(z)^2$, we have

$$(1 + zR(z))\sigma_1(z)^2 = R(z)\sigma_0(z)^2 \bmod g(z).$$

Because $g(z)$ is irreducible, $R(z)$ can be inverted modulo $g(z)$. We put $h(z) = z + R(z)^{-1} \bmod g(z)$ and we have

$$h(z)\sigma_1(z)^2 = \sigma_o(z)^2 \bmod g(z).$$

The mapping $f(z) \mapsto f(z)^2 \bmod g(z)$ is bijective and linear over $\mathbf{F}_2^{tm}$, there is a unique polynomial $S(z)$ such that $S(z)^2 = h(z) \bmod g(z)$. We have

$$S(z)\sigma_1(z) = \sigma_0(z) \bmod g(z).$$

The polynomial $\sigma_0(z), \sigma_1(z)$ are the unique solution of the equation

$$\begin{cases}
S(z)\sigma_1(z) = \sigma_0(z) \bmod g(z) \\
\deg \sigma_0 \le t/2 \\
\deg \sigma_1 \le (t-1)/2
\end{cases} \tag{3}$$

The three steps of the algorithm are the following

1. Compute $h(z) = z + R(z)^{-1} \bmod g(z)$ using the extended Euclidian algorithm.
2. Compute $S(z) = \sqrt{h(z)} \bmod g(z)$
   If $s(z)$ such that $s(z)^2 = z \bmod g(z)$ has been precomputed and $h(z) = h_0 + h_1 z + \ldots + h_{t-1}z^{t-1}$, we have

$$S(z) = \sum_{i=0}^{(t-1)/2} h_{2i}^{2^{m-1}} z^i + \sum_{i=0}^{t/2-1} h_{2i+1}^{2^{m-1}} z^i s(z)$$

3. Compute $(\sigma_0(z), \sigma_1(z))$ as in (3) using the extended Euclidian algorithm.

The polynomial $\sigma(z) = \sigma_0(z)^2 + z\sigma_1(z)^2$ is returned.

Merkle Tree Traversal Revisited

Johannes Buchmann, Erik Dahmen, and Michael Schneider

Technische Universität Darmstadt
Department of Computer Science
Hochschulstraße 10, 64289 Darmstadt, Germany
{buchmann,dahmen,mischnei}@cdc.informatik.tu-darmstadt.de

Abstract. We propose a new algorithm for computing authentication paths in the Merkle signature scheme. Compared to the best algorithm for this task, our algorithm reduces the worst case running time considerably.

Keywords: Authentication path computation, digital signatures, Merkle signatures, Merkle tree traversal, post-quantum cryptography.

1 Introduction

Digital signatures are extremely important for the security of computer networks such as the Internet. For example, digital signatures are widely used to ensure authenticity and integrity of updates for operating systems and other software applications. Currently used signature schemes like RSA and ECDSA base their security on the hardness of factoring and computing discrete logarithms. In the past 20 years, there has been significant progress in solving these problems which is why the key sizes for RSA and ECDSA are constantly increased [9]. The security of RSA and ECDSA is also threatened by large quantum computers that, if built, are able to solve the underlying problems in linear time and thus are able to completely break RSA and ECDSA [12]. The research on alternative signature schemes, so-called post quantum signature schemes, is therefore of extreme importance.

One of the most interesting post-quantum signature schemes is the Merkle signature scheme (MSS)[10]. Its security can be reduced to the collision resistance of the used hash function [4]. The best known quantum algorithm to find collisions of hash functions achieves only a square root speed-up compared to the birthday attack [6]. Therefore, the security of MSS is only marginally affected if large quantum computers are built. If a specific hash function is found to be insecure, MSS is easily saved by using a new, secure hash function. This makes MSS an intriguing candidate for a post-quantum signature scheme. It is therefore important to implement the Merkle signature scheme as efficiently as possible. In recent years, many improvements for MSS were proposed [2, 3, 5, 11]. With those improvements, the performance of MSS is now competitive. However, signing with MSS is in most cases still slower than signing with ECDSA. This paper proposes an MSS improvement that reduces the signing time.

The time required for generating a Merkle signature is dominated by the time for computing the authentication path, that later allows the verifier to deduce

J. Buchmann and J. Ding (Eds.): PQCrypto 2008, LNCS 5299, pp. 63–78, 2008.

the validity of the one-time verification key from the validity of the MSS public key. Current algorithms [1, 7, 10, 13, 14] for computing authentication paths have fairly unbalanced running times. The best case runtime of those algorithms is significantly shorter than the worst case runtime. So the computation of some authentication paths is very slow while other authentication paths can be computed very quickly.

Here we propose an authentication path algorithm which is significantly faster in the worst case than the best algorithm known so far. This is Szydlo's algorithm from [13] which provides the optimal time-memory trade-off. In fact, the worst case runtime of our algorithm is very close to its average case runtime which, in turn, equals the average case runtime of the best known algorithm proposed in [13]. The idea of our algorithm is to balance the number of leaves that are computed in each authentication path computation, since leaves are by far the most expensive nodes in the Merkle tree. All other known approaches balance the number of nodes. This does not balance the running time since computing an inner node only requires one hash function evaluation, while computing a leaf takes several hundred hash function evaluations; this is because leaves are essentially one-time verification keys and thus the cost for computing a leaf is determined by the key pair generation cost of the respective one-time signature scheme. This problem is pointed out in [1, 11] but no solution has been provided so far. Our algorithm balances the number of leaves that are computed in each round. Inner nodes are computed as required and since their cost is negligible compared to leaves, the worst case time required by our algorithm is extremely close to the average case time. To be more precise, for each authentication path our algorithm computes $H/2$ leaves and $3/2(H-3)+1$ inner nodes in the worst case and $(H-1)/2$ leaves and $(H-3)/2$ inner nodes on average, where H is the height of the Merkle tree. Our algorithm needs memory to store $3.5H - 4$ nodes.

Previous work. There are two different approaches to compute authentication paths. In [10] Merkle proposes to compute each authentication node separately. This idea is adopted by Szydlo [14], where he implements a better scheduling of the node calculations and achieves the optimal trade-off, that is $O(H)$ time and $O(H)$ space. In [13], Szydlo further improves the constants. For each authentication path his algorithm computes H nodes of the Merkle tree and requires storage for $3H - 2$ nodes.

The second approach is called fractal Merkle tree traversal [7]. This approach splits the Merkle tree into smaller subtrees and stores a stacked series of subtrees that contain authentication paths for several succeeding leaves. Varying the height h of the subtrees allows a trade-off between time and space needed for the tree traversal. Using the low space solution ($h = \log H$) requires $O(H/\log H)$ time and $O(H^2/\log H)$ space. In [1], the authors improve the constants of this algorithm and prove the optimality of the fractal time-memory trade-off.

Organisation. Section 2 describes a simplified version of our algorithm for Merkle trees of even height. The general algorithm is presented in Appendix A. Section 3 compares the new algorithm with that of Szydlo [13]. Section 4 states our conclusion. Appendix B considers the computation of leaves using a PRNG.

2 Authentication Path Computation

In this section we describe our new algorithm to compute authentication paths. It is based on Szydlo's algorithm from [13]. We describe the algorithm in detail, prove its correctness, and estimate the worst case and average case runtime as well as the required space.

Definitions and notations. In the following, $H \geq 2$ denotes the height of the Merkle tree. The index of the current leaf is denoted by $\varphi \in \{0, \ldots, 2^H - 1\}$. The nodes in the Merkle tree are denoted by $y_h[j]$, where $h = 0, \ldots, H$ denotes the height of the node in the tree (leaves have height 0 and the root has height H) and $j = 0, \ldots, 2^{H-h} - 1$ denotes the position of this node in the tree counting from left to right. Further, let $f : \{0,1\}^* \rightarrow \{0,1\}^n$ be a cryptographic hash function. Using this notation, inner nodes of a Merkle tree are computed as

$$y_h[j] = f\left(y_{h-1}[2j] \parallel y_{h-1}[2j+1]\right), \tag{1}$$

for $h = 1, \ldots, H$ and $j = 0, \ldots, 2^{H-h} - 1$.

Next, we define the value τ. In round $\varphi \in \{0, \ldots, 2^H - 1\}$, we define τ as the height of the first parent of leaf φ which is a left node. If leaf φ is a left node itself, then $\tau = 0$. Otherwise τ is given as $\tau = \max\{h : 2^h | (\varphi + 1)\}$. Figure 1 shows an example.

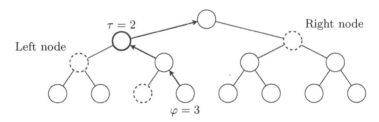

Fig. 1. The height of the first parent of leaf φ that is a left node is $\tau = 2$. The dashed nodes denote the authentication path for leaf φ. The arrows indicate the path from leaf φ to the root.

The value τ tells us on which heights the authentication path for leaf $\varphi + 1$ requires new nodes. It requires new right nodes on heights $h = 0, \ldots, \tau - 1$ and a single new left node on height τ.

Computing inner nodes. A basic tool to compute inner nodes of a Merkle tree is the treehash algorithm shown in Algorithm 1. This algorithm uses a stack STACK with the usual push and pop operations and the LEAFCALC(φ) routine which computes the φth leaf[1]. To compute a node on height h, Algorithm 1 must be executed 2^h times and requires the leaf indices to be input successively from

---

[1] That is, it computes the φth one-time key pair and obtains the leaf from the one-time verification key.

left to right, i.e. $\varphi = 0, \ldots, 2^h - 1$. In total, the computation of 2^h leaves and $2^h - 1$ hashes (inner nodes) is required. After the last call the stack contains one node, the desired inner node on height h. The treehash algorithm stores at most h nodes, so-called tail nodes, on the stack.

Algorithm 1. Treehash

Input: Leaf index φ, stack STACK
Output: Updated stack STACK

1. LEAF ← LEAFCALC(φ)
2. **while** LEAF has the same height in the tree as the top node on STACK **do**
   (a) TOP ← STACK.pop()
   (b) LEAF ← f(TOP ∥ LEAF)
3. STACK.push(LEAF)
4. **Return** STACK

2.1 Our Authentication Path Algorithm

We now describe our Merkle tree traversal algorithm in detail. We begin with a simplified version that requires the height of the Merkle tree to be even. The general version, which comprises a time-memory trade-off suggested by Szydlo, is discussed in Appendix A. Like Szydlo's algorithm [13], we deploy two different strategies to compute authentication nodes, depending on whether the node is a left child (left authentication node, left node) or a right one. The difference to Szydlo's algorithm is, that we only schedule the computation of leaves and not tree nodes in general.

Data structures. Our algorithm uses the following data structures:

- AUTH$_h$, $h = 0, \ldots, H - 1$. An array of nodes that stores the current authentication path.
- RETAIN. The single right authentication node on height $H - 2$.
- STACK. A stack of nodes with the usual push and pop operations.
- TREEHASH$_h$, $h = 0, \ldots, H - 3$. These are instances of the treehash algorithm. All these treehash instances share the stack STACK. Further, each instance has the following entries and methods.

  - TREEHASH$_h$.node. This entry stores a single tail node. This is the first node Algorithm 1 pushes on the stack. The remaining tail nodes are pushed on the stack STACK.
  - TREEHASH$_h$.initialize(φ). This method initializes this instance with the index φ of the leaf to begin with.
  - TREEHASH$_h$.update(). This method executes Algorithm 1 once, meaning that it computes the next leaf (Line 1) and performs the necessary hash function evaluations to compute this leaf's parents (Line 2b), if tail nodes are stored on the stack.

– TREEHASH$_h$.height. This entry stores the height of the lowest tail node stored by this treehash instance, either on the stack STACK or in the entry TREEHASH$_h$.node. If TREEHASH$_h$ does not store any tail nodes TREEHASH$_h$.height = h holds. If TREEHASH$_h$ is finished or not initialized TREEHASH$_h$.height = ∞ holds.

• KEEP$_h$, $h = 0, \ldots, H - 2$. An array of nodes that stores certain nodes for the efficient computation of left authentication nodes.

Initialization. The initialization of our algorithm is done during the MSS key pair generation. We store the authentication path for the first leaf ($\varphi = 0$): AUTH$_h$ = $y_h[1]$, $h = 0, \ldots, H - 1$. We also store the next right authentication node in the treehash instances: TREEHASH$_h$.node = $y_h[3]$, for $h = 0, \ldots, H - 3$. Finally we store the single next right authentication node on height $H - 2$: RETAIN = $y_{H-2}[3]$. Figure 2 shows which nodes are stored during the initialization.

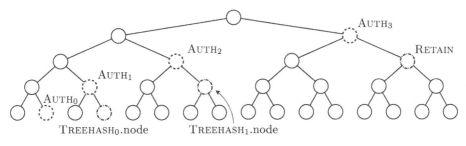

Fig. 2. Initialization of our algorithm. Dashed nodes denote the authentication path for leaf ($\varphi = 0$). Dash-dotted nodes denote the nodes stored in the treehash instances and the single node RETAIN.

Update and output phase. In the following we describe the update and output phase of our algorithm. Algorithm 2 shows a pseudo-code description. Input is the index of the current leaf $\varphi \in \{0, \ldots, 2^H - 2\}$, the height of the Merkle tree $H \geq 2$, where H must be even, and the algorithm state AUTH, KEEP, RETAIN, and TREEHASH prepared in previous rounds or during the initialization. Our algorithm first generates the authentication path for the next leaf $\varphi + 1$ and then computes the algorithm state for the next step. Output is the authentication path for leaf $\varphi + 1$.

Computing left authentication nodes. We review the computation of left nodes due to [13]. The basic idea is to store certain right nodes in an array KEEP$_h$, $h = 0, \ldots, H - 2$ and use them later to compute left authentication nodes using only one evaluation of the hash function.

If in round $\varphi \in \{0, \ldots, 2^H - 2\}$, the parent of leaf φ on height $\tau + 1$ is a left node (this can be verified by checking if $\lfloor \varphi / 2^{\tau+1} \rfloor$ is even), then AUTH$_\tau$ is a right node and we store it in KEEP$_\tau$ (Line 2). In round $\varphi' = \varphi + 2^\tau$ the authentication path for leaf $\varphi' + 1$ requires a new left authentication node on height $\tau' = \tau + 1$. The left child of this authentication node is the authentication node on height $\tau' - 1$ of leaf φ'. The right child of this node was stored in $\text{KEEP}_{\tau'-1}$ in round φ. The new left authentication node on height τ' is then computed as $\text{AUTH}_{\tau'} = f(\text{AUTH}_{\tau'-1} \parallel \text{KEEP}_{\tau'-1})$ (Line 4a). For those rounds φ where $\tau = 0$ holds, the single new left node required for the authentication path of leaf $\varphi + 1$ is the current leaf φ. We compute it using the algorithm LEAFCALC, i.e. we set $\text{AUTH}_0 = \text{LEAFCALC}(\varphi)$ (Line 3).

Computing right authentication nodes. Unlike left authentication nodes, right authentication nodes must be computed from scratch, i.e. starting from the leaves. This is because none of their child nodes were used in previous authentication paths. We use one TREEHASH instance for each height where right authentication nodes must be computed, i.e. for heights $h = 0, \ldots, H - 3$.

In round $\varphi \in \{0, \ldots, 2^H - 2\}$, the authentication path for leaf $\varphi + 1$ requires new right authentication nodes on heights $h = 0, \ldots, \tau - 1$. Our algorithm is constructed such that for $h \leq H - 3$ these nodes are already computed and stored in $\text{TREEHASH}_h.\text{node}$. If a new authentication node is required on height $h = H - 2$ we copy it from the node RETAIN. Note that there is only one new right node required on this height during the whole runtime of Algorithm 2. The authentication path for leaf $\varphi + 1$ is obtained by copying the nodes from $\text{TREEHASH}_h.\text{node}$ and RETAIN to AUTH_h for $h = 0, \ldots, \tau - 1$ (Line 4b).

After copying the right nodes, all treehash instances on height $h = 0, \ldots, \tau - 1$ are initialized for the computation of the next right authentication node. The index of the leaf to begin with is $\varphi + 1 + 3 \cdot 2^h$. If $\varphi + 1 + 3 \cdot 2^h \geq 2^H$ holds, then no new right node will be required on this height and the treehash instance is not initialized anymore (Line 4c).

The last step of the algorithm is to update the treehash instances using the $\text{TREEHASH}_h.\text{update}()$ method (Line 5). We perform $H/2 - 1$ updates in each round. One update corresponds to one execution of Algorithm 1, i.e. one update requires the computation of one leaf and the necessary hash function evaluations to compute this leaf's parents. We use the strategy from [13] to decide which of the $H - 2$ treehash instances receives an update. The treehash instance that receives an update is the instance where $\text{TREEHASH}_h.\text{height}$ contains the smallest value. If there is more than one such instance, we choose the one with the lowest index (Line 5a).

2.2   Correctness

In this section we show the correctness of Algorithm 2. First we show that the budget of $H/2 - 1$ updates per round is sufficient for the treehash instances to compute the required authentication nodes on time. Then we will show that it is possible for all treehash instances to share a single stack.

Nodes are computed on time. If TREEHASH_h is initialized in round φ, the authentication node on height h computed by this instance is required in round $\varphi + 2^{h+1}$. During these 2^{h+1} rounds there are $(H - 2)2^h$ updates available and TREEHASH_h requires 2^h updates to complete.

Algorithm 2. Authentication path computation, simplified version

---

Input: $\varphi \in \{0, \ldots, 2^H - 2\}$, $H \geq 2$ even, and the algorithm state.
Output: Authentication path for leaf $\varphi + 1$

1. Let $\tau = 0$ if leaf φ is a left node or let τ be the height of the first parent of leaf φ which is a left node:
   $\tau \leftarrow \max\{h : 2^h | (\varphi + 1)\}$
2. If the parent of leaf φ on height $\tau + 1$ is a left node, store the current authentication node on height τ in KEEP_τ:
   if $\lfloor \varphi/2^{\tau+1} \rfloor$ is even **and** $\tau < H - 1$ **then** $\text{KEEP}_\tau \leftarrow \text{AUTH}_\tau$
3. If leaf φ is a left node, it is required for the authentication path of leaf $\varphi + 1$:
   if $\tau = 0$ **then** $\text{AUTH}_0 \leftarrow \text{LEAFCALC}(\varphi)$
4. Otherwise, if leaf φ is a right node, the authentication path for leaf $\varphi + 1$ changes on heights $0, \ldots, \tau$:
   if $\tau > 0$ **then**
   (a) The authentication path for leaf $\varphi + 1$ requires a new left node on height τ. It is computed using the current authentication node on height $\tau - 1$ and the node on height $\tau - 1$ previously stored in $\text{KEEP}_{\tau-1}$. The node stored in $\text{KEEP}_{\tau-1}$ can then be removed:
   $\text{AUTH}_\tau \leftarrow f(\text{AUTH}_{\tau-1} \| \text{KEEP}_{\tau-1})$, remove $\text{KEEP}_{\tau-1}$
   (b) The authentication path for leaf $\varphi + 1$ requires new right nodes on heights $h = 0, \ldots, \tau - 1$. For $h \leq H - 3$ these nodes are stored in TREEHASH_h and for $h = H - 2$ in RETAIN:
   for $h = 0$ **to** $\tau - 1$ **do**
       if $h \leq H - 3$ **then** $\text{AUTH}_h \leftarrow \text{TREEHASH}_h.\text{node}$
       if $h = H - 2$ **then** $\text{AUTH}_h \leftarrow \text{RETAIN}$
   (c) For heights $0, \ldots, \tau - 1$ the treehash instances must be initialized anew. The treehash instance on height h is initialized with the start index $\varphi + 1 + 3 \cdot 2^h$ if this index is smaller than 2^H:
   for $h = 0$ **to** $\tau - 1$ **do**
       if $\varphi + 1 + 3 \cdot 2^h < 2^H$ **then** $\text{TREEHASH}_h.\text{initialize}(\varphi + 1 + 3 \cdot 2^h)$
5. Next we spend the budget of $H/2 - 1$ updates on the treehash instances to prepare upcoming authentication nodes:
   repeat $H/2 - 1$ **times**
   (a) We consider only stacks which are initialized and not finished. Let s be the index of the treehash instance whose lowest tail node has the lowest height. In case there is more than one such instance we choose the instance with the lowest index:
   $$s \leftarrow \min \left\{ h : \text{TREEHASH}_h.\text{height} = \min_{j=0,\ldots,H-3} \{\text{TREEHASH}_j.\text{height}\} \right\}$$
   (b) The treehash instance with index s receives one update:
   $\text{TREEHASH}_s.\text{update}()$
6. The last step is to output the authentication path for leaf $\varphi + 1$:
   return $\text{AUTH}_0, \ldots, \text{AUTH}_{H-1}$.

On height $i = 0, \ldots, h-1$, a new instance is initialized every 2^{i+1} rounds, each requiring 2^i updates to complete. During the 2^{h+1} available rounds, $2^{h+1}/2^{i+1}$ treehash instances are initialized on heights $i = 0, \ldots, h - 1$. All these lower instances are completed before TREEHASH$_h$ (Line 5a).

In addition, active treehash instances on heights $i = h + 1, \ldots, H - 3$ might receive updates until their lowest tail node has height h. Once they have a tail node on height h they don't receive further updates while the instance on height h is active (Line 5a). Computing a tail node on height h requires at most 2^h updates.

The number of updates required to complete TREEHASH$_h$ on time is at most

$$\sum_{i=0}^{h-1} \frac{2^{h+1}}{2^{i+1}} \cdot 2^i + 2^h + \sum_{i=h+1}^{H-3} 2^h = (H-2)2^h \tag{2}$$

This shows that the budget of $H/2 - 1$ leaves per round suffices. For $h = H - 3$ this bound is tight.

Sharing a single stack works. To show that it is possible for all treehash instances to share a single stack, we have to show that if TREEHASH$_h$ receives an update and has previously stored tail nodes on the stack, all these tail nodes are on top of the stack.

When TREEHASH$_h$ receives its first update, the height of the lowest tail node of TREEHASH$_i$, $i \in \{h+1, \ldots, H-3\}$ is at least h. Otherwise, one of the instances on height i would receive an update (Line 5a). This means that TREEHASH$_h$ is completed before TREEHASH$_i$ receives another update and thus tail nodes of higher treehash instances do not interfere with tail nodes of TREEHASH$_h$.

While TREEHASH$_h$ is active and stores tail nodes on the stack, it is possible that treehash instances on lower heights $i \in \{0, \ldots, h - 1\}$ receive updates and store nodes on the stack. If TREEHASH$_i$ receives an update, the height of the lowest tail node of TREEHASH$_h$ has height $\geq i$. This implies that TREEHASH$_i$ is completed before TREEHASH$_h$ receives another update and therefore doesn't store tail nodes on the stack anymore.

2.3   Time and Space Bounds

This section considers the time and space requirements of Algorithm 2. We will show that

i) On average, our algorithm computes $(H - 1)/2$ leaves and $(H - 3)/2$ inner nodes.

ii) The number of tail nodes stored on the stack is bounded by $H - 4$.

iii) The number of inner nodes computed by all treehash instances per round is bounded by $3/2(H - 3)$.

iv) The number of nodes stored in KEEP is bounded by $H/2 + 1$.

For the space, we have to add the H nodes stored in AUTH, the $H - 2$ nodes TREEHASH.node and the single node stored in RETAIN. For the worst case time, we have to add the $H/2 - 1$ leaves to compute right nodes and one leaf and one inner node to compute left nodes (Lines 3, 4a in Algorithm 2). All together we get the following theorem:

Theorem 1. *Let $H \geq 2$ be even. Algorithm 2 needs to store at most $3.5H - 4$ nodes and needs to compute at most $H/2$ leaves and $3/2(H-3)+1$ inner nodes per step to successively compute authentication paths. On average, Algorithm 2 computes $(H-1)/2$ leaves and $(H-3)/2$ inner nodes per step.*

Average costs. We now estimate the average cost of our algorithm in terms of leaves (L) and inner nodes (I) to compute. We begin with the right nodes. On height $h = 0$ there are 2^{H-1} right leaves to compute. On heights $h = 1, \ldots, H-3$, there are 2^{H-h-1} right nodes to compute. Each of these nodes requires the computation of 2^h leaves and $2^h - 1$ inner nodes. For the left nodes, we must compute one leaf and one inner node every second step, alternating. This makes a total of 2^{H-1} leaves and inner nodes. Summing up yields

$$\left(\sum_{h=0}^{H-3} 2^{H-h-1} \cdot 2^h + 2^{H-1} \right) L + \left(\sum_{h=1}^{H-3} 2^{H-h-1} \cdot (2^h - 1) + 2^{H-1} \right) I \quad (3)$$

$$= \left(\frac{H-1}{2} \cdot 2^H \right) L + \left(\frac{H-3}{2} \cdot 2^H + 4 \right) I \quad (4)$$

as total number of leaves and inner nodes that must be computed. To obtain the average cost per step we divide by 2^H.

Space required by the stack. We will show that the stack stores at most one tail node on each height $h = 0, \ldots, H - 5$ at a time.

TREEHASH$_h$, $h \in \{0, \ldots, H - 3\}$ stores up to h tail nodes on different heights to compute the authentication node on height h. The tail node on height $h-1$ is stored in TREEHASH$_h$.node and the remaining tail nodes on heights $0, \ldots, h - 2$ are stored on the stack. When TREEHASH$_h$ receives its first update, the following two conditions hold:

1. All treehash instances on heights $< h$ are either empty or completed and store no tail nodes on the stack.
2. All treehash instances on heights $> h$ are either empty or completed or have tail nodes of height at least h.

Both conditions follow directly from Line 5a in Algorithm 2. These conditions imply that while TREEHASH$_h$ is active, all tail nodes on the stack that have height at most $h - 2$ are on different heights.

If a treehash instance on height $i = h + 1, \ldots, H - 3$ stores a tail node on the stack, then all treehash instances on heights $i + 1, \ldots, H - 3$ have tail nodes of height at least i, otherwise the treehash instance on height i wouldn't have received any updates in the first place (recall that TREEHASH$_i$.height $= i$ holds if TREEHASH$_i$ was just initialized). This implies that all tail nodes on the stack that have height at least h and at most $H - 5$ are on different heights.

If a treehash instance on height $j < h$ is initialized while TREEHASH_h is active, the same arguments can be applied to the instance on height j.

In total, there is at most one tail node on each height $h = 0, \ldots, H - 5$ which bounds the number of nodes stored on the stack by $H - 4$. This bound is tight for round $\varphi = 2^{H-1} - 2$, before the update that completes the treehash instance on height $H - 3$.

Inner nodes computed by treehash. For now we assume that the maximum number of inner nodes is computed in the following case: TREEHASH_{H-3} receives all $u = H/2 - 1$ updates and is completed in this round. On input an index φ, the number of inner nodes computed by treehash in the worst case equals the height of the first parent of leaf φ which is a left node, if the corresponding tail nodes are stored on the stack. On height h, a left node occurs every 2^h leaves, which means that every 2^h updates at most h inner nodes are computed by treehash. This implies that during the u available updates, at most one inner node on height h is computed every $\lceil u/2^h \rceil$ updates for $h = 1, \ldots, \lceil \log_2 u \rceil$. The last update requires the computation of $H - 3 = 2u - 1$ inner nodes to obtain the desired node on height $H - 3$, i.e. completing this treehash instance. So far only $\lceil \log_2 u \rceil$ inner nodes were counted, so *additional* $2u - 1 - \lceil \log_2 u \rceil$ inner nodes must be added. In total, we get the following upper bound for the number of inner nodes computed per round.

$$B = \sum_{h=1}^{\lceil \log_2 u \rceil} \left\lceil \frac{u}{2^h} \right\rceil + 2u - 1 - \lceil \log_2 u \rceil \tag{5}$$

In round $\varphi = 2^{H-1} - 2$ this bound is tight. This is the last round before the treehash instance on height $H - 3$ must be completed and as we saw in Section 2.2, all available updates are required in this case. The desired upper bound is estimated as follows:

$$B \leq \sum_{h=1}^{\lceil \log_2 u \rceil} \left(\frac{u}{2^h} + 1 \right) + 2u - 1 - \lceil \log_2 u \rceil$$

$$= u \sum_{h=1}^{\lceil \log_2 u \rceil} \frac{1}{2^h} + 2u - 1 = u \left(1 - \frac{1}{2^{\lceil \log_2 u \rceil}} \right) + 2u - 1$$

$$\leq u \left(1 - \frac{1}{2u} \right) + 2u - 1 = 3u - \frac{3}{2} = \frac{3}{2}(H - 3)$$

The next step is to show that the above mentioned case is indeed the worst case. If a treehash instance on height $< H - 3$ receives all updates and is completed in this round, less than B hashes are required. The same holds if the treehash instance receives all updates but is not completed in this round. The last case to consider is the one where the u available updates are spend on treehash instances on different heights. If the active treehash instance TREEHASH_h stores a tail node ν on height j, it will receive updates until it has a tail node on height $j+1$. This requires 2^j updates and the computation of 2^j inner nodes. *Additional*

$t \in \{1 \ldots H - j - 4\}$ inner nodes are computed to obtain ν's parent on height $j + t + 1$, if $\mathrm{TREEHASH}_h$ stores tail nodes on heights $j + 1 \ldots j + t$ on the stack and in $\mathrm{TREEHASH}_h$.node. The next treehash instance that receives the remaining updates has a tail node on height $\geq j$. This instance computes *additional* inner nodes only, if there are enough updates left to compute an inner node on height $\geq j + t$, the height of the next tail node possibly stored on the stack. But this is the same scenario that appears in the above mentioned worst case, i.e. if a node on height $j + 1$ is computed, the tail nodes on the stack are used to compute its parent on height $j + t + 1$ and the same instance receives the next update.

Space required to compute left nodes. First we remark that because of Steps 2 and 4a in Algorithm 2, the node stored in KEEP_{h-1} is removed whenever an authentication node is stored in KEEP_h in the same round, $h = 1, \ldots, H - 2$. Next we show that if a node gets stored in KEEP_h, $h = 0, \ldots, H - 3$, then KEEP_{h+1} is empty. To see this we have to consider in which rounds a node is stored in KEEP_{h+1}. This happens in rounds $\varphi \in S_a = \{2^{h+1} - 1 + a \cdot 2^{h+3}, \ldots, 2^{h+2} - 1 + a \cdot 2^{h+3}\}, a \in \mathbb{N}_0$. In rounds $\varphi' = 2^h - 1 + b \cdot 2^{h+2}, b \in \mathbb{N}_0$, a node gets stored in KEEP_h. It is straight forward to compute that $\varphi' \in S_a$ implies that $2a + 1/4 \leq b \leq 2a + 3/4$ which is a contradiction to $b \in \mathbb{N}_0$.

As a result, at most $H/2$ nodes are stored in KEEP at a time and two consecutive nodes can share one entry. One additional entry is required to temporarily store the authentication node on height h (Step 2) until node on height $h - 1$ is removed (Step 4a).

3   Comparison

We now compare our algorithm with Szydlo's algorithm from [13]. We compare the number of leaves, inner nodes, and total hash function evaluations computed per step in the worst case and the average case.

The computation of an inner node costs one hash function evaluation. This follows directly from the construction rule for Merkle trees of Equation (1). The cost to compute one leaf, in terms of hash function evaluations, depends on the one-time signature scheme used for the MSS. The Lamport–Diffie one-time signature scheme [8] requires $2n$ evaluations of the hash function, where n is the output length of the hash function. The Winternitz one-time signature scheme [5] roughly requires $2^w \cdot n/w$ evaluations of the hash function, where w is the Winternitz parameter. For our comparison, we use a cost of 100 hash function evaluations for each leaf calculation.

Table 1 shows the number of leaves, inner nodes, and total hash function evaluations computed per step in the worst case and the average case. These values were obtained experimental. The number of leaves and inner nodes our algorithm requires according to Theorem 1 are given in parentheses.

This table shows, that the cost for the inner nodes is negligible compared to the cost for the leaf calculations. Our algorithm reduces the total number of hash function evaluations required in the worst case by more than $49\%, 27\%, 28\%, 15\%$ for $H = 4, 10, 14, 20$, respectively, even when using the comparatively low ratio

Table 1. Comparison of the worst case and average case runtime of our algorithm and Szydlos algorithm from [13]. The values according to Theorem 1 are given in parentheses.

H	Our Algorithm			Szydlo's Algorithm		
	leaves	inner nodes	hashes	leaves	inner nodes	hashes
Worst case						
4	2 (2)	1 (2.5)	201	4	0	400
10	5 (5)	8 (11.5)	508	7	4	704
14	7 (7)	14 (17.5)	714	10	4	1000
20	10 (10)	24 (26.5)	1024	12	8	1208
Average case						
4	1.2 (1.5)	0.6 (0.5)	120.6	1.5	0.6	150.6
10	4.0 (4.5)	3.0 (3.5)	403.0	4.5	3.5	453.5
14	6.0 (6.5)	5.0 (5.5)	605.0	6.5	5.5	655.5
20	9.0 (9.5)	8.0 (8.5)	908.0	9.5	8.5	958.5

of 100 hash function evaluations per leaf. When using larger ratios, as they occur in practice, the advantage of our algorithm is more distinct. We state the comparison only for Merkle trees up to a height of $H = 20$, since for larger heights the MSS key pair generation becomes too inefficient so that Merkle trees of height $H > 20$ cannot be used in practice [2].

For $H = 4, 10, 14, 20$, our algorithm needs to store $10, 31, 45, 66$ nodes and Szydlo's algorithm needs to store $10, 28, 40, 58$ nodes, respectively. Although Szydlo's algorithm requires slightly less storage, additional implementing effort and possibly overhead must be taken into account when using Szydlo's algorithm on platforms without dynamic memory allocation. This is because Szydlo's algorithm uses separate stacks for each of the H treehash instances, where, roughly speaking, each stack can store up to $O(H)$ nodes but all stacks together never store more than $O(H)$ nodes at a time. The simple approach of reserving the maximal required memory for each stack yields memory usage quadratic in H.

Table 1 also shows, that our algorithm on average performs slightly better than Szydlo's algorithm. This is a result of the slightly increased memory usage of our algorithm. More importantly, comparing the average case and worst case runtime shows, that the worst case runtime of our algorithm is extremely close to its average case runtime. This certifies that our algorithm provides balanced timings for the authentication path generation and thus the MSS signature generation.

4   Conclusion

We proposed a new algorithm for the computation of authentication paths in a Merkle tree. In the worst case, our algorithm is significantly faster than the best algorithm known so far, namely Szydlo's algorithm from [13]. In fact, the worst case runtime of our algorithm is very close to its average case runtime which, in turn, equals the average case runtime of Szydlo's algorithm. The main idea of our algorithm is to distinguish between leaves and inner nodes of the Merkle tree and balance the number of leaves computed in each step.

In detail, our algorithm computes $H/2$ leaves and $3/2(H - 3) + 1$ inner nodes in the worst case and $(H - 1)/2$ leaves and $(H - 3)/2$ inner nodes on average. For example, we reduce the worst case cost for computing authentication paths in a Merkle tree of height $H = 20$ by more than 15% compared to Szydlo's algorithm. When implementing our algorithm, the space bound of $3.5H - 4$ nodes can be achieved without additional effort, even on platforms that do not offer dynamic memory allocation.

References

1. Berman, P., Karpinski, M., Nekrich, Y.: Optimal trade-off for Merkle tree traversal. Theoretical Computer Science 372(1), 26–36 (2007)
2. Buchmann, J., Coronado, C., Dahmen, E., Döring, M., Klintsevich, E.: CMSS — an improved Merkle signature scheme. In: Barua, R., Lange, T. (eds.) INDOCRYPT 2006. LNCS, vol. 4329, pp. 349–363. Springer, Heidelberg (2006)
3. Buchmann, J., Dahmen, E., Klintsevich, E., Okeya, K., Vuillaume, C.: Merkle signatures with virtually unlimited signature capacity. In: Katz, J., Yung, M. (eds.) ACNS 2007. LNCS, vol. 4521, pp. 31–45. Springer, Heidelberg (2007)
4. Coronado, C.: On the security and the efficiency of the Merkle signature scheme. Cryptology ePrint Archive, Report 2005/192 (2005), http://eprint.iacr.org/
5. Dods, C., Smart, N., Stam, M.: Hash based digital signature schemes. In: Smart, N. (ed.) Cryptography and Coding 2005. LNCS, vol. 3796, pp. 96–115. Springer, Heidelberg (2005)
6. Grover, L.K.: A fast quantum mechanical algorithm for database search. In: Proceedings of the Twenty-Eighth Annual Symposium on the Theory of Computing, pp. 212–219. ACM Press, New York (1996)
7. Jakobsson, M., Leighton, T., Micali, S., Szydlo, M.: Fractal Merkle tree representation and traversal. In: Joye, M. (ed.) CT-RSA 2003. LNCS, vol. 2612, pp. 314–326. Springer, Heidelberg (2003)
8. Lamport, L.: Constructing digital signatures from a one way function. Technical Report SRI-CSL-98, SRI International Computer Science Laboratory (1979)
9. Lenstra, A.K., Verheul., E.R.: Selecting cryptographic key sizes. Journal of Cryptology 14(4), 255–293 (2001); updated version (2004), http://plan9.bell-labs.com/who/akl/index.html
10. Merkle, R.C.: A certified digital signature. In: Brassard, G. (ed.) CRYPTO 1989. LNCS, vol. 435, pp. 218–238. Springer, Heidelberg (1990)
11. Naor, D., Shenhav, A., Wool, A.: One-time signatures revisited: Practical fast signatures using fractal merkle tree traversal. In: IEEE – 24th Convention of Electrical and Electronics Engineers in Israel, pp. 255–259 (2006)
12. Shor, P.W.: Algorithms for quantum computation: Discrete logarithms and factoring. In: Proc. 35th Annual Symposium on Foundations of Computer Science, pp. 124–134. IEEE Computer Society Press, Los Alamitos (1994)

13. Szydlo, M.: Merkle tree traversal in log space and time (preprint, 2003),
    http://www.szydlo.com/
14. Szydlo, M.: Merkle tree traversal in log space and time. In: Cachin, C., Camenisch,
    J.L. (eds.) EUROCRYPT 2004. LNCS, vol. 3027, pp. 541–554. Springer, Heidelberg
    (2004)

A   General Version of the Authentication Path Algorithm

We now describe the general version of our algorithm that is able to handle
Merkle trees of odd height. The general version also provides an additional trade-
off between the computation time and the storage needed, as suggested by Szydlo
in [13]. The basic idea is to store more right authentication nodes (like the
single node RETAIN) to obtain an even number of treehash instances that need
updating. The parameter K denotes the number of upper levels where all right
nodes are stored permanently. We must choose $K \geq 2$, such that $H - K$ is
even. Instead of a single node RETAIN, we now use stacks RETAIN_h, $h = H -
K, \ldots, H - 2$, to store all right authentication nodes during the initialization:
$\text{RETAIN}_h.\text{push}(y_h[2j + 3])$, for $h = H - K, \ldots, H - 2$ and $j = 2^{H-h-1} - 2, \ldots, 0$.
The pseudo-code of the general version is shown in Algorithm 3. Including the
parameter K in Theorem 1 yields Theorem 2.

Theorem 2. *Let $H \geq 2$ and $K \geq 2$ such that $H - K$ is even. Algorithm 3 needs
to store at most $3H + \lfloor H/2 \rfloor - 3K - 2 + 2^K$ nodes and needs to compute at most
$(H - K)/2 + 1$ leaves and $3(H - K - 1)/2 + 1$ inner nodes per step to successively
compute authentication paths. On average, Algorithm 3 computes $(H - K + 1)/2$
leaves and $(H - K - 1)/2$ inner nodes per step.*

The simplified version described in Section 2 corresponds to the choice $K = 2$.
The proofs for the correctness and the time and space bounds of the general
version can be obtained by substituting $H - K + 2$ for H in the proofs for the
simplified version.

B   Computing Leaves Using a PRNG

In [2], the authors propose to use a forward secure PRNG to successively compute
the one-time signature keys. The benefit is that the storage cost for the private
key is reduced drastically, since only one seed must be stored instead of 2^H
one-time signature keys. Let SEED_φ denote the seed required to compute the
one-time key pair corresponding to leaf φ.

During the authentication path computation, leaves which are up to $3 \cdot 2^{H-K-1}$
steps away from the current leaf must be computed. Calling the PRNG that
many times to obtain the seed required to compute this leaf is too inefficient.
Instead we propose the following scheduling strategy that requires $H - K$ calls
to the PRNG in each round to compute the seeds. We have to store two seeds
for each height $h = 0, \ldots, H - K - 1$. The first (SEEDACTIVE) is used to successively compute the leaves for the authentication node currently constructed

---

Algorithm 3. Authentication path computation, general version

---

Input: $\varphi \in \{0, \ldots, 2^H - 2\}$, H, K and the algorithm state.
Output: Auththentication path for leaf $\varphi + 1$

1. Let $\tau = 0$ if leaf φ is a left node or let τ be the height of the first parent of leaf φ which is a left node:
$$\tau \leftarrow \max\{h : 2^h | (\varphi + 1)\}$$

2. If the parent of leaf φ on height $\tau + 1$ is a left node, store the current authentication node on height τ in KEEP_τ:
if $\lfloor \varphi / 2^{\tau+1} \rfloor$ is even **and** $\tau < H - 1$ **then** $\text{KEEP}_\tau \leftarrow \text{AUTH}_\tau$

3. If leaf φ is a left node, it is required for the authentication path of leaf $\varphi + 1$:
if $\tau = 0$ **then** $\text{AUTH}_0 \leftarrow \text{LEAFCALC}(\varphi)$

4. Otherwise, if leaf φ is a right node, the authentication path for leaf $\varphi + 1$ changes on heights $0, \ldots, \tau$:
if $\tau > 0$ **then**

   (a) The authentication path for leaf $\varphi + 1$ requires a new left node on height τ. It is computed using the current authentication node on height $\tau - 1$ and the node on height $\tau - 1$ previously stored in $\text{KEEP}_{\tau-1}$. The node stored in $\text{KEEP}_{\tau-1}$ can then be removed:
   $\text{AUTH}_\tau \leftarrow f(\text{AUTH}_{\tau-1} \| \text{KEEP}_{\tau-1})$, remove $\text{KEEP}_{\tau-1}$

   (b) The authentication path for leaf $\varphi + 1$ requires new right nodes on heights $h = 0, \ldots, \tau - 1$. For $h \leq H - K - 1$ these nodes are stored in TREEHASH_h and for $h \geq H - K$ in RETAIN_h:
   for $h = 0$ **to** $\tau - 1$ **do**
       if $h \leq H - K - 1$ **then** $\text{AUTH}_h \leftarrow \text{TREEHASH}_h.\text{node}$
       if $h > H - K - 1$ **then** $\text{AUTH}_h \leftarrow \text{RETAIN}_h.\text{pop}()$

   (c) For heights $0, \ldots, \min\{\tau - 1, H - K - 1\}$ the treehash instances must be initialized anew. The treehash instance on height h is initialized with the start index $\varphi + 1 + 3 \cdot 2^h$ if this index is smaller than 2^H:
   for $h = 0$ **to** $\min\{\tau - 1, H - K - 1\}$ **do**
       if $\varphi + 1 + 3 \cdot 2^h < 2^H$ **then** $\text{TREEHASH}_h.\text{initialize}(\varphi + 1 + 3 \cdot 2^h)$

5. Next we spend the budget of $(H - K)/2$ updates on the treehash instances to prepare upcoming authentication nodes:
repeat $(H - K)/2$ **times**

   (a) We consider only stacks which are initialized and not finished. Let s be the index of the treehash instance whose lowest tail node has the lowest height. In case there is more than one such instance we choose the instance with the lowest index:
   $$s \leftarrow \min\left\{ h : \text{TREEHASH}_h.\text{height}() = \min_{j=0,\ldots,H-K-1} \{\text{TREEHASH}_j.\text{height}()\} \right\}$$

   (b) The treehash instance with index s receives one update:
   $\text{TREEHASH}_s.\text{update}()$

6. The last step is to output the authentication path for leaf $\varphi + 1$:
return $\text{AUTH}_0, \ldots, \text{AUTH}_{H-1}$.

---

by TREEHASH$_h$ and the second (SEEDNEXT) is used for upcoming right nodes on this height. SEEDNEXT is updated using the PRNG in each round. During the initialization, we set SEEDNEXT$_h$ = SEED$_{3 \cdot 2^h}$ for $h = 0, \ldots, H - K - 1$. In each round, at first all seeds SEEDNEXT$_h$ are updated using the PRNG. If in round φ a new treehash instance is initialized on height h, we copy SEEDNEXT$_h$ to SEEDACTIVE$_h$. In that case SEEDNEXT$_h$ = SEED$_{\varphi+1+3 \cdot 2^h}$ holds and thus is the correct seed to begin computing the next authentication node on height h.

Explicit Hard Instances of the Shortest Vector Problem

Johannes Buchmann, Richard Lindner, and Markus Rückert

Technische Universität Darmstadt, Department of Computer Science
Hochschulstraße 10, 64289 Darmstadt, Germany
{buchmann,rlindner,rueckert}@cdc.informatik.tu-darmstadt.de

Abstract. Building upon a famous result due to Ajtai, we propose a sequence of lattice bases with growing dimension, which can be expected to be hard instances of the shortest vector problem (SVP) and which can therefore be used to benchmark lattice reduction algorithms.

The SVP is the basis of security for potentially post-quantum cryptosystems. We use our sequence of lattice bases to create a challenge, which may be helpful in determining appropriate parameters for these schemes.

Keywords: Lattice reduction, lattice-based cryptography, challenge.

1   Introduction

For the construction of post-quantum cryptosystems, it is necessary to identify computational problems, whose difficulty can be used as a basis of the security for such systems, and that remain difficult even in the presence of quantum computers. One candidate is the problem of approximating short vectors in a lattice (shortest vector problem — SVP). The quantum-hardness of this problem was analyzed by Ludwig [25] and Regev [33]. They both find that the computational advantage gained with quantum computers is marginal. There are several cryptographic schemes whose security is based on the intractability of the SVP in lattices of sufficiently large dimension (e.g. [3, 16, 17, 34]). To determine appropriate parameters for these cryptosystems, it is necessary to assess the practical difficulty of this problem as precisely as possible.

In this paper, we present a sequence of lattice bases with increasing dimension, which we propose as a world wide challenge. The construction of these lattices is based both on theoretical and on practical considerations. On the theoretical side, we apply a result of Ajtai [2]. It states that being able to find a sufficiently short vector in a random lattice from a certain set, which also contains our challenge lattices, implies the ability to solve supposedly hard problems (cf. [35]) in all lattices with a slightly smaller dimension than that of the random lattice. Furthermore, we invoke a theorem of Dirichlet on Diophantine approximation (cf. [20]). It guarantees the existence of a short vector in each challenge lattice. On the practical side, using an analysis by Gama and Nguyen [13], we argue

J. Buchmann and J. Ding (Eds.): PQCrypto 2008, LNCS 5299, pp. 79–94, 2008.

that finding this vector is hard for the lattices in our challenge. We also present first experimental results that confirm the analysis.

Our challenge at `http://www.latticechallenge.org` can be considered as an analogue of similar challenges for the integer factoring problem [36] and the problems of computing discrete logarithms in the multiplicative group of a finite field [27], or in the group of points on an elliptic curve over a finite field [10].

Our aim is to evaluate the current state-of-the-art in practical lattice basis reduction by providing means for an immediate and well-founded comparison. As a first application of the proposed challenge, we compare the performance of LLL-type reduction methods — LLL [24], Stehlé's fpLLL [30], Koy and Schnorr's segment LLL (sLLL) [22] — and block-type algorithms — Schnorr's BKZ [38, 39], Koy's primal-dual (PD) [21], Ludwig's practical random sampling [1] (PSR) [26]. To our knowledge, this is the first comparison of these algorithms.

Related work. Lattice reduction has been subject to intense studies over the last decades, where a couple of methods and reduction schemes, in particular the LLL algorithm by Lenstra, Lenstra, and Lovász [24], have been developed and successively improved. Especially, the block Korkine Zolorarev algorithm (BKZ), due to Schnorr [38, 39], has become the standard method when strong lattice basis reduction is required.

There have been several approaches to measure the effectiveness of known lattice reduction algorithms, especially in the context of the NTRU cryptosystem [17]. Some of them, as in [18, 19], base their analysis on cryptosystems while others, like [13, 31], make a more general approach using random lattices.

To our knowledge, there has never been a unified challenge, one that is independent of a specific cryptosystem, for lattice reduction algorithms. In all previous challenges, the solution was always known to the creator.

Organization. In Section 2, we provide a brief introduction to lattices and state some fundamental definitions. In Section 3, we define a family of lattices and prove two properties, which are fundamental for our explicit construction presented in Section 4. Then, we give first experimental results comparing the performance of various lattice reduction algorithms in Section 5. Finally, Section 6 introduces the actual lattice challenge.

2   Preliminaries

Let $\mathbb{R}^n$ denote the n-dimensional real vectorspace. We write the vectors of this space in boldface to distinguish them from numbers. Any two vectors $\mathbf{v}, \mathbf{w} \in \mathbb{R}^n$ have an inner product $\langle \mathbf{v}, \mathbf{w} \rangle = \mathbf{v}^T \mathbf{w}$. Any $\mathbf{v} \in \mathbb{R}^n$ has a length given by the Euclidean norm $\|\mathbf{v}\|_2 = \sqrt{\langle \mathbf{v}, \mathbf{v} \rangle} = \sqrt{v_1^2 + \cdots + v_n^2}$. In addition to the Euclidean norm, we also use the maximum norm $\|\mathbf{v}\|_\infty = \max_{i=1,\ldots,n}\{|v_i|\}$.

A lattice in $\mathbb{R}^n$ is a set $L = \{\sum_{i=1}^m x_i \mathbf{b}_i \mid x_i \in \mathbb{Z}\}$, where $\mathbf{b}_1, \ldots, \mathbf{b}_m$ are linearly independent over $\mathbb{R}$. The matrix $B = [\mathbf{b}_1, \ldots, \mathbf{b}_m]$ is called a *basis* of the lattice L

---

[1] A practical variant of Schnorr's random sampling reduction [40].

and we write $L = L(B)$. The number of linearly independent vectors in the basis is the dimension of the lattice. If $\dim(L(B)) = n$ the lattice is full-dimensional.

An m-dimensional lattice $L = L(B)$ has many different bases, namely all the matrices in the orbit $B\,\mathrm{GL}_m(\mathbb{Z}) = \{BT \mid T \in \mathrm{GL}_m(\mathbb{Z})\}$. If the lattice is full-dimensional and integral, that is $L \subseteq \mathbb{Z}^n$, then there exists a unique basis $B = (b_{i,j})$ of L, which is in Hermite normal form (HNF), i.e.

i. $b_{i,j} = 0$ for all $1 \leq j < i \leq m$
ii. $b_{i,i} > b_{i,j} \geq 0$ for all $1 \leq i < j \leq m$

Furthermore, the volume $\mathrm{vol}(L)$ of a full-dimensional lattice is defined as $|\det(B)|$, for any basis B of L. For every m-dimensional lattice L there is a dual (or polar, reciprocal) lattice $L^* = \{\mathbf{x} \in \mathbb{R}^m \mid \forall \mathbf{y} \in L : \langle \mathbf{x}, \mathbf{y} \rangle \in \mathbb{Z}\}$. For any full-dimensional lattice $L = L(B)$, it holds that $L^* = L((B^{-1})^T)$. The length of the shortest lattice vector, denoted with $\lambda_1 = \lambda_1(L)$, is called first successive minimum.

3   Foundations of the Challenge

In this section, we define a family of sets containing lattices, where each set will have two important properties:

1. All lattices in the set contain non-obvious short vectors;
2. Being able to find a short vector in a lattice chosen uniformly at random from the set, implies being able to solve difficult computational problems in all lattices of a certain smaller dimension.

The family of lattice sets. Let $n \in \mathbb{N}$, $c_1, c_2 \in \mathbb{R}_{>0}$, such that

$$\frac{1}{2\ln(2)} \leq c_2 \leq \frac{c_1}{4} \ln\left(\frac{n}{c_1 \ln(n)}\right) . \tag{1}$$

Furthermore, let

$$m = \lfloor c_1 n \ln(n) \rfloor , \tag{2}$$
$$q = \lfloor n^{c_2} \rfloor , \tag{3}$$

and $\mathbb{Z}_q = \{0, \ldots, q-1\}$. For a matrix $X \in \mathbb{Z}_q^{n \times m}$, with column vectors $\mathbf{x}_1, \ldots, \mathbf{x}_m$, let

$$L(c_1, c_2, n, X) = \left\{ (v_1, \ldots, v_m) \in \mathbb{Z}^m \;\middle|\; \sum_{i=1}^{m} v_i \mathbf{x}_i \equiv 0 \pmod{q} \right\} .$$

All lattices in the set $L(c_1, c_2, n, \cdot) = \{L(c_1, c_2, n, X) \mid X \in \mathbb{Z}_q^{n \times m}\}$ are of dimension m and the family of lattices $\mathfrak{L}$ is the set of all $L(c_1, c_2, n, \cdot)$, such that c_1, c_2, n are chosen according to (1).

In the following theorems, we prove that all lattices in the sets of the family $\mathfrak{L}$ have the desired properties.

Existence of short vectors. We prove that all lattices in $L(c_1, c_2, n, \cdot)$ of the family $\mathfrak{L}$ contain a vector with Euclidean norm less than n.

Theorem 1. *Let $n \in \mathbb{N}, c_1, c_2 \in \mathbb{R}_{>0}$, and $q, m \in \mathbb{N}$ be as described above. Then, any lattice in $L(c_1, c_2, n, \cdot) \in \mathfrak{L}$ contains a vector with Euclidean norm less than n.*

Proof. Let $L(c_1, c_2, n, X) \in L(c_1, c_2, n, \cdot) \in \mathfrak{L}$. We first show that any solution of a certain Diophantine approximation problem corresponds to a vector in $L(c_1, c_2, n, X)$. Then, we use a theorem of Dirichlet to establish the existence of a non-zero lattice vector of length less than n.

Let $\mathbf{v} \in L(c_1, c_2, n, X)$, then there exists $\mathbf{w} \in \mathbb{Z}^n$, such that

$$\frac{1}{q} X \mathbf{v} - \mathbf{w} = 0.$$

This is equivalent to

$$\left\| \frac{1}{q} X \mathbf{v} - \mathbf{w} \right\|_\infty < \frac{1}{q}. \tag{4}$$

Dirichlet's theorem (cf. [20, 37]) states that for any $t > 1$, there is $\mathbf{v} \in \mathbb{Z}^m$ and $\mathbf{w} \in \mathbb{Z}^n$, such that

$$\left\| \frac{1}{q} X \mathbf{v} - \mathbf{w} \right\|_\infty < e^{-\frac{t}{n}} \qquad \text{and} \tag{5}$$

$$\|\mathbf{v}\|_\infty < e^{\frac{t}{m}}. \tag{6}$$

We set $t = n \ln(q)$. Then, (5) implies that (4) is satisfied. It remains to prove that $\|\mathbf{v}\|_\infty < n/\sqrt{m}$ because this implies $\|\mathbf{v}\|_2 < n$. Using (6), we have

$$\|\mathbf{v}\|_\infty < e^{\frac{t}{m}} \le e^{\frac{n \ln(q)}{m}} \le e^{\frac{n \ln(\lfloor n^{c_2} \rfloor)}{\lceil c_1 n \ln(n) \rceil}} \overset{*}{\le} e^{\frac{2 n c_2 \ln(n)}{c_1 n \ln(n)}} \le e^{\frac{2 c_2}{c_1}}.$$

For a rigorous proof of inequality $*$ see Appendix A. Together with (1), this evaluates to

$$e^{\frac{2 c_2}{c_1}} \le e^{\frac{2 c_1}{4 c_1} \ln\left(\frac{n}{c_1 \ln(n)}\right)} \le \sqrt{\frac{n}{c_1 \ln(n)}} \le \frac{n}{\sqrt{m}},$$

which completes the proof. $\qquad\qquad\qquad\qquad\qquad\qquad\qquad\qquad\qquad\qquad\square$

Hardness of finding short vectors. In the following, we show that being able to find short vectors in an m-dimensional lattice chosen uniformly at random from $L(c_1, c_2, n, \cdot) \in \mathfrak{L}$, implies being able to solve (conjectured) hard lattice problems for *all* lattices of dimension n.

In his seminal work [2], Ajtai proved the following theorem that connects average-case instances of certain lattice problems to worst-case instances. The problems are defined as follows.

Lattice problems. Let $L \subseteq \mathbb{Z}^n$ be an n-dimensional lattice and $\gamma \ge 1$. We define the

- Approximate shortest length problem (γ-SLP):
  Find $l \in \mathbb{R}$, such that $l \le \lambda_1(L) \le \gamma l$.

- Approximate shortest vector problem (γ-SVP):
  Find a vector $\mathbf{v} \in L \setminus \{\mathbf{0}\}$, such that for all $\mathbf{w} \in L : \|\mathbf{v}\|_2 \leq \gamma \|\mathbf{w}\|_2$.
- Approximate shortest basis problem (γ-SBP):
  Find a basis B of L, such that for all $C \in B\,\mathrm{GL}_m(\mathbb{Z})$:

$$\max_{i=1,2,\ldots,n} \|\mathbf{b}_i\|_2 \leq \gamma \max_{i=1,2,\ldots,n} \|\mathbf{c}_i\|_2 .$$

Theorem 2 ([2, Theorem 1]). *Let $c > 1$ be an absolute constant. If there exists a probabilistic polynomial time (in n) algorithm $\mathcal{A}$ that finds a vector of norm $< n$ in a random m-dimensional lattice from $L(c_1, c_2, n, \cdot) \in \mathfrak{L}$ with probability $\geq 1/2$ then there exists*

1. *an algorithm $\mathcal{B}_1$ that solves the γ-SLP;*
2. *an algorithm $\mathcal{B}_2$ that solves the SVP, provided that the shortest vector is γ-unique [2];*
3. *an algorithm $\mathcal{B}_3$ that solves the γ-SBP.*

Algorithms $\mathcal{B}_1, \mathcal{B}_2, \mathcal{B}_3$ solve the respective problem (each with $\gamma = n^c$) with probability exponentially close to 1 in all lattices of dimension n, i.e. especially in the worst-case. $\mathcal{B}_1, \mathcal{B}_2,$ and $\mathcal{B}_3$ run in probabilistic polynomial time in n.

As for the constant c in Theorem 2, there have been several improvements to Ajtai's reduction with $c \geq 8$ [9]. The first improvement ($c = 3.5 + \epsilon$) is due to Cai and Nerurkar [9], whereas the most recent works by Miccancio [28] and Micciancio and Regev [29], improve c to almost [3] 1.

Asymptotic and practical hardness of the above problems depends on the choice of γ. A recent survey [35] by Regev states the currently known "approximability" and "inapproximability" results. As for the complexity of lattice problems, it focuses on the works of Lagarias, Lenstra, and Schnorr [23], Banaszczyk [7], Goldreich and Goldwasser [15], Ajtai, Kumar, and Sivakumar [4], Aharonov and Regev [1], and Peikert [32]. Since it is very helpful and descriptive, we adopted Figure 1 from the survey.

On the left, there are provably NP-hard problems, followed by a gap for which the hardness is unknown. In the center, there are problems conjectured not to be NP-hard because their NP-hardness would contradict the general perception that coNP $\neq$ NP. Finally, on the right, there are problems that can be solved in probabilistic polynomial time.

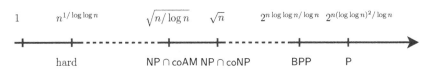

Fig. 1. The complexity of γ-SVP for increasing γ (some constants omitted)

---

[2] A shortest vector $\mathbf{v} \in L$ is γ-*unique* if for all $\mathbf{w} \in L$ with $\|\mathbf{w}\|_2 \leq \gamma \|\mathbf{v}\|_2 \Rightarrow \mathbf{w} = \pm\mathbf{v}$.
[3] Omitting poly-logarithmic terms in the resulting approximation factor.

We emphasize that the problems in Theorem 2 are *not* believed to be NP-hard because $\gamma > \sqrt{n}$. Nevertheless, there is no known algorithm that efficiently solves worst-case instances of lattice problems for sufficiently large dimensions n, with an approximation factor polynomial in n. So Theorem 2 strongly supports our claim that computing short vectors in the lattice family is hard. This is also supported by a heuristic argument of Gama and Nguyen [13], which we refer to in Section 4.

4   Construction of Explicit Bases

Ajtai's construction in [2] defines all lattices implicitly. In this section, we show how to generate explicit integral bases for these lattices.

For any $m \geq 500$, we now construct a lattice L_m of dimension m, which is our hard instance of the SVP. The lattice L_m is of the form $L(c_1, c_2, n, X)$, where the parameters c_1, c_2, n, X are chosen as a function of the dimension m as follows.

We start with a desired lattice dimension m, set $c_2 = 1$, and choose $c_1, n = n(m)$ such that (1) and (2) hold. This is done by setting

$$c_1 = \inf\{c \in \mathbb{R} \mid \exists n \in \mathbb{N} : m = \lfloor cn \ln(n) \rfloor \wedge c_2 \leq c \ln(n/(c \ln(n)))/4\}, \quad (7)$$

$$n(m) = \max\{n \in \mathbb{N} \mid m = \lfloor c_1 n \ln(n) \rfloor \wedge c_2 \leq c_1 \ln(n/(c_1 \ln(n)))/4\}. \quad (8)$$

With $m = 500$, for example, we get $c_1 = 1.9453, c_2 = 1$, and $n = q = 63$.

Having selected the set $L(c_1, c_2, n, \cdot)$, we "randomly" pick a lattice from it. We use the digits of π as a source of "randomness" [4]. This approach is supported by the conjectured normalcy of π in [5, 6]. We write

$$3.\pi_1 \pi_2 \pi_3 \pi_4 \cdots,$$

so π_i, for $i \geq 1$, is the ith decimal digit of π in the expansion after the decimal point. In order to compensate for potential statistical bias, we define

$$\pi_i^* = \pi_{2i} + \pi_{2i-1} \mod 2 \qquad \text{for } i \geq 1.$$

Now, we use the sequence $(\pi_1^*, \pi_2^*, \pi_3^*, \pi_4^*, \ldots)$ as a substitute for a sequence of uniformly distributed random bits.

The matrix $X = (x_{i,j}) \in \mathbb{Z}_q^{n \times m}$ is chosen via

$$x_{i,j} = \sum_{l=k}^{k+\lfloor \log_2(q) \rfloor} 2^{l-k} \pi_l^* \mod q \qquad \text{for } 1 \leq i \leq n, 1 \leq j \leq m,$$

with $\quad k = k(i,j) = ((i-1)m + (j-1))\lfloor \log_2(q) \rfloor + 1.$

With that, we have selected a "random" element $L(c_1, c_2, n, X)$, for which we will now generate an integral basis.

---

[4] The digits of π can be optained from `ftp://pi.super-computing.org/`.

Let I_m be the m-dimensional identity matrix. We start with the matrix

$$Y_1 = (X^T \mid q\,I_m) = \begin{pmatrix} x_{1,1} & \cdots & x_{n,1} & q & 0 & \cdots & 0 \\ x_{1,2} & \cdots & x_{n,2} & 0 & q & & \vdots \\ \vdots & \ddots & \vdots & \vdots & & \ddots & 0 \\ x_{1,m} & \cdots & x_{n,m} & 0 & \cdots & 0 & q \end{pmatrix}.$$

Let Y_2 be the Hermite normal form of Y_1, we compute the transformation matrix T_1, which satisfies

$$Y_2\,T_1 = Y_1 = (X^T \mid qI_m).$$

We set T_2 to be equal to T_1, but without the n leading columns. This guarantees that

$$Y_2\,T_2 = q\,I_m. \tag{9}$$

Finally, we set the basis to $B = T_2^T$.

Now, we have to show that B is an integral basis of $L(c_1, c_2, n, X)$. Clearly, B is an integral matrix because the transformation T_1, given by the HNF computation, is in $\mathbb{Z}^{m \times (n+m)}$ and T_2 is the same matrix with the n leading columns removed.

By the uniqueness of inverses, (9) shows that $B = ((Y_2/q)^{-1})^T$. This implies that B is a basis for the dual lattice of $L(Y_2/q)$ (cf. Section 2). Since Y_2 is an integral transformation of Y_1, they span the same lattice. Thus, $L(Y_2/q) = L(Y_1/q)$.

By the defining property of the dual lattice, we have that for any $\mathbf{v} \in L(B)$ and $\mathbf{w} \in L(Y_1/q)$, it holds that $\langle \mathbf{v}, \mathbf{w} \rangle \in \mathbb{Z}$. So especially for all columns $\mathbf{x}$ of X^T, it holds that $\langle \mathbf{v}, \mathbf{x}/q \rangle \in \mathbb{Z}$, or equivalently $\langle \mathbf{v}, \mathbf{x} \rangle \in q\mathbb{Z}$. This implies $\langle \mathbf{v}, \mathbf{x} \rangle \bmod q = 0$, which in turn gives us $L(B) \subseteq L(c_1, c_2, n, X)$.

Now let $\mathbf{v} \in L(c_1, c_2, n, X)$, so for any column $\mathbf{x}$ of X^T we have that the inner product $\langle \mathbf{v}, \mathbf{x} \rangle \bmod q = 0$, or equivalently $\langle \mathbf{v}, \mathbf{x}/q \rangle \in \mathbb{Z}$. Since we know $L(c_1, c_2, n, X) \subseteq \mathbb{Z}^m$, it also holds that $\langle \mathbf{v}, \mathbf{e} \rangle \in \mathbb{Z}$ for any column $\mathbf{e}$ of the identity matrix I_m. Since $\mathbf{v}$ has an integral inner product with each column vector in Y_1/q, this means $\mathbf{v}$ is in the dual lattice of $L(Y_1/q)$, which we know to be $L(B)$. Finally, we have $L(B) = L(c_1, c_2, n, X)$.

For a small example of such a basis, refer to Appendix C.

The choice of parameters. We now argue that our choice of the paramters leads to m-dimensional lattices $L_m = L(c_1, c_2, n, X)$, in which vectors of norm less than $n(m)$ are hard to find.

We have chosen $c_2 = 1$. By Theorem 1, this guarantees the existence of lattice vectors with norm less than $n(m) = q$ in L_m.

A choice of $c_2 < 1$, and thus $q < n$, would imply that all q-vectors, namely vectors that are zero except for one entry q, in $\mathbb{Z}^m$ have Euclidean norm less than $n(m)$. This renders the lattice challenge preposterous because q-vectors are easy to find. Moreover, Theorem 1 only guarantees the existence of one short vector, which in this case might be a q-vector.

Table 1. Lattice parameters with the necessary Hermite factor γ

m	n, q	γ
500	63	1.0072^m
825	127	1.0050^m
1000	160	1.0042^m
1250	208	1.0036^m
1500	256	1.0031^m
1750	304	1.0027^m
2000	348	1.0024^m

On the other hand, choosing $c_2 > 1$ enlarges c_1, and because of (2) decreases $n(m)$. Then, the hardness of lattice problems in a large dimension m would be based on the worst-case hardness of lattice problems in a very small dimension n. As n decreases, our hardness argument becomes less meaningful because even worst-case lattice problems in small dimensions are believed to be easy.

Table 1 shows how m and n are related for the selected lattices L_m. For a graphical overview, up to $m = 2000$, refer to Appendix B. Thus, in order to apply Theorem 2 as a strong indication for hardness, we keep $n(m)$ close to m in the above construction. We choose a pseudo-random X to get a random element in $L(c_1, c_2, n, \cdot)$, as required by Theorem 2. Using the recent improvement of Ajtai's result due to Gentry, Peikert, and Vaikuntanathan [14], it is possible to choose c_2 arbitrarily close to 1. Their results can also be used to improve our construction, by providing an even stronger indication of hardness. For this, we refer the reader to the extended version [8].

To give an even stronger argument for the hardness of the SVP in our lattices, we use a result by Gama and Nguyen [13]. They argue that finding vectors $\mathbf{v}$ in a lattice L is difficult if

$$\|\mathbf{v}\| < \gamma \text{vol}(L)^{1/m}, \tag{10}$$

where $\gamma \leq 1.01^m$ and m is the dimension of L. In this inequality, γ is called Hermite factor. For $\gamma \leq 1.005^m$ Gama and Nguyen state that computing vectors $\mathbf{v}$ that satisfy (10) is "totally out of reach".

Finding a vector $\mathbf{v} \in L_m$ of length less than $n(m)$ means finding a vector $\mathbf{v}$ that satisfies (10) with Hermite factor

$$\gamma < \frac{n(m)}{\text{vol}(L_m)^{1/m}}.$$

Such Hermite factors are tabulated in column 3 of Table 1.

In combination with the analysis of Gama and Nguyen, the table suggests that while finding a vector shorter than $n(m)$ in L_{500} is still possible, the respective problem in L_{825} will be very hard in practice. As the dimension increases, the necessary Hermite factor falls below 1.004^n and 1.003^n. We think that finding short vectors in the corresponding lattices will require entirely new algorithms.

5   Experiments with Lattice Reduction Algorithms

As a first application of our explicit construction of lattices L_m, we show how various lattice reduction algorithms perform on them. Basically, there are two types of algorithms: the LLL-type and the block-type. Building upon LLL, block-type algorithms are typically stronger, in the sense that they are able to find significantly shorter vectors. Block-type algorithms, however, are impractical for large block sizes because their running time increases at least exponentially in this parameter.

Toy challenges. In Section 4, we have seen that the problem of finding a vector of length less than $n(m)$ in lattices L_m starts to become difficult for $m \geq 500$ and it should be infeasible for $m \geq 825$.

Thus, we define a relaxed variant of the family $\mathfrak{L}$. It is the family of all lattice sets $L(2, 1, n, \cdot)$, i.e. we set $c_2 = 1$ and $c_1 = 2$, so (1) does not necessarily hold. Although, in such lattices, there is no guarantee for the existence of lattice vectors of norm less than $n(m)$, such vectors indeed exist in practice. Moreover, our explicit construction in Section 4 still works and produces bases for lattices L_m, $m < 500$. In the following, the lattices L_m, $200 \leq m < 500$, will be referred to as toy challenges. Explicit parameters for this range can be found in Appendix D. There, we also compute the necessary Hermite factor as in Section 4. The factors suggest that current lattice reduction methods are supposed to find lattice vectors of norm less than $n(m)$. Our experiments with block-type methods confirm this.

All experiments were run on a single core AMD Opteron at 2.6 GHz, using Shoup's NTL [41] in version 5.4.2 and GCC 4.1.2. .

Implementations. For LLL and BKZ, we used the famous implementations integrated in the NTL. We thank Filipović and Koy for making available their implementations of sLLL and PD, which were part of the diploma thesis [12]. We also thank Ludwig for making available and updating his implementation of PSR that was part of his PhD thesis [26]. Finally, we thank Cadé and Stehlé for making available their implementation of fpLLL. It was obtained from [42].

Figure 2 and Figure 3 depict the performance, i.e. the length of the shortest obtained vector and the logarithmic running time in seconds, for LLL-type and block-type methods, respectively. The boxed line in the left figures shows the norm bound $n(m)$ that has to be undercut. While block-type methods reliably find vectors of norm less than $n(m)$ up to a dimension around 500, the best LLL-type algorithms merely succeed in dimensions < 300.

While being arguably efficient with our choice of parameters, sLLL is unable to find sufficiently short vectors even in dimension 200. For larger dimensions,

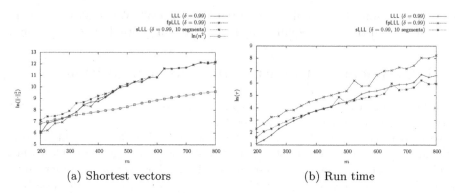

(a) Shortest vectors   (b) Run time

Fig. 2. Performance of LLL-type lattice reduction with comparable parameters

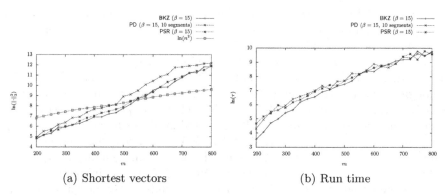

(a) Shortest vectors   (b) Run time

Fig. 3. Performance of block-type lattice reduction with comparable parameters

however, the approximation results of all LLL-type algorithms seem to converge, whereas the running time performance of fpLLL is significantly surpassed by that of the other two. Note that we use the default wrapper method of fpLLL. Damien Stehlé pointed out that one should rather use its faster heuristics (see [8]).

In Figure 3a, observe that BKZ and PSR perform slightly better than PD, which is mostly due to the internal sLLL step in PD. Accordingly, the graphs seem to converge at the right end, similarly to those in Figure 2a. While the approximation performance of block-type algorithms can be further improved using higher block sizes, this approach is limited by the resulting running time. Extrapolating to higher dimensions, it becomes obvious that finding sufficiently short vectors in L_m requires a significantly larger effort for dimensions that are somewhat higher than 600. This coincides with our observation on the Hermite factor in Section 4.

As for the running time performance of the block-type schemes, observe in Figure 3b that all three behave similarly. In lower dimensions, up to about $m = 450$, BKZ performs strictly better. In higher dimensions, the differences even out and the random character of PSR becomes obvious in its slightly erratic timing.

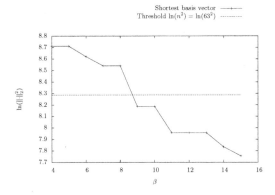

Fig. 4. Shortest vectors found by β-BKZ in dimension $m = 500$

To conclude, we have reviewed the current state-of-the-art performance of lattice reduction algorithms, using reasonable parameters. We did not, however, explore the limits of the block-type methods. This assessment, we leave to the contestants of the actual lattice challenge that is defined in the next section.

6 The Challenge

In Section 4, we have constructed challenge lattices L_m of dimension m, for $m \geq 500$. The results in Section 3 together with the pseudo-random choice of L_m guarantee the existence of vectors $\mathbf{v} \in L_m$ with $\|\mathbf{v}\|_2 < n(m)$, which are hard to find. For a toy example, refer to Appendix C.

As stated before, we want the lattice challenge to be *open* in the sense that it does not terminate when the *first* short vector is found. Having proven the existence of just one solution might suggest that there are no more, but during practical experiments, we found that many successively shorter vectors exist. For example in Figure 4, we display that in dimension $m = 500$ BKZ with increasing block size subsequently finds smaller and smaller lattice vectors.

We propose the following challenge to all researchers and students.

Lattice Challenge

The contestants are given lattice bases of lattices L_m, together with a norm bound ν. Initially, we set $\nu = n(m)$.

The goal is to find a vector $\mathbf{v} \in L_m$, with $\|\mathbf{v}\|_2 < \nu$.
Each solution $\mathbf{v}$ to the challenge decreases ν to $\|\mathbf{v}\|_2$.
The challenge is hosted at http://www.latticechallenge.org.

Acknowledgements

We would like to thank Oded Regev for his helpful remarks and suggestions. Furthermore, we thank the program committee and the anonymous reviewers for their valuable comments.

References

1. Aharonov, D., Regev, O.: Lattice problems in NP ∩ coNP. J. ACM 52(5), 749–765 (2005)
2. Ajtai, M.: Generating hard instances of lattice problems. In: Proceedings of the Annual Symposium on the Theory of Computing (STOC), pp. 99–108. ACM Press, New York (1996)
3. Ajtai, M., Dwork, C.: A public-key cryptosystem with worst-case/average-case equivalence. In: Proceedings of the Annual Symposium on the Theory of Computing (STOC), pp. 284–293. ACM Press, New York (1997)
4. Ajtai, M., Kumar, R., Sivakumar, D.: A sieve algorithm for the shortest lattice vector problem. In: Proceedings of the Annual Symposium on the Theory of Computing (STOC), pp. 601–610. ACM Press, New York (2001)
5. Bailey, D., Crandall, R.: On the random character of fundamental constant expansions. Experimental Mathematics 10(2), 175–190 (2001)
6. Bailey, D., Crandall, R.: Random generators and normal numbers. Experimental Mathematics 11(4), 527–546 (2002)
7. Banaszczyk, W.: New bounds in some transference theorems in the geometry of numbers. Mathematische Annalen 296(4), 625–635 (1993)
8. Buchmann, J., Lindner, R., Rückert, M.: Explicit hard instances of the shortest vector problem (extended version). Cryptology ePrint Archive, Report 2008/333 (2008), http://eprint.iacr.org/2008/333
9. Cai, J., Nerurkar, A.: An improved worst-case to average-case connection for lattice problems. In: Proceedings of the Annual Symposium on Foundations of Computer Science (FOCS), pp. 468–477 (1997)
10. Certicom Corp. The Certicom ECC Challenge, http://www.certicom.com/index.php/the-certicom-ecc-challenge
11. Coppersmith, D., Shamir, A.: Lattice Attacks on NTRU. In: Fumy, W. (ed.) EUROCRYPT 1997. LNCS, vol. 1233, pp. 52–61. Springer, Heidelberg (1997)
12. Filipović, B.: Implementierung der gitterbasenreduktion in segmenten. Master's thesis, Johann Wolfgang Goethe-Universität Frankfurt am Main (2002)
13. Gama, N., Nguyen, P.Q.: Predicting lattice reduction. In: Smart, N.P. (ed.) EUROCRYPT 2008. LNCS, vol. 4965, pp. 31–51. Springer, Heidelberg (2008)
14. Gentry, C., Peikert, C., Vaikuntanathan, V.: Trapdoors for hard lattices and new cryptographic constructions. In: Ladner, R.E., Dwork, C. (eds.) STOC, pp. 197–206. ACM Press, New York (2008)
15. Goldreich, O., Goldwasser, S.: On the limits of nonapproximability of lattice problems. J. Comput. Syst. Sci. 60(3), 540–563 (2000)
16. Goldreich, O., Goldwasser, S., Halevi, S.: Public-key cryptosystems from lattice reduction problems. In: Kaliski Jr., B.S. (ed.) CRYPTO 1997. LNCS, vol. 1294, pp. 112–131. Springer, Heidelberg (1997)
17. Hoffstein, J., Pipher, J., Silverman, J.H.: NTRU: A ring-based public key cryptosystem. In: Buhler, J. (ed.) ANTS 1998. LNCS, vol. 1423, pp. 267–288. Springer, Heidelberg (1998)

18. Hoffstein, J., Silverman, J.H., Whyte, W.: Estimated breaking times for NTRU lattices. Technical Report 012, Version 2, NTRU Cryptosystems (2003), http://ntru.com/cryptolab/tech_notes.htm
19. Howgrave-Graham, N., Pipher, H.J.J., Whyte, W.: On estimating the lattice security of NTRU. Technical Report 104, Cryptology ePrint Archive (2005), http://eprint.iacr.org/2005/104/
20. Kleinbock, D., Weiss, B.: Dirichlet's theorem on diophantine approximation and homogeneous flows. J.MOD.DYN. 4, 43 (2008)
21. Koy, H.: Primale-duale Segment-Reduktion (2004), http://www.mi.informatik.uni-frankfurt.de/research/papers.html
22. Koy, H., Schnorr, C.-P.: Segment LLL-reduction of lattice bases. In: Silverman, J.H. (ed.) CaLC 2001. LNCS, vol. 2146, pp. 67–80. Springer, Heidelberg (2001)
23. Lagarias, J.C., Lenstra Jr., H.W., Schnorr, C.-P.: Korkin-Zolotarev bases and successive minima of a lattice and its reciprocal lattice. Combinatorica 10(4), 333–348 (1990)
24. Lenstra, A., Lenstra, H., Lovász, L.: Factoring polynomials with rational coefficients. Mathematische Annalen 261(4), 515–534 (1982)
25. Ludwig, C.: A faster lattice reduction method using quantum search. In: Ibaraki, T., Katoh, N., Ono, H. (eds.) ISAAC 2003. LNCS, vol. 2906, pp. 199–208. Springer, Heidelberg (2003)
26. Ludwig, C.: Practical Lattice Basis Sampling Reduction. PhD thesis, Technische Universität Darmstadt (2005), http://elib.tu-darmstadt.de/diss/000640/
27. McCurley, K.S.: The discrete logarithm problem. In: Pomerance, C. (ed.) Cryptology and computational number theory, Providence, pp. 49–74. American Mathematical Society (1990)
28. Micciancio, D.: Almost perfect lattices, the covering radius problem, and applications to Ajtai's connection factor. SIAM Journal on Computing 34(1), 118–169 (2004)
29. Micciancio, D., Regev, O.: Worst-case to average-case reductions based on gaussian measures. SIAM Journal on Computing 37(1), 267–302 (2007)
30. Nguyen, P.Q., Stehlé, D.: Floating-point LLL revisited. In: Cramer, R. (ed.) EUROCRYPT 2005. LNCS, vol. 3494, pp. 215–233. Springer, Heidelberg (2005)
31. Nguyen, P.Q., Stehlé, D.: LLL on the average. In: Hess, F., Pauli, S., Pohst, M.E. (eds.) ANTS 2006. LNCS, vol. 4076, pp. 238–256. Springer, Heidelberg (2006)
32. Peikert, C.: Limits on the hardness of lattice problems in ℓ_p norms. In: IEEE Conference on Computational Complexity, pp. 333–346. IEEE Computer Society Press, Los Alamitos (2007)
33. Regev, O.: Quantum computation and lattice problems. SIAM J. Comput. 33(3), 738–760 (2004)
34. Regev, O.: On lattices, learning with errors, random linear codes, and cryptography. In: Proceedings of the 37th annual ACM symposium on Theory of computing, pp. 84–93. ACM Press, New York (2005)
35. Regev, O.: On the complexity of lattice problems with polynomial approximation factors. In: A survey for the LLL+25 conference (2007)
36. RSA Security Inc. The RSA Challenge Numbers, http://www.rsa.com/rsalabs/node.asp?id=2093
37. Schmidt, W.: Diophantine Approximation. Lecture Notes in Mathematics, vol. 785. Springer, Heidelberg (1980)
38. Schnorr, C.: A hierarchy of polynomial time lattice basis reduction algorithms. Theoretical Computer Science 53, 201–224 (1987)
39. Schnorr, C.: Block reduced lattice bases and successive minima. Combinatorics, Probability and Computing 4, 1–16 (1994)

40. Schnorr, C.: Lattice reduction by random sampling and birthday methods. In: Alt, H., Habib, M. (eds.) STACS 2003. LNCS, vol. 2607, pp. 146–156. Springer, Heidelberg (2003)
41. Shoup, V.: Number theory library (NTL) for C++, http://www.shoup.net/ntl/
42. Stehlé, D.: Damien Stehlé's homepage at école normale supérieure de Lyon, http://perso.ens-lyon.fr/damien.stehle/english.html

A   Completing the Proof of Theorem 1

With parameters c_1, c_2, n as in the theorem, we want to show that

$$\lfloor c_1 n \ln(n) \rfloor \geq c_1 n \ln(n)/2 \tag{11}$$

holds. By (1), we have that $c_1 \geq 1/(2\ln(2))$. Evaluating both sides of (11) with $n = 1, 2, 3$, we find that the inequality holds for these n. For all $n \geq 4$, consider the following.

We have that $c_1 \geq 1/(2\ln(2)) \geq 2/4\ln(4)$, which implies

$$
\begin{aligned}
\lfloor c_1 n \ln(n) \rfloor &\geq c_1 n \ln(n) - 1 \\
&\geq c_1 n \ln(n)/2 + c_1 n \ln(n)/2 - 1 \\
&\geq c_1 n \ln(n)/2 + c_1 4 \ln(4)/2 - 1 \\
&\geq c_1 n \ln(n)/2
\end{aligned}
$$

This completes the proof.

B   Ratio between m and n

In order to get an idea of the ratio m/n in our challenge lattices, refer to Figure 5. The bend at $m = 500$ reflects our choice of c_1 and c_2 in the toy challenges, where we "cap" the value of c_2 at 2.0.

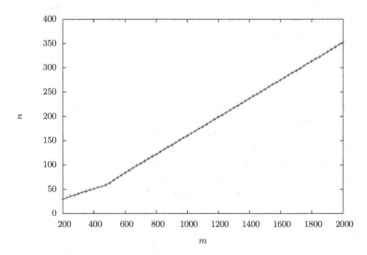

Fig. 5. Ratio between challenge dimension m and reference dimension n

C   Challenge Example

The following low-dimensional example gives an idea of what the challenge lattices, and the short vectors in them, essentially look like. Its block structure is similar to the one found by Coppersmith and Shamir for NTRU lattices [11]. This is not surprising because both belong to the class of modular lattices.

Example 1. The transposed challenge basis for $m = 30, n = q = 8$ looks like:

```
[
[1 0 0 0 0 0 0 0 0 0 0 0 0 0 0 0 0 0 0 0 0 0 -4 -7 -4 -7 -6 -2 -3 -7]
[0 1 0 0 0 0 0 0 0 0 0 0 0 0 0 0 0 0 0 0 0 0 -7 -4 -1  0 -6 -7 -1 -5]
[0 0 1 0 0 0 0 0 0 0 0 0 0 0 0 0 0 0 0 0 0 0 -2 -2 -6 -2 -6 -6 -4 -6]
[0 0 0 1 0 0 0 0 0 0 0 0 0 0 0 0 0 0 0 0 0 0 -6 -7 -1 -5 -5 -1 -4 -3]
[0 0 0 0 1 0 0 0 0 0 0 0 0 0 0 0 0 0 0 0 0 0 -7 -4 -2 -3 -1  0 -1 -3]
[0 0 0 0 0 1 0 0 0 0 0 0 0 0 0 0 0 0 0 0 0 0 -6 -3 -5 -7 -3 -7  0 -2]
[0 0 0 0 0 0 1 0 0 0 0 0 0 0 0 0 0 0 0 0 0 0 -5 -1 -6 -6 -6 -4 -3 -5]
[0 0 0 0 0 0 0 1 0 0 0 0 0 0 0 0 0 0 0 0 0 0  0  0 -1  0 -2 -2 -2 -7]
[0 0 0 0 0 0 0 0 1 0 0 0 0 0 0 0 0 0 0 0 0 0 -4 -4 -3  0 -5 -7 -6 -4]
[0 0 0 0 0 0 0 0 0 1 0 0 0 0 0 0 0 0 0 0 0 0 -3 -2 -4 -6 -4 -3 -2 -3]
[0 0 0 0 0 0 0 0 0 0 1 0 0 0 0 0 0 0 0 0 0 0 -7 -6 -4  0  0 -2 -7 -4]
[0 0 0 0 0 0 0 0 0 0 0 1 0 0 0 0 0 0 0 0 0 0 -4 -1  0  0 -7 -3 -7  0]
[0 0 0 0 0 0 0 0 0 0 0 0 1 0 0 0 0 0 0 0 0 0 -1 -6 -3  0 -4 -1 -2 -3]
[0 0 0 0 0 0 0 0 0 0 0 0 0 1 0 0 0 0 0 0 0 0 -3 -1  0 -4 -3 -3 -2  0]
[0 0 0 0 0 0 0 0 0 0 0 0 0 0 1 0 0 0 0 0 0 0 -6 -6 -2 -2 -1 -3 -6 -6]
[0 0 0 0 0 0 0 0 0 0 0 0 0 0 0 1 0 0 0 0 0 0  0 -7 -7 -4 -2 -1 -2 -5]
[0 0 0 0 0 0 0 0 0 0 0 0 0 0 0 0 1 0 0 0 0 0 -6 -2 -1 -4 -4 -3 -2 -6]
[0 0 0 0 0 0 0 0 0 0 0 0 0 0 0 0 0 1 0 0 0 0 -2 -6 -1 -1 -5 -4 -3 -3]
[0 0 0 0 0 0 0 0 0 0 0 0 0 0 0 0 0 0 1 0 0 0 -4  0 -5 -4 -6 -7 -5 -2]
[0 0 0 0 0 0 0 0 0 0 0 0 0 0 0 0 0 0 0 1 0 0 -4 -3 -3  0 -5 -3 -3 -7]
[0 0 0 0 0 0 0 0 0 0 0 0 0 0 0 0 0 0 0 0 1 0 -4  0 -3 -2 -2 -6 -4 -4]
[0 0 0 0 0 0 0 0 0 0 0 0 0 0 0 0 0 0 0 0 0 1 -5 -5 -3  0 -1 -3  0 -6]
[0 0 0 0 0 0 0 0 0 0 0 0 0 0 0 0 0 0 0 0 0 0  8  0  0  0  0  0  0  0]
[0 0 0 0 0 0 0 0 0 0 0 0 0 0 0 0 0 0 0 0 0 0  0  8  0  0  0  0  0  0]
[0 0 0 0 0 0 0 0 0 0 0 0 0 0 0 0 0 0 0 0 0 0  0  0  8  0  0  0  0  0]
[0 0 0 0 0 0 0 0 0 0 0 0 0 0 0 0 0 0 0 0 0 0  0  0  0  8  0  0  0  0]
[0 0 0 0 0 0 0 0 0 0 0 0 0 0 0 0 0 0 0 0 0 0  0  0  0  0  8  0  0  0]
[0 0 0 0 0 0 0 0 0 0 0 0 0 0 0 0 0 0 0 0 0 0  0  0  0  0  0  8  0  0]
[0 0 0 0 0 0 0 0 0 0 0 0 0 0 0 0 0 0 0 0 0 0  0  0  0  0  0  0  8  0]
[0 0 0 0 0 0 0 0 0 0 0 0 0 0 0 0 0 0 0 0 0 0  0  0  0  0  0  0  0  8]
]
```

The shortest vector in the respective lattice is

```
[0 0 0 0 -1 1 0 0 -1 0 0 0 1 0 0 0 0 0 1 0 0 0 0 -1 0 0 1 0 0 0]
```

and its Euclidean norm is $\sqrt{7} < n = 8$.

D   Toy Challenges

Table 2 depicts the parameters of our toy challenges.

Table 2. Lattice parameters with the necessary Hermite factor γ

m	n, q	γ
200	30	1.0146^m
225	33	1.0133^m
250	36	1.0123^m
275	38	1.0115^m
300	41	1.0107^m
325	44	1.0101^m
350	46	1.0095^m
375	49	1.0091^m
400	51	1.0086^m
425	54	1.0082^m
450	56	1.0079^m
475	59	1.0075^m

Practical-Sized Instances of Multivariate PKCs: Rainbow, TTS, and ℓIC-Derivatives

Anna Inn-Tung Chen[1], Chia-Hsin Owen Chen[2], Ming-Shing Chen[2], Chen-Mou Cheng[1], and Bo-Yin Yang[2,*]

[1] Department of Electrical Engineering, National Taiwan University, Taipei, Taiwan
{anna1110,doug}@crypto.tw
[2] Institute of Information Science, Academia Sinica, Taipei, Taiwan
{mschen,owenhsin,by}@crypto.tw

Abstract. We present instances of MPKCs (multivariate public key cryptosystems) with design, given the best attacks we know, and implement them on commodity PC hardware. We also show that they can hold their own compared to traditional alternatives. In fact, they can be up to an order of magnitude faster.

Keywords: Gröbner basis, multivariate public key cryptosystem.

1 Introduction

MPKCs (multivariate public key cryptosystems) [14,31] are PKCs whose public keys are multivariate polynomials in many small variables. It has two properties that are often touted: Firstly, it is considered a significant possibility for Post-Quantum Cryptography, with potential to resist future attacks with quantum computers. Secondly, it is often considered to be faster than the competition.

Extant MPKCs almost always hide the private map $\mathcal{Q}$ via composition with two affine maps S, T. So, $\mathcal{P} = (p_1, \ldots, p_m) = T \circ \mathcal{Q} \circ S : \mathbb{K}^n \to \mathbb{K}^m$, or

$$\mathcal{P} : \mathbf{w} = (w_1, \ldots, w_n) \overset{S}{\mapsto} \mathbf{x} = \mathrm{M}_S \mathbf{w} + \mathbf{c}_S \overset{\mathcal{Q}}{\mapsto} \mathbf{y} \overset{T}{\mapsto} \mathbf{z} = \mathrm{M}_T \mathbf{y} + \mathbf{c}_T = (z_1, \ldots, z_m) \tag{1}$$

The public key consists of the polynomials in $\mathcal{P}$. $\mathcal{P}(0)$ is always taken to be zero.

In any given scheme, the *central map* $\mathcal{Q}$ belongs to a certain class of quadratic maps whose inverse can be computed relatively easily. The maps S, T are affine (sometimes linear) and full-rank. The x_j are called the central variables. The polynomials giving y_i in $\mathbf{x}$ are called the central polynomials; when necessary to distinguish between the variable and the value, we will write $y_i = q_i(\mathbf{x})$. The key of a MPKC is the design of the central map because, solving a generic multivariate quadratic system is hard, so the best solution for finding $\mathbf{w}$ given $\mathbf{z}$ invariably turns to other means, which depend on the structure of $\mathcal{Q}$.

---

* Corresponding author.

J. Buchmann and J. Ding (Eds.): PQCrypto 2008, LNCS 5299, pp. 95–108, 2008.

1.1   Questions

Four or five years ago, it was shown that instances of TTS and C^{*-}, specifically TTS/4 and SFLASH, are faster signature schemes than traditional competition using RSA and ECC [1, 10, 33]. These two instances both been broken in the meantime [18, 20]. Now that the width of a typical ALU is 64 bits, commodity PC hardware has never been more friendly to RSA and ECC. While multivariates still represent a future-proofing effort, can we still say that MPKCs are efficient on commodity hardware?

1.2   Our Answers

Currently the fastest multivariate PKCs seems to be from the Rainbow and ℓIC families [16, 17]. We run comparisons using Pentium III (P3) machines (on which NESSIE contestants are tested) and modern Core 2 and Opteron (hereafter C2 an K8) machines. On these test runs, we can say that compared to implementations using standard PKCs (DSA, RSA, ECDSA), present instances of MPKCs with design security levels of around 2^{80} can hold their own in terms of efficiency.

In this paper, we describe how we select our Rainbow and ℓIC-derived instances sketch our implementation. We also suggest the new approach of using bit-slicing when evaluating in GF(16) or other small fields during the construction of the private map.

In the comparison here, we use D. J. Bernstein's eBATs system to do benchmarking. We can conclude that

1. $3IC^-p$ is comparable to SFLASH, but not as fast as Rainbow.
2. Rainbow is fast and TTS faster, although the security is not as well studied.
3. $2IC^+i$ is a very fast way to build an encryption scheme.

Table 1. Current Multivariate PKCs Compared on a Pentium III 500

Scheme	result	SecrKey	PublKey	KeyGen	SecrMap	PublMap
RSA-1024	1024b	128 B	320 B	2.7 sec	84 ms	2.00 ms
ECC-GF(2^{163})	320b	48 B	24 B	1.6 ms	1.9 ms	5.10 ms
PMI+$(136, 6, 18, 8)$	144b	5.5 kB	165 kB	1.1 sec	1.23 ms	0.18 ms
rainbow $(2^8, 18, 12, 12)$	336b	24.8 kB	22.5 kB	0.3 sec	0.43 ms	0.40 ms
rainbow $(2^4, 24, 20, 20)$	256b	91.5 kB	83 kB	1.6 sec	0.93 ms	0.73 ms
TTS $(2^8, 18, 12, 12)$	336b	3.5kB	22.5kB	0.04 sec	0.11 ms	0.40 ms
TTS $(2^4, 24, 20, 20)$	256b	5.6kB	83kB	0.43 sec	0.22 ms	0.74 ms
2IC$^+$i $(128,6,16)$	144b	5 kB	165 kB	1 sec	0.03 ms	0.17 ms
2IC$^+$i $(256,12,32)$	288b	18.5 kB	1184 kB	14.9 sec	0.24 ms	2.60 ms
QUARTZ	128b	71.0 kB	3.9 kB	3.1 sec	11 sec	0.24 ms
3IC-p$(2^4, 32, 1)$	380b	9 kB	148 kB	0.6 sec	2.00 ms	1.90 ms
pFLASH	292b	5.5 kB	72 kB	0.3 sec	5.7 ms	1.70 ms

Table 2. Comparison on One core of an Intel Core 2 (C2)

Scheme	result	SecrKey	PublKey	KeyGen	SecrMap	PublMap
PMI+$(136,6,18,8)$	144b	5.5 kB	165 kB	350.8 Mclk	335.4 kclk	51.4 kclk
PMI+$(136,6,18,8)$64b	144b	5.5 kB	165 kB	350.4 Mclk	333.9 kclk	46.5 kclk
rainbow $(2^8,18,12,12)$	336b	24.8 kB	22.5 kB	110.7 Mclk	143.9 kclk	121.4 kclk
rainbow $(2^4,24,20,20)$	256b	91.5 kB	83 kB	454.0 Mclk	210.2 kclk	153.8 kclk
rainbow $(2^4,24,20,20)$64b	256b	91.5 kB	83 kB	343.8 Mclk	136.8 kclk	79.3 kclk
TTS $(2^8,18,12,12)$	336b	3.5kB	22.5kB	11.5 Mclk	35.9 kclk	121.4 kclk
TTS $(2^4,24,20,20)$	256b	5.6kB	83kB	175.7 Mclk	64.8 kclk	78.9 kclk
2IC$^+$i (128,6,16)	144b	5 kB	165 kB	324.7 Mclk	8.3 kclk	52.0 kclk
2IC$^+$i (128,6,16)64b	144b	5 kB	165 kB	324.9 Mclk	6.7 kclk	46.9 kclk
2IC$^+$i (256,12,32)	288b	18.5 kB	1184 kB	4119.7 Mclk	26.7 kclk	385.6 kclk
2IC$^+$i (256,12,32)64b	288b	18.5 kB	1184 kB	4418.2 Mclk	23.0 kclk	266.9 kclk
3IC-p$(2^4,32,1)$	380b	9 kB	148 kB	173.6 Mclk	503 kclk	699 kclk
pFLASH	292b	5.5 kB	72 kB	86.6 Mclk	2410 kclk	879 kclk
DSA/ElGamal 1024b		148B	128B	1.08 Mclk	1046 kclk	1244 kclk
RSA 1024b		148B	128B	108 Mclk	2950 kclk	121 kclk
ECC 256b		96B	64B	2.7 Mclk	2850 kclk	3464 kclk

Table 3. Comparison on One Core of an Opteron/Athlon64 (K8)

Scheme	result	SecrKey	PublKey	KeyGen	SecrMap	PublMap
PMI+$(136,6,18,8)$	144b	5.5 kB	165 kB	425.4 Mclk	388.8 kclk	63.9 kclk
PMI+$(136,6,18,8)$64b	144b	5.5 kB	165 kB	424.7 Mclk	393.3 kclk	60.4 kclk
rainbow $(2^8,18,12,12)$	336b	24.8 kB	22.5 kB	234.6 Mclk	297.0 kclk	224.4 kclk
rainbow $(2^4,24,20,20)$	256b	91.5 kB	83 kB	544.6 Mclk	224.4 kclk	164.0 kclk
rainbow $(2^4,24,20,20)$64b	256b	91.5 kB	83 kB	396.2 Mclk	138.7 kclk	83.9 kclk
TTS $(2^8,18,12,12)$	336b	3.5kB	22.5kB	20.4 Mclk	69.1 kclk	224.4 kclk
TTS $(2^4,24,20,20)$	256b	5.6kB	83kB	225.2 Mclk	103.8 kclk	84.8 kclk
2IC$^+$i (128,6,16)	144b	5 kB	165 kB	382.6 Mclk	8.7 kclk	64.2 kclk
2IC$^+$i (128,6,16)64b	144b	5 kB	165 kB	382.1 Mclk	7.5 kclk	60.1 kclk
2IC$^+$i (256,12,32)	288b	18.5 kB	1184 kB	5155.5 Mclk	31.1 kclk	537.0 kclk
2IC$^+$i (256,12,32)64b	288b	18.5 kB	1184 kB	5156.1 Mclk	26.6 kclk	573.9 kclk
3IC-p$(2^4,32,1)$	380b	9 kB	148 kB	200.7 Mclk	645 kclk	756 kclk
pFLASH	292b	5.5 kB	72 kB	126.9 Mclk	5036 kclk	872 kclk
DSA/ElGamal 148B		148B	128B	0.864 Mclk	862 kclk	1018 kclk
RSA 1024b		148B	128B	150 Mclk	2647 kclk	117 kclk
ECC 256b		96B	64B	2.8 Mclk	3205 kclk	3837 kclk

1.3   Previous Work

In [4], Berbain, Billet and Gilbert describe several ways to compute the *public maps* of MPKCs and compare their efficiency. However, they do not describe the evaluation of the *private maps*.

[18] summarizes the state of the art against generalized Rainbow/TTS schemes. The school of Stern *et al* developed differential attacks that breaks minus variants

[24, 20] and internal perturbation [23]. Ways to circumvent these attacks are proposed in [13, 19].

The above attacks the cryptosystem as an EIP or "structural" problem. To solve the system of equations, we have this

Problem $\mathcal{MQ}(q; n, m)$**:** Solve the system $p_1(\mathbf{x}) = p_2(\mathbf{x}) = \cdots = p_m(\mathbf{x}) = 0$, where each p_i is a quadratic in $\mathbf{x} = (x_1, \ldots, x_n)$. All coefficients and variables are in $\mathbb{K} = \mathrm{GF}(q)$, the field with q elements.

Best known methods for generic $\mathcal{MQ}$ are $\mathbf{F_4}$-$\mathbf{F_5}$ or XL whose complexities [11, 21, 22, 32] are very hard to evaluate; asymptotic formulas can be found in [2, 3, 32].

1.4   Summary and Future Work

Our programs are not very polished; it merely serves to show that MPKCs can still be fairly fast compared to the state-of-the-art traditional PKCs even on the most modern and advanced microprocessors. There are some recent advances in algorithms also, such as computations based on the inverted twisted Edwards curves [5, 6, 7], which shows that when tuned for the platform, the traditional cryptosystems can get quite a bit faster. It still remains to us to optimize more for specific architectures including embedded platforms. Further, it is an open question on whether the TTS schemes, with some randomness in the central maps, can be made with comparable security as equally sized Rainbow schemes. So far we do not have a conclusive answer.

2   Rainbow and TTS Families

We characterize a Rainbow [16] type PKC with u stages:

- The segment structure is given by a sequence $0 < v_1 < v_2 < \cdots < v_{u+1} = n$.
- For $l = 1, \ldots, u + 1$, set $S_l := \{1, 2, \ldots, v_l\}$ so that $|S_l| = v_l$ and $S_0 \subset S_1 \subset \cdots \subset S_{u+1} = S$. Denote by $o_l := v_{l+1} - v_l$ and $O_l := S_{l+1} \setminus S_l$ for $l = 1 \cdots u$.
- The central map $\mathcal{Q}$ has component polynomials $y_{v_1+1} = q_{v_1+1}(\mathbf{x})$, $y_{v_1+2} = q_{v_1+2}(\mathbf{x}), \ldots, y_n = q_n(\mathbf{x})$ — *notice unusual indexing* — of the following form

$$y_k = q_k(\mathbf{x}) = \sum_{i=1}^{v_l} \sum_{j=i}^{n} \alpha_{ij}^{(k)} x_i x_j + \sum_{i < v_{l+1}} \beta_i^{(k)} x_i, \text{ if } k \in O_l := \{v_l + 1 \cdots v_{l+1}\}.$$

  In every q_k, where $k \in O_l$, there is no cross-term $x_i x_j$ where both i and j are in O_l at all. So given all the y_i with $v_l < i \leq v_{l+1}$, and all the x_j with $j \leq v_l$, we can compute $x_{v_l+1}, \ldots, x_{v_{l+1}}$.

  S_i is the i-th vinegar set and O_i the corresponding i-th oil set.

- To expedite computations, some coefficients $(\alpha_{ij}^{(k)})$ may be fixed (e.g., set to zero), chosen at random (and included in the private key), or be interrelated in a predetermined manner.

– To invert $\mathcal{Q}$, determine (usu. at random) $x_1, \ldots x_{v_1}$, i.e., all x_k, $k \in S_1$. From the components of $\mathbf{y}$ that corresponds to the polynomials $p'_{v_1+1}, \ldots p'_{v_2}$, we obtain a set of o_1 equations in the variables x_k, $(k \in O_1)$. We may repeat the process to find all remaining variables.

For historical reasons, a Rainbow type signature scheme is said to be a TTS [33] scheme if the coefficients of $\mathcal{Q}$ are sparse.

2.1 Known Attacks and Security Criteria

1. Rank (or Low Rank, MinRank) attack to find a central equation with least rank [33].
$$C_{\text{low rank}} \approx \left[q^{v_1+1} m(n^2/2 - m^2/6)/ \right] \mathfrak{m}.$$
Here as below, the unit $\mathfrak{m}$ is a multiplications in $\mathbb{K}$, and v_1 the number of vinegars in layer 1. This is the "MinRank" attack of [25]. as improved by [8,33].
2. Dual Rank (or High Rank) attack [9,25], which finds a variable appearing the fewest number of times in a central equation cross-term [18,33]:

$$C_{\text{high rank}} \approx \left[q^{o_n - v'} n^3/6 \right] \mathfrak{m},$$

where v' counts the vinegar variables that never appears until the final segment.
3. Trying for a direct solution. The complexity is roughly as $\mathcal{MQ}(q; m, m)$.
4. Using the Reconciliation Attack [18], the complexity is as $\mathcal{MQ}(q; v_u, m)$.
5. Using the Rainbow Band Separation from [18], the complexity is determined by that of $\mathcal{MQ}(q; n, m + n)$.
6. Against TTS, there is Oil-and-Vinegar Separation [30,26,27], which finds an Oil subspace that is sufficiently large (estimates as corrected in [33]).

$$C_{\text{UOV}} \approx \left[q^{n-2o-1} o^4 + (\text{some residual term bounded by } o^3 q^{m-o}/3) \right] \mathfrak{m}.$$

o is the max. *oil set* size, i.e., there is a set of o central variables which are never multiplied together in the central equations, and no more.

2.2 Choosing Rainbow Instances

First suppose that we wish to use SHA-1, which has 160 bits. It is established by [18] that using $GF(2^8)$ there is no way to get to 2^{80} security using roughly that length hash, unpadded.

Specifically, to get the complexity of $\mathcal{MQ}(2^8, m, m)$, to above 2^{80} (the direct attack) we need about $m = 24$. Then we need $\mathcal{MQ}(2^8, n, n+m)$ to get above 2^{80} (the Rainbow Band Separation), which requires at least $n = 42$. This requires an 192-bit hash digest plus padding and a signature length of 336 bits with the vinegar sequence $(18, 12, 12)$.

If we look at smaller fields, that's a different story. If we use $GF(2^4)$, we need 20 oil variables each in the last segment and at least 20 vinegar variables in the first segment to get by the minrank and high rank attacks. To be comparable to the sizes of $3IC$-p, we choose the vinegar (structural) sequence $(24, 20, 20)$. The digest is 160 bits and the signature 192. We use random parameters under this framework and don't do TTS. The implementations are described below. In each of the two instances, the central map is inverted by setting up and solving two identically-sized linear systems.

2.3   Choosing TTS Instances

TTS of the same size over $\mathrm{GF}(2^8)$ or $\mathrm{GF}(2^4)$ are 2× or more the speed of than a Rainbow instance. They also tend to have instances also have much lower memory requirement. But we don't really know about their security.

The following are TTS instances built with exactly the same rainbow structural parameters and called henceforth TTS/7. They have exactly the same size input and output as the corresponding Rainbow instances:

TTS $(2^8, 18, 12, 12)$ $\mathbb{K} = \mathrm{GF}(2^8)$, $n = 42$, $m = 24$. $\mathcal{Q}$ is structured as follows:

$$y_i = x_i + a_{i1}x_{\sigma_i} + a_{i2}x_{\sigma_i'} + \sum_{j=0}^{11} p_{ij}x_{j+18}x_{\pi_i(j)}$$

$$+ p_{i,12}x_{\pi_i(12)}x_{\pi_i(15)} + p_{i,13}x_{\pi_i(13)}x_{\pi_i(16)} + p_{i,14}x_{\pi_i(14)}x_{\pi_i(17)}, \ i = 18 \cdots 29$$

[indices $0 \cdots 17$ appears exactly once in each random permutation π_i, and exactly once among the σ, σ' (where six σ_i' slots are empty)];

$$y_i = x_i + a_{i1}x_{\sigma_i} + a_{i2}x_{\sigma_i'} + a_{i3}x_{\sigma_i''} + \sum_{j=0}^{11} x_{j+29}\left(p_{ij}x_{\pi_i(j)} + p_{i,j+12}x_{\pi_i(j+12)}\right)$$

$$+ p_{i,24}x_{\pi_i(24)}x_{\pi_i(27)} + p_{i,25}x_{\pi_i(25)}x_{\pi_i(28)} + p_{i,26}x_{\pi_i(26)}x_{\pi_i(29)}, \ i = 30 \cdots 41$$

[indices $0 \cdots 29$ appears exactly once in each random permutation π_i, and exactly once among the σ, σ', σ'' (where six σ_i'' slots are empty)].

TTS $(2^4, 24, 20, 20)$ $\mathbb{K} = \mathrm{GF}(2^4)$, $n = 64$, $m = 40$.

$$y_i = x_i + a_{i1}x_{\sigma_i} + a_{i2}x_{\sigma_i'} + \sum_{j=0}^{19} p_{ij}x_{j+23}x_{\pi_i(j)}$$

$$+ p_{i,20}x_{\pi_i(20)}x_{\pi_i(22)} + p_{i,21}x_{\pi_i(21)}x_{\pi_i(23)}, \ i = 24 \cdots 43$$

[indices $0 \cdots 23$ appears exactly once in each random permutation π_i, and exactly once among the σ, σ' (there are only four σ_i')];

$$y_i = x_i + a_{i1}x_{\sigma_i} + a_{i2}x_{\sigma_i'} + a_{i3}x_{\sigma_i''} + \sum_{j=0}^{19} x_{j+44}\left(p_{ij}x_{\pi_i(j)} + p_{i,j+20}x_{\pi_i(j+20)}\right)$$

$$+ p_{i,40}x_{\pi_i(40)}x_{\pi_i(42)} + p_{i,41}x_{\pi_i(41)}x_{\pi_i(43)}, \ i = 44 \cdots 63$$

[indices $0 \cdots 43$ appears exactly once in each random permutation π_i, and exactly once among the σ, σ', σ'' (there are only four σ_i'')].

3   The ℓ-Invertible Cycle (ℓIC) and Derivatives

The ℓ-invertible cycle [17] can be best considered an improved version or extension of Matsumoto-Imai, otherwise known as C^* [28]. Let's review first the latter.

Triangular (and Oil-and-Vinegar, and variants thereof) systems are sometimes called "single-field" or "small-field" approaches to MPKC design, in contrast to the approach taken by Matsumoto and Imai in 1988. In such "big-field" variants, the central map is really a map in a larger field $\mathbb{L}$, a degree n extension of a finite field $\mathbb{K}$. To be quite precise, we have a map $\overline{\mathcal{Q}} : \mathbb{L} \to \mathbb{L}$ that we can invert, and pick a $\mathbb{K}$-linear bijection $\phi : \mathbb{L} \to \mathbb{K}^n$. Then we have the following multivariate polynomial map, which is presumably quadratic (for efficiency):

$$\mathcal{Q} = \phi \circ \overline{\mathcal{Q}} \circ \phi^{-1}. \tag{2}$$

then, one "hide" this map $\mathcal{Q}$ by composing from both sides by two invertible affine linear maps S and T in $\mathbb{K}^n$, as in Eq. 1.

Matsumoto and Imai suggest that we pick a $\mathbb{K}$ of characteristic 2 and this map $\overline{\mathcal{Q}}$

$$\overline{\mathcal{Q}} : \mathbf{x} \longmapsto \mathbf{y} = \mathbf{x}^{1+q^\alpha}, \tag{3}$$

where $\mathbf{x}$ is an element in $\mathbb{L}$, and such that $\gcd(1 + q^\alpha, q^n - 1) = 1$. The last condition ensures that the map $\overline{\mathcal{Q}}$ has an inverse, which is given by

$$\overline{\mathcal{Q}}^{-1}(\mathbf{x}) = \mathbf{x}^h, \tag{4}$$

where $h(1 + q^\alpha) = 1 \bmod (q^n - 1)$. This ensures that we can decrypt any secret message easily by this inverse. *Hereafter we will simply identify a vector space $\mathbb{K}^k$ with larger field $\mathbb{L}$, and $\mathcal{Q}$ with $\overline{\mathcal{Q}}$, totally omitting the isomorphism ϕ from formulas.*

ℓIC also uses an intermediate field $\mathbb{L} = \mathbb{K}^k$ and extends C^* by using the following central map from $(\mathbb{L}^*)^\ell$ to itself:

$$\mathcal{Q} : (X_1, \ldots, X_\ell) \mapsto (Y_1, \ldots, Y_\ell) \tag{5}$$
$$:= (X_1 X_2, X_2 X_3, \ldots, X_{\ell-1} X_\ell, X_\ell X_1^{q^\alpha}).$$

For "standard 3IC", $\ell = 3$, $\alpha = 0$. Invertion in $(\mathbb{L}^*)^3$ is then easy.

$$\mathcal{Q}^{-1} : (Y_1, Y_2, Y_3) \in (\mathbb{L}^*)^3 \mapsto (\sqrt{Y_1 Y_3/Y_2}, \sqrt{Y_1 Y_2/Y_3}, \sqrt{Y_2 Y_3/Y_1},). \tag{6}$$

Most of the analysis of the properties of the 3IC map can be found in [17] — the 3IC and C^* maps has a lot in common. Typically, we take out $1/3$ of the variables with a minus variation (3IC$^-$).

For encryption schemes, "2IC" or $\ell = 2$, $q = 2$, $\alpha = 1$ is suggested.

$$\mathcal{Q}_{2\text{IC}} : (X_1, X_2) \mapsto (X_1 X_2, X_1 X_2^2), \qquad \mathcal{Q}_{2\text{IC}}^{-1} : (Y_1, Y_2) \mapsto (Y_1/Y_2^2, Y_2/Y_1). \tag{7}$$

We construct 2ICi like we do PMI [12]: Take $\mathbf{v} = (v_1, \dots, v_r)$ to be an r-tuple of random affine forms in the variables $\mathbf{x}$. Let $\mathbf{f} = (f_1, \dots, f_n)$ be a random r-tuple of quadratic functions in $\mathbf{v}$. Let our new $\mathcal{Q}$ be defined by

$$\mathbf{x} \mapsto \mathbf{y} = \mathcal{Q}_{2\text{IC}}(\mathbf{x}) + \mathbf{f}(\mathbf{v}(\mathbf{x}))$$

where the power operation assumes the vector space to represent a field. *The number of Patarin relations decrease quickly down to 0* as r increases. For every $\mathbf{y}$, we may find $\mathcal{Q}^{-1}(\mathbf{y})$ by guessing at $\mathbf{v}(\mathbf{x}) = \mathbf{b}$, finding a candidate $\mathbf{x} = \mathcal{Q}_{2\text{IC}}^{-1}(\mathbf{y} + \mathbf{b})$ and checking the initial assumption that $\mathbf{v}(\mathbf{x}) = \mathbf{b}$. Since we repeat the high going-to-the-h-th-power procedure q^r times, we are almost forced to let $q = 2$ and make r as low as possible.

3.1   Known Attacks to Internal Perturbation and Defenses

ℓIC has so much in common with C^* that we need the same variations. In other words, we need to do 3IC$^-$p (with minus and projection) and 2IC$^+$i (with internal perturbation and plus), paralleling C^{*-}p and C^{*+}i (a.k.a. PMI+).

The cryptanalysis of PMI and hence 2ICi depends on the idea that for a randomly chosen $\mathbf{b}$, the probability is q^{-r} that it lies in the kernel $\mathcal{K}$ of the linear part of $\mathbf{v}$. When that happens, $\mathbf{v}(\mathbf{x} + \mathbf{b}) = \mathbf{v}(\mathbf{x})$ for any $\mathbf{x}$. Since q^{-r} is not too small, if we can distinguish between a vector $\mathbf{b} \in T^{-1}\mathcal{K}$ (back-mapped into $\mathbf{x}$-space) and $\mathbf{b} \notin T^{-1}\mathcal{K}$, we can bypass the protection of the perturbation, find our bilinear relations and accomplish the cryptanalysis.

In [23], Fouque, Granboulan and Stern built a *one-sided distinguisher* using a test on the kernel of the *polar form* or *symmetric difference* $D\mathcal{P}(\mathbf{w}, \mathbf{b}) = \mathcal{P}(\mathbf{b} + \mathbf{w}) - \mathcal{P}(\mathbf{b}) - \mathcal{P}(\mathbf{w})$. We say that $t(\mathbf{b}) = 1$ if $\dim \ker_{\mathbf{w}} D\mathcal{P}(\mathbf{b}, \mathbf{w}) = 2^{\gcd(n,\alpha)} - 1$, and $t(\mathbf{b}) = 0$ otherwise. If $\mathbf{b} \in \mathcal{K}$, then $t(\mathbf{b}) = 1$ with probability one, otherwise it is less than one. In fact if $\gcd(n, \alpha) > 1$, it is is an almost perfect distinguisher. We omit the gory details and refer the reader to [23] for the complete differential cryptanalysis.

Typically, to defeat this attack, we need to add a random equations to the central map. For 2ICi as for PMI, both a and r are roughly proportional to n creating 2IC$^+$i like we did PMI+ [13]. PMI+(n, r, a, α) refers to a map from GF(2^n) with r perturbations, a extra variables, and a central map of $\mathbf{x} \to \mathbf{x}^{2^\alpha + 1}$. Similarly, 2IC$^+i(n, r, a)$ refers to 2IC with r perturbations dimensions and a added equations.

3.2   Known Attacks to Minus Variants and Defenses

The attack found by Stern etc. can be explained by considering the case of C^* cryptosystem. We recollect that the symmetric differential of any function G, defined formally:

$$DG(\mathbf{a}, \mathbf{x}) := G(\mathbf{x} + \mathbf{a}) - G(\mathbf{x}) - G(\mathbf{a}) + G(0).$$

is bilinear and symmetric in its variables $\mathbf{a}$ and $\mathbf{x}$. Let ζ be an element in the big field $\mathbb{L}$. Then we have

$$DQ(\zeta \cdot a, x) + DQ(a, \zeta \cdot x) = (\zeta^{q^\alpha} + \zeta)DQ(a, x).$$

Clearly the public key of C^{*-} inherits some of that symmetry. Now not every skew-symmetric action by a matrix M_ζ that corresponds to an $\mathbb{L}$-multiplication that result in $M_\zeta^T H_i + H_i M_\zeta$ being in the span of the public-key differential matrices, because $S := \text{span}\{H_i : i = 1 \cdots n - r\}$ as compared to $\text{span}\{H_i : i = 1 \cdots n\}$ is missing r of the basis matrices. However, as the authors of [20] argued heuristically and backed up with empirical evidence, if we just pick the first three $M_\zeta^T H_i + H_i M_\zeta$ matrices, or any three random linear combinations of the form $\sum_{i=1}^{n-r} b_i(M_\zeta^T H_i + H_i M_\zeta)$ and demand that they fall in S, then

1. There is a good chance to find a nontrivial M_ζ satisfying that requirement;
2. This matrix really correspond to a multiplication by ζ in $\mathbb{L}$;
3. Applying the skew-symmetric action of this M_ζ to the public-key matrices leads to other matrices in $\text{span}\{H_i : i = 1 \cdots n\}$ that is not in S.

Why *three*? There are $n(n - 1)/2$ degrees of freedom in the H_i, so to form a span of $n - r$ matrices takes $n(n-3)/2 + r$ linear relations among its components ($n - r$ and not n because if we are attacking C^{*-}, we are missing r components of the public key). There are n^2 degrees of freedom in an $n \times n$ matrix U. So, if we take a random public key, it is always possible to find a U such that

$$U^T H_1 + H_1 U, \, U^T H_2 + H_2 U \in S = \text{span}\{H_i : i = 1 \cdots n - r\},$$

provided that $3n > 2r$. However, if we ask that

$$U^T H_1 + H_1 U, \, U^T H_2 + H_2 U, \, U^T H_3 + H_3 U \in S,$$

there are many more conditions than degrees of freedom, hence it is unlikely to find a nontrivial solution for truly random H_i. Conversely, for a set of public keys from C^*, tests [20] shows that it almost surely eventually recovers the missing r equations and break the scheme.

Similarly, [24] and the related [29] shows a similar attack (with a more complex backend) almost surely breaks $3IC^-$ and any other ℓIC^-. For the ℓIC case, the point is the differential expose the symmetry for a linear map $(X_1, X_2, X_3) \mapsto (\xi_1 X_1, \xi_2 X_2, \xi_3 X_3)$. Exactly the same symmetric property is found enabling the same kind of attacks.

It was pointed out [15] that *Internal Perturbation* is almost exactly equal to *both Vinegar* variables *and Projection*, or fixing the input to an affine subspace. Let s be one, two or more. We basically set s variables of the public key to be zero to create the new public key. However, in the case of signature schemes, each projected dimension will slow down the signing process by a factor of q. A differential attack looks for an invariant or a symmetry. Restricting to a subspace of the original **w**-space breaks a symmetry. Something like the *Minus* variant destroys an invariant. Hence the use of projection by itself prevents some attacks.

In [19], it was checked experimentally, for various C^* parameters n and θ, the effect of restricting the internal function to a randomly chosen subspace H of various dimensions s. This is a projected C^{*-} instance of parameters (q, n, r, s). We repeated this check for 3IC$^-$ and discover that again the attacks from [24,29] are prevented. We call this setup 3IC$^-$p(q, k, s).

3.3 Choosing Instances

For signature schemes, we choose C^{*-}p$(2^4, 74, 22, 1)$, which uses 208-bit hashes and is related to the original FLASH by the fact that it uses half as wide variables and project one. We also choose 3IC$^-$p$(2^4, 32, 1)$, which acts on 256-bit hashes.

To invert the public map of projected minus signature schemes:

1. Put in random numbers to the "minus" coordinates.
2. Invert the linear transformation T to get **y**.
3. Invert the central map C^* or 3IC to get **x**.
4. Invert the final linear transformation S to get **w**.
5. If the last component (nybble) of **w** is zero, return the rest, else go to step 1 and repeat.

For the encryptions schemes, we choose PMI+$(136, 6, 18, 8)$ and 2IC $(128,6,16)$ and $(256,12,32)$.

To invert the public map of internally perturbed plus encryption schemes:

1. Invert the linear transformation T to get **y**.
2. Guess the vector $\mathbf{b} = \mathbf{v}(\mathbf{x})$.
3. Invert the central map C^* or 3IC on $\mathbf{y} - \mathbf{b}$ to get **x**.
4. Verify $\mathbf{b} = \mathbf{v}(\mathbf{x})$ and the extra a central equations; if they don't hold, then return to step 2 and repeat.
5. Invert the final linear S to get **w**.

4   Implementation Techniques

Most of the techniques here are not new, just implemented here. However, we do suggest that the bit-sliced Gaussian Elimination idea is new.

4.1   Evaluation of Public Polynomials

We pretty much follow the suggestions of [4] for evaluation of the public polynomials. I.e., over GF(2^8) we use traditional methods, i.e., logarithmic and exponential tables (full 64kB multiplication is faster for long streaming work but has a much higher up-front time cost for one-time use). Over GF(2^4) we use bit-slicing and build lookup tables of all the cross-terms. Over GF(2) we evaluate only the non-zero polynomials.

4.2   Operating on Tower Fields

During working with the inversion of the central map, we operate the big-field systems using as much of tower fields as we can. We note that firstly, $GF(2) = \{(0)_2, (1)_2\}$, where $(\cdot)_2$ means the binary representation. Then $t^2 + t + (1)_2$ is irreducible over $GF(2)$. We can implement $GF(2^{2^i})$ recursively. With a proper choice of α_i, we let $GF(2^{2^i}) = GF(2^{2^{i-1}})[t_i]/(t_i^2 + t_i + \alpha_i)$.. One can also verify that $\alpha_{i+1} := \alpha_i t_i$ will lead to a good series of extensions.

For $a, b, c, d \in GF(2^{2^{i-1}})$, we can do Karatsuba-style

$$(at_i + b)(ct_i + d) = [(a + b)(c + d) + bd]t_i + [ac\alpha_i + bd]$$

where the addition is the bitwise XOR and the multiplication of expressions of a, b, c, d and α_i are done in $GF(2^{2^{i-1}})$. Division can be effected via $(at_i + b)^{-1} = (at_i + a + b)(ab + b^2 + a^2\alpha_i)^{-1}$.

While most of the instances we work with only looks at tower fields going up powers of two, a degree-three extension is similar with the extension being quotiented against $t^3 + t + 1$ and similar polynomials, and a three-way Karatsuba is relatively easy. We can do a similar thing for raising to a power of five.

4.3   Bit-Sliced GF(16) Rainbow Implementations

It is noted in [4] that GF(4) and GF(16) can be bitsliced for good effect. Actually, any $GF(2^k)$ for small k can be bitsliced this way. In particular, it is possible to exploit the bitslicing to evaluate the private map.

1. Invert the linear transformation T to get $\mathbf{y}$ from $\mathbf{z}$. We can use bitslicing here to multiply each z_i to one columne of the matrix M_T^{-1}.
2. Guess at the initial block of vinegar variables
3. Compute the first system to be solved.
4. Solve the first system via Gauss-Jordan elimination with bitslice.
5. Compute the second system to be solved.
6. Solve the second system via Gauss-Jordan elimination with bitslice. We have computed all of $\mathbf{x}$.
7. Invert the linear transformation S to get $\mathbf{w}$ from $\mathbf{x}$.

Note that during the bitslice solving, every equation can be stored as four bit-vectors (here 32-bit or double words suffices), which stores every coefficient along with the constant term. In doing Gauss-Jordan elimination, we use a sequence of bit test choices to multiply the pivot equation so that the pivot coefficient becomes 1, and then use bit-slicing SIMD multiplication to add the correct multiple to every other equation. Bit-Sliced GF(16) is not used for TTS since the set-up takes too much time.

4.4   TTS Implementations

There are a few things to note:

1. Due to the sparsity of the central maps, setting up the Gaussian elimination to run using bitslice takes too much time. Hence, for TTS in GF(16) we complete the entire computation of the private map expressing each GF(16) element as a nybble (4 bits or half a byte) and start the evaluation of the public map by converting the nybble vector packed two to a byte, to the bitslice form.

2. Again for GF(16), we maintain two 4kByte multiplication tables that allows us to lookup either abc or ab and ac at the same time.

3. We use the special form of key generation mentioned in [33, 34]. That is, following Imai and Matsumoto [28], we divide the coefficients involved in each public key polynomial into linear, square, and crossterm portions thus:

$$z_k = \sum_i P_{ik} w_i + \sum_i Q_{ik} w_i^2 + \sum_{i<j} R_{ijk} w_i w_j = \sum_i w_i \left[P_{ik} + Q_{ik} w_i + \sum_{i<j} R_{ijk} w_j \right].$$

R_{ijk}, which comprise most of the public key, may be computed as in [34]:

$$R_{ijk} = \sum_{\ell=n-m}^{n-1} \left[(M_T)_{k,(\ell-n+m)} \left(\sum_{p\, x_\alpha x_\beta \text{ in } y_\ell} p\left((M_S)_{\alpha i}(M_S)_{\beta j} + (M_S)_{\alpha j}(M_S)_{\beta i} \right) \right) \right]$$

The second sum is over all cross-terms $p\ x_\alpha x_\beta$ in the central equation for y_ℓ. For every pair $i < j$, we can compute at once R_{ijk} for every k in $O(n^2)$ totalling $O(n^4)$. Similar computations for P_{ik} and Q_{ik} take even less time.

The instances that we chose are tested not to suffer the same kind of attacks that fell previous TTS schemes, but we still don't have any conclusive evidence one way or the other of how likely this type of system can stand in the long run.

Acknowledgements

The authors thank Prof. Jintai Ding and Pei-Yuan Wu for invaluable comments and discussions, and also to National Science Council for sponsorship under Grant 96-2221-E-001-031-MY3.

References

1. Akkar, M.-L., Courtois, N.T., Duteuil, R., Goubin, L.: A fast and secure implementation of SFLASH. In: Desmedt, Y.G. (ed.) PKC 2003. LNCS, vol. 2567, pp. 267–278. Springer, Heidelberg (2002)
2. Bardet, M., Faugère, J.-C., Salvy, B.: On the complexity of Gröbner basis computation of semi-regular overdetermined algebraic equations. In: Proceedings of the International Conference on Polynomial System Solving, pp. 71–74, Previously INRIA report RR-5049 (2004)

3. Bardet, M., Faugère, J.-C., Salvy, B., Yang, B.-Y.: Asymptotic expansion of the degree of regularity for semi-regular systems of equations. In: Gianni, P. (ed.) MEGA 2005 Sardinia (Italy) (2005)
4. Berbain, C., Billet, O., Gilbert, H.: Efficient implementations of multivariate quadratic systems. In: Biham, E., Youssef, A.M. (eds.) SAC 2006. LNCS, vol. 4356, pp. 174–187. Springer, Heidelberg (2007)
5. Bernstein, D.J., Birkner, P., Joye, M., Lange, T., Peters, C.: Twisted edwards curves. In: Vaudenay, S. (ed.) AFRICACRYPT 2008. LNCS, vol. 5023, pp. 389–405. Springer, Heidelberg (2008)
6. Bernstein, D.J., Lange, T.: Faster addition and doubling on elliptic curves. In: Kurosawa, K. (ed.) ASIACRYPT 2007. LNCS, vol. 4833, pp. 29–50. Springer, Heidelberg (2007)
7. Bernstein, D.J., Lange, T.: Inverted edwards coordinates. In: Boztaş, S., Lu, H.-F. (eds.) AAECC 2007. LNCS, vol. 4851, pp. 20–27. Springer, Heidelberg (2007)
8. Billet, O., Gilbert, H.: Cryptanalysis of rainbow. In: De Prisco, R., Yung, M. (eds.) SCN 2006. LNCS, vol. 4116, pp. 336–347. Springer, Heidelberg (2006)
9. Coppersmith, D., Stern, J., Vaudenay, S.: The security of the birational permutation signature schemes. Journal of Cryptology 10, 207–221 (1997)
10. Courtois, N., Goubin, L., Patarin, J.: SFLASH: Primitive specification (second revised version), Submissions, Sflash, 11 pages (2002), https://www.cosic.esat.kuleuven.be/nessie
11. Courtois, N.T., Klimov, A., Patarin, J., Shamir, A.: Efficient algorithms for solving overdefined systems of multivariate polynomial equations. In: Preneel, B. (ed.) EUROCRYPT 2000. LNCS, vol. 1807, pp. 392–407. Springer, Heidelberg (2000), http://www.minrank.org/xlfull.pdf
12. Ding, J.: A new variant of the Matsumoto-Imai cryptosystem through perturbation. In: Bao, F., Deng, R., Zhou, J. (eds.) PKC 2004. LNCS, vol. 2947, pp. 305–318. Springer, Heidelberg (2004)
13. Ding, J., Gower, J.: Inoculating multivariate schemes against differential attacks. In: Yung, M., Dodis, Y., Kiayias, A., Malkin, T. (eds.) PKC 2006. LNCS, vol. 3958. Springer, Heidelberg (2006), http://eprint.iacr.org/2005/255
14. Ding, J., Gower, J., Schmidt, D.: Multivariate Public-Key Cryptosystems. In: Advances in Information Security. Springer, Heidelberg (2006)
15. Ding, J., Schmidt, D.: Cryptanalysis of HFEv and internal perturbation of HFE. In: Vaudenay, S. (ed.) PKC 2005. LNCS, vol. 3386, pp. 288–301. Springer, Heidelberg (2005)
16. Ding, J., Schmidt, D.: Rainbow, a new multivariable polynomial signature scheme. In: Ioannidis, J., Keromytis, A., Yung, M. (eds.) ACNS 2005. LNCS, vol. 3531, pp. 164–175. Springer, Heidelberg (2005)
17. Ding, J., Wolf, C., Yang, B.-Y.: ℓ-invertible cycles for multivariate quadratic public key cryptography. In: Okamoto, T., Wang, X. (eds.) PKC 2007. LNCS, vol. 4450, pp. 266–281. Springer, Heidelberg (2007)
18. Ding, J., Yang, B.-Y., Chen, C.-H.O., Chen, M.-S., Cheng, C.-M.: New differential-algebraic attacks and reparametrization of rainbow. In: Bellovin, S.M., Gennaro, R., Keromytis, A., Yung, M. (eds.) ACNS 2008. LNCS, vol. 5037, pp. 242–257. Springer, Heidelberg (2008), http://eprint.iacr.org/2008/108
19. Ding, J., Yang, B.-Y., Dubois, V., Cheng, C.-M., Chen, O.C.-H.: Breaking the symmetry: a way to resist the new differential attack. In: ICALP 2008. LNCS. Springer, Heidelberg (2008), http://eprint.iacr.org/2007/366

20. Dubois, V., Fouque, P.-A., Shamir, A., Stern, J.: Practical cryptanalysis of SFLASH. In: Menezes, A. (ed.) CRYPTO 2007. LNCS, vol. 4622, pp. 1–12. Springer, Heidelberg (2007)
21. Faugère, J.-C.: A new efficient algorithm for computing Gröbner bases (F_4). Journal of Pure and Applied Algebra 139, 61–88 (1999)
22. Faugère, J.-C.: A new efficient algorithm for computing Gröbner bases without reduction to zero (F_5). In: International Symposium on Symbolic and Algebraic Computation — ISSAC 2002, pp. 75–83. ACM Press, New York (2002)
23. Fouque, P.-A., Granboulan, L., Stern, J.: Differential cryptanalysis for multivariate schemes. In: Cramer, R. (ed.) EUROCRYPT 2005. LNCS, vol. 3494, pp. 341–353. Springer, Heidelberg (2005)
24. Fouque, P.-A., Macario-Rat, G., Perret, L., Stern, J.: Total break of the ℓIC- signature scheme. In: Public Key Cryptography, pp. 1–17 (2008)
25. Goubin, L., Courtois, N.T.: Cryptanalysis of the TTM cryptosystem. In: Okamoto, T. (ed.) ASIACRYPT 2000. LNCS, vol. 1976, pp. 44–57. Springer, Heidelberg (2000)
26. Kipnis, A., Patarin, J., Goubin, L.: Unbalanced Oil and Vinegar signature schemes. In: Stern, J. (ed.) EUROCRYPT 1999. LNCS, vol. 1592, pp. 206–222. Springer, Heidelberg (1999)
27. Kipnis, A., Shamir, A.: Cryptanalysis of the oil and vinegar signature scheme. In: Krawczyk, H. (ed.) CRYPTO 1998. LNCS, vol. 1462, pp. 257–266. Springer, Heidelberg (1998)
28. Matsumoto, T., Imai, H.: Public quadratic polynomial-tuples for efficient signature verification and message-encryption. In: Günther, C.G. (ed.) EUROCRYPT 1988. LNCS, vol. 330, pp. 419–545. Springer, Heidelberg (1988)
29. Ogura, N., Uchiyama, S.: Remarks on the attack of fouque et al. against the ℓic scheme. Cryptology ePrint Archive, Report 2008/208 (2008), http://eprint.iacr.org/
30. Wolf, C., Braeken, A., Preneel, B.: Efficient cryptanalysis of RSE(2)PKC and RSSE(2)PKC. In: Blundo, C., Cimato, S. (eds.) SCN 2004. LNCS, vol. 3352, pp. 294–309. Springer, Heidelberg (2005), http://eprint.iacr.org/2004/237
31. Wolf, C., Preneel, B.: Taxonomy of public key schemes based on the problem of multivariate quadratic equations. Cryptology ePrint Archive, Report 2005/077, 64 pages, May 12 (2005), http://eprint.iacr.org/2005/077/
32. Yang, B.-Y., Chen, J.-M.: All in the XL family: Theory and practice. In: Park, C.-s., Chee, S. (eds.) ICISC 2004. LNCS, vol. 3506, pp. 67–86. Springer, Heidelberg (2005)
33. Yang, B.-Y., Chen, J.-M.: Building secure tame-like multivariate public-key cryptosystems: The new TTS. In: Boyd, C., González Nieto, J.M. (eds.) ACISP 2005. LNCS, vol. 3574, pp. 518–531. Springer, Heidelberg (2005)
34. Yang, B.-Y., Chen, J.-M., Chen, Y.-H.: TTS: High-speed signatures on a low-cost smart card. In: Joye, M., Quisquater, J.-J. (eds.) CHES 2004. LNCS, vol. 3156, pp. 371–385. Springer, Heidelberg (2004)

Digital Signatures Out of Second-Preimage Resistant Hash Functions

Erik Dahmen[1], Katsuyuki Okeya[2], Tsuyoshi Takagi[3], and Camille Vuillaume[2]

[1] Technische Universität Darmstadt
dahmen@cdc.informatik.tu-darmstadt.de
[2] Hitachi, Ltd., Systems Development Laboratory
{katsuyuki.okeya.ue,camille.vuillaume.ch}@hitachi.com
[3] Future University, Hakodate
takagi@fun.ac.jp

Abstract. We propose a new construction for Merkle authentication trees which does not require collision resistant hash functions; in contrast with previous constructions that attempted to avoid the dependency on collision resistance, our technique enjoys provable security assuming the well-understood notion of second-preimage resistance. The resulting signature scheme is existentially unforgeable when the underlying hash function is second-preimage resistant, yields shorter signatures, and is affected neither by birthday attacks nor by the recent progresses in collision-finding algorithms.

Keywords: Merkle signatures, provable security, second-preimage resistance.

1 Introduction

In 1979, Ralph Merkle proposed a digital signature scheme constructed out of cryptographic hash functions only [7]. The interest of this scheme is that, unlike most public-key cryptosystems, its security does not rely on number-theoretic problems. Even if a particular hash function appears insecure, the scheme can be easily repaired by using a different hash function. Finally, the current research suggests that the Merkle signature scheme (MSS) will be only marginally affected if large quantum computers are built, something that is not true for popular public-key cryptosystems such as RSA and ECC.

The security of the original construction of the MSS relies on a collision resistant hash function for the hash tree and a preimage resistant function for the one-time signature stage [3]. Regarding security, this construction has two drawbacks. First, recent attacks on the collision resistance of popular hash functions such as MD5 [15] and SHA1 [14] show that collision resistance is a goal which is hard to achieve. Second, the security level of Merkle signatures is determined by the collision resistance property of the hash function and therefore affected by birthday attacks.

In [8], the authors argue, without proof, that the security level of the MSS should be determined by the second-preimage resistance property of the hash

J. Buchmann and J. Ding (Eds.): PQCrypto 2008, LNCS 5299, pp. 109–123, 2008.

function. Although no attack based on a collision finder is known for the MSS, its security proof does not exclude the existence of such attacks. In addition, Rohatgi proposes using target-collision resistant hash functions for achieving goals that are similar to ours [11]. Unfortunately, practical hash functions were not designed with target-collision resistance in mind, and keyed hash functions such as HMAC lose all of their security properties when their key is revealed, and as such, cannot be regarded as target-collision resistant. Although we agree with [8] that second-preimage resistance *should* be at the heart of the security of the MSS, we emphasize that until now, no satisfactory solution is known, at least from a provable security perspective.

In this paper, we propose a new construction for Merkle authentication trees and show that the resulting signature scheme is secure against adaptive chosen message attacks, assuming a second-preimage resistant hash function and a secure one-time signature scheme. Our construction is inspired by the XOR tree proposed by Bellare and Rogaway for building universal one-way hash functions out of universal one-way compression functions [1]. However, we use the XOR tree for a totally different purpose, namely establishing the unforgeability of the Merkle signature scheme, and we relax the assumption on the compression function to second-preimage resistance. Even for hash functions with short output size, our scheme *provably* yields a high security level; compared to the original MSS, not only security is improved, but the size of signatures is reduced as well.

The paper is organized as follows: in Section 2 we review security notions for hash functions and signature schemes. In Section 3 we introduce the new construction and its security proof. In Section 4 we estimate the security level of the new scheme. In Section 5 we consider the problem of signing arbitrarily long messages. In Section 6 we present practical considerations. In Section 7 we state our conclusion.

2   Hash Functions and Signature Schemes

Hash Functions. We call $\mathcal{H}_K = \left\{ H_k : \{0,1\}^* \to \{0,1\}^n \right\}_{k \in K}$ a family of hash functions, parameterized by a key $k \in K$, that map bit strings of arbitrary length to bit strings of length n. There exist various security notions for hash functions, see [10] for an overview. In this paper we focus on the three most popular ones, namely preimage resistance, second-preimage resistance and collision resistance. In the following, $x \in_R X$ means that x is chosen uniformly at random.

Preimage resistance. For any key $k \in_R K$ and $y \in_R H_k(\{0,1\}^n)$ it is computationally infeasible to compute $x \in \{0,1\}^*$ such that $H_k(x) = y$.

Second-preimage resistance. For any key $k \in_R K$ and $x \in_R \{0,1\}^n$ it is computationally infeasible to compute $x' \in \{0,1\}^*$ such that $x' \neq x$ and $H_k(x) = H_k(x')$.

Collision resistance. For any key $k \in_R K$ it is computationally infeasible to compute $x, x' \in \{0,1\}^*$ such that $x' \neq x$ and $H_k(x) = H_k(x')$.

We call a family $\mathcal{H}_k$ of hash functions $(t_{\mathrm{ow}}, \epsilon_{\mathrm{ow}})$ preimage resistant (respectively $(t_{\mathrm{SPR}}, \epsilon_{\mathrm{SPR}})$ second-preimage resistant or $(t_{\mathrm{CR}}, \epsilon_{\mathrm{CR}})$ collision resistant), if for any adversary $\mathcal{A}$ that runs in time at most t_{OW} (resp. t_{SPR} or t_{CR}), the probability of finding a preimage (resp. second-preimage or collision) is smaller than ϵ_{OW} (resp. ϵ_{SPR} or ϵ_{CR}).

Using generic (brute-force) attacks to compute preimages or second-preimages, one requires $t_{\text{OW}} = t_{\text{SPR}} = 2^{n-k}$ evaluations of the hash function, to find a preimage or second preimage with probability $\epsilon_{\text{OW}} = \epsilon_{\text{SPR}} = 1/2^k$. Due to the birthday paradox, one requires $t_{\text{CR}} = 2^{n/2}$ evaluations of the hash function to find a collision with probability $\epsilon_{\text{CR}} = 1/2$.

Signatures Schemes. A signature scheme SIGN is defined as the triple (GEN, SIG, VER). GEN is the key pair generation algorithm that on input a security parameter 1^n produces a pair (sk, pk), where sk is the private key or signature key and pk is the public key or verification key, (sk, pk) $\leftarrow$ GEN(1^n). SIG is the signature generation algorithm that on input a message M and private key sk produces a signature $\sigma(M) \leftarrow$ SIG(M, sk). VER is the verification algorithm that on input $(M, \sigma(M), \text{pk})$ checks whether the signature is valid, i.e. it outputs **true** if and only if the signature is valid and **false** otherwise [4]. In the following, let $t_{\text{GEN}}, t_{\text{SIG}}, t_{\text{VER}}$ be the time algorithms GEN, SIG, VER require for key generation, signing and verification, respectively.

Let SIGN = (GEN, SIG, VER) be a signature scheme. We call SIGN a (t, ϵ, Q) signature scheme or (t, ϵ, Q) existentially unforgeable under an adaptive chosen message attack (CMA-secure), if for any forger $\text{FOR}^{\text{SIG}_{\text{sk}}(\cdot)}(\text{pk})$, that has access to a signing oracle $\text{SIG}_{\text{sk}}(\cdot)$ and that runs in time at most t, the success probability in forging a signature is at most ϵ, where $\text{FOR}^{\text{SIG}_{\text{sk}}(\cdot)}(\text{pk})$ can query the signing oracle at most Q times [4].

3 Merkle Signatures Using Second-Preimage Resistance

In this section we describe our construction for the Merkle authentication tree, from now on called SPR-Merkle tree, and prove that the CMA-security of the resulting signature scheme (SPR-MSS) can be reduced to the second-preimage resistance of the used hash function and the CMA-security of the chosen one-time signature scheme (OTS). In the following, let $\mathcal{H}_K = \{H_k : \{0,1\}^{2n} \to \{0,1\}^n\}_{k \in K}$ be a family of $(t_{\text{SPR}}, \epsilon_{\text{SPR}})$ second-preimage resistant hash functions.

Our construction differs to the original construction proposed by Merkle in the following way: before applying the hash function to the concatenation of two child nodes to compute their parent, both child nodes are XORed with a randomly chosen mask. Also, a leaf of the SPR-Merkle tree is not the hash value of the concatenation of the bit strings in the OTS verification key, but the bit strings themselves. The SPR-Merkle tree is constructed starting directly from these bit strings. For that reason, it is sufficient that the hash functions $H_k \in \mathcal{H}_K$ accept only bit strings of length at most $2n$ as input. In this section we restrict the length of the message to be signed to n bits. The problem of signing arbitrarily long messages is considered in Section 5.

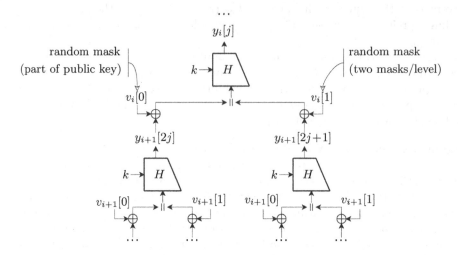

Fig. 1. XOR construction for the SPR-Merkle tree

Key Pair Generation. The key pair generation of our scheme works as follows. First choose $h \geq 1$, to determine the number of signatures that can be generated with this key pair, i.e. 2^h many. Next compute 2^h OTS key pairs (X_j, Y_j), for $j = 0, \ldots, 2^h - 1$. We assume that each signature key and verification key consists of 2^l bit strings each of length n. Then choose a key for the hash function $k \in_R K$ and masks $v_i[0], v_i[1] \in_R \{0,1\}^n$ uniformly at random for $i = 0, \ldots, h+l-1$. The $2^h \cdot 2^l$ n-bit strings from the verification keys form the leaves of the SPR-Merkle tree, which in total yields a tree of height $h + l$. The nodes are denoted by $y_i[j]$, where $i = 0, \ldots, h + l$ denotes the height of the node in the tree (the root has height 0 and the leaves have height $h + l$) and $j = 0, \ldots, 2^i - 1$ denotes the position of the node on that height, counting from left to right. The inner nodes are computed as

$$y_i[j] = H_k\Big(\big(y_{i+1}[2j] \oplus v_i[0]\big) \parallel \big(y_{i+1}[2j + 1] \oplus v_i[1]\big)\Big)$$

for $i = h+l-1, \ldots, 0$ and $j = 0, \ldots, 2^i-1$, see Figure 1. The SPR-MSS private key consists of the 2^h OTS signature keys X_j and the SPR-MSS public key consists of

1. The key for the hash function k,
2. The XOR masks $v_0[0], v_0[1], \ldots, v_{h+l-1}[0], v_{h+l-1}[1]$, and
3. The root of the Merkle tree $y_0[0]$.

Remark 1. In case the number of bit strings L in the verification key of the chosen OTS is not a power of 2, the resulting SPR-Merkle tree has height $h + \lceil \log_2 L \rceil$. The SPR-Merkle tree is constructed such that the subtrees below the 2^h nodes $y_h[j]$ are unbalanced trees of height $\lceil \log_2 L \rceil$.

Signature Generation. For $s \in \{0, \ldots, 2^h - 1\}$, the sth signature of message $M = (m_0, \ldots, m_{n-1})_2$ is $\sigma_s(M) = (s, \sigma_{\mathrm{OTS}}(M), Y_s, A_s)$, where

- s is the index of the signature,
- $\sigma_{\mathrm{OTS}}(M)$ is the one-time signature of M, generated with X_s,
- Y_s is the sth verification key, and
- $A_s = (a_h, \ldots, a_1)$ is the authentication path for Y_s, where a_i is the sibling of the node at height i on the path from $y_h[s]$ to the root $y_0[0]$, i.e.

$$a_i = \begin{cases} y_i[s/2^{h-i} - 1], \text{if } s/2^{h-i} \equiv 1 \bmod 2 \\ y_i[s/2^{h-i} + 1], \text{if } s/2^{h-i} \equiv 0 \bmod 2 \end{cases}, \quad \text{for } i = 1, \ldots, h.$$

Verification. The verification consists of two steps. First the verifier verifies the one-time signature of message M using the supplied verification key Y_s. Then he verifies the authenticity of Y_s as follows: first he uses the 2^l bit strings in Y_s to compute the inner node $y_h[s]$ as

$$y_i[j] = H_k\big(y_{i+1}[2j] \oplus v_i[0] \,\|\, y_{i+1}[2j + 1] \oplus v_i[1]\big)$$

for $i = h + l - 1, \ldots, h$ and $j = s2^{i-h}, \ldots, (s + 1)2^{i-1} - 1$. Then he uses the authentication path A_s and recomputes the path from $y_h[s]$ to the root $y_0[0]$ as

$$p_i = \begin{cases} H_k\Big(\big(a_{i+1} \oplus v_i[0]\big) \,\|\, \big(p_{i+1} \oplus v_i[1]\big)\Big), \text{if } s/2^{h-i+1} \equiv 1 \bmod 2 \\ H_k\Big(\big(p_{i+1} \oplus v_i[0]\big) \,\|\, \big(a_{i+1} \oplus v_i[1]\big)\Big), \text{if } s/2^{h-i+1} \equiv 0 \bmod 2 \end{cases}$$

for $i = h - 1, \ldots, 0$ and $p_h = y_h[s]$. The signature is valid if p_0 equals the signers public root $y_0[0]$ and the verification of $\sigma_{\mathrm{OTS}}(M)$ was successful. Figure 2

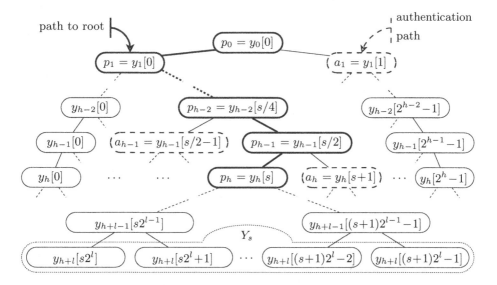

Fig. 2. Notations of the SPR-MSS

illustrates how the authentication path can be utilized in order to recompute the root $y_0[0]$.

3.1   Security of the SPR-MSS

We now reduce the CMA-security of the SPR-MSS to the second-preimage resistance of $\mathcal{H}_K$ and the CMA-security of the used OTS. We do so by showing in Algorithm 1 how a forger $\text{FOR}^{\text{SIG}_{\text{sk}}(\cdot)}(\text{pk})$ for the SPR-MSS can be used to construct an adversary $\text{ADV}_{\text{SPR,OTS}}$ that either finds a second-preimage for a random element of $\mathcal{H}_K$ or breaks the CMA-security for a certain instance of the underlying OTS. In Algorithm 1, we use the convention that when algorithms called by $\text{ADV}_{\text{SPR,OTS}}$ fail, so does $\text{ADV}_{\text{SPR,OTS}}$.

Algorithm 1. $\text{ADV}_{\text{SPR,OTS}}$

INPUT: Hash function key $k \in_R K$, tree height $h \geq 1$, first-preimage $x \in_R \{0,1\}^{2n}$, OTS instance with verification key Y and signing oracle $\text{SIG}_X(\cdot)$
OUTPUT: Second-preimage $x' \in \{0,1\}^{2n}$ with $x' \neq x$ and $H_k(x) = H_k(x')$, **or** existential forgery for the supplied instance of the OTS, **or failure**

---

1. Choose $c \in_R \{0, \ldots, 2^h - 1\}$ uniformly at random.
2. Generate OTS key pairs $(X_j, Y_j), j = 0, \ldots, 2^h - 1, j \neq c$ and set $Y_c \leftarrow Y$.
3. Choose $(a, b) \in_R \{(i, j) : i \in \{0, \ldots, h + l - 1\}, j \in \{0, \ldots, 2^i - 1\}\}$.
4. Choose random masks $v_i[0], v_i[1] \in_R \{0,1\}^n, i = 0, \ldots, h + l - 1, i \neq a$.
5. Construct the Merkle tree up to height $a + 1$.
6. Choose $v_a[0], v_a[1] \in \{0,1\}^n$ such that

$$x = \big(y_{a+1}[2b] \oplus v_a[0]\big) \parallel \big(y_{a+1}[2b + 1] \oplus v_a[1]\big).$$

   Note that $y_a[b] = H_k(x)$.
7. Use $v_a[0], v_a[1]$ to complete the key pair generation.
8. Run $\text{FOR}^{\text{SIG}_{\text{sk}}(\cdot)}(\text{pk})$.
9. When $\text{FOR}^{\text{SIG}_{\text{sk}}(\cdot)}(\text{pk})$ asks its qth oracle query with message M_q:
   (a) **if** $q = c$ **then** obtain the one-time signature of M_q using the signing oracle $\text{SIG}_X(\cdot)$ provided as input: $\sigma_{\text{OTS}}(M_q) \leftarrow \text{SIG}_X(M_q)$.
   (b) **else** compute $\sigma_{\text{OTS}}(M_q)$ using the qth OTS signature key X_q.
   (c) Respond to forger with signature $\sigma_q(M_q) = (q, \sigma_{\text{OTS}}(M_q), Y_q, A_q)$.
10. When $\text{FOR}^{\text{SIG}_{\text{sk}}(\cdot)}(\text{pk})$ outputs signature $\sigma'(M')$ for M':
    (a) Verify the signature $\sigma'(M') = (s, \sigma_{\text{OTS}}(M'), Y'_s, A'_s)$.
    (b) **if** $(Y'_s, A'_s) \neq (Y_s, A_s)$:
        i. **if** $y_a[b]$ is computed during the verification as $y_a[b] = H_k(x')$ and $x' \neq x$ holds **then return** x' as second-preimage of x.
        ii. **else return failure**.
    (c) **else** (in that case $(Y'_s, A'_s) = (Y_s, A_s)$):
        i. **if** $s = c$ **then return** $(\sigma_{\text{OTS}}(M'), M')$ as forgery for the supplied instance of the OTS.
        ii. **else return failure**.

Note that since the first-preimage x is chosen uniformly at random, so are the masks $v_a[0], v_a[1]$. As a consequence, the adversary $\mathrm{ADV_{SPR,OTS}}$ creates an environment identical to the signature forging game played by the forger. We will now compute the success probability of $\mathrm{ADV_{SPR,OTS}}$.

Case 1 $(Y'_s, A'_s) \neq (Y_s, A_s)$. The fact that the verification key Y'_s can be authenticated against the root $y_0[0]$ implies a collision of H_k, see Appendix C. This collision can either occur during the computation of the inner node $y_h[s]$ or during the computation of the path from $y_h[s]$ to the root $y_0[0]$. The adversary $\mathrm{ADV_{SPR,OTS}}$ is successful in finding a second-preimage of x if the node $y_a[b]$ is computed as $y_a[b] = H_k(x')$ with $x \neq x'$. Since the position of node $y_a[b]$ was chosen at random, the probability that the collision occurs precisely at this position is at least $1/(2^{h+l} - 1)$. In total, the success probability of $\mathrm{ADV_{SPR,OTS}}$ is at least $\epsilon/(2^{h+l} - 1)$, where ϵ is the success probability of the forger.

Case 2 $(Y'_s, A'_s) = (Y_s, A_s)$. In this case $(\sigma_{\mathrm{OTS}}(M'), M') \neq (\sigma_{\mathrm{OTS}}(M_s), M_s)$ holds which implies that $\mathrm{FOR}^{\mathrm{SIG_{sk}(\cdot)}}(\mathrm{pk})$ generated an existential forgery for one instance of the underlying OTS. The probability that $\mathrm{FOR}^{\mathrm{SIG_{sk}(\cdot)}}(\mathrm{pk})$ breaks CMA-security of the supplied instance $(s = c)$ is at least $1/2^h$. In total, the success probability of $\mathrm{ADV_{SPR,OTS}}$ is at least $\epsilon/2^h$, where ϵ is the success probability of the forger.

Note that since both cases are complementary, one occurs with probability at least $1/2$. This leads to the following theorem:

Theorem 1 (Security of SPR-MSS). *If $\mathcal{H}_K = \{H_k : \{0,1\}^{2n} \to \{0,1\}^n\}_{k \in K}$ is a family of $(t_{\mathrm{SPR}}, \epsilon_{\mathrm{SPR}})$ second-preimage resistant hash functions with $\epsilon_{\mathrm{SPR}} \leq 1/(2^{h+l+1} - 2)$ and the used OTS is a $(t_{\mathrm{OTS}}, \epsilon_{\mathrm{OTS}}, 1)$ signature scheme with $\epsilon_{\mathrm{OTS}} \leq 1/2^{h+1}$, then the SPR-MSS is a $(t, \epsilon, 2^h)$ signature scheme with*

$$\epsilon \leq 2 \cdot \max\left\{(2^{h+l} - 1) \cdot \epsilon_{\mathrm{SPR}}, 2^h \cdot \epsilon_{\mathrm{OTS}}\right\}$$
$$t = \min\left\{t_{\mathrm{SPR}}, t_{\mathrm{OTS}}\right\} - 2^h \cdot t_{\mathrm{SIG}} - t_{\mathrm{VER}} - t_{\mathrm{GEN}}.$$

4 Comparison

Security Level. We compute the security level of the SPR-MSS and compare it with the original MSS that relies on collision resistance (CR-MSS). As OTS we use the Lamport–Diffie one-time signature scheme (LD–OTS) [6]. The following theorem establishes the security of the LD–OTS (details of the reduction can be found in Appendix A).

Theorem 2 (Security of LD-OTS). *If $\mathcal{F}_K = \{F_k : \{0,1\}^n \to \{0,1\}^n\}_{k \in K}$ is a family of $(t_{\mathrm{OW}}, \epsilon_{\mathrm{OW}})$ one-way functions with $\epsilon_{\mathrm{OW}} \leq 1/4n$, then the LD–OTS is a $(t, \epsilon, 1)$ signature scheme with*

$$\epsilon \leq 4n \cdot \epsilon_{\mathrm{OW}}$$
$$t = t_{\mathrm{OW}} - t_{\mathrm{SIG}} - t_{\mathrm{GEN}}$$

By combining Theorems 1 and 2, we get

$$\epsilon \leq 2 \cdot \max\left\{(2^{h+\log_2 2n} - 1) \cdot \epsilon_{\mathrm{SPR}}, 2^{h+\log_2 4n} \cdot \epsilon_{\mathrm{OW}}\right\}$$
$$t = \min\left\{t_{\mathrm{SPR}}, t_{\mathrm{OW}}\right\} - 2^h \cdot t_{\mathrm{SIG}} - t_{\mathrm{VER}} - t_{\mathrm{GEN}}. \tag{1}$$

Note that we can replace t_{OTS} by t_{OW} rather than $t_{\mathrm{OW}} - t_{\mathrm{SIG}} - t_{\mathrm{GEN}}$ since the time the OTS requires for signing and key generation are already included in Theorem 1.

The security level is computed as the quotient t/ϵ. For the values $t_{\mathrm{OW}}, t_{\mathrm{SPR}}, \epsilon_{\mathrm{OW}}$ and ϵ_{SPR} we consider the generic attacks of Section 2 and set

$$\epsilon_{\mathrm{OW}} = 1/2^{h+\log_2 4n+1} \qquad t_{\mathrm{OW}} = 2^{n-h-\log_2 4n-1}$$
$$\epsilon_{\mathrm{SPR}} = 1/(2^{h+\log_2 2n+1} - 2) \qquad t_{\mathrm{SPR}} = 2^{n-\log_2(2^{h+\log_2 2n+1}-2)} \tag{2}$$

which yields $\epsilon = 1$ in Equation (1). The times for signing, verifying, and key generation are stated in terms of evaluations of F_k and H_k. We set $t_{\mathrm{SIG}} = (h+1) \cdot n$ (n to compute the LD–OTS signature and $h \cdot n$ as the average cost for the authentication path computation using Szydlo's algorithm [13]), $t_{\mathrm{VER}} = 3n+h-1$ (n to verify the LD–OTS signature, $2n - 1$ to compute the inner node $y_h[s]$, and h to compute the path to the root), and $t_{\mathrm{GEN}} = 2^{h+\log_2 2n+1} - 1$ ($2^h \cdot 2n$ to compute the LD–OTS verification keys and $2^{h+\log_2 2n} - 1$ to compute the root). By substituting these values, we get

$$t/\epsilon = 2^{n-h-\log_2 4n-1} - 2^{h+\log_2(h+1)n} - 2^{\log_2(3n+h-1)} - 2^{h+\log_2 2n+1} + 1.$$

The values for $t_{\mathrm{SIG}}, t_{\mathrm{VER}}$ and t_{GEN} affect the security level only for large h. Otherwise the security level can be estimated as $2^{n-h-\log_2 n-4}$.

A similar result can be obtained for the security of the CR-MSS with the following theorem (details of the reduction can be found in Appendix B).

Theorem 3 (Security of CR-MSS). *If $\mathcal{G}_K = \left\{G_k : \{0,1\}^{2n} \to \{0,1\}^n\right\}_{k \in K}$ is a family of $(t_{\mathrm{CR}}, \epsilon_{\mathrm{CR}})$ collision resistant hash functions with $\epsilon_{\mathrm{CR}} \leq 1/2$ and the underlying OTS is a $(t_{\mathrm{OTS}}, \epsilon_{\mathrm{OTS}}, 1)$ signature scheme with $\epsilon_{\mathrm{OTS}} \leq 1/2^{h+1}$, then the CR-MSS is a $(t, \epsilon, 2^h)$ signature scheme with*

$$\epsilon \leq 2 \cdot \max\left\{\epsilon_{\mathrm{CR}}, 2^h \cdot \epsilon_{\mathrm{OTS}}\right\}$$
$$t = \min\left\{t_{\mathrm{CR}}, t_{\mathrm{OTS}}\right\} - 2^h \cdot t_{\mathrm{SIG}} - t_{\mathrm{VER}} - t_{\mathrm{GEN}}$$

By combining Theorems 2 and 3, we get

$$\epsilon \leq 2 \cdot \max\left\{\epsilon_{\mathrm{CR}}, 2^{h+\log_2 4n} \cdot \epsilon_{\mathrm{OW}}\right\}$$
$$t = \min\left\{t_{\mathrm{CR}}, t_{\mathrm{OW}}\right\} - 2^h \cdot t_{\mathrm{SIG}} - t_{\mathrm{VER}} - t_{\mathrm{GEN}}. \tag{3}$$

We now set $\epsilon_{\mathrm{CR}} = 1/2$ and $t_{\mathrm{CR}} = 2^{n/2}$ (see Section 2) and use the values for $\epsilon_{\mathrm{OW}}, t_{\mathrm{OW}}$ from Equation (2) which yields $\epsilon = 1$ in Equation (3). We further set $t_{\mathrm{SIG}} = (h+1) \cdot n$, $t_{\mathrm{VER}} = n+1+h$ and $t_{\mathrm{GEN}} = 2^h \cdot 2n + 2^{h+1} - 1$ and get

$$t/\epsilon = 2^{n/2} - 2^{h+\log_2(h+1)n} - 2^{\log_2(n+1+h)} - 2^{h+\log_2 2n} - 2^{h+1} + 1.$$

Again, the values for $t_{\mathrm{SIG}}, t_{\mathrm{VER}}$ and t_{GEN} affect the security level only for large h. Otherwise, the security level can be estimated as $2^{n/2-1}$.

Table 1. Security level of SPR-MSS and CR-MSS using the LD–OTS

Output length n	128	160	224	256
Security level of SPR-MSS	2^{118-h}	$2^{148.67-h}$	$2^{212.19-h}$	2^{244-h}
Maximal height of tree h	$h \leq 52$	$h \leq 67$	$h \leq 98$	$h \leq 114$
Security level of CR-MSS	2^{63}	2^{79}	2^{111}	2^{127}
Maximal height of tree h	$h \leq 50$	$h \leq 65$	$h \leq 96$	$h \leq 112$

Remark 2. It is possible to choose different trade-offs for the values in Equation (2). This however would not affect the resulting security level but only the upper bound for h. We chose these values because they correspond to the extreme case $\epsilon = 1$ in Equation (1), where Theorems 1 and 3 still hold.

Table 1 shows the security level of SPR-MSS and CR-MSS for different values of n. It also shows the upper bounds for h such that the security level of SPR-MSS and CR-MSS can be estimated as $2^{n-h-\log_2 n-4}$ and $2^{n/2-1}$, respectively.

Table 1 shows that the security level is increased drastically when using the SPR-MSS. As a consequence, the SPR-MSS not only has weaker security assumptions, but hash functions with much smaller output size suffice to obtain the same security level as the CR-MSS. Nowadays, a security level of at least 2^{80} is required. When using $n = 128$, the SPR-MSS achieves a security level greater than 2^{80} for $h \leq 38$. To obtain a similar security level with CR-MSS, one must use $n = 224$.

Sizes. The CR-MSS public key consists of the root of the Merkle tree and the key for the hash function. Assuming this key has bit length n, the size of an CR-MSS public key is $2 \cdot n$ bits. The SPR-MSS public key must also contain the $2(h + l)$ XOR masks, each of bit length n. Therefore, in total the size of an SPR-MSS public key is $2(h + l + 1) \cdot n$ bits. In case of the LD–OTS we have $l = \lceil \log_2 2n \rceil$. Using the same hash function, the signature size is the same for the CR-MSS and the SPR-MSS. When using the LD–OTS, the one-time signature of the message consists of n bit strings of length n. The verification key also consists of n bit strings of length n, since half of the verification key can be computed from the signature. The authentication path consists of h bit strings of length n. In total, the size of a signature is $(2n + h) \cdot n$ bits. Table 2 compares the signature and public key size of the SPR-MSS and the CR-MSS when using $h = 20$.

Table 2 shows that in addition to its superior security, the SPR-MSS also provides smaller signatures than the CR-MSS, at the expense of larger public keys. In fact, in many cases the signer's public key, embedded in a certificate, is part of the signature; for that reason the sum of the sizes of the public key and the signature is often relevant. However, even in this case, the SPR-MSS is still superior to the CR-MSS.

Table 2. Sizes of SPR-MSS and CR-MSS using the LD–OTS

	Public key size	Signature size	Security level
SPR-MSS ($n = 128$)	7, 424 bits	35, 328 bits	2^{98}
CR-MSS ($n = 160$)	320 bits	54, 400 bits	2^{79}
CR-MSS ($n = 224$)	448 bits	104, 832 bits	2^{111}

5   Signing Arbitrarily Long Data

In Section 3 we restricted the length of the message to be signed to n bits. We now give some suggestions for signing arbitrarily long messages. The most straightforward way is to use a collision resistant hash function anyway. Although this solution requires stronger security assumptions, the SPR-MSS would still provide smaller signatures.

A better approach is to use target collision resistant (TCR) hash functions [1,9]. Recall that in the TCR game, the adversary must first commit to a message M, then receives the key K, and wins if he can output another message M' such that $H_K(M) = H_K(M')$. The security notion TCR is stronger than second-preimage resistance, but weaker than collision resistance [10]. In the TCR-hash-and-sign paradigm, the signature of a message M is the pair $\big(\sigma(K \| H_K(M)),\ K\big)$, i.e. the key K must be signed as well. In [1], Bellare and Rogaway show how a TCR hash function can be constructed from a TCR compression function using the XOR tree we used in SPR-MSS. In this case, the length of the hash key depends on the message length. If M has bit length $n \cdot b$, the bit length of the key K is $2n \cdot \lceil \log_2 b \rceil$. In [12] Shoup proposed a linear construction for TCR hash functions that reduce the bit length of the key to $n \cdot \lceil \log_2 b \rceil$. However, even with Shoup's hash function, the key size still depends (logarithmically) on the message length, and can be relatively large. In order to solve the problem of long keys, Bellare and Rogaway suggested iterating TCR hash functions [1]. For example, the TCR hash function can be iterated with three different keys K_1, K_2 and K_3 as depicted in Figure 3; in this case, although the three keys must be transmitted with the signature, only K_3 must be signed. Since each round reduces the size of the input to the next hash function, assuming a message with b blocks, after three iterations, the size of the final key K_3 will have about $\log_2(\log_2(\log_2(b)))$ blocks of n bits. With a 128-bit hash function, if K_3 is allowed to have at most 3 blocks, then messages up to 2^{63} blocks (or 2^{71} bits) can be signed.

Unfortunately, even when TCR hash functions are iterated, the signature size is somewhat large: if K_3 has three blocks, the input to the signature scheme has $4n$ bits, and the signature size is about $4n^2$ bits. In [5] Halevi and Krawczyk introduce yet another security notion, which they call enhanced target collision resistance (eTCR). Unlike the TCR game, the adversary commits to a message M, receives the key K, and wins if he finds another key and another message such that $H_K(M) = H_{K'}(M')$. When using eTCR hash functions, it is no longer necessary to sign the key. Furthermore, Halevi and Krawczyk proved that an

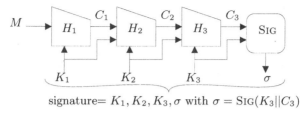

signature= K_1, K_2, K_3, σ with $\sigma = \text{SIG}(K_3 || C_3)$

Fig. 3. Iterating TCR hash functions

eTCR hash function can be instantiated by a real-world hash function, where the blocks of the input message are randomized with a single key, and the key is appended to the message [5]. Their proof assumes that the underlying compression function has second-preimage resistance-like properties, which they call eSPR (evaluated second-preimage resistance). Using an eTCR hash function and assuming eSPR for the underlying compression function, our scheme yields signatures of only about n^2 bits.

6   Practical Considerations

Using a Real-World Hash Function. Most of our proofs are based on a second-preimage resistant family of hash functions. Although there is no explicit family for SHA1 or MD5, one can regard the initial chaining value as a key [10], or consider the hash functions themselves to be the key, through the random choices made by their designers [1]. However, in that case, the key is known by adversaries *before* starting the experiment, and not randomly chosen in the experiment; the corresponding security notion is called *always* second-preimage resistant by Rogaway and Shrimpton [10]. Our theorems apply to any second-preimage-resistant hash function, including always second-preimage resistant hash functions.

Using a Pseudo-Random Number Generator. In the description of our signature scheme, we assumed that the 2^h one-time signature secret keys X_j are completely stored by the signer. In practice, if the number of signatures 2^h is large, this is of course completely out of question. Instead of randomly generating the OTS secret keys X_j, one can take them as output of a pseudo-random number generator with a unique seed, which totally eliminates the issue of storage. The resulting scheme can be proven to be secure with the additional assumption that the output of the PRNG is indistinguishable from a truly random number [3].

Shorter One-Time Signatures. The main drawback of Merkle signatures is their long signature size. In fact, the one-time signature scheme is mostly responsible for these lengthy signatures, because one-time signatures typically have a number of *blocks* proportional to the number of *bits* to sign. Improving on the original idea of Lamport, Merkle proposed using one block for each message bit, where a checksum is appended to the message [7]. In addition, Winternitz suggested processing message bits by blocks of w consecutive bits, at the expense of some more hash computations [7]. Combining these ideas, the number of bit strings for one instance of the OTS is $l = \lceil n^2/w \rceil + \lceil \lceil \log_2(n/w) \rceil /w \rceil$, the size of one-time signatures $l * n$ and the number of hash evaluations for signing (and verifying) is on average $2^{w-1} * l$ [2]. Although there are other techniques for constructing one-time signature schemes out of hash functions, and especially using graphs instead of trees, practical implementations of one-time signatures using the improvements from Merkle and Winternitz often outperform graph-base one-time signatures [2].

7   Conclusion

We proposed SPR-MSS, a variant of the Merkle signature scheme with much weaker security assumptions than the original construction. More precisely, our scheme is existentially unforgeable under adaptive chosen message attacks, assuming second-preimage and preimage resistant hash functions. Compared to the original Merkle signature which relies on a collision-resistant hash function, SPR-MSS provides a higher security level even when the underlying hash function has a smaller output size. For instance, when using a 128-bit hash function such as MD5, which is still secure in view of second-preimage resistance, SPR-MSS offers a security level better than 2^{80} for trees of height up to 38.

References

1. Bellare, M., Rogaway, P.: Collision-resistant hashing: Towards making UOWHFs practical. In: Kaliski Jr., B.S. (ed.) CRYPTO 1997. LNCS, vol. 1294, pp. 470–484. Springer, Heidelberg (1997)
2. Dods, C., Smart, N., Stam, M.: Hash based digital signature schemes. In: Smart, N. (ed.) Cryptography and Coding 2005. LNCS, vol. 3796, pp. 96–115. Springer, Heidelberg (2005)
3. García, L.C.C.: On the security and the efficiency of the merkle signature scheme. Cryptology ePrint Archive, Report 2005/192 (2005), http://eprint.iacr.org/
4. Goldwasser, S., Micali, S., Rivest, R.L.: A digital signature scheme secure against adaptive chosen-message attacks. SIAM Journal on Computing 17(2), 281–308 (1988)
5. Halevi, S., Krawczyk, H.: Strengthening digital signatures via randomized hashing. In: Dwork, C. (ed.) CRYPTO 2006. LNCS, vol. 4117, pp. 41–59. Springer, Heidelberg (2006)
6. Lamport, L.: Constructing digital signatures from a one way function. Technical Report SRI-CSL-98, SRI International Computer Science Laboratory (1979)
7. Merkle, R.C.: A certified digital signature. In: Brassard, G. (ed.) CRYPTO 1989. LNCS, vol. 435, pp. 218–238. Springer, Heidelberg (1990)
8. Naor, D., Shenhav, A., Wool, A.: One-time signatures revisited: Have they become practical. Cryptology ePrint Archive, Report 2005/442 (2005), http://eprint.iacr.org/

9. Naor, M., Yung, M.: Universal one-way hash functions and their cryptographic applications. In: 21st Annual ACM Symposium on Theory of Computing - STOC 1989, pp. 33–43. ACM Press, New York (1989)

10. Rogaway, P., Shrimpton, T.: Cryptographic hash-function basics: Definitions, implications, and separations for preimage resistance, second-preimage resistance, and collision resistance. In: Roy, B., Meier, W. (eds.) FSE 2004. LNCS, vol. 3017, pp. 371–388. Springer, Heidelberg (2004)

11. Rohatgi, P.: A compact and fast hybrid signature scheme for multicast packet authentication. In: ACM Conference on Computer and Communications Security - CSS 1999, pp. 93–100. ACM Press, New York (1999)

12. Shoup, V.: A composition theorem for universal one-way hash functions. In: Preneel, B. (ed.) EUROCRYPT 2000. LNCS, vol. 1807, pp. 445–452. Springer, Heidelberg (2000)

13. Szydlo, M.: Merkle tree traversal in log space and time. In: Cachin, C., Camenisch, J.L. (eds.) EUROCRYPT 2004. LNCS, vol. 3027, pp. 541–554. Springer, Heidelberg (2004)

14. Wang, X., Yin, Y.L., Yu, H.: Finding collisions in the full SHA-1. In: Shoup, V. (ed.) CRYPTO 2005. LNCS, vol. 3621, pp. 17–36. Springer, Heidelberg (2005)

15. Wang, X., Yu, H.: How to break MD5 and other hash functions. In: Cramer, R. (ed.) EUROCRYPT 2005. LNCS, vol. 3494, pp. 19–35. Springer, Heidelberg (2005)

A Security of the Lamport–Diffie One-Time Signature Scheme

This Section describes the Lamport–Diffie one-time signature scheme (LD–OTS) [6] and states a security reduction to the used one-way function. Let $\mathcal{F}_K = \left\{ F_k : \{0,1\}^n \to \{0,1\}^n \right\}_{k \in K}$ be a family of one-way functions. The one-time signature key of the LD–OTS consists of the $2n$ n-bit strings $x_i[0], x_i[1] \in_R \{0,1\}^n, i = 0, \ldots, n-1$ and a key for the one-way function $k \in_R K$. The verification key Y consists of the $2n$ n-bit strings $\left(y_i[0], y_i[1] \right) = \left(F_k(x_i[0]), F_k(x_i[1]) \right)$ for $i = 0, \ldots, n-1$ and the key k. The signature of an n-bit message $M = (m_0, \ldots, m_{n-1})_2$ is given as $\sigma_i = x_i[m_i], i = 0, \ldots, n-1$, i.e. the bit strings from the signature key are chosen according to the bits of the message; $x_i[0]$ if $m_i = 0$ and $x_i[1]$ if $m_i = 1$. To verify a signature one has to check if $F_k(\sigma_i) = y_i[m_i]$ holds for all $i = 0, \ldots, n-1$. The time required by the LD–OTS for key generation, signing and verifying in terms of evaluations of F_k are $t_{\text{GEN}} = 2n$, $t_{\text{SIG}} = n$ and $t_{\text{VER}} = n$, respectively. We disregard the time required to randomly choose the signature key and assume the signer does not store the verification key.

Algorithm 2 shows how a forger $\text{FOR}^{\text{SIG}_X(\cdot)}(Y)$ for the LD–OTS can be used to construct an inverter for an random element of $\mathcal{F}_K$. In other words, the security of the LD–OTS is reduced to the preimage resistance of $\mathcal{F}_K$.

The adversary ADV_{Pre} is successful in finding a preimage of y if and only if $\text{FOR}^{\text{SIG}_X(\cdot)}(Y)$ queries an M with $m_a = (1 - b)$ (Line 5a) and returns a valid signature for M' with $m'_a = b$ (Line 6a). The probability for $m_a = (1 - b)$ is $1/2$. Since M' must be different from the queried message M, there exists at

---

Algorithm 2. ADV$_{\text{Pre}}$

INPUT: $k \in_R K$ and $y \in F_k(\{0,1\}^n)$
OUTPUT: x such that $y = F_k(x)$ or **failure**

1. Generate LD–OTS key pair (X, Y).
2. Choose $a \in_R \{1, \ldots, n\}$ and $b \in_R \{0, 1\}$.
3. Replace $y_a(b)$ with y in the LD–OTS verification key Y.
4. Run $\text{FOR}^{\text{SIG}_X(\cdot)}(Y)$.
5. When $\text{FOR}^{\text{SIG}_X(\cdot)}(Y)$ asks its only oracle query with $M = (m_0, \ldots, m_{n-1})_2$:
   (a) **if** $m_a = (1 - b)$ **then** sign M and respond to $\text{FOR}^{\text{SIG}_X(\cdot)}$.
   (b) **else return failure**.
6. When $\text{FOR}^{\text{SIG}_X(\cdot)}$ outputs signature for message $M' = (m'_0, \ldots, m'_{n-1})_2$:
   (a) **if** $m'_a = b$ **then return** σ_a as preimage of y.
   (b) **else return failure**.

---

least one index c such that $m'_c = 1 - m_c$. ADV$_{\text{Pre}}$ is successful if $a = c$, which happens with probability at least $1/2n$. This result is summarized in Theorem 2 in Section 4.

B   Security of the Original Merkle Signature Scheme

This section states a security reduction for the original Merkle signature scheme to the collision resistance of the used compression function and the CMA-security of the underlying OTS. The reduction is similar to what was shown in Section 3.1; the main difference being that we are satisfied if we find a collision *anywhere* in the tree. Let $\mathcal{G}_K = \{G_k : \{0,1\}^{2n} \to \{0,1\}^n\}_{k \in K}$ be a family of collision resistant hash functions. Algorithm 3 shows how a forger $\text{FOR}^{\text{SIG}_{\text{sk}}(\cdot)}(\text{pk})$ for the MSS can be used to construct a collision finder for a random element of $\mathcal{G}_K$.

To compute the success probability of ADV$_{\text{CR,OTS}}$ we have to distinguish two cases.

Case 1 $(Y'_s, A'_s) \neq (Y_s, A_s)$: The fact that the verification key Y'_s can be authenticated against the root $y_0[0]$ implies a collision of G_k, see Appendix C. The success probability of finding a collision is at least ϵ, the success probability of the forger.

Case 2 $(Y'_s, A'_s) = (Y_s, A_s)$: In this case $(\sigma_{\text{OTS}}(M'), M') \neq (\sigma_{\text{OTS}}(M_s), M_s)$ holds which implies that $\text{FOR}^{\text{SIG}_{\text{sk}}(\cdot)}(\text{pk})$ generated an existential forgery for one instance of the underlying OTS. The probability that $\text{FOR}^{\text{SIG}_{\text{sk}}(\cdot)}(\text{pk})$ breaks CMA-security of the supplied instance $(s = c)$ is at least $1/2^h$. In total, the success probability of ADV$_{\text{SPR,OTS}}$ is at least $\epsilon/2^h$, where ϵ is the success probability of the forger.

Note that since both cases are complementary, one occurs with probability at least $1/2$. This result is summarized in Theorem 3 in Section 4.

Algorithm 3. ADV$_{\text{CR,OTS}}$

INPUT: Key for the hash function $k \in_R K$, height of the tree $h \geq 1$, an instance of the underlying OTS consisting of a verification key Y and the corresponding signing oracle SIG$_X(\cdot)$
OUTPUT: Collision of G_k, existential forgery for the supplied instance of the OTS, or
failure

1. Choose $c \in_R \{0, \ldots, 2^h - 1\}$ uniformly at random.
2. Generate OTS key pairs $(X_j, Y_j), j = 0, \ldots, 2^h - 1, j \neq c$ and set $Y_c \leftarrow Y$.
3. Complete the key pair generation.
4. Run FOR$^{\text{SIG}_{\text{sk}}(\cdot)}$(pk).
5. When FOR$^{\text{SIG}_{\text{sk}}(\cdot)}$(pk) asks its qth oracle query with message M_q:
   (a) **if** $q = c$ **then** obtain the one-time signature of M_q using the signing oracle SIG$_X(\cdot)$ provided as input: $\sigma_{\text{OTS}}(M_q) \leftarrow \text{SIG}_X(M_q)$.
   (b) **else** compute $\sigma_{\text{OTS}}(M_q)$ using the qth OTS signature key X_q.
   (c) Generate the MSS signature $\sigma_q(M_q) = (q, \sigma_{\text{OTS}}(M_q), Y_q, A_q)$ and respond to the forger.
6. When FOR$^{\text{SIG}_{\text{sk}}(\cdot)}$(pk) outputs signature $\sigma'_s(M') = (s, \sigma_{\text{OTS}}(M'), Y'_s, A'_s)$ for M':
   (a) verify the signature $\sigma'_s(M')$.
   (b) **if** $(Y'_s, A'_s) \neq (Y_s, A_s)$ **then return** a collision of G_k.
   (c) **else** (if $(Y'_s, A'_s) = (Y_s, A_s)$):
       i. **if** $s = c$ **then return** $(\sigma_{\text{OTS}}(M'), M')$ as forgery for the supplied instance of the OTS.
       ii. **else return** failure.

C $(Y'_s, A'_s) \neq (Y_s, A_s)$ Implies a Collision

Case 1 $A'_s \neq A_s$: Let $h \geq \delta > 0$ be the index where the authentication paths are different, i.e. $a'_\delta \neq a_\delta$. Further let $(p'_h, \ldots, p'_0), (p_h, \ldots, p_0)$ be the paths from node $y_h[s]$ to the root $y_0[0]$ constructed using the authentication paths A'_s, A_s, respectively. We certainly know that $p'_0 = p_0$ holds. If $p'_{\delta-1} = p_{\delta-1}$, then $(a'_\delta \parallel p'_\delta), (a_\delta \parallel p_\delta)$ is a collision for H_k. Otherwise, there exists an index $\delta > \gamma > 0$ such that $p'_\gamma \neq p_\gamma$ and $p'_{\gamma-1} = p_{\gamma-1}$. Then, $(a'_\gamma \parallel p'_\gamma), (a_\gamma \parallel p_\gamma)$ is a collision for H_k. Note, that the order in which a_i and p_i are concatenated depends on the index s in the signature.

Case 2 $Y'_s \neq Y_s$: Let $s \cdot 2^l \leq \delta < (s+1) \cdot 2^l$ be the index where the bit strings in the verification keys are different, i.e. $y'_\delta \neq y_\delta$. If $y'_h[s] = y_h[s]$, there exists an index $h + l \geq \gamma > h$ such that $y'_\gamma[\beta] \neq y_\gamma[\beta]$ and $y'_{\gamma-1}[\lfloor \beta/2 \rfloor] = y_{\gamma-1}[\lfloor \beta/2 \rfloor]$, with $\beta = \delta/2^{h+l-\gamma}$. Then a collision for H_k is given as

$$\begin{cases} (y'_\gamma[\beta] \parallel y'_\gamma[\beta + 1]), (y_\gamma[\beta] \parallel y_\gamma[\beta + 1]) \text{ , if } \beta \equiv 0 \mod 2 \\ (y'_\gamma[\beta - 1] \parallel y'_\gamma[\beta]), (y_\gamma[\beta - 1] \parallel y_\gamma[\beta]) \text{ , if } \beta \equiv 1 \mod 2. \end{cases}$$

Otherwise, that is if $y'_h[s] \neq y_h[s]$, similar arguments as in Case 1 can be used to find a collision.

Cryptanalysis of Rational Multivariate Public Key Cryptosystems

Jintai Ding and John Wagner

Department of Mathematical Sciences
University of Cincinnati,
Cincinnati, OH, 45220, USA
ding@math.uc.edu, wagnerjh@email.uc.edu

Abstract. In 1989, Tsujii, Fujioka, and Hirayama proposed a family of multivariate public key cryptosystems, where the public key is given as a set of multivariate rational functions of degree 4. These cryptosystems are constructed via composition of two quadratic rational maps. In this paper, we present the cryptanalysis of this family of cryptosystems. The key point of our attack is to transform a problem of decomposition of two rational maps into a problem of decomposition of two polynomial maps. We develop a new improved 2R decomposition method and other new techniques, which allows us to find an equivalent decomposition of the rational maps to break the system completely. For the example suggested for practical applications, it is very fast to derive an equivalent private key, and it requires only a few seconds on a standard PC.

1 Introduction

Multivariate public key cryptosystems have undergone very fast development in the last 20 years. They are considered one of the promising families of alternatives for post-quantum cryptography, which are cryptosytems that could resist attacks by the quantum computers of the future [1]. Though most people think that Diffie and Fell wrote the first paper on the multivariate public key cryptosystems [3], Tsujii, Kurosawa and etc actually did similar work at the same time [7]. Though this family of cryptosystems is almost 20 years old, it is not so well known. It actually included several methods rediscovered later, which is partially due to the fact that they were written in Japanese and were published inside Japan. Recently it is pointed out by Tsujii [6] that there is not yet any successful attack on the degree 4 rational multivariate public key cryptosystem designed at that time (1989)[5].

This family of multivariate public key cryptosystem is very different from most of the known cryptosystems, namely the public key functions are rational functions instead of polynomial functions and the total degree of the polynomials components are of degree 4 instead of degree 2. The public key is presented as:
$$P(x_1, .., x_n) = (P_1(x_1, .., x_n)/P_{n+1}(x_1, .., x_n), \cdots, P_n(x_1, .., x_n)/P_{n+1}(x_1, .., x_n)),$$
where $P_i(x_1, .., x_n)$ are degree 4 polynomials over a finite field k. We call this

J. Buchmann and J. Ding (Eds.): PQCrypto 2008, LNCS 5299, pp. 124–136, 2008.

family of cryptosystems rational multivariate public key cryptosystems (RMP-KCs).

The construction of this family of cryptosystems relies on three basic methods. The first one is called the core transformation, which is essentially an invertible rational map with two variables. The second one is called the sequential solution method, which is essentially invertible rational triangular maps. This ideas was used later in the name of tractable rational maps in [8], but the authors [8] were not aware of the work of Tsujii's group. The last one is the method of composition of nonlinear maps, which was also used later by Goubin and Patarin [4] again without knowing the works of Tsujii's group. The public key therefore has following expression: $P = L_3 \circ G \circ L_2 \circ F \circ L_1$, where $\circ$ stands for map composition and L_i are invertible affine maps. G and F are degree two rational maps: $F = (F_1/F_{n+1}, \cdots, F_n/F_{n+1};)$ $G = (G_1/G_{n+1}, \cdots, G_n/G_{n+1})$, where F_i and G_i are quadratic polynomials and F and G utilize both the core transformation and the triangular method.

The designers of this family of cryptosystem also employed two very interesting ideas to reduce the public key size, which is a key constraint with the potential to render a multivariate public key cryptosystem application less efficient. The first idea is to use functions of a small number of variables over a relatively large field. Since the the public key size is $\mathcal{O}(n^4)$, using fewer variables greatly reduces the public key size.

The second idea is to build a public key using a field k, then use an extension field of k, say K, as the field from which the plaintext is defined. If $|k|^e = |K|$, then the public key size required is only $\frac{1}{e}$ as large as if K were used to define the public key. Mathematically, the public key lies in the function ring over k^n, a subring of the function ring over K^n. Encryption and decryption occur using the larger function ring. This idea was used later in Sflash Version-1 [10].

In 1989, the designers proposed a practical application using k of size 2^8, K of size 2^{32} and $n = 5$. This application encrypts blocks of 20 bytes using a 756 byte public key. This family of cryptosystems seems to be very interesting and worthy of further exploration.

As we mentioned before, there is a related cryptosystem called 2R by Patarin, which is very similar except that F and G are replaced by 2 quadratic polynomial maps, but this cryptosystem is broken by a decomposition method using partial derivatives [9]. It is clear this method cannot be directly used on RMPKCs because of more complicated expressions for derivatives of rational functions.

Our new method begins by viewing separately the denominator and the numerators of the public key as polynomial functions. We would like to decompose these quartic polynomials into quadratic components. We will use these quadratics to reconstruct the given public key polynomials, but we first have to transform them so that the reconstruction is done is a way that we have a complete alternate private key for the cryptosystem. This alternate private key gives us the ability to invert ciphertext just as easily as the owner of the original private key.

To see how we accomplish this, let's refer to the polynomial expressions in the denominator and the numerators of the public key as $p_i = g_i \circ (f_1, \ldots, f_{n+1})$. We first find $\mathcal{S} = Span \{ f_j : 1 \leq j \leq n+1 \}$. From $\mathcal{S}$, we carefully choose a basis that will enable us to invert the resulting rational maps when we reconstruct the public key. After choosing this basis, it is easy to find each g_i. We will have to transform in a similar way the components of $Span \{ g_j : 1 \leq j \leq n+1 \}$.

We would like to emphasize that our attack is not just application of known methods. In particular, the design of these RMPKCs create two especially interesting challenges for us. The first challenge is to find $Span \{ f_j : 1 \leq j \leq n+1 \}$, and it turns out that the 2R decomposition method alone can not fiund this space by just applying the partial derivative attack directly to the quartic polynomials p_i. Mathematically, our new idea is to use subplanes of our function space, and the computational means that to do this is very simple: we merely set some of the variables equal to zero. By combining results from three or more of such subplanes, we successfully identify $Span \{ f_j : 1 \leq j \leq n+1 \}$. This new extension of 2R decompostion is very different from that in [2].

The second challenge comes from the use of a common denominator in both F and G. We must identify each of these two denominators exactly (up to a scaling factor). This step is necessary to complete the reconstruction of the public key. To find the exact denominator of F, we capitalize on a weakness in the design of the core transformation of G. This weakness results in a portion (subspace) of $Span \{ p_j : 1 \leq j \leq n+1 \}$ in which the polynomial elements have the denominator of F as a factor. We find it using linear algebra techniques. Finding the exact denominator of G comes to us automatically as we solve for the g_i's in the equations $p_i = g_i \circ (f_1, \ldots, f_{n+1})$.

The paper is arranged as follows. In Section 2, we will present the specifics of the cryptosystems we will attack. In Section 3, we will present the details of the cryptanalysis of this family of cryptosystems; we will include our experimental results and relevant information on computational complexity. In the last section, we will summarize our learnings.

2   The RMPKC Cryptosystem

In this section, we will present the design of the rational multivariate public key cryptosystem [5]. Let k be a finite field and k^n the n-dimensional vector space over k.

1. **The public key.** The public key is given as a set of rational degree 4 functions: $P(x_1, \ldots x_n) = (\frac{P_1(x_1,\ldots,x_n)}{P_{n+1}(x_1,\ldots,x_n)}, \cdots, \frac{P_n(x_1,\ldots,x_n)}{P_{n+1}(x_1,\ldots,x_n)})$, where each P_i is a degree 4 polynomial over k. P is constructed as the composition of the five maps: $P = L_3 \circ G \circ L_2 \circ F \circ L_1 = (P_1/P_{n+1}, \cdots, P_n/P_{n+1})$. Here L_1, L_2, L_3 are invertible, linear transformations over k^n. Both F and G are quadratic rational maps, i.e. each consists of n quadratic rational functions, $k^n \rightarrow k$. $F = (F_1/F_{n+1}, \cdots, F_n/F_{n+1})$ and $G = (G_1/G_{n+1}, \cdots, G_n/G_{n+1})$, where for $1 \leq i \leq n+1$, F_i and G_i are quadratic polynomials in $(x_1, \ldots, x_n)$. The details of the construction of F and G are provided below in the section explaining the private key. F and G are constructed identically, with different choices of random parameters.

Note the denominators used in both rational maps are the same in the two nonlinear map respectively. G_{n+1} is the common denominator for G; it enables the public key to consist of exactly $n+1$ polynomials. F_{n+1} is the common denominator for F; it enables the composition of degree 2 rational functions to result in a degree 4 rational function, not that of higher degree. To see how this works, we'll introduce a division function, $\phi : k^{n+1} \longrightarrow k^n$ with $\phi(x_1, \ldots, x_{n+1}) = (\frac{x_1}{x_{n+1}}, \cdots, \frac{x_n}{x_{n+1}})$. Also let $\bar{F}, \bar{G} : k^n \longrightarrow k^{n+1}$ each be quadratic polynomials that satisfy

$$\phi \circ \bar{G} = L_3 \circ G \quad \text{and} \quad \phi \circ \bar{F} = L_2 \circ F \circ L_1$$

resulting in $P = \phi \circ \bar{G} \circ \phi \circ \bar{F} = \phi \circ (\bar{G} \circ \phi) \circ \bar{F}$.

Now let $\tilde{G}$ be the homogenization of $\bar{G}$, i.e. $\tilde{G} : k^{n+1} \to k^{n+1}$ where

$$\forall\, 1 \leq i \leq n+1, \tilde{G}_i(v_1, \ldots, v_{n+1}) = v_{n+1}^2 \bar{G}_i(\frac{v_1}{v_{n+1}}, \cdots, \frac{v_n}{v_{n+1}}) =$$
$$v_{n+1}^2 \bar{G}_i \circ \phi(v_1, \ldots, v_{n+1}).$$

Note that $\tilde{G} \neq \bar{G} \circ \phi$, but $\phi \circ \tilde{G} = \phi \circ \bar{G} \circ \phi$. So $P = \phi \circ \tilde{G} \circ \bar{F}$ where $\tilde{G}$ and $\bar{F}$ are quadratic polynomials. The public key, then, contains the ordered list of n+1 quartic polynomials $(P_1, \ldots, P_{n+1})$ where $\forall\, 1 \leq i \leq n+1$, $P_i(x_1, \ldots, x_n) = \tilde{G}_i \circ \bar{F}(x_1, \ldots, x_n)$.

2. **Encryption.** Given a plaintext $X = (X_1', \cdots, X_n') \in k^n$ one computes the ciphertext $Y' = (Y_1', \cdots, Y_n') \in k^n$ as

$$(Y_1', \cdots, Y_n') = (\frac{P_1(X_1', \ldots, X_n')}{P_{n+1}(X_1', \ldots, X_n')}, \cdots, \frac{P_n(X_1', \ldots, X_n')}{P_{n+1}(X_1', \ldots, X_n')}).$$

3. **The private key.** The private key is the set of the five maps F, G, L_1, L_2, L_3 and the key to invert the non-linear maps F and G. The map P can illustrated as: $k^n \xrightarrow{L_1} k^n \xrightarrow{F} k^n \xrightarrow{L_2} k^n \xrightarrow{G} k^n \xrightarrow{L_3} k^n$.

The design principles of the quadratic rational components, F and G, are identical, except that they use different choices for the random parameters involved. A two-part construction is used. The first part is what the designers call a core transformation. The second part is called the sequential part, since inversion is accomplished sequentially. Its structure can be seen as triangular. The core tranformation is applied only to the last two components, namely $C = (\frac{F_{n-1}}{F_{n+1}}, \frac{F_n}{F_{n+1}})$, which can be viewed as a map $k^2 \longrightarrow k^2$. To construct F_{n-1}, F_n, F_{n+1}, we first randomly choose 12 elements in k: $\alpha_1, \ldots, \alpha_6$ and $\beta_1, \ldots, \beta_6$. C has an inverse which is given by:

$$C^{-1}(y_{n-1}, y_n) = (\,\frac{\alpha_1 y_{n-1} + \alpha_2 y_n + \alpha_3}{\alpha_4 y_{n-1} + \alpha_5 y_n + \alpha_6}, \frac{\beta_1 y_{n-1} + \beta_2 y_n + \beta_3}{\beta_4 y_{n-1} + \beta_5 y_n + \beta_6}\,).$$

Then F_{n-1}, F_n and F_{n+1} are defined as follows:

$$\forall\, n-1 \leq i \leq n+1, \quad F_i(x_{n-1}, x_n) = \tau_{i,1} x_{n-1} x_n + \tau_{i,2} x_{n-1} + \tau_{i,3} x_n + \tau_{i,4}$$

where the $\tau_{i,j}$ is defined as follows:

$\tau_{n-1,1} = \alpha_6\beta_5 - \alpha_5\beta_6$	$\tau_{n,1} = \alpha_6\beta_4 - \alpha_4\beta_6$	$\tau_{n+1,1} = \alpha_5\beta_4 - \alpha_4\beta_5$
$\tau_{n-1,2} = \alpha_3\beta_5 - \alpha_5\beta_3$	$\tau_{n,2} = \alpha_3\beta_4 - \alpha_4\beta_3$	$\tau_{n+1,2} = \alpha_1\beta_4 - \alpha_4\beta_1$
$\tau_{n-1,3} = \alpha_6\beta_2 - \alpha_2\beta_6$	$\tau_{n,3} = \alpha_6\beta_1 - \alpha_1\beta_6$	$\tau_{n+1,3} = \alpha_5\beta_2 - \alpha_2\beta_5$
$\tau_{n-1,4} = \alpha_3\beta_2 - \alpha_2\beta_3$	$\tau_{n,4} = \alpha_3\beta_1 - \alpha_1\beta_3$	$\tau_{n+1,4} = \alpha_1\beta_2 - \alpha_2\beta_1$

The rest of the components are given in a triangular form:

$$\forall 1 \leq i \leq n-2, \ F_i(x_1, \ldots, x_n) = a_i(x_{i+1}, \ldots, x_n)x_i + b_i((x_{i+1}, \ldots, x_n),$$

where the a_i's are randomly chosen linear polynomials and the b_i's are randomly chosen quadratic polynomials.

4. **Decryption.** To decrypt, we need to invert the map P, which is done as follows: $P^{-1}(Y_1', \ldots, Y_n') = L_1^{-1} \circ F^{-1} \circ L_2^{-1} \circ G^{-1} \circ L_3^{-1}(Y_1', \ldots, Y_n') = (X_1', \ldots, X_n')$. The holder of the private key has the means to find the inverse of each of L_3, G, L_2, F, L_1. Performing the calculations in order yields $(X_1', \ldots, X_n')$. Inversion of the linear transformations is obvious.

To invert the map F is to find the solution of equation: $F(x_1, ..., x_n) = (y_1', ..., y_n')$ for a given vector $(y_1', ..., y_n')$. We first use the inverse of C to calculate $(x_{n-1}', x_n') = C^{-1}(y_{n-1}', y_n')$. Then we plug the resulting values into the third last component function of F. This gives us the following linear equation in x_{n-2}:

$$y_{n-2}' = \frac{F_{n-2}(x_{n-2}, x_{n-1}', x_n')}{F_{n+1}(x_{n-1}', x_n')} = \frac{a_{n-2}(x_{n-1}', x_n') * x_{n-2} + b_{n-2}(x_{n-1}', x_n')}{\tau_{n-2,1} x_{n-1}' x_n' + \tau_{n-2,2} x_{n-1}' + \tau_{n-2,3} x_n' + \tau_{n-2,4}}$$

yielding $x_{n-2}' = \frac{y_{n-2}' * (\tau_{n-2,1} x_{n-1}' x_n' + \tau_{n-2,2} x_{n-1}' + \tau_{n-2,3} x_n' + \tau_{n-2,4}) - b_{n-2}(x_{n-1}', x_n')}{a_{n-2}(x_{n-1}', x_n')}.$

After obtaining x_{n-2}', we can plug known values into the fourth last component function of F and derive x_{n-3}'. This sequential solution method is continued to find the rest of $(x_1', \ldots, x_n')$ which gives us a solution for $F(x_1, ..., x_n) = (y_1', ..., y_n')$. Inversion of G is performed in the exact same manner as F.

Note that in the inversion process, division is required in the calculation of each of the components of $(x_1', \ldots, x_n')$. In each case, the expression for the divisor is linear in terms of known values of input variables $(x_{i+1}', \ldots, x_n')$ and the given values of output variables $(y_i', \ldots, y_n')$. In both cases, the probability of valid division is approximately $\frac{q-1}{q}$. The probability of successfully inverting both F and G, and thus P, therefore, is approximately $\left(\frac{q-1}{q}\right)^{2n}$.

3   Cryptanalysis of RMPKC

Our attack can be viewed as the decomposition of maps. The cryptanalysis of RMPKC is performed as follows: given P, the composition of $L_3 \circ G \circ L_2 \circ F \circ L_1$, generate a new set of maps L_3', G', L_2', F', and L_1' such that

$$L_3 \circ G \circ L_2 \circ F \circ L_1 = L_3' \circ G' \circ L_2' \circ F' \circ L_1',$$

and G' and F' can be inverted in the same way as G and F, with the keys to inversion obtained during the process. This new set of maps can be viewed as a private key equivalent to the original one, thus can be used to defeat the RMPKC cryptosystem.

To decompose RMPKC, we will use the partial derivative method, which takes the composition of two homogeneous quadratic polynomial maps forming a homogeneous quartic map, and decomposes it into quadratic maps which, when composed together, form the original quartic map [9]. Consider $g \circ f$ where $g = ((g_1(x_1,\ldots,x_m), \ldots, g_m(x_1,\ldots,x_m)))$, $f = ((f_1(x_1,\ldots,x_m), \ldots, f_m(x_1,\ldots,x_m)))$ and each of the g_i's and the f_i's are homogeneous quadratic polynomials. The first step is to find $\mathcal{F} = Span \{ f_i : 1 \le i \le m \}$, a vector space over k.

Once found, one can select linearly independent quadratics from it, say $(f'_1,\ldots,f'_m)$. Then by solving a set of linear equations, one can find $(g'_1,\ldots,g'_m)$ such that $\forall\ 1 \le i \le m$, $g'_i \circ f' = g_i \circ f$ where $f' = (f'_1,\ldots,f'_m)$.

The critical step of this process is finding $\mathcal{F}$. The following definitions are needed: $D = Span \{ \frac{\partial}{\partial x_j} g_i \circ f(x_1,\ldots,x_m) : 1 \le i,j \le m \}$;

$\Lambda = \{ x_j f : 1 \le j \le m, f \in \mathcal{F} \}$; $R = \{ \theta : \forall\ 1 \le i \le m,\ x_i \theta \in D \}$. When each of the f_i's and g_i's are homogeneous quadratic polynomials, $D \subseteq \Lambda$. This is true basically because

$$\frac{\partial}{\partial x_j}(g_i \circ f) = \sum_{r=1}^{m} \frac{\partial}{\partial w_r} g_i(f) \times \frac{\partial}{\partial x_j} f_r(x_1,\ldots,x_m)$$

where $\frac{\partial}{\partial w_r} g_i(f)$ is linear in the f's and $\frac{\partial}{\partial x_j} f(x_1,\ldots,x_m)$ is linear in the $(x_1,\ldots,x_m)$.

We calculate D and R from $g \circ f$. If $D = \Lambda$, then $R = \mathcal{F}$ and this step is complete. When $D \subset \Lambda$, $R \subset \mathcal{F}$. Why $R \subseteq \mathcal{F}$ and $D = \Lambda \Longleftrightarrow R = \mathcal{F}$ should be fairly easy to see.

Application of the partial derivative attack to RMPKC requires some additional work. As we saw in the explanation of the public key, we have access to $n + 1$ polynomials of the form $P_i = \tilde{G}_i \circ \bar{F}(x_1,\ldots,x_n)$ where $\tilde{G}_i$ is a homogeneous quadratic polynomial and $\bar{F}$ consists of non-homogeneous quadratic polynomials. Our first step is to homogenize each of the P_i's, which effectively homogenizes each of the $\bar{F}_i$'s, yielding the following:

$$\tilde{P}_i(x_1,\ldots,x_{n+1}) = \tilde{G}_i \circ \tilde{F}(x_1,\ldots,x_{n+1})$$

where each of the $\tilde{P}_i$'s are homogeneous quartic polynomials and each of the $\tilde{G}_i$'s and $\tilde{F}_i$'s are homogeneous quadratic polynomials.

Then we begin the partial derivative attack, by calculating D from $\tilde{G}_i \circ \tilde{F}(x_1,\ldots,x_{n+1})$. We never get $D = \Lambda$, due to the triangular structure of G and the use of k which has characteristic 2. We are able to recover $\mathcal{F}$ by applying the attack with a new method of projection of our functions to subplanes; the details will be provided in the section that follows. After finding $\mathcal{F}$, we de-homogenize the space by setting $x_{n+1} = 1$.

The second challenge that the specifics of RMPKC present to the partial derivative attack is the challenge to select the polynomials $F'_1,\ldots,F'_{n+1}$ from $\mathcal{F}|_{x_{n+1}=1}$ in such a way that they may be easily inverted. The procedure we use to find such $F'_1,\ldots,F'_{n+1}$ is described below. The process results in a linear transformation L'_1 and a quadratic rational map F', which inverts in the same manner as F for the holder of the private key.

Then to continue the partial derivative attack we can find the g_i's that satisfy $P_i = g_i \circ F'$; but these g_i's would not invert easily. So we define $\mathcal{G}' = Span \{ g_i :$

$1 \leq i \leq n+1$ } and select polynomials from $\mathcal{G}'$ which we can invert. This process generates linear transformations L_2' and L_3', and quadratic rational map G', which inverts in the same manner as G in the private key. Then we have $P = L_3' \circ G' \circ L_2' \circ F' \circ L_1'$, an alternative private key, thus breaking the RMPKC.

We organize our attack into four phases. The sections that follow will present an explanation in further detail of each phase.

1. Find $\mathcal{F} = Span\{ \tilde{F}_i : 1 \leq i \leq n+1 \}$.
2. Determine F' and L_1'.
3. Find $\mathcal{G}' = Span\{ g_i' \mid g_i' \circ F' \circ L_1' = P_i : 1 \leq i \leq n+1 \}$.
4. Determine G', L_2', and L_3'.

3.1   Phase I: Find $\mathcal{F} = Span\{ \tilde{F}_i : 1 \leq i \leq n+1 \}$

We start with the public key, $P = \tilde{G} \circ \bar{F} = (P_1, \ldots, P_{n+1})$ and homogenize by creating $\tilde{P} = (\tilde{P}_1, \ldots, \tilde{P}_{n+1})$ using $\forall 1 \leq i \leq n+1$, $\tilde{P}_i(x_1, \ldots, x_{n+1}) = x_{n+1}^4 P_i(\frac{x_1}{x_{n+1}}, \cdots, \frac{x_n}{x_{n+1}})$. This gives us $\tilde{P} = \tilde{G} \circ \tilde{F}$ where $\tilde{F} = (\tilde{F}_1, \ldots, \tilde{F}_{n+1})$ and $\forall 1 \leq i \leq n+1$, $\tilde{F}_i(x_1, \ldots, x_{n+1}) = x_{n+1}^2 \bar{F}_i(\frac{x_1}{x_{n+1}}, \cdots, \frac{x_n}{x_{n+1}})$.

To proceed we need to define $H_i \forall i \in \{ 1, 2, 3 \}$ as the set of all homogeneous polynomials in $k[x_1, \ldots, x_{n+1}]$ of degree i. Each H_i is a vector space over k as well as a subset of $k[x_1, \ldots, x_{n+1}]$. For notational simplification, we will use context to distinguish between these uses of H_i.

We now define D, R, and Λ for $\tilde{G} \circ \tilde{F}$. Recall we calculate D and R from $\tilde{P}$.

$$D = Span\{ \frac{\partial}{\partial x_j} \tilde{G}_i \circ \tilde{F}(x_1, \ldots, x_{n+1}) : 1 \leq i, j \leq n+1 \} \subset \mathcal{H}_3$$

$$\Lambda = \{ x_j f : 1 \leq j \leq n+1, f \in \mathcal{F} \} \subset \mathcal{H}_3$$

$$R = \{ f \in \mathcal{H}_2 : \forall 1 \leq i \leq n+1, x_i f \in D \}.$$

Since the polynomials of $\tilde{G}$ and $\tilde{F}$ are homogeneous quadratics, we are guaranteed $D \subseteq \Lambda$ and $R \subseteq \mathcal{F}$. We also have $D = \Lambda \iff R = \mathcal{F}$. Because of the structure of the original polynomials in G and the use of a field of characteristic 2, we will always find $D \subset \Lambda$ and therefore $R \subset \mathcal{F}$. So we use the following definitions of Γ and γ to help explain how to see what is happening with individual f's in $\mathcal{F}$, why they do not find themselves in R, and how we are going to eventually find them with our alternative approach.

$$\Gamma(f) = \{ \theta \in \mathcal{H}_1 : \theta f \in D \} \quad \text{and} \quad \gamma(f) = dim(\Gamma(f)).$$

Clearly, $f \in R \iff \gamma(f) = n+1$. We always get $\gamma(f) \leq n+1$, and $Min\{ \gamma(f) : f \in \mathcal{F} \}$ describes how far away from obtaining $R = \mathcal{F}$ for any given application of RMPKC. For $n = 5$ and $n = 6$, we find $Min\{ \gamma(f) : f \in \mathcal{F} \} = n$ almost every time. For $n = 7$ we usually get $Min\{ \gamma(f) : f \in \mathcal{F} \} = n - 1$. And for $n \geq 8$ we most likely get $Min\{ \gamma(f) : f \in \mathcal{F} \} = n-2$. Our alternative approach works most simply for $Min\{ \gamma(f) : f \in \mathcal{F} \} = n$. We will describe this now in detail; then briefly show how we accomplish this for $Min\{ \gamma(f) : f \in \mathcal{F} \} < n$. We again start with the key definitions, valid $\forall 1 \leq s \leq n+1$; and we have access to each D_s and R_s.

$$\mathcal{F}_s = Span\ \{\ f(x_1,\ldots,x_{s-1},0,x_{s+1},\ldots,x_{n+1}) : \forall\ f \in \mathcal{F}\ \}\ .$$

$$D_s = Span\ \{\ \tfrac{\partial}{\partial x_j}\tilde{G}_i \circ \tilde{F}(x_1,\ldots,x_{s-1},0,x_{s+1},\ldots,x_{n+1}) :\ 1 \le i,j \le n+1\ \}\ .$$

$$\Lambda_s = \{\ x_i f : 1 \le i \le n+1 (i \ne s), f \in \mathcal{F}_s\ \}\ .$$

$$R_s = \{\ f \in \mathcal{H}_2 : \forall\ 1 \le i \le n+1 (i \ne s),\ x_i f \in D_s\ \}\ .$$

$$\Gamma_s(f) = \{\ \theta \in \mathcal{H}_1 : \theta f \in D_s\ \}\ ,\qquad \gamma_s(f) = dim(\ \Gamma_s(f)\ ).$$

Now we always get $D_s \subseteq \Lambda_s$, $R_s \subseteq \mathcal{F}_s$, and $D_s = \Lambda_s \iff R_s = \mathcal{F}_s \iff$ $Min\ \{\ \gamma_s(f) : f \in \mathcal{F}_s\ \} = n$. Fortunately for this attack, with high probability, $\gamma_s(f) = Min\ \{\ \gamma(f), n\ \}$. This is a crucial point. At this time, we do not have a mathematical explanation for why it is so; our experiments confirm it with consistent results. Once we get $\forall\ 1 \le s \le n+1, R_s = \mathcal{F}_s$, finding $\mathcal{F}$ is easy.

Let $R_s^+ = R_s + Span\ \{\ x_s x_i : 1 \le i \le n+1\ \}$. When $R_s = \mathcal{F}_s$, $\mathcal{F} \subset R_s^+$. Furthermore, if $\forall\ 1 \le s \le n+1, R_s = \mathcal{F}_s$, then $\mathcal{F} = \overset{n+1}{\underset{s=1}{\cap}} R_s^+$, completing the task of finding $\mathcal{F}$.

For the cases of $Min\ \{\ \gamma(f) : f \in \mathcal{F}\ \} < n$, we expand our alternative approach one or more levels further. Notice above the spaces R_s^+, which are created by setting $x_s = 0$, finding D_s and R_s, then adding $Span\ \{\ x_s x_i : 1 \le i \le n+1\ \}$. For $n = 7$, when we have $Min\ \{\ \gamma(f) : f \in \mathcal{F}\ \} = n-1$, we use $x_{s_1} = 0 = x_{s_2}$ where $s_1 \ne s_2$. Following the same manner we form D_{s_1,s_2} and R_{s_1,s_2}. Then we let $R_{s_1,s_2}^+ = R_{s_1,s_2} + Span\ \{\ x_{s_1} x_i : 1 \le i \le n+1\ \} + Span\ \{\ x_{s_2} x_i : 1 \le i \le n+1\ \}$. With consistency, we do get $\mathcal{F} = \underset{\substack{1 \le s_1, s_2 \le n+1 \\ s_1 \ne s_2}}{\cap} R_{s_1,s_2}^+$.

For $n \ge 8$, when we have $Min\ \{\ \gamma(f) : f \in \mathcal{F}\ \} = n-2$, we use $x_{s_1} = 0 = x_{s_2} = 0 = x_{s_3}$ where $s_1 \ne s_2 \ne s_3 \ne s_1$. Following the same manner we form D_{s_1,s_2,s_3} and R_{s_1,s_2,s_3}. Then we let $R_{s_1,s_2,s_3}^+ = R_{s_1,s_2,s_3} + Span\ \{\ x_{s_1} x_i : 1 \le i \le n+1\ \} + Span\ \{\ x_{s_2} x_i : 1 \le i \le n+1\ \} + Span\ \{\ x_{s_3} x_i : 1 \le i \le n+1\ \}$. Again we consistently get $\mathcal{F} = \underset{\substack{1 \le s_1, s_2, s_3 \le n+1 \\ s_1 \ne s_2 \ne s_3 \ne s_1}}{\cap} R_{s_1,s_2,s_3}^+$.

3.2   Phase II: Choose F′ and L′₁

In this phase we will determine the quadratic polynomials of $F' = (\frac{F_1'}{F_{n+1}'},\cdots,$ $\frac{F_n'}{F_{n+1}'})$ and the linear transformation, L_1' such that

$$Span\ \{\ F_i' \circ L_1' : 1 \le i \le n+1\ \} = Span\ \{\ F_i \circ L_1 : 1 \le i \le n+1\ \}\ ,$$

and F' can be easily inverted just like F.

However, we do need one additional condition on our new map, namely we must have $F_{n+1}' \circ L_1' = \lambda F_{n+1} \circ L_1$ for some $\lambda \in k$. This is necessary in order to find the proper G', which will be determined later, to be chosen so that it too can be inverted in the same manner as G.

Our first step is to determine a core transformation in F'. From the definition in Section 2, we can see that there is a subspace spanned by two linearly independent linear functions in $\mathcal{F}$, which actually lies in the space spanned by F_{n-1}, F_n, F_{n+1}. Therefore F' also contains a subspace that is contained in $Span \{ \theta'_{n-1}, \theta'_n, 1 \}$ for some $\theta'_{n-1}, \theta'_n \in \mathcal{H}_1$. This space can be found easily, and it is clear that we have $Span \{ \theta'_{n-1}, \theta'_n \} = Span \{ L_{1,n-1}, L_{1,n} \}$, where $L_{1,n-1}$ and $L_{1,n}$ are the last two components of the linear transformation L_1. Next we find the three-dimensional subspace of $\mathcal{F}$ which forms the core transformation, i.e. let $\mathcal{R} = \mathcal{F} \cap Span \{ \theta'^2_{n-1}, \theta'^2_n, \theta'_{n-1}\theta'_n, \theta'_{n-1}, \theta'_n, 1 \}$.

By construction, we know not only that $\exists R_1, R_2, R_3 \in \mathcal{R}$ such that $\mathcal{R} = Span \{ R_1, R_2, R_3 \}$ and $R_3 \in Span \{ \theta_{n-1}^2, \theta_n^2, \theta_{n-1}\theta_n, 1 \}$ and $R_1, R_2 \in Span \{ \theta'_{n-1}, \theta'_n, 1 \}$, but also that $\exists \theta_{n-1}, \theta_n \in Span \{ \theta'_{n-1}, \theta'_n \}$ where $R_1, R_2 \in Span \{ \theta_{n-1}, \theta_n, 1 \}$ and $R_3 \in Span \{ \theta_{n-1}\theta_n, 1 \}$. Furthermore, R_3 can be chosen so that $R_3 = \theta'^2_{n-1} + a\theta'_{n-1}\theta'_n + b\theta'^2_n + c$. We can find appropriately $\theta_{n-1} = \theta'_{n-1} + s\theta'_n$ and $\theta_n = \theta'_{n-1} + t\theta'_n$ by finding the right values for s and t.

We solve for s and t by equating the quadratic terms of our chosen R_3, i.e. $\theta'^2_{n-1} + a\theta'_{n-1}\theta'_n + b\theta'^2_n = (\theta'_{n-1} + s\theta'_n)(\theta'_{n-1} + t\theta'_n)$. So $s + t = a$ and $st = b$. Thus $s(a - s) = b$, i.e. $s^2 - as + b = 0$. In characteristic 2, this last equation is actually linear and can be solved for s.

This choice of θ_i allows us to calculate an inversion function for the core transformation (described below), just like the inversion function of F. Coincidently, either $\theta_{n-1} = \lambda_1 L_{1,n-1}$ and $\theta_n = \lambda_2 L_{1,n}$ for some $\lambda_1, \lambda_2 \in k$ or $\theta_{n-1} = \lambda_1 L_{1,n}$ and $\theta_n = \lambda_2 L_{1,n-1}$ for some $\lambda_1, \lambda_2 \in k$; but we don't care which nor do we use this result directly.

To get $F'_{n+1} \circ L'_1 = \lambda F_{n+1} \circ L_1$ for some $\lambda \in k$, we choose $f_{n+1} \in \mathcal{R}$ such that $f_{n+1}|\rho$ for some nonzero $\rho \in \mathcal{P} = Span \{ P_i : 1 \leq i \leq n+1 \}$. This works to identify $f_{n+1} = \lambda F_{n+1} \circ L_1$ for some $\lambda \in k$ because the quadratic polynomials of G become homogeneous when composed with the rational functions in F, making the linear subspace of the polynomials of G become a subspace divisible by $F_{n+1} \circ L_1$ (the denominator) when composed with $L_2 \circ F \circ L_1$.

We randomly choose $f_{n-1}, f_n \in \mathcal{R}$ such that $\mathcal{R} = Span \{ f_i : n - 1 \leq i \leq n + 1 \}$. We then determine $f_1, \ldots, f_{n-2}$ and $\theta_1, \ldots, \theta_{n-2}$ sequentially, by first choosing f_{n-2} and θ_{n-2}, then working our way to f_1 and θ_1. Our procedure is as follows:

$\forall\ i = (n - 2, n - 3, \cdots, 2)$ find $\theta_i \notin Span \{ \theta_{i+1}, \ldots, \theta_n \}$ and $f_i \in \mathcal{F}$ such that $f_i \in Span \{ \theta_j\theta_k : \begin{smallmatrix} i \leq j \leq k \leq n+1 \\ k \neq i \end{smallmatrix} \} + Span \{ \theta_j : i \leq j \leq n + 1 \} + 1$.

The last components, f_1 and θ_1, can be chosen randomly as long as $Span \{ f_i : 1 \leq i \leq n+1 \} = \mathcal{F}$ and $Span \{ \theta_i : 1 \leq i \leq n + 1 \} = Span \{ x_i : 1 \leq i \leq n \}$.

$\theta_1, \ldots, \theta_n$ are the components of L'_1. It is easy to calculate $F_1, \ldots, F_{n+1}$ such that $\forall\ 1 \leq i \leq n + 1, f_i = F_i \circ L'_1$.

Now that we have determined L_1 and F', we can find the inversion function parameters ($\alpha'_1, \ldots, \alpha'_6, \beta'_1, \ldots, \beta'_6$) for the core transformation of F' by considering

$$x_{n-1} = \frac{\alpha'_1 \frac{F'_{n-1}(x_{n-1}, x_n)}{F'_{n+1}(x_{n-1}, x_n)} + \alpha'_2 \frac{F'_n(x_{n-1}, x_n)}{F'_{n+1}(x_{n-1}, x_n)} + \alpha'_3}{\alpha'_4 \frac{F'_{n-1}(x_{n-1}, x_n)}{F'_{n+1}(x_{n-1}, x_n)} + \alpha'_5 \frac{F'_n(x_{n-1}, x_n)}{F'_{n+1}(x_{n-1}, x_n)} + \alpha'_6} =$$

$$\frac{\alpha'_1 F'_{n-1}(x_{n-1}, x_n) + \alpha'_2 F'_n(x_{n-1}, x_n) + \alpha'_3 F'_{n+1}(x_{n-1}, x_n)}{\alpha'_4 F'_{n-1}(x_{n-1}, x_n) + \alpha'_5 F'_n(x_{n-1}, x_n) + \alpha'_6 F'_{n+1}(x_{n-1}, x_n)}$$

or equivalently

$$x_{n-1}\big(\alpha'_4 F'_{n-1}(x_{n-1}, x_n) + \alpha'_5 F'_n(x_{n-1}, x_n) + \alpha'_6 F'_{n+1}(x_{n-1}, x_n)\big) =$$
$$\alpha'_1 F'_{n-1}(x_{n-1}, x_n) + \alpha'_2 F'_n(x_{n-1}, x_n) + \alpha'_3 F'_{n+1}(x_{n-1}, x_n)$$

We equate the coefficients of the terms $(1, x_{n-1}, x_n, (x_{n-1})^2, x_{n-1}x_n$, and $(x_{n-1})^2 x_n)$ and simultaneously solve for the $\alpha'_1, \ldots, \alpha'_6$. In the same manner we find $\beta'_1, \ldots, \beta'_6$ by starting with

$$x_n = \frac{\beta'_1 \frac{F'_{n-1}(x_{n-1}, x_n)}{F'_{n+1}(x_{n-1}, x_n)} + \beta'_2 \frac{F'_n(x_{n-1}, x_n)}{F'_{n+1}(x_{n-1}, x_n)} + \beta'_3}{\beta'_4 \frac{F'_{n-1}(x_{n-1}, x_n)}{F'_{n+1}(x_{n-1}, x_n)} + \beta'_5 \frac{F'_n(x_{n-1}, x_n)}{F'_{n+1}(x_{n-1}, x_n)} + \beta'_6} =$$
$$\frac{\beta'_1 F'_{n-1}(x_{n-1}, x_n) + \beta'_2 F'_n(x_{n-1}, x_n) + \beta'_3 F'_{n+1}(x_{n-1}, x_n)}{\beta'_4 F'_{n-1}(x_{n-1}, x_n) + \beta'_5 F'_n(x_{n-1}, x_n) + \beta'_6 F'_{n+1}(x_{n-1}, x_n)}$$

Phase III: Find $\mathcal{G}'$ $\forall\ 1 \leq i \leq n+1$, find linear combinations of $\{ (F'_j \circ L'_1)(F'_r \circ L'_1) : 1 \leq j \leq r \leq n+1 \}$ which are equal to P_i. The coefficients of these combinations are the coefficients of the homogeneous polynomials $\bar{G}'_i$.

Let $\mathcal{G}' = Span\ \{\ \bar{G}'_i : 1 \leq i \leq n+1\ \}$.

3.3   Phase IV: Choose G', L'₂ and L'₃

In this phase we will determine the quadratic polynomials of $G' = \begin{pmatrix} G'_1/G'_{n+1} \\ \vdots \\ G'_n/G'_{n+1} \end{pmatrix}$;

and the linear transformations, L'_2 and L'_3 such that $\forall\ 1 \leq i \leq n+1, P_i = (L'_3)_i \circ G' \circ L'_2 \circ F' \circ L'_1$, and G' can be easily inverted just like G.

Our first step is to determine a core transformation in G'. We easily find two linearly independent linear vectors in $\mathcal{G}'$, ϕ'_{n-1} and ϕ'_n. Let $\mathcal{U}=Span\ \{\ \phi'_{n-1}, \phi'_n\ \}$. That makes $\mathcal{U} = Span\ \{\ L_{2,n-1}, L_{2,n}\ \}$. Next we find the three-dimensional subspace of $\mathcal{G}'$ which forms the core transformation, i.e.

let $\mathcal{V} = \mathcal{G}' \cap Span\ \{\ {\phi'_{n-1}}^2, {\phi'_n}^2, \phi'_{n-1}\phi'_n, \phi'_{n-1}, \phi'_n, 1\ \}$.

Now we find ϕ_{n-1} and ϕ_n in $\mathcal{U}$ such that $\forall\ g \in \mathcal{V}, g \in Span\ \{\ \phi_{n-1}\phi_n, \phi_{n-1}, \phi_n, 1\ \}$. This choice of ϕ's allows us to calculate an inversion function for the core transformation, just like the inversion function of G. Coincidently, either $\phi_{n-1} = \lambda_1 L_{2,n-1}$ and $\phi_n = \lambda_2 L_{2,n}$ for some $\lambda_1, \lambda_2 \in k$ or $\phi_{n-1} = \lambda_1 L_{2,n}$ and $\phi_n = \lambda_2 L_{2,n-1}$ for some $\lambda_1, \lambda_2 \in k$; but we don't care which nor do we use this result directly.

Up to this point, our work with G' has been identical to the work with F'. The method to determine G'_{n+1} is the first place where we differ. G'_{n+1} will be the quadratic polynomial in two variables such that $G'_{n+1}(\phi_{n-1}, \phi_n) = \bar{G}'_{n+1}(x_1, \ldots, x_n, 1)$.

Now we randomly choose $g_{n-1}, g_n \in \mathcal{V}$ such that $\mathcal{V} = Span\ \{\ g_i : n-1 \leq i \leq n+1\ \}$. We then determine $g_1, \ldots, g_{n-2}$ and $\phi_1, \ldots, \phi_{n-2}$ sequentially, by first choosing g_{n-2} and ϕ_{n-2}, then working our way to g_1 and ϕ_1. Our procedure is as follows:

$\forall\ i = (n-2, n-3, \cdots, 2)$ find $\phi_i \notin Span\ \{\ \phi_{i+1}, \ldots, \phi_n\ \}$ and $g_i \in \mathcal{G}'$ such that $g_i \in Span\ \{\ \phi_j\phi_k : \begin{smallmatrix} i \leq j \leq k \leq n+1 \\ k \neq i \end{smallmatrix}\ \} + Span\ \{\ \phi_j : i \leq j \leq n+1\ \} + 1.$

The last components, g_1 and ϕ_1, can be chosen randomly as long as $Span\ \{\ g_i : 1 \leq i \leq n+1\ \} = \mathcal{G}'$ and $Span\ \{\ \phi_i : 1 \leq i \leq n+1\ \} = Span\ \{\ x_i : 1 \leq i \leq n\ \}.$

$\phi_1, \ldots, \phi_n$ are the components of L_2'. And again we must differ in our approach to G' from the approach to F'. At this point, we have for $1 \leq i \leq n, \bar{G}_i$ is a linear combination of $\{\ g_j : 1 \leq j \leq n+1\ \}$. We need to have $\forall 1 \leq i \leq n, \bar{G}_i$ is a linear combination of only $\{\ g_j : 1 \leq j \leq n\ \}$, (excluding g_{n+1}).

To explain how we do this is best done using $(n+1)$ x $(n+1)$ matrices. Let χ be the matrix of the linear transformation $(k^{n+1} \longrightarrow k^{n+1})$ such that

$$\begin{pmatrix} \\ \chi \\ \\ \end{pmatrix} \begin{pmatrix} g_1 \circ L_2' \\ \vdots \\ g_{n+1} \circ L_2' \end{pmatrix} = \begin{pmatrix} \bar{G}_1' \\ \vdots \\ \bar{G}_{n+1}' \end{pmatrix}. \ \chi \text{ is in the form } \begin{pmatrix} * & \cdots & * & * \\ \vdots & \ddots & \vdots & \vdots \\ * & \cdots & * & * \\ 0 & \cdots & 0 & * \end{pmatrix} \text{ but } \begin{pmatrix} * & \cdots & * & 0 \\ \vdots & \ddots & \vdots & \vdots \\ * & \cdots & * & 0 \\ 0 & \cdots & 0 & * \end{pmatrix}$$

is the form which we need.

So we find an invertible upper triangular matrix π and an invertible matrix ν of the desired form such that $\nu\chi = \pi$. The zero entries of π provide linear equations to solve for the entries of ν with coefficients from χ, which are known.

Now we have $\chi = \nu^{-1}\pi$. So let $G' = \begin{pmatrix} G_1'/G_{n+1}' \\ \vdots \\ G_n'/G_{n+1}' \end{pmatrix}$ where $\begin{pmatrix} G_1' \\ \vdots \\ G_{n+1}' \end{pmatrix} = \pi \begin{pmatrix} g_1 \\ \vdots \\ g_{n+1} \end{pmatrix}$;

and let $L_3' = \nu^{-1}$.

$$\text{Thus } \begin{pmatrix} \bar{G}_1' \\ \vdots \\ \bar{G}_{n+1}' \end{pmatrix} = \chi \begin{pmatrix} g_1 \circ L_2' \\ \vdots \\ g_{n+1} \circ L_2' \end{pmatrix} = \nu^{-1}\pi \begin{pmatrix} g_1 \circ L_2' \\ \vdots \\ g_{n+1} \circ L_2' \end{pmatrix} = L_3' \begin{pmatrix} G_1' \circ L_2' \\ \vdots \\ G_{n+1}' \circ L_2' \end{pmatrix}.$$

Furthermore, $P = L_3' \circ G' \circ L_2' \circ F' \circ L_1'$ and our decomposition is complete.

We can find the inversion function parameters ($\delta_1', \ldots, \delta_6', \gamma_1', \ldots, \gamma_6'$) for the core transformation of G' in the exact same manner that we found $\alpha_1', \ldots, \alpha_6'$ and $\beta_1', \ldots, \beta_6'$ for F'.

In summary, we have created an alternate CQRM cryptosystem using L_1', F', L_2', G', and L_3' such that $L_3' \circ G' \circ L_2' \circ F' \circ L_1' = L_3 \circ G \circ L_2 \circ F \circ L_1$ and both G' and F' are invertible, just like G and F; so cryptanalysis of CQRM is complete.

3.4   Experimental Results and Computational Complexity

The proposal for RMPKC in 1989 suggested an implementation with k of size 2^8 and $n = 5$. Our attack programmed in Magma completes cryptanalysis consistently in less than six seconds running on a personal computer with a Pentium 4 1.5 GHz processor and 256 MB of RAM. We ran several experiments at higher values of n and for larger fields k.

Increasing the size of the field increases the run time of the program linearly. The larger values of n cause a much greater run time and manifest the critical elements of both the public key size of the cryptosystem and the computational complexity of our cryptanalysis. Since the public key is a set of $n + 1$ quartic polynomials, its size is of order $\mathcal{O}(n^4)$.

The following table indicates the public key size, median total run time, and median percent of total run time for each of the four steps, for various values of n as indicated. We used $|k| = 2^{16}$, which seems to be reasonable. A k of size 2^{32} would be quite reasonable as well.

n	Public Key (kBytes)	Total Run Time (sec)	Step 1 Find $\mathcal{F}$ (%)	Step 2 Define L'_1 & F' (%)	Step 3 Find $\mathcal{G}'$ (%)	Step 4 Define L'_2, G' & L'_3 (%)
5	1.5	10.8	11	78	8	3
6	2.9	40.0	9	80	8	2
10	22.0	1949	15	76	8	1
14	91.8	33654	10	80	9	1

Step 2 clearly comprises the bulk of the run time. Finding of the exact denominator of F takes almost all of this time, requiring $\frac{1}{24}(16n^6 + 131n^5 + 440n^4 + 595n^3 + 419n^2 + 114n)$ operations. However, step 1 has computational complexity of $\mathcal{O}(n^7)$ and step 3 has computational complexity of $\mathcal{O}(n^9)$ so eventually at higher values for n step 3 will comprise the bulk of the run time.

Remark. *The steps above shows our attack is not a simple application of any one existing attack method, let alone, just the Minrank attack alone. The key is that we need first to accomplish a polynomial map decomposition and then recover a subtle rational map decomposition equivalent to the original one, which requires much more than the Minrank method. One more important point is the direct algebraic attack, namely from the public key, we can derive a set of polynomial equations once we are given the ciphertext,* **but these are degree 4 equations not degree 2 equations,** *whose computation complexity, as we all know, is much higher than the case of degree 2 equations. This is further complicated by the fact that we are working on the field of size of 2^{32}, where the field equations can not be used. This is confirmed by our experiments, for example, Magma F4 implementation failed to solve even the cases $n = 5$ on an ordinary PC, which was proposed more than 20 years ago.*

4   Conclusion

We develop a new improved 2R decomposition method to break the family of rational multivariate public key cryptosystems proposed by Tsujii, Fujioka, and Hirayama in 1989. We show that it is polynomial time to break this family of cryptosystems in terms of the number of variables, the critical parameter of the system. We demonstrate in experiments that our method is very efficient and we can break the scheme originally suggested for practical applications in a few seconds on a standard PC. The main contribution is that we develop new techniques to improve the original 2R decomposition such that it can be used successfully to attack a special family of rational maps. Although we defeat the cryptosystems, we still believe that this family of cryptosystems contains some very interesting ideas that may be utilized effectively.

References

1. International Workshop on Post-Quantum Cryptography. Katholieke Universiteit Leuven, Belgium, May 24–26 (2006), http://postquantum.cr.yp.to
2. Faugere, J.-C., Perret, L.: Cryptanalysis of 2R- Schemes. In: Dwork, C. (ed.) CRYPTO 2006. LNCS, vol. 4117, pp. 357–372. Springer, Heidelberg (2006)
3. Fell, H., Diffie, W.: Analysis of a public key approach based on polynomial substitution. In: Williams, H.C. (ed.) CRYPTO 1985. LNCS, vol. 218, pp. 340–349. Springer, Heidelberg (1986)
4. Goubin, L., Patarin, J.: Asymmetric Cryptography with S-Boxes, Extended Version, http://citeseer.ist.psu.edu/patarin97asymmetric.html
5. Tsujii, S., Fujioka, A., Hirayama, Y.: Generalization of the public key cryptosystem based on the difficulty of solving a system of non-linear equations. ICICE Transactions (A) J72-A 2, 390–397 (1989), http://eprint.iacr.org/2004/336
6. Tsujii, S., Tadaki, K., Fujita, R.: Piece In Hand Concept for Enhancing the Security of Multivariate Type Public Key Cryptosystems: Public Key Without Containing All the Information of Secret Key, Cryptology ePrint Archive, Report 2004/366 (2004), http://eprint.iacr.org/2004/366
7. Tsujii, S., Kurosawa, K., Itoh, T., Fujioka, A., Matsumoto, T.: A public key cryptosystem based on the difficulty of solving a system of nonlinear equations. ICICE Transactions (D) J69-D 12, 1963–1970 (1986)
8. Lih-Chung, W., Yuh-Hua, H., Lai, F., Chun-Yen, C., Bo-Yin, Y.: Tractable rational map signature. In: Vaudenay, S. (ed.) PKC 2005. LNCS, vol. 3386, pp. 244–257. Springer, Heidelberg (2005)
9. Ye, D.F., Lam, K.Y., Dai, Z.D.: Cryptanalysis of 2R Schemes. In: Wiener, M. (ed.) CRYPTO 1999. LNCS, vol. 1666, pp. 315–325. Springer, Heidelberg (1999)
10. Specifications of SFLASH, NESSIE documentation, https://www.cosic.esat.kuleuven.ac.be/nessie/workshop/

Syndrome Based Collision Resistant Hashing

Matthieu Finiasz

ENSTA

Abstract. Hash functions are a hot topic at the moment in cryptography. Many proposals are going to be made for SHA-3, and among them, some provably collision resistant hash functions might also be proposed. These do not really compete with "standard" designs as they are usually much slower and not well suited for constrained environments. However, they present an interesting alternative when speed is not the main objective. As always when dealing with provable security, hard problems are involved, and the fast syndrome-based cryptographic hash function proposed by Augot, Finiasz and Sendrier at Mycrypt 2005 relies on the problem of Syndrome Decoding, a well known "Post Quantum" problem from coding theory. In this article we review the different variants and attacks against it so as to clearly point out which choices are secure and which are not.

Keywords: hash functions, syndrome decoding, provable security.

1 Introduction

At Mycrypt 2005 Augot, Finiasz and Sendrier proposed a new "provably collision resistant" family of hash functions [1]. This family, called Fast Syndrome Based hash function (or simply FSB), is provably collision resistant in the sense that finding a collision for FSB requires to solve a hard problem of coding theory, namely, the Syndrome Decoding problem. However, even if finding collisions requires to solve an NP-complete problem, some algorithms still exist to solve it and choosing secure parameters for the function turned out to be harder than expected. As a consequence, some attacks were found making some of the originally proposed parameters unsafe. The aim of this article is to review the different FSB variants and the various attacks against them, and to clearly point out which parameters are insecure and which are not.

The FSB construction is based on the Merkle-Damgård design. Therefore, we only describe the compression function which is then iterated in order to obtain the hash function. As a result, if finding collisions for this compression function is hard, then finding collisions for the full hash function will also be hard. The goal of this design is to be able to reduce the problem of finding collisions to the syndrome decoding problem.

The compression function is composed of two sub-functions:

- First a *constant weight encoding* function which takes the s input bits of the compression function and outputs a binary word of length n and Hamming weight w,

J. Buchmann and J. Ding (Eds.): PQCrypto 2008, LNCS 5299, pp. 137–147, 2008.
© Springer-Verlag Berlin Heidelberg 2008

- Then a *syndrome computation* function which multiplies the previously obtained constant weight word by a $r \times n$ binary matrix $\mathcal{H}$ and outputs the resulting r bits (which in coding theory are usually called a *syndrome*). In practice, as w is usually small, this multiplication is simply the XOR of w columns of $\mathcal{H}$.

Depending on the choice of the constant weight encoding algorithm and of the matrix the FSB hash function can either be faster or safer, depending on what matters the most. Up to now, two different choices have been proposed, and some attacks on specific parameters sets have followed. In this article we first recall these two constructions (see Section 2) and then present all the known attacks against them (see Section 3). In Section 4 we discuss some other issues concerning the FSB construction and eventually propose some up to date candidates in Section 5.

2   Description

As explained, the FSB compression function is composed of two sub-functions : the constant weight encoding function takes s input bits and outputs a word of length n and weight w, the syndrome computation function uses a binary matrix $\mathcal{H}$ of size $r \times n$ and multiplies it by the previous low weight word to output r bits.

2.1   Original Version

The original version of FSB was first presented in [1]. It uses *regular words* for constant weight encoding and matrix $\mathcal{H}$ is a random matrix.

Definition 1. *A regular word of weight w and length n is a binary word of length n containing exactly one non-zero bit in each of its w intervals of length $\frac{n}{w}$.*

The reasons for these encoding/matrix choices are quite simple:

- Regular word encoding is the fastest possible constant weight encoding. If $\frac{n}{w}$ is a power of two, then, the constant weight encoding simply consists in reading $\log_2 \frac{n}{w}$ input bits at a time in order to get the index of a column of $\mathcal{H}$.
- A random matrix was chosen for $\mathcal{H}$ for security reasons: it is widely believed among coding theorists that random linear codes have good properties making them hard to decode. As we will see in Section 3, finding collisions for FSB is equivalent to decoding in a code of parity check matrix $\mathcal{H}$, thus, using a random matrix is probably a good choice.

2.2   Quasi-Cyclic Version

The main drawback of the original version is the size of the matrix $\mathcal{H}$. The parameters proposed in [1] all involve using a matrix of at least a few hundred kilobytes (if not a few megabytes), which is a lot for most constrained environments. For this reason, an improved version was presented in [6], still using regular words for constant weight encoding, but this time using a quasi-cyclic binary matrix $\mathcal{H}$.

Definition 2. *A* $r \times n$ quasi-cyclic *matrix is a matrix composed of* $\frac{n}{r}$ *cyclic blocs. Each* $r \times r$ *cyclic bloc is such that the* i-*th line of the bloc is a cyclic shift by* $i - 1$ *positions of the first line of the bloc.*

A quasi-cyclic matrix is thus entirely defined by its first line, and the size of the cyclic blocs.

Quasi-cyclic codes are very interesting as they decrease the size of the description of the hash function a lot (a single line is enough). Moreover, it is proven in [8] that when the size of the cyclic blocs is a prime p (and 2 is a generator of $GF(p)$), these codes have properties similar to random codes.

Unfortunately, some of the parameters proposed in [6] were awkwardly selected, making them subject to new attacks that we will present in the following section.

3   Known Attacks

The aim of our hash function construction is to be collision resistant. As it uses the Merkle-Damgård design, it is sufficient that our compression function is collision resistant. We thus want to evaluate the complexity of the best collision search algorithms against it. In practice, there are two ways to find a collision in the FSB compression function:

- Either find a collision in the constant weight encoding algorithm: choosing an injective encoding is enough to guarantee that no such collision exists,
- Or find two words of weight w having the same syndrome: that is, find two words c and c' such that $\mathcal{H} \times c = \mathcal{H} \times c'$.

As our compression function needs to compress, this second type of collision always exists, our goal is thus only to make them hard to find!

Problem 1 (Collision search). Given a binary matrix $\mathcal{H}$ and a weight w, find a word c of non-zero weight $\leq 2w$ such that $\mathcal{H} \times c = 0$.

In other words, finding collisions for FSB requires to find a set of $2w$ or less columns of $\mathcal{H}$ which XOR to zero.

3.1   Decoding Attack

The most natural algorithms to solve the collision problem for FSB are decoding algorithms: if one considers $\mathcal{H}$ as the parity check matrix of a binary code, finding a collision consists in looking for a code word of weight $\leq 2w$ (which is roughly equivalent to a decoding problem). Depending on the choice for the matrix $\mathcal{H}$, this requires to either find a structure in $\mathcal{H}$ making this search easier, or find a low weight code word in a random code (that is, assume that $\mathcal{H}$ contains no specific structure making decoding easier).

For the original version of FSB, a truly random matrix is used for $\mathcal{H}$, therefore, the probability that a structure exists in $\mathcal{H}$ is negligible. For the quasi-cyclic version, an obvious structure exists: the matrix is quasi-cyclic. Nevertheless, if the quasi-cyclic length is well chosen, no specific decoding algorithm is known and decoding can only be done as in a random code. However, as we will see in Section 3.4, a bad choice for the quasi-cyclic length can make the search for low weight code words much easier.

Considering no structure can be found in $\mathcal{H}$, the best decoding algorithm for a random binary code is the Canteaut-Chabaud algorithm [4]. This algorithm is the most advanced of the information set decoding algorithms family and is specifically designed to solve the hardest decoding instances, that is, finding words of weight w close to the Gilbert-Varshamov bound when a single solution exists. Here, the weights we are looking for are much larger (otherwise no compression is possible) which places us in a domain where decoding is somehow easier and where a large number of solutions exist. Giving a closed formula for the complexity of this algorithm is very difficult, especially when many solutions exist, but it is however possible to program an algorithm computing the best possible work factor for a given set of parameters. Additionally, for the domain of parameters we are considering, the Canteaut-Chabaud algorithm is almost always slower than the generalized birthday technique we describe in the next section. When choosing parameters we thus simply checked that the work factor for this attack was above the expected security level, and this was always the case.

3.2   Wagner's Generalized Birthday Technique

Wagner's generalized birthday technique [10] is an extension of the standard birthday collision search technique that uses any power of two number of lists instead of only two. This technique takes advantage of the large number of solutions and looks for specific solutions which can be found more efficiently. It was first applied to FSB in [5].

Standard Birthday Technique. We are looking for $2w$ columns of $\mathcal{H}$ which XOR to 0. These columns are r bits long so we know that if we can build two lists of $2^{\frac{r}{2}}$ elements containing XORs of w columns of $\mathcal{H}$, there is a high probability that these two lists contain an identical element. Building these lists and finding this collision can be done in time/space complexity $O(2^{\frac{r}{2}})$.

Generalized Birthday Technique. With Wagner's generalized technique, one has to build 2^a lists of $2^{\frac{r}{a+1}}$ elements containing XORs of $\frac{w}{2^a}$ columns of $\mathcal{H}$. These lists are then merged pairwise to obtain 2^{a-1} lists of XORs of $\frac{w}{2^{a-1}}$ columns of $\mathcal{H}$. However, in the resulting lists, instead of keeping all the possible elements, only those starting with $\frac{r}{a+1}$ zeros are kept: this way, the size of the lists will not increase. Then, these lists are once again merged pairwise, canceling $\frac{r}{a+1}$

bits again and so on, until only two lists are left and the standard birthday technique can be used. With this technique, collisions can be found in time/space complexity of $O(2^{\frac{r}{a+1}})$, for any value of a such that enough elements are found to populate the 2^a starting lists.

Depending on s and r, the size of the input and output of the compression function, it is easy to evaluate the largest possible value for a, and thus the best possible complexity for this attack. There are s input bits to the function, meaning that 2^s different inputs exist. Thus, 2^s words of weight w can be built. The number L of different words of weight $\frac{w}{2^a-1}$ that can be built must thus verify $\binom{L}{2^a-1} \leq 2^s$. Additionally, if we want the attack to be possible, the size L of the starting lists must be large enough, meaning that we need $L \geq 2^{\frac{r}{a+1}}$. Thus, any valid parameter a must verify:

$$\binom{2^{\frac{r}{a+1}}}{2^a-1} \leq 2^s \quad \Longleftrightarrow \quad \frac{r}{a+1} - a + 1 \leq \frac{s}{2^a-1} \quad \overset{a \text{ small}}{\Longleftrightarrow} \quad \frac{2^a-1}{a+1} \leq \frac{s}{r}. \quad (1)$$

For $s = r$, it is interesting to note that $a = 3$ verifies the inequality. If we want the function to compress (that is, $s > r$), $a = 3$ will thus always be possible, and a security higher than $2^{\frac{r}{4}}$ is never possible. This is why a final compression function (see Section 4.2) will always be necessary.

3.3   Linearization

The linearization attack against FSB was presented in [9]. The idea of this attack is that when w becomes large enough, the problem of finding a collision can be linearized in order to reduce it to a linear algebra problem. A collision can then be found in polynomial time!

There are two forms to this attack: first the straight-forward linearization, then a extension making it possible to use this attack in some cases where it could not normally apply.

Simple Linearization. Suppose $w = \frac{r}{2}$. In this case, finding a collision consists in finding r columns of $\mathcal{H}$ XORing to 0. Now, instead of looking for any word of weight r and length n we restrict ourselves to very specific words: each of the r columns of $\mathcal{H}$ will be chosen among one pair of columns, meaning that the i-th column will be either h_i^0 or h_i^1, where all the $h_i^{\{0,1\}}$ are different columns of $\mathcal{H}$. Finding a collision now requires to determine a binary vector B of length r where the i-th bit of B decides which column to choose between h_i^0 and h_i^1. Now comes the linearization: we build a matrix $\mathcal{H}'$ such that the i-th columns of $\mathcal{H}'$ is $h_i' = h_i^1 - h_i^0$. Now, we simply need to find B such that:

$$\mathcal{H}' \times B = \sum_{i=1}^{r} h_i^0.$$

This is a linear system to solve and it is done in polynomial time. Thus, as soon as $2w \geq r$, finding a collision for FSB can be done in polynomial time.

Extension of the Attack. When $w < \frac{r}{2}$, the previous attack can still be applied, but the matrix $\mathcal{H}'$ will no longer be square and the probability that a solution B exists will probably be negligible. To improve this, one can use a larger alphabet: instead of choosing two columns one can choose three columns of $\mathcal{H}$ at a time and code two bits of B with them. However, three columns give three possibilities and two bits of B require four columns (with the fourth column being the XOR of the second and the third). Thus, each solution vector B using extended alphabets will have probability $\frac{1}{4}$ per set of three columns of being invalid. This solution will thus increase the chance that a solution vector B can be found, but will decrease the probability that this solution is realizable in practice. According to [9], if $2w + 2w' = r$ (with $w' \le w$), the probability that a valid solution is found is:

$$\left(\frac{3}{4}\right)^{2w'} \times 0.28879 \simeq 2^{-0.830w'-1.792}.$$

This attack is thus usable as soon as $w \ge \frac{r}{4}$, but it will mostly be of interest when w is close to $\frac{r}{2}$.

3.4 Quasi-Cyclic Divisibility

This attack was presented in [7] and it exploits the divisibility of the cycle length in the quasi-cyclic version of FSB. Suppose $\mathcal{H}$ is built of $\frac{n}{r}$ cyclic blocs of size $r \times r$ and there exists a divisor p or r such that $r = p \times r'$. Then, Wagner's generalized birthday technique can be applied on the length r' instead of r. Instead of looking for any word of weight w and length n, we focus on words having a "cyclic" syndrome: each time the i-th column of a bloc of $\mathcal{H}$ is chosen, the $p - 1$ columns at position $i + r'$, $i + 2r'$,... cyclicly to $i - r'$, are also chosen. This way, a bloc-wise cyclic shift by r' positions of the input word keeps it unchanged. This means that the syndrome of a word selected this way also remains unchanged when cyclicly shifted by r' positions. Thus, if the r' top positions of the syndrome are null, the whole syndrome is also null.

Focusing on the r' top rows of $\mathcal{H}$ and selecting only the previously described words, we now need to apply Wagner's technique to the following problem: find $\frac{w}{p}$ columns of a $r' \times \frac{n}{p}$ binary matrix XORing to 0. The largest possible value for the parameter a of Wagner's algorithm is smaller than before, but the attack applies to r' bits only and the final complexity drops significantly. When selecting parameters for FSB, it is important that such an attack cannot be applied.

4   Other Issues

4.1   IV Weakness

As pointed out in [7] another weakness of the original FSB compression function lies in the way the input to the compression function is handled. In particular, the chaining bits (or IV) and the message bits are simply concatenated, and no mixing whatsoever is applied. When using regular words, this means that the output of the compression function is simply the XOR of two independent hashes: one resulting from the IV bits, the other one from the message bits. If one can find a collision on the message part of the compression function (this will be somehow harder than a normal collision as less input bits are available), then this collision is IV independent. This has no influence on the collision resistance of the function, but it is a problem when using the hash function as a MAC or as a PRF for example: the resistance to some attacks falls from the cost of an inversion (or second preimage) to the cost of building a message only collision (which will probably be just above the cost for building a standard collision).

In order to avoid such problems, the best thing would be to mix the input bits through a diffusion function. However, such a mixing is quite costly and would severely reduce the throughput of the hash function. The best solution is thus probably to integrate this diffusion in the constant weight encoding function. As stated in Section 5.1, a simple interleaving of the message bits with the IV bits is enough to avoid this problem.

4.2   Final Compression Function

Another issue with the FSB compression function is the ratio between the security against collision and the output size of the function. A hash function is expected to have a security of $2^{\frac{r}{2}}$ against collisions if it outputs r-bits hashes. With FSB, we have seen in Section 3.2 that if our compression function is to compress, an attack in $2^{\frac{r}{4}}$ will always be possible. The solution is thus to use a final compression function: use FSB to hash the message into a large hash, and then use a final compression function g to reduce the size of the hash from r to r' bits, where r' is twice the bit security of FSB against collisions. However, finding a suitable function g is not straight-forward:

- If g is collision resistant, then using FSB hash and then g will lead to a collision resistant hash function. However, even if g is not collision resistant, building a collisions on the complete hash from a collision on g will not be easy: it requires to invert FSB. So requiring collision resistance for g is clearly too much.
- If g is a linear function, then g can be applied to all the columns of $\mathcal{H}$ and finding a collision on the whole function will only require to find a collision on a matrix $\mathcal{H}'$ of size $r' \times n$. Thus the security against collisions will be less than $2^{\frac{r'}{4}}$.

Apart from this, it is hard to state anything relevant about the final compression function and we believe that most non-linear compression function could do the trick. However, as far as provable security is concerned, choosing a provably collision resistant function g is probably the only choice at the moment.

5   Possible Candidates

5.1   Constant Weight Encoding

There are many ways to perform constant weight encoding, spanning from the one to one encoding where all words of weight w are equiprobable, to the regular word encoding. The first one is the most bit efficient (the compression function will have the largest possible input for some given parameters n and w), the second one is the fastest. When dealing with hash functions, speed is usually a very important factor and fast constant weight encoding would be a natural choice, however, concerning security, all results on the hardness of syndrome decoding consider random words of weight w, not regular words (or words with any other structure). Luckily, when looking for collisions, a collision for any given constant weight encoding is also a collision for the one to one encoding: any pair of words of weight w (even with a strong structure) can be coded with the one to one equiprobable encoding. Thus, finding collisions for FSB using regular words can not be easier than finding collisions for FSB using a more bit efficient encoding.

However, no proof can be given that finding collisions for regular words is indeed harder than with the one to one equiprobable encoding. Thus, when choosing parameters for FSB, we will consider the security of FSB with one to one constant weight encoding, even if a faster encoding is used in practice.

The conclusion of this is that using regular word encoding is certainly the best choice for efficiency. However, as seen in Section 4.1, using such an encoding causes IV weakness issues. In order to avoid these issues it is necessary that every index of a non-zero bit of the constant weight word depends from the value of both the IV and the message. This way, no IV independent collision can be built. Interleaving the bits coming from the IV (or chaining value) with those of the message is thus a solution. Depending on the parameters chosen for the function, different interleavings will be possible.

5.2   Matrix Choice

The choice of the matrix $\mathcal{H}$ is also very important for the efficiency of FSB. Of course, for optimal security, nothing can be better than a truly random matrix, but in this case the description of the hash function will be very large and will not be suitable for memory constraint devices and for most hardware implementations. Thus, using matrices that can be described with a single line is important if FSB is ever to be used in practice.

The results of Gaborit and Zémor [8] tend to prove that well chosen quasi-cyclic codes have good properties making them suitable candidates. However, this requires that r is a prime number, which will certainly make implementation less efficient than using powers of two. Our idea is thus to use a *truncated quasi-cyclic* matrix instead of a standard quasi-cyclic matrix.

Definition 3. *A $r \times n$ matrix $\mathcal{H}$ is a* truncated quasi-cyclic *matrix if it can be divided in $\frac{n}{r}$ blocs of size $r \times r$ and each bloc is the top left sub-bloc of a $p \times p$ cyclic bloc.*

With this definition, any matrix $\mathcal{H}$ built of blocks which are Toeplitz matrices will be a truncated quasi-cyclic matrix with $p > 2r$, but in order to be as close as possible to standard quasi-cyclic matrices, we will always choose r very close to p. Then, the description of the $r \times n$ matrix $\mathcal{H}$ can be reduced to a "first line" of $\frac{n}{r} \times p$ bits and the values of p and r.

As explained in [8], in order for p to be a suitable choice it must be prime, and 2 must be a generator of $GF(p)$. Hence, it is easy to check the best p for a given r: one simply needs to test the primes greater than r one by one until 2 is a generator. For example, for $r = 512$ we get $p = 523$, for $r = 768$ we get $p = 773$ and for $r = 1024$ we get $p = 1061$.

5.3   Choosing Parameters

When choosing parameters we want Wagner's attack to be the most efficient so that we precisely control the security of FSB. As seen in Section 3.2, this security only depends on the output size r and the input size s of the compression function. As stated in Section 5.1 we want to measure the security of the construction when using a one to one constant weight encoding, which means, s is not the effective number of bits that the compression function will read, but $s = \log_2 \binom{n}{w}$. Once r and s are chosen to obtain the desired security level, one simply needs to select a convenient value for w (and deduce n), such that linearization attacks are impossible.

Concerning previously proposed parameters, all those proposed in [6] use a quasi-cyclic matrix of cyclicity a power of 2 and are thus all subject to the attack of Section 3.4: none of these parameters should be used. Three sets of parameters were proposed in the original paper [1]:

- Short hash has its security reduced to $2^{72.2}$ as the security gained from using regular words is no longer taken into account.
- Fast hash is subject to the extended linearization attack and has its security reduced to $2^{59.9}$.
- The Intermediate proposal however still has a security above 2^{80} and can still be considered safe.

Parameters for 80-bit Security. Choosing $r = 512$ and a security of 2^{80} against collisions we get from Equation (1) that $s \leq 1688$. Now, to avoid linearization attacks we need $w \leq \frac{r}{4} = 128$. If we choose $w = 128$, we get for $n = 2^{18}$ a value $s = 1587$ which is suitable. Our first proposition is thus to use:

$$r = 512, n = 2^{18}, w = 128,$$

with regular word encoding, and a truncated quasi-cyclic matrix with $p = 523$. For the IV interleaving, each of the w positions are coded by 11 input bits, 4 of which are taken from the IV and the rest from the message. With these parameters FSB reads input blocs of 896 bits and outputs 512 bits. These bits can then be compressed to 160 bits using a suitable final compression function. The matrix $\mathcal{H}$ is described by $267\,776$ bits (~ 32.7kB).

Parameters for 128-bit Security. For 128-bit security we need r larger than 512. We can use $r = 768$ and obtain $s \leq 2048$. If we pick $w = 192$ and $n = 3 \times 2^{15}$ we get $s = 1999$ and linearization attacks are impossible. Our proposition is to use:

$$r = 768, n = 3 \times 2^{15}, w = 192,$$

with regular word encoding, and a truncated quasi-cyclic matrix with $p = 773$. Each position is coded using 9 input bits, so the IV interleaving will take 4 bits from the IV and 5 bits from the message each time. FSB thus reads input blocs of 960 bits and output 768 bits which, at the end, need to be compressed to 256 bits. The matrix $\mathcal{H}$ is described by 98 944 bits ($\sim$ 12kB).

The same parameters, using a shorter $n = 3 \times 2^{14}$ will probably be more efficient as each position will be coded with 8bits, 4 from the IV and 4 from the message, even if only 768 bit blocs are read instead of 960 bit blocs. Moreover, it will have a shorter description ($\sim$ 6kB) and the security against collisions will be a little higher (about 2^{133}).

6   Conclusion

Taking into account all the different attacks against FSB, it is still possible to select parameters that offer both a high level of security (relying on well identified problems) and a satisfying efficiency. Also, apart from the choice of the final compression function, the other choices that had to be made for FSB seem clear: use regular word encoding (with IV interleaving) and a truncated quasi-cyclic matrix. For the final compression function, using a provably secure pseudo-random generator could be a good choice: use the output of FSB as an IV and generate the desired number of bits of output. One could then use the generators of Blum-Blum-Shub [3], or preferably for post-quantum security QUAD [2].

References

1. Augot, D., Finiasz, M., Sendrier, N.: A family of fast syndrome based cryptographic hash functions. In: Dawson, E., Vaudenay, S. (eds.) Mycrypt 2005. LNCS, vol. 3715, pp. 64–83. Springer, Heidelberg (2005)
2. Berbain, C., Gilbert, H., Patarin, J.: QUAD: a practical stream cipher with provable security. In: Vaudenay, S. (ed.) EUROCRYPT 2006. LNCS, vol. 4004, pp. 109–128. Springer, Heidelberg (2006)
3. Blum, L., Blum, M., Shub, M.: Comparison of two pseudo-random number generators. In: Chaum, D., Rivest, R.L., Sherman, A. (eds.) Crypto 1982, pp. 61–78. Plenum (1983)
4. Canteaut, A., Chabaud, F.: A new algorithm for finding minimum-weight words in a linear code: Application to McEliece's cryptosystem and to narrow-sense BCH codes of length 511. IEEE Transactions on Information Theory 44(1), 367–378 (1998)

5. Coron, J.-S., Joux, A.: Cryptanalysis of a provably secure cryptographic hash function. IACR eprint archive (2004), `http://eprint.iacr.org/2004/013`
6. Finiasz, M., Gaborit, P., Sendrier, N.: Improved fast syndrome based cryptographic hash functions. In: Rijmen, V. (ed.) ECRYPT Workshop on Hash Functions (2007)
7. Fouque, P.-A., Leurent, G.: Cryptanalysis of a hash function based on quasi-cyclic codes. In: Malkin, T. (ed.) CT-RSA 2008. LNCS, vol. 4964, pp. 19–35. Springer, Heidelberg (2008)
8. Gaborit, P., Zémor., G.: Asymptotic improvement of the Gilbert-Varshamov bound for linear codes. In: IEEE Conference, ISIT 2006, pp. 287–291 (2006)
9. Saarinen, M.-J.O.: Linearization attacks against syndrome based hashes. In: Srinathan, K., Rangan, C.P., Yung, M. (eds.) INDOCRYPT 2007. LNCS, vol. 4859, pp. 1–9. Springer, Heidelberg (2007)
10. Wagner, D.: A generalized birthday problem. In: Yung, M. (ed.) CRYPTO 2002. LNCS, vol. 2442, pp. 288–304. Springer, Heidelberg (2002)

Nonlinear Piece In Hand Perturbation Vector Method for Enhancing Security of Multivariate Public Key Cryptosystems

Ryou Fujita[1], Kohtaro Tadaki[2], and Shigeo Tsujii[1]

[1] Institute of Information Security
2–14–1 Tsuruya-cho, Kanagawa-ku, Yokohama-shi, 221–0835 Japan
[2] Research and Development Initiative, Chuo University
1–13–27 Kasuga, Bunkyo-ku, Tokyo, 112–8551 Japan

Abstract. The piece in hand (PH) is a general scheme which is applicable to any reasonable type of multivariate public key cryptosystems for the purpose of enhancing their security. In this paper, we propose a new class PH method called NLPHPV (NonLinear Piece in Hand Perturbation Vector) method. Although our NLPHPV uses similar perturbation vectors as are used for the previously known internal perturbation method, this new method can avoid redundant repetitions in decryption process. With properly chosen parameter sizes, NLPHPV achieves an observable gain in security from the original multivariate public key cryptosystem. We demonstrate these by both theoretical analyses and computer simulations against major known attacks and provides the concrete sizes of security parameters, with which we even expect the grater security against potential quantum attacks.

Keywords: public key cryptosystem, multivariate polynomial, multivariate public key cryptosystem, piece in hand concept, perturbation vector.

1 Introduction

Multivariate Public Key Cryptosystems (MPKCs, for short) originally proposed in 80's as possible alternatives to the traditional, widely-used public key cryptosystems, such as RSA and ElGamal cryptosystems. One of the motivations for researching MPKC is that the public key cryptosystems based on the intractability of prime factorization or discrete logarithm problem are presently assumed to be secure, but their security will not be guaranteed in the quantum computer age. On the other hand, no quantum algorithm is known so far to be able to solve efficiently the underlying problem of MPKCs, i.e., the problem of solving a set of multivariate quadratic or higher degree polynomial equations over a finite field.

Since the original research of MPKCs was started, many new schemes have been proposed so far. At the same time, many new methods to cryptanalyze

J. Buchmann and J. Ding (Eds.): PQCrypto 2008, LNCS 5299, pp. 148–164, 2008.

MPKCs have also been discovered. Recently, for the purpose of resisting these attacks, the research on the method for enhancing security of MPKCs is becoming one of the main themes of this area. The piece in hand (PH, for short) matrix method aims to bring the computational complexity of cryptanalysis close to exponential time by adding random polynomial terms to original MPKC. The PH methods were introduced and studied in a series of papers [27, 28, 29, 30, 31, 32, 33, 34]. Among them, there are primary two types of the PH matrix methods; the linear PH matrix methods and the nonlinear PH matrix methods. In particular, the papers [31, 32, 33, 34] proposed the linear PH matrix method with random variables and the nonlinear PH matrix method, and showed that these PH matrix methods lead to the substantial gain in security against the Gröbner basis attack under computer experiments.

Because of the nonlinearity of the PH matrix, the nonlinear PH matrix methods are expected to enhance the security of the original MPKC more than the linear PH matrix methods in general. Thus, in the present paper, we propose a new PH method, called NonLinear Piece in Hand Perturbation Vector (NLPHPV, for short) method, which can be applied to both encryption schemes and signature schemes in general.[1] The adopted application of perturbation vector is similar to the internal perturbation method [3] and the construction of R-SE(2)PKC [13], where random transformation is mixed with the "non-singular" transformation. In particular, on the internal perturbation method, computational complexity by the Gröbner basis attack is reported in [5], the paper showed that when r is not too small (i.e., $r \gtrsim 6$), the perturbed Matsumoto-Imai cryptosystem [3] is secure against the Gröbner basis attack, where r is the perturbation dimension. Note, however, that in exchange for enhancing the security, the decryption process of the internal perturbation method becomes q^r times slower than unperturbed one, where q is the number of field elements. This fact contrasts with our NLPHPV method in a sense that it does not require repeated processes of decryption process which grows exponentially, though the cipher text size becomes slightly large. From this point of view of efficiency, NLPHPV method can be a good alternative to the internal perturbation method. We also discuss on security benefit of the NLPHPV method against major known attacks, i.e., the Gröbner basis attack, the rank attack [37], and the differential attack [9]. Based on also our security considerations, we suggest concrete parameter sizes for the NLPHPV method.

This paper is organized as follows. We begin in Section 2 with some basic notation and a brief introduction of the schemes of MPKCs in general. We introduce the NLPHPV method in Section 3. We then show, based on computer experiments, that the NLPHPV method properly provides substantial security against the Gröbner basis attack in Section 4. We discuss the immunity of the NLPHPV method against known attacks in Section 5. Based on the discussion, we suggest parameters for the NLPHPV method in Section 6. We conclude this paper with the future direction of our work in Section 7.

---

[1] In signature scheme, the parameters of the NLPHPV method are restricted to some region. We will deal with the issue in Section 3 and Subsection 5.2.

2 Preliminaries

In this section we review the schemes of MPKCs in general after introducing some notations about fields, polynomials, and matrices.

2.1 Notations

We represent a column vector in general by bold face symbols such as $\boldsymbol{p}$, $\boldsymbol{E}$, and $\boldsymbol{X}$.

- $\mathbf{F}_q$: finite field which has q elements with $q \geq 2$.
- $\mathbf{F}_q[x_1, \ldots, x_k]$: set of all polynomials in variables $x_1, x_2, \ldots, x_k$ with coefficients in $\mathbf{F}_q$.
- $S^{n \times l}$: set of all $n \times l$ matrices whose entries are in a nonempty set S with positive integers n and l. Let $S^{n \times 1} = S^n$.
- S^n: set of all column vectors consisting n entries in S.
- $A^T \in S^{l \times n}$: transpose of A for matrix $A \in S^{n \times l}$.
- $\boldsymbol{f}(\boldsymbol{g}) = (h_1, \ldots, h_n)^T \in \mathbf{F}_q[x_1, \ldots, x_m]^n$: *substitution* of $\boldsymbol{g}$ for the variables in $\boldsymbol{f}$, where $\boldsymbol{f} = (f_1, \ldots, f_n)^T \in \mathbf{F}_q[x_1, \ldots, x_k]^n$, $\boldsymbol{g} = (g_1, \ldots, g_k)^T \in \mathbf{F}_q[x_1, \ldots, x_m]^k$ are polynomial column vectors. Each h_i is the polynomial in $\mathbf{F}_q[x_1, \ldots, x_m]$ obtained by substituting $g_1, \ldots, g_k$ for the variables $x_1, \ldots, x_k$ in f_i, respectively.
- $\boldsymbol{f}(\boldsymbol{p}) \in \mathbf{F}_q^n$: vector obtained by substituting $p_1, \ldots, p_k$ for the variables $x_1, \ldots, x_k$ in $\boldsymbol{f}$, respectively, for $\boldsymbol{f} \in \mathbf{F}_q[x_1, \ldots, x_k]^n$ and $\boldsymbol{p} \in \mathbf{F}_q^k$, where $\boldsymbol{p} = (p_1, \ldots, p_k)^T$ with $p_1, \ldots, p_k \in \mathbf{F}_q$.

2.2 MPKCs in General

A MPKC as in [3, 12, 13, 14, 17, 18, 19, 21, 25, 26, 36, 38] are often made by the following building blocks:

Secret key: The secret key includes the following:
- the two invertible matrices $A_0 \in \mathbf{F}_q^{k \times k}$, $B_0 \in \mathbf{F}_q^{n \times n}$;
- the polynomial transformation $\boldsymbol{G} \in \mathbf{F}_q[x_1, \ldots, x_k]^n$ whose inverse is efficiently computable.

Public key: The public key includes the following:
- the finite field $\mathbf{F}_q$ including its additive and multiplicative structure;
- the polynomial vector $\boldsymbol{E} = B_0 \boldsymbol{G}(A_0 \boldsymbol{x}) \in \mathbf{F}_q[x_1, \ldots, x_k]^n$, where $\boldsymbol{x} = (x_1, \ldots, x_k)^T \in \mathbf{F}_q[x_1, \ldots, x_k]^k$.

Encryption: Given a plain text vector $\boldsymbol{p} = (p_1, \ldots, p_k)^T \in \mathbf{F}_q^k$, the corresponding cipher text is the vector $\boldsymbol{c} = \boldsymbol{E}(\boldsymbol{p})$.

Decryption: Given the cipher text vector $\boldsymbol{c} = (c_1, \ldots, c_n)^T \in \mathbf{F}_q^n$, decryption includes the following steps:
(i) Compute $\boldsymbol{w} = B_0^{-1} \boldsymbol{c} \in \mathbf{F}_q^n$,
(ii) Compute $\boldsymbol{v} \in \mathbf{F}_q^k$ from $\boldsymbol{w}$ by using the inverse transformation of $\boldsymbol{G}$,
(iii) Compute $\boldsymbol{p} = A_0^{-1} \boldsymbol{v} \in \mathbf{F}_q^k$.

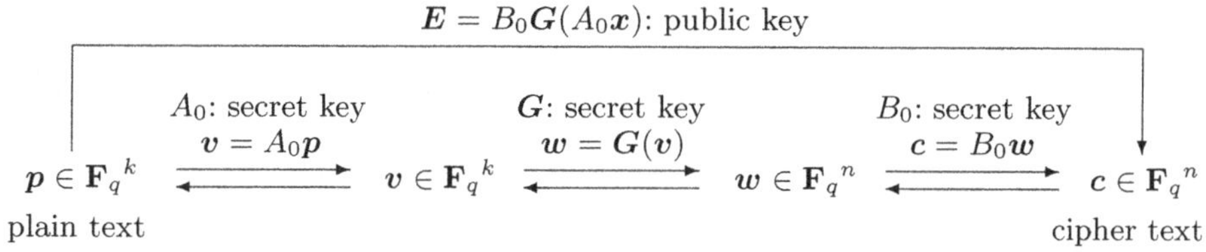

$$\boldsymbol{E} = B_0 G(A_0 \boldsymbol{x}): \text{public key}$$

A_0: secret key G: secret key B_0: secret key

$\boldsymbol{v} = A_0 \boldsymbol{p}$ $\boldsymbol{w} = G(\boldsymbol{v})$ $\boldsymbol{c} = B_0 \boldsymbol{w}$

$\boldsymbol{p} \in \mathbf{F}_q{}^k$ $\xrightarrow{\hspace{2cm}}$ $\boldsymbol{v} \in \mathbf{F}_q{}^k$ $\xrightarrow{\hspace{2cm}}$ $\boldsymbol{w} \in \mathbf{F}_q{}^n$ $\xrightarrow{\hspace{2cm}}$ $\boldsymbol{c} \in \mathbf{F}_q{}^n$

plain text   cipher text

Fig. 1. Scheme of Multivariate Public Key Cryptosystem

3   Nonlinear Piece In Hand Perturbation Vector (NLPHPV) Method

Let $\mathcal{K}$ be an arbitrary MPKC whose public key polynomial vector is given by $\boldsymbol{E} \in \mathbf{F}_q[x_1, \ldots, x_k]^n$, as described in Subsection 2.2. Let f, l and h be any positive integers. We set $g \overset{\text{def}}{=} n + l + h$. Let p and z be any positive integers with $p \leq k \leq z$, and let t be any nonnegative integer with $t \leq z - p$. The relation between these parameters and correspondence to plain text and random number is given in Figure 2.

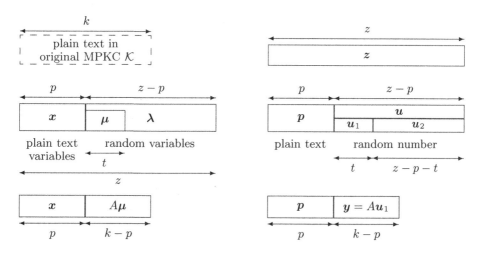

Fig. 2. Plain text and random number

Let $A \in \mathbf{F}_q{}^{(k-p) \times t}$ and $C \in \mathbf{F}_q{}^{f \times z}$ be randomly chosen matrices. Let $\boldsymbol{r} \in \mathbf{F}_q[x_1, \ldots, x_z]^h$ be a randomly chosen polynomial vector. In the NLPHPV method, a new MPKC $\widetilde{\mathcal{K}}$ is constructed from the given MPKC $\mathcal{K}$ for the purpose of enhancing the security. A public key $\widetilde{\boldsymbol{E}} \in \mathbf{F}_q[x_1, \ldots, x_z]^g$ of $\widetilde{\mathcal{K}}$ is constructed from the original public key $\boldsymbol{E}$ of $\mathcal{K}$.

Secret key: The secret key includes the following:
- secret key of $\mathcal{K}$;
- randomly chosen invertible matrix $B \in \mathbf{F}_q{}^{g \times g}$;

- polynomial transformation $H \in \mathbf{F}_q[x_1, \ldots, x_f]^l$ whose inverse is efficiently computable;
- the *nonlinear piece in hand perturbation vector* $Q \in \mathbf{F}_q[x_1, \ldots, x_f]^n$, which is randomly chosen.

Public key: The public key includes the following:
  - the finite field $\mathbf{F}_q$ including its additive and multiplicative structure;
  - the number of plain text variables in the NLPHPV method p;
  - the polynomial vector $\widetilde{E} \in \mathbf{F}_q[x_1, \ldots, x_z]^g$. $\widetilde{E}$ is constructed as the following equation:

$$\widetilde{E} \underset{\text{def}}{=} B \begin{pmatrix} E\begin{pmatrix} x \\ A\mu \end{pmatrix} + Q(f) \\ H(f) \\ r \end{pmatrix}. \tag{1}$$

Here $x = (x_1, \ldots, x_p)^T \in \mathbf{F}_q[x_1, \ldots, x_p]^p$, $\mu = (x_{p+1}, \ldots, x_{p+t})^T \in \mathbf{F}_q[x_{p+1}, \ldots, x_{p+t}]^t$, $\lambda = (x_{p+1}, \ldots, x_z)^T \in \mathbf{F}_q[x_{p+1}, \ldots, x_z]^{z-p}$, $f = (f_1, \ldots, f_f)^T = C\begin{pmatrix} x \\ \lambda \end{pmatrix} \in \mathbf{F}_q[x_1, \ldots, x_z]^f$. Note that, in the right-hand side of (1), the vector $A\mu \in \mathbf{F}_q[x_{p+1}, \ldots, x_{p+t}]^{k-p}$ is substituted for the variables $x_{p+1}, \ldots, x_k$ in the original public key E while keeping the variables $x_1, \ldots, x_p$ in E unchanged. $Q(f)$ plays a role in masking the original public key E and randomizing it. r is appended to the polynomial sets in order to cope with the differential attack [6, 9].

Note that t random variables $x_{p+1}, \ldots, x_{p+t}$ in μ are included in E from $z-p$ random variables $x_{p+1}, \ldots, x_z$ in λ. Then, increasing the value $\binom{z-p}{t}$ makes these random variables indistinguishable.

Remark 1. We may replace $E\begin{pmatrix} x \\ A\mu \end{pmatrix}$ in (1) with $E\left(D\begin{pmatrix} x \\ \mu \end{pmatrix}\right)$ in a more general form. Here $D \in \mathbf{F}_q^{k \times (p+t)}$ is a randomly chosen matrix such that, for any $p, p' \in \mathbf{F}_q^p$ and any $u_1, u_1' \in \mathbf{F}_q^t$, if $D\begin{pmatrix} p \\ u_1 \end{pmatrix} = D\begin{pmatrix} p' \\ u_1' \end{pmatrix}$, then $p = p'$. This condition on D is needed to recover the plain text uniquely. However, D can be rewritten as $D = U\begin{pmatrix} I_p & 0 \\ 0 & A \end{pmatrix}$ for some invertible matrix $U \in \mathbf{F}_q^{k \times k}$. Thus, the transformation $E\begin{pmatrix} x \\ A\mu \end{pmatrix}$ is equivalent to $E\left(D\begin{pmatrix} x \\ \mu \end{pmatrix}\right)$ since A_0 is randomly chosen in original MPKC $\mathcal{K}$.

In signature scheme, the requirement of the uniqueness in decryption is removed. Thus, the matrix D can be randomly chosen and the distinction between plain text and random variables is also removed.

Encryption: Given a plain text vector $p = (p_1, \ldots, p_p)^T \in \mathbf{F}_q^p$ and a random number $u = (u_1, \ldots, u_{z-p})^T \in \mathbf{F}_q^{z-p}$, the corresponding cipher text is the vector $\widetilde{c} = \widetilde{E}\begin{pmatrix} p \\ u \end{pmatrix}$.

Decryption: Given the cipher text vector $\tilde{c} = (\tilde{c}_1, \ldots, \tilde{c}_g)^T \in \mathbf{F}_q{}^g$, decryption includes the following steps:

(i) Compute $B^{-1}\tilde{c}$. By (1), we see that

$$B^{-1}\tilde{c} = \begin{pmatrix} E\begin{pmatrix} p \\ y \end{pmatrix} + Q(f(z)) \\ H(f(z)) \\ r(z) \end{pmatrix},$$

where $z \underset{\text{def}}{=} \begin{pmatrix} p \\ u \end{pmatrix} \in \mathbf{F}_q{}^z$, $u = \begin{pmatrix} u_1 \\ u_2 \end{pmatrix} \in \mathbf{F}_q{}^{z-p}$, $u_1 \in \mathbf{F}_q{}^t$, $u_2 \in \mathbf{F}_q{}^{z-p-t}$, $y \underset{\text{def}}{=} Au_1 \in \mathbf{F}_q{}^{k-p}$.

(ii) Compute $f(z)$ from the value $H(f(z))$ by using the inverse transformation of H.

(iii) Compute $Q(f(z))$ by substitution of $f(z)$ for Q.

(iv) Compute $E\begin{pmatrix} p \\ y \end{pmatrix}$ from the value $E\begin{pmatrix} p \\ y \end{pmatrix} + Q(f(z))$.

(v) Compute $\begin{pmatrix} p \\ y \end{pmatrix}$ by using the secret key of $\mathcal{K}$. Note that y is discarded after the decryption.

In signature scheme, the matrices A and C are included in the secret key, and it is needed to compute u by solving linear equation $\begin{pmatrix} 0 & A & 0 \\ & C & \end{pmatrix}\begin{pmatrix} p \\ \lambda \end{pmatrix} = \begin{pmatrix} y \\ f(z) \end{pmatrix}$ for unknown λ, and to check if $r\begin{pmatrix} p \\ u \end{pmatrix} = r(z)$ for the solution

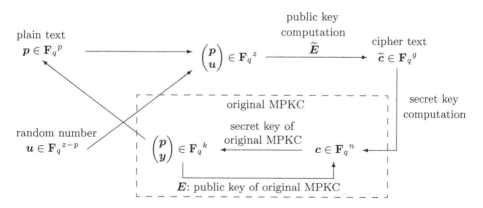

Fig. 3. NonLinear Piece in Hand Perturbation Vector method

u, where $r(z)$ is the value given above.[2] Since the probability that $\begin{pmatrix} p \\ u \end{pmatrix}$ satisfies this criteria is $1/q^h$ on average, h must be small as possible in signature scheme.

The encryption and decryption processes in the NLPHPV method are schematically represented in Figure 3.

4   Experimental Results

In this section, based on computer experiments, we clarify the enhancement of the security by the NLPHPV method proposed in the previous section.

Recently, Faugère and Joux [8] showed in an experimental manner that computing a Gröbner basis (GB, for short) of the public key is likely to be an efficient attack to HFE [21], which is one of major MPKCs. In fact, they broke the first HFE challenge (80bits) proposed by Patarin. The attack used by them is to compute a Gröbner basis for the ideal generated by polynomial components in $E - c$, where E is a public key and c is a cipher text vector.

Table 1. Computational times of the GB attack for PMI+

Parameters			Computational times
k	r	a	in second
28	6	0	845
28	6	5	733
28	6	10	563
28	6	15	436
29	6	15	747
30	6	15	1305

k: number of plain text variables
r: perturbation dimension
a: number of Plus polynomials

Table 2. Computational times of the GB attack for the enhanced MI by the NLPHPV method

Parameters			Computational times
k	l	h	in second
28	17	3	290
28	17	4	289
28	17	5	263
29	17	3	537
29	17	8	402
29	17	10	349
30	17	3	936
30	17	8	701
30	17	13	513

We report in Table 1 and Table 2 the time required for the GB attack against the perturbed Matsumoto-Imai-Plus cryptosystem (PMI+, for short) [6] and the Matsumoto-Imai cryptosystem (MI, for short) [18] enhanced by the NLPHPV method. Note that $n = k$ and $q = 2$ for the public keys $E \in \mathbf{F}_q[x_1, \ldots, x_k]^n$ of MI by its specification. We deal with the case of $p = z = k$, $f = l$ in

---

[2] The equation is replaced with $\begin{pmatrix} D & 0 \\ & C \end{pmatrix} \begin{pmatrix} x \\ \lambda \end{pmatrix} = \begin{pmatrix} D \begin{pmatrix} p \\ u_1 \end{pmatrix} \\ f(z) \end{pmatrix}$ for unknown x and λ when the matrix D above is randomly chosen.

the NLPHPV method. As an practical example of the polynomial transformation H in the NLPHPV method, we use the public key polynomials of the HFE in which the degree of the secret univariate polynomial is more than 128,[3] though we can choose any H. The computation times are evaluated on PRO-SIDE edAEW416R2 workstation with AMD Opteron Model 854 processors at 2.80GHz and 64GB of RAM. We use the algorithm F_4 implemented on the computational algebra system Magma V2.12-21. In Table 1 and Table 2, due to the constraint of computing ability, only the cases of $k = 28, 29, 30$ are computed. Since MI may have polynomial time complexity about $O(k^7)$ of cryptanalysis, as shown in [5] and our preliminary experimental results, it is quite difficult at present to compare MI with the enhanced MI in a practical length of a plain text such as 200bits. If we can experimentally cryptanalyze the MI enhanced by the NLPHPV method in the practical length of a plain text in order to compare it with the original MI, then this implies that the cryptosystem enhanced by NLPHPV method is useless in itself. This is a limitation and dilemma of the security evaluation by computer experiments. On the other hand, our another computer experiments with the same facilities show that it takes about 0.07 seconds to cryptanalyze the plain MI with $k = 30$ by the GB attack. Since plain MI with $k = 30$ was cryptanalyzed within about 0.07 seconds under our environment, it would be estimated that the perturbation by internal or NLPHPV enhances the F_4 time complexity by about 10^4 times. This fact shows that the internal perturbation method and the NLPHPV method enhance the security of MI against the GB attack.

We now consider the applicability of the internal perturbation method and the NLPHPV method. The internal perturbation method requires q^r times decryption complexity of the original MPKC. On the other hand, the NLPHPV method requires at most a few times decryption complexity of the original MPKC regardless of the value of q. Though the application of the NLPHPV method requires the increase of cipher text size, in terms of the decryption time, the NLPHPV method seems to be a possible alternative to the internal perturbation method in the enhancement of the security against the GB attack.

Remark 2. In the above, we only dealt with the case that no random variable was introduced. For the purpose of enhancing the security further, it is possible to introduce random variables. As shown in Appendix A, the increase of the number $z - p$ of random variables $x_{p+1}, \ldots, x_z$ increases the time required for the GB attack against the enhanced cryptosystem $\widetilde{\mathcal{K}}$ and provides substantial security against the GB attack.

5 Discussion on Security

In this section, we discuss the security of the NLPHPV method against major known attacks. The main purpose of this section is to enclose the secure parameter region of the NLPHPV method by both theoretical and experimental observations.

---

[3] The optimal choice of H is still open. We will clarify this point in the future work.

5.1   GB Attack

As stated in the previous section, based on computer experiments, the NLPHPV method properly provides substantial security, and enhances the security of the Matsumoto-Imai cryptosystem against the GB attack. In the case where the original MPKC is other than Matsumoto-Imai cryptosystem, or in the case where signature scheme is considered, we will clarify their security against the GB attack in the full version of this paper. A purely theoretical treatment of their security is also an issue in the future.

5.2   Rank Attack

In 2004 Wolf, Braeken, and Preneel [37] introduced an attack against a class of MPKCs, called *step-wise triangular schemes* (STS, for short), based on the rank calculation of the public key (see also [1, 10, 23]). On the other hand, recently, Ito, Fukushima, and Kaneko [11] proposed an attack against the MPKC which is obtained by applying the linear PH matrix method to the sequential solution method as an original MPKC. Their attack makes use of an STS-like structure of the MPKC.

In fact, the structure of the public key of the NLPHPV method can be seen as a gSTS (general step-wise triangular structure) [37]. The detailed description is given below. Let $A' = \begin{pmatrix} C \\ \begin{matrix} I_p & 0 \\ 0 & A & 0 \end{matrix} \\ R \end{pmatrix} \in \mathbf{F}_q{}^{z \times z}$ be an invertible matrix, where A, C are as in Section 3, I_p is the identity matrix in $\mathbf{F}_q{}^{p \times p}$, and R is a specific matrix in $\mathbf{F}_q{}^{(z-k-f) \times z}$. For A', we define $\boldsymbol{x}' = (x_1', \ldots, x_f', \ldots, x_{f+k}', \ldots, x_z')^T \underset{\mathrm{def}}{=} A' \begin{pmatrix} \boldsymbol{x} \\ \boldsymbol{\lambda} \end{pmatrix}$, where $\boldsymbol{x}$, $\boldsymbol{\lambda}$ are as in Section 3. Let $\boldsymbol{x}_1' = (x_1', \ldots, x_f')^T$, $\boldsymbol{x}_2' = (x_{f+1}', \ldots, x_{f+k}')^T$, and $\boldsymbol{x}_3' = (x_{f+k+1}', \ldots, x_z')^T$ be parts of $\boldsymbol{x}'$. Then, $\boldsymbol{x}_1' = C \begin{pmatrix} \boldsymbol{x} \\ \boldsymbol{\lambda} \end{pmatrix}$, $\boldsymbol{x}_2' = \begin{pmatrix} \boldsymbol{x} \\ A\boldsymbol{\mu} \end{pmatrix}$, where $\boldsymbol{\mu}$ is as in Section 3. We denote $\boldsymbol{H} = (h_1, \ldots, h_l)^T \in \mathbf{F}_q[x_1, \ldots, x_f]^l$, $\boldsymbol{Q} = (q_1, \ldots, q_n)^T \in \mathbf{F}_q[x_1, \ldots, x_f]^n$, $\boldsymbol{E} = (e_1, \ldots, e_n)^T \in \mathbf{F}_q[x_1, \ldots, x_k]^n$, where $\boldsymbol{H}$, $\boldsymbol{Q}$, and $\boldsymbol{E}$ are as in Section 3. By substitution of $\boldsymbol{x}_1'$ for the variables in $\boldsymbol{H}$, we obtain $\boldsymbol{H}(\boldsymbol{x}_1')$, which is equal to $\boldsymbol{H}(\boldsymbol{f})$ in (1). Similarly, $\boldsymbol{Q}(\boldsymbol{x}_1')$ and $\boldsymbol{E}(\boldsymbol{x}_2')$ are equal to $\boldsymbol{Q}(\boldsymbol{f})$ and $\boldsymbol{E} \begin{pmatrix} \boldsymbol{x} \\ A\boldsymbol{\mu} \end{pmatrix}$ in (1), respectively. We define $\boldsymbol{r}' = (r_1', \ldots, r_h')^T \underset{\mathrm{def}}{=} \boldsymbol{r} \left((A')^{-1} \boldsymbol{X} \right) \in \mathbf{F}_q[x_1, \ldots, x_z]^h$, where $\boldsymbol{X} = (x_1, \ldots, x_z)^T \in \mathbf{F}_q[x_1, \ldots, x_z]^z$ and $\boldsymbol{r}$ is as in Section 3. Then, $\boldsymbol{r}'(\boldsymbol{x}') = \boldsymbol{r} \left((A')^{-1} A' \begin{pmatrix} \boldsymbol{x} \\ \boldsymbol{\lambda} \end{pmatrix} \right) = \boldsymbol{r} \begin{pmatrix} \boldsymbol{x} \\ \boldsymbol{\lambda} \end{pmatrix} = \boldsymbol{r}$.

Using $\boldsymbol{H}(\boldsymbol{x}_1')$, $\boldsymbol{Q}(\boldsymbol{x}_1')$, $\boldsymbol{E}(\boldsymbol{x}_2')$, and $\boldsymbol{r}'(\boldsymbol{x}')$ above, we construct the gSTS corresponding to (1) as follows:

$$\text{Step 1} \begin{cases} y'_1 = h_1(x'_1, \ldots, x'_f), \\ \quad \vdots \\ y'_l = h_l(x'_1, \ldots, x'_f), \end{cases}$$
$$\text{Step 2} \begin{cases} y'_{l+1} = q_1(x'_1, \ldots, x'_f) + e_1(x'_{f+1}, \ldots, x'_{f+k}), \\ \quad \vdots \\ y'_{l+n} = q_n(x'_1, \ldots, x'_f) + e_n(x'_{f+1}, \ldots, x'_{f+k}), \end{cases} \tag{2}$$
$$\text{Step 3} \begin{cases} y'_{l+n+1} = r'_1(x'_1, \ldots, x'_f, \ldots, x'_{f+k}, \ldots, x'_z), \\ \quad \vdots \\ y'_g = r'_h(x'_1, \ldots, x'_f, \ldots, x'_{f+k}, \ldots, x'_z). \end{cases}$$

We denote $y' = (y'_1, \ldots, y'_g)^T$. Then, $\widetilde{E} = By'$, where $\widetilde{E}$, B are as in Section 3.

In this gSTS, the number of layers is 3, the numbers of new variables (step-width) are f, k, $z - k - f$, and the numbers of equations (step-height) are l, n, h, respectively. This structure may bring down undesirable vulnerability against the rank attack. In the following, we discuss the security of the NLPHPV method against two rank attacks; high rank attack and low rank attack.

High Rank Attack. In the high rank attack against the gSTS, to separate the part of Step 3 in (2) from the public key, the attacker searches vectors $v = (v_1, \ldots, v_g)^T \in \mathbf{F}_q{}^g$. The vectors form together an invertible matrix whose row is a row of the secret key B^{-1} or its linear equivalent copy, since multiplying B^{-1} to the public key $\widetilde{E}$ separates their layers. The attacker can find each of the vectors v with a probability $1/q^h$ by checking whether

$$\text{rank} \left(\sum_{i=1}^{g} v_i P_i \right) \leq f + k,$$

for randomly chosen $v_1, \ldots v_g \in \mathbf{F}_q$, where P_i are matrices, in a quadratic form, of the public key polynomial vector $\widetilde{E} = (\widetilde{e}_1, \ldots, \widetilde{e}_g)^T = (X^T P_1 X, \ldots, X^T P_g X)^T$, with $X = (x_1, \ldots, x_z)^T \in \mathbf{F}_q[x_1, \ldots, x_z]^z$.

One of the simple countermeasures is to make the step-height of Step 3 thick, i.e., to make the number h of polynomials in the randomly chosen polynomial vector r in the NLPHPV method large. If q^h is large enough, the probability $1/q^h$ becomes negligible. However, larger h loses efficiency of cryptosystem in signature scheme as mentioned in Section 3.

In the case that h is not too large, one of the countermeasures against the weakness is to combine Step 2 with Step 3, i.e., to set $f + k = z$. Then, both on Step 2 and on Step 3 in (2), the rank is $z = f + k$, and the difference of the rank between these steps disappears. Also, the combination of Step 2 and Step 3 replaces the probability $1/q^h$ by $1/q^{n+h}$. In the case where n is large enough, this probability becomes negligible, and therefore the high rank attack could be intractable.

Low Rank Attack. In the low rank attack against the gSTS, the attacker can find $w = (w_1, \ldots, w_g)^T \in \mathbf{F}_q{}^z$ with a probability $1/q^f$ by checking whether the unknown $v = (v_1, \ldots, v_g)$ has f solutions in equation

$$\left(\sum_{i=1}^{g} v_i P_i \right) w = 0,$$

for randomly chosen $w_1, \ldots w_g \in \mathbf{F}_q$.

One of the countermeasures against the weakness is to widen the step-width of Step 1, i.e., to choose f to be large enough. Then, the probability $1/q^f$ becomes small, and therefore the low rank attack could be intractable.

5.3 Differential Attack

In 2005 Fouque, Granboulan, and Stern [9] adapted the differential cryptanalysis to MPKCs in order to break MI and its variant, called PMI [3]. In the differential attack, the attacker tries to find $v = (v_1, \ldots, v_z)^T \in \mathbf{F}_q{}^z$ such that $\dim (\ker (L_v)) = \delta$, where $L_v \in \mathbf{F}_q{}^{z \times z}$, $L_v X = \widetilde{E}(X + v) - \widetilde{E}(X) - \widetilde{E}(v) + \widetilde{E}(0)$, $X = (x_1, \ldots, x_z)^T \in \mathbf{F}_q[x_1, \ldots, x_z]^z$, and δ is a specific value.

We confirmed, by computer experiments, that the dimensions of the kernel in the NLPHPV method are the same in almost all cases. Moreover, note that the differential cryptanalysis might be applied only to Matsumoto-Imai type cryptosystems and the application of Plus method might recover their security against the cryptanalysis [6]. In the NLPHPV method proposed in this paper, the original MPKC $\mathcal{K}$ can be chosen to be any MPKC, not limited to Matsumoto-Imai type cryptosystems, and the NLPHPV method has a structure like Plus method. Thus, the NLPHPV method might be immune against the differential cryptanalysis. We will clarify this point in the future work.

6 Consideration on Secure Parameter Setting

Based on the discussion on the security in the previous section, we suggest a secure parameter setting of the NLPHPV method in Table 3.

Table 3. Parameter Setting

	Parameters										Public Key Size
	q	p	k	n	z	g	f	l	h	t	
Encryption scheme	256		260	260							8.89 MB
The enhanced encryption scheme by the NLPHPV method	256	256	260	260	420	300	20	20	20	82	26.65 MB
Signature scheme	256		30	20							9.92 KB
The enhanced signature scheme by the NLPHPV method	256		30	20	50	30	20				39.78 KB

In recently proposed major MPKCs, public key sizes for encryption schemes are 175 KB in PMI+ [6] and 160.2 KB in ℓIC i+ [7], and for signature schemes 15 KB in Rainbow [4] and 9.92 KB in ℓIC- [7]. The main purpose of these schemes is to implement them on small devices with limited computing resources. On the other hand, we assume the situation in the future when quantum computers appear, and place much more value on the security than the efficiency, such as the reduction of key size. Let us consider the security level of the quantum computer age where quantum computers are available. Then, the simple application of the Grover's algorithm to exhaustive search of 2^N candidates reduces the time complexity $O(2^N)$ to $O(\sqrt{2^N})$. On the other hand, nowadays, the exhaustive search of 2^{80} candidates is thought to be impossible and the complexity 2^{80} is selected as the standard security level in present cryptographic community. Therefore, we assume that the security level of the quantum computer age is greater than the complexity 2^{160}. Note that we omit the evaluation of the size of secret key below. This is because the size of secret key of a MPKC is much smaller than that of public key and different in various MPKCs.

6.1   Encryption Scheme

The plain text size is 2048 bits. Information transmission rate (i.e., the size of plain text divided by the size of cipher text) is $256/300 \approx 0.853$. The public key size increases about 3 times from the original encryption scheme. In the original encryption scheme, the numbers of plain text and cipher text variables are 260.

In the high rank attack against this scheme, the probability with which the attacker finds each of the vectors v is $1/q^h$. Therefore, the attack complexity of the high attack is $q^h = 2^{160}$ on average. On the other hand, in the low rank attack, the probability with which the attacker finds w is $1/q^f$. Therefore, the attack complexity of the low rank attack is $q^f = 2^{160}$ on average. For these reasons, these rank attacks are intractable. Also, since $\binom{z-p}{t} = \binom{164}{82} \approx 2^{160}$, it is also intractable to distinguish random variables.

6.2   Signature Scheme

The signature size is 400 bits. In the original signature scheme, the number of input variables is 20, and 30 output variables. The public key size increases about 4 times from the original signature scheme.

In the high rank attack against this scheme, the probability with which the attacker finds each of the vectors v is $1/q^{n+h}$ not $1/q^h$, since $z = f + k$ as noted in Subsection 5.2. Therefore, the attack complexity of the high rank attack is $q^{n+h} > q^n = 2^{720}$. On the other hand, in the low rank attack, the probability with which the attacker finds w is $1/q^f$. Therefore, the attack complexity of the low rank attack is $q^f = 2^{160}$ on average. For these reasons, these rank attacks are intractable.

7   Concluding Remarks

In this paper, we proposed a new class of PH methods called NonLinear Piece in Hand Perturbation Vector (NLPHPV) method. NLPHPV is more efficient than previously known internal perturbation methods in terms of the decryption process avoiding redundant repetitive steps. Based on computer experiments, we have shown the enhancement of the security of the Matsumoto-Imai cryptosystem by the method against the Gröbner basis attack. Then, by considering the security against known other attacks, we have suggested a secure parameter setting of the NLPHPV method for the quantum computer age. From the practical view point of current interest, it is also important to evaluate the efficiency of both encryption and decryption in the cryptosystem enhanced by the method. However, since the aim of the present paper is mainly to develop the framework of nonlinear PH matrix methods as a potential countermeasure against the advent of quantum computers in the future, this practical issue is not considered in this paper but discussed in another paper. Because of the same reason, we have not considered some provable security, for example IND-CCA of the class of PH methods for encryption but considered just the encryption primitive $\widetilde{E}$ for an MPKC which is obtained by applying the NLPHPV method. We leave the consideration of the stronger security to a future study.

Acknowledgments

The authors are grateful to Dr. Tomohiro Harayama and Mr. Masahito Gotaishi for helpful discussions and comments.

This work is supported by the "Strategic information and COmmunications R&D Promotion programmE" (SCOPE) from the Ministry of Internal Affairs and Communications of Japan.

References

1. Coppersmith, D., Stern, J., Vaudenay, S.: Attacks on the birational permutation signature schemes. In: Stinson, D.R. (ed.) CRYPTO 1993. LNCS, vol. 773, pp. 435–443. Springer, Heidelberg (1994)
2. Courtois, N., Klimov, A., Patarin, J., Shamir, A.: Efficient algorithms for solving overdefined systems of multivariate polynomial equations. In: Preneel, B. (ed.) EUROCRYPT 2000. LNCS, vol. 1807, pp. 392–407. Springer, Heidelberg (2000)
3. Ding, J.: A new variant of the Matsumoto-Imai cryptosystem through perturbation. In: Bao, F., Deng, R., Zhou, J. (eds.) PKC 2004. LNCS, vol. 2947, pp. 305–318. Springer, Heidelberg (2004)
4. Ding, J., Schmidt, D.: Rainbow, a new multivariable polynomial signature scheme. In: Ioannidis, J., Keromytis, A., Yung, M. (eds.) ACNS 2005. LNCS, vol. 3531, pp. 164–175. Springer, Heidelberg (2005)
5. Ding, J., Gower, J.E., Schmidt, D., Wolf, C., Yin, Z.: Complexity estimates for the F4 attack on the perturbed Matsumoto-Imai cryptosystem. In: Smart, N. (ed.) Cryptography and Coding 2005. LNCS, vol. 3796, pp. 262–277. Springer, Heidelberg (2005)

6. Ding, J., Gower, J.E.: Inoculating multivariate schemes against differential attacks. In: Yung, M., Dodis, Y., Kiayias, A., Malkin, T. (eds.) PKC 2006. LNCS, vol. 3958, pp. 290–301. Springer, Heidelberg (2006)

7. Ding, J., Wolf, C., Yang, B.Y.: ℓ-Invertible Cycles for $\mathcal{M}$ultivariate $\mathcal{Q}$uadratic ($\mathcal{MQ}$) public key cryptography. In: Okamoto, T., Wang, X. (eds.) PKC 2007. LNCS, vol. 4450, pp. 266–281. Springer, Heidelberg (2007)

8. Faugère, J.C., Joux, A.: Algebraic cryptanalysis of hidden field equation (HFE) cryptosystems using Gröbner bases. In: Boneh, D. (ed.) CRYPTO 2003. LNCS, vol. 2729, pp. 44–60. Springer, Heidelberg (2003)

9. Fouque, P.A., Granboulan, L., Stern, J.: Differential cryptanalysis for multivariate schemes. In: Cramer, R. (ed.) EUROCRYPT 2005. LNCS, vol. 3494, pp. 341–353. Springer, Heidelberg (2005)

10. Goubin, L., Courtois, N.: Cryptanalysis of the TTM cryptosystem. In: Okamoto, T. (ed.) ASIACRYPT 2000. LNCS, vol. 1976, pp. 44–57. Springer, Heidelberg (2000)

11. Ito, D., Fukushima, Y., Kaneko, T.: On the security of piece in hand concept based on sequential solution method. Technical Report of IEICE, ISEC2006-30, SITE2006-27 (2006-7) (July 2006) (in Japanese)

12. Kasahara, M., Sakai, R.: A new principle of public key cryptosystem and its realization. Technical Report of IEICE, ISEC2000-92 (2000-11) (November 2000) (in Japanese)

13. Kasahara, M., Sakai, R.: A construction of public key cryptosystem for realizing ciphertext of size 100 bit and digital signature scheme. IEICE Transactions on Fundamentals E87-A(1), 102–109 (2004)

14. Kasahara, M., Sakai, R.: A construction of public-key cryptosystem based on singular simultaneous equations. IEICE Transactions on Fundamentals E88-A(1), 74–80 (2005)

15. Kipnis, A., Patarin, J., Goubin, L.: Unbalanced Oil and Vinegar signature schemes. In: Stern, J. (ed.) EUROCRYPT 1999. LNCS, vol. 1592, pp. 206–222. Springer, Heidelberg (1999)

16. Kipnis, A., Shamir, A.: Cryptanalysis of the HFE public key cryptosystem by relinearization. In: Wiener, M. (ed.) CRYPTO 1999. LNCS, vol. 1666, pp. 19–30. Springer, Heidelberg (1999)

17. Matsumoto, T., Imai, H., Harashima, H., Miyakawa, H.: A class of asymmetric cryptosystems using obscure representations of enciphering functions. In: 1983 National Convention Record on Information Systems, IECE Japan, pp. S8-5 (1983) (in Japanese)

18. Matsumoto, T., Imai, H.: Public quadratic polynomial-tuples for efficient signature-verification and message-encryption. In: Günther, C.G. (ed.) EUROCRYPT 1988. LNCS, vol. 330, pp. 419–453. Springer, Heidelberg (1988)

19. Moh, T.T.: A public key system with signature and master key functions. Communications in Algebra 27, 2207–2222 (1999)

20. Patarin, J.: Cryptanalysis of the Matsumoto and Imai public key scheme of Eurocrypt 1988. In: Coppersmith, D. (ed.) CRYPTO 1995. LNCS, vol. 963, pp. 248–261. Springer, Heidelberg (1995)

21. Patarin, J.: Hidden fields equations (HFE) and isomorphisms of polynomials (IP): two new families of asymmetric algorithms. In: Maurer, U.M. (ed.) EUROCRYPT 1996. LNCS, vol. 1070, pp. 33–48. Springer, Heidelberg (1996)

22. Patarin, J., Goubin, L., Courtois, N.: C^*_{-+} and HM: Variations around two schemes of T. Matsumoto and H. Imai. In: Ohta, K., Pei, D. (eds.) ASIACRYPT 1998. LNCS, vol. 1514, pp. 35–49. Springer, Heidelberg (1998)

23. Shamir, A.: Efficient signature schemes based on birational permutations. In: Stinson, D.R. (ed.) CRYPTO 1993. LNCS, vol. 773, pp. 1–12. Springer, Heidelberg (1994)
24. Tadaki, K., Tsujii, S.: On the enhancement of security by piece in hand matrix method for multivariate public key cryptosystems. In: Proc. SCIS 2007, vol. 2C1-3 (2007)
25. Tsujii, S., Kurosawa, K., Itoh, T., Fujioka, A., Matsumoto, T.: A public-key cryptosystem based on the difficulty of solving a system of non-linear equations. IECE Transactions (D) J69-D(12), 1963–1970 (1986) (in Japanese)
26. Tsujii, S., Fujioka, A., Hirayama, Y.: Generalization of the public-key cryptosystem based on the difficulty of solving a system of non-linear equations. IEICE Transactions (A) J72-A(2), 390–397 (1989) (in Japanese) (An English translation of [26] is included in [29] as an appendix)
27. Tsujii, S.: A new structure of primitive public key cryptosystem based on soldiers in hand matrix. Technical Report TRISE 02-03, Chuo University (July 2003)
28. Tsujii, S., Fujita, R., Tadaki, K.: Proposal of MOCHIGOMA (piece in hand) concept for multivariate type public key cryptosystem. Technical Report of IEICE, ISEC2004-74 (2004-09) (September 2004)
29. Tsujii, S., Tadaki, K., Fujita, R.: Piece in hand concept for enhancing the security of multivariate type public key cryptosystems: public key without containing all the information of secret key. Cryptology ePrint Archive, Report 2004/366 (December 2004), http://eprint.iacr.org/2004/366
30. Tsujii, S., Tadaki, K., Fujita, R.: Piece in hand concept for enhancing the security of multivariate type public key cryptosystems: public key without containing all the information of secret key. In: Proc. SCIS 2005, vol. 2E1-3, pp. 487–492 (2005), http://lab.iisec.ac.jp/~tsujii/SCIS2005-2E1-3.pdf
31. Tsujii, S., Tadaki, K., Fujita, R.: Proposal for piece in hand (soldiers in hand) matrix — general concept for enhancing security of multivariate public key cryptosystems — Ver.2. In: Proc. SCIS 2006, vol. 2A4-1 (2006) (in Japanese), http://lab.iisec.ac.jp/~tsujii/SCIS2006-2A4-1.pdf
32. Tsujii, S., Tadaki, K., Fujita, R.: Proposal for piece in hand matrix ver.2: general concept for enhancing security of multivariate public key cryptosystems. In: Workshop Record of the International Workshop on Post-Quantum Cryptography (PQCrypto 2006), pp. 103–117 (2006), http://postquantum.cr.yp.to/pqcrypto2006record.pdf
33. Tsujii, S., Tadaki, K., Fujita, R.: Proposal for piece in hand matrix: general concept for enhancing security of multivariate public key cryptosystems. IEICE Transactions on Fundamentals E90-A(5), 992–999 (2007), http://lab.iisec.ac.jp/~tsujii/TTF07.pdf
34. Tsujii, S., Tadaki, K., Fujita, R.: Nonlinear piece in hand matrix method for enhancing security of multivariate public key cryptosystems. In: Proceedings of the First International Conference on Symbolic Computation and Cryptography (SCC 2008), pp. 124–144 (2008)
35. Wang, L.C., Hu, Y.H., Lai, F., Chou, C.Y., Yang, B.Y.: Tractable rational map signature. In: Vaudenay, S. (ed.) PKC 2005. LNCS, vol. 3386, pp. 244–257. Springer, Heidelberg (2005)
36. Wang, L.C., Yang, B.Y., Hu, Y.H., Lai, F.: A medium-field multivariate public-key encryption scheme. In: Pointcheval, D. (ed.) CT-RSA 2006. LNCS, vol. 3860, pp. 132–149. Springer, Heidelberg (2006)
37. Wolf, C., Braeken, A., Preneel, B.: Efficient cryptanalysis of RSE(2)PKC and RSSE(2)PKC. In: Blundo, C., Cimato, S. (eds.) SCN 2004. LNCS, vol. 3352, pp. 294–309. Springer, Heidelberg (2005)

38. Wolf, C., Preneel, B.: Taxonomy of Public Key Schemes based on the problem of Multivariate Quadratic equations. Cryptology ePrint Archive, Report 2005/077 (December 2005), http://eprint.iacr.org/2005/077

A   Experimental Results in NLPHPV Method with Random Variables

We report in Table 4 and Table 5 the time required for the GB attack against MPKC (MI or R-SE(2)PKC (RSE, for short)) and the MPKC enhanced by the NLPHPV method. Note that $n = k$ and $q = 2$ for the public keys $\boldsymbol{E} \in \mathbf{F}_q[x_1, \ldots, x_k]^n$ of MI and RSE by their specifications. Table 4 and Table 5 give the comparison of the particular case with a plain text of 15 bits (MI with $k = 15$ and the enhanced MI with $z = 47$, $g = 35$, or RSE with $k = 15$ and the enhanced RSE with $z = 44$, $g = 35$). This shows that the time required for cryptanalysis is increased by more than 10^5 times by the application of the NLPHPV method. This fact shows that the NLPHPV method enhances the security of MI and RSE against the GB attack. Table 4 and Table 5 show that the increase of the number $z - p$ of random variables $x_{p+1}, \ldots, x_z$ increases the time required for the GB attack against the enhanced cryptosystem $\widetilde{\mathcal{K}}$ and provides substantial security against the GB attack.

Table 4. Comparison between computational times of the GB attack for MI and the enhanced MI by the NLPHPV method

Cryptosystems	Parameters								Computational times in second
	p	k	z	g	f	l	h	t	
MI		15							$< 10^{-2}$
		20							0.01
		25							0.03
		30							0.07
		35							0.2
		40							0.4
		45							0.7
		50							1
		55							2
		60							4
The enhanced MI by the NLPHPV method	15	20	40	35	10	10	5	10	75
	15	20	43	35	10	10	5	10	129
	15	20	45	35	10	10	5	10	260
	15	20	46	35	10	10	5	10	320
	15	20	47	35	10	10	5	10	1029
	15	20	40	40	10	10	10	10	97
	15	20	43	40	10	10	10	10	161
	15	20	47	40	10	10	10	10	284
	15	20	48	40	10	10	10	10	495
	15	20	49	40	10	10	10	10	1077

Table 5. Comparison between computational times of the GB attack for RSE and the enhanced RSE by the NLPHPV method

Cryptosystems	Parameters								Computational times in second
	p	k	z	g	f	l	h	t	
RSE		15							0.01
		20							0.03
		25							0.1
		30							0.2
		35							0.5
		40							1
		45							2
		50							5
		55							9
		60							16
The enhanced RSE by the NLPHPV method	15	20	40	35	10	10	5	10	40
	15	20	41	35	10	10	5	10	71
	15	20	42	35	10	10	5	10	179
	15	20	43	35	10	10	5	10	713
	15	20	44	35	10	10	5	10	2791
	15	20	40	40	10	10	10	10	51
	15	20	42	40	10	10	10	10	82
	15	20	44	40	10	10	10	10	231
	15	20	45	40	10	10	10	10	877
	15	20	46	40	10	10	10	10	2327

On the Power of Quantum Encryption Keys

Akinori Kawachi and Christopher Portmann

Department of Mathematical and Computing Sciences, Tokyo Institute of
Technology, 2-12-1 Ookayama, Meguro-ku, Tokyo 152-8552, Japan
kawachi@is.titech.ac.jp, portmann.c.aa@m.titech.ac.jp

Abstract. The standard definition of quantum state randomization,
which is the quantum analog of the classical one-time pad, consists in
applying some transformation to the quantum message conditioned on a
classical secret key k. We investigate encryption schemes in which this
transformation is conditioned on a quantum encryption key state ρ_k instead of a classical string, and extend this symmetric-key scheme to an
asymmetric-key model in which copies of the same encryption key ρ_k
may be held by several different people, but maintaining information-
theoretical security. We find bounds on the message size and the number
of copies of the encryption key which can be safely created in these two
models in terms of the entropy of the decryption key, and show that the
optimal bound can be asymptotically reached by a scheme using classical
encryption keys. This means that the use of quantum states as encryption keys does not allow more of these to be created and shared, nor
encrypt larger messages, than if these keys are purely classical.

1 Introduction

1.1 Quantum Encryption

To encrypt a quantum state σ, the standard procedure consists in applying some
(unitary) transformation U_k to the state, which depends on a classical string k.
This string serves as secret key, and anyone who knows this key can perform the
reverse operation and obtain the original state. If the transformations $U_1, U_2, \ldots$
are chosen with probabilities $p_1, p_2, \ldots$, such that when averaged over all possible
choices of key,

$$\mathcal{R}(\sigma) = \sum_k p_k U_k \sigma U_k^\dagger, \tag{1}$$

the result looks random, i.e., close to the fully mixed state, $\mathcal{R}(\sigma) \approx \mathbb{I}/d$, this
cipher can safely be transmitted on an insecure channel. This procedure is called
approximate quantum state randomization or *approximate quantum one-time
pad* [1, 2, 3] or *quantum one-time pad, quantum Vernam cipher* or *quantum
private channel* in the case of perfect security [4, 5, 6], and is the quantum
equivalent of the classical one-time pad.

An encryption scheme which uses such a randomization procedure is called
symmetric, because the same key is used to encrypt and decrypt the message.

J. Buchmann and J. Ding (Eds.): PQCrypto 2008, LNCS 5299, pp. 165–180, 2008.
© Springer-Verlag Berlin Heidelberg 2008

An alternative paradigm is *asymmetric-key cryptography*, in which a different key is used for encryption and decryption. In such a cryptosystem the encryption key may be shared amongst many different people, because possessing this key is not sufficient to perform the reverse operation, decryption. This can be seen as a natural extension of symmetric-key cryptography, because this latter corresponds to the special case in which the encryption and decryption keys are identical and can be shared with only one person.

Although the encryption model given in Eq. (1) is symmetric, by replacing the classical encryption key with a quantum state we can make it asymmetric. To see this, let us rewrite Eq. (1) as

$$\mathcal{R}(\sigma) = \sum_k p_k \operatorname{tr}_K \left[U \left(|k\rangle\langle k|^K \otimes \sigma^S \right) U^\dagger \right], \tag{2}$$

where $U := \sum_k |k\rangle\langle k| \otimes U_k$. The encryption key in Eq. (2), $|k\rangle\langle k|$, is diagonal in the computational basis, i.e., classical, but an arbitrary quantum state, ρ_k, could be used instead, e.g.,

$$\mathcal{R}(\sigma) = \sum_k p_k \operatorname{tr}_K \left[U \left(\rho_k^K \otimes \sigma^S \right) U^\dagger \right], \tag{3}$$

for some set of quantum encryption keys $\{\rho_k\}_k$.

If the sender only holds such a quantum encryption key state ρ_k without knowing the corresponding decryption key k, then the resulting model is asymmetric in the sense that possessing this copy of the encryption key state is enough to perform the encryption, but not to decrypt. So many different people can hold copies of the encryption key without compromising the security of the scheme. It is generally impossible to distinguish between non-orthogonal quantum states with certainty (we refer to the textbook by Nielsen and Chuang [7] for an introduction to quantum information), so measuring a quantum state cannot tell us precisely what it is, and possessing a copy of the encryption key state does not allow us to know how the quantum message got transformed, making it impossible to guess the message, except with exponentially small probability.

Up to roughly $\log N$ copies of a state can be needed to discriminate between N possible states [8], so such a scheme could allow the same encryption key to be used several times, if multiple copies of this quantum key state are shared with any party wishing to encrypt a message. The scheme will stay secure as long as the number of copies created stays below a certain threshold. What is more, the security which can be achieved is information-theoretic like for standard quantum state randomization schemes [9], not computational like most asymmetric-key encryption schemes.

Such an asymmetric-key cryptosystem is just a possible application of a quantum state randomization scheme which uses quantum keys. It is also interesting to study quantum state randomization with quantum keys for itself (in the symmetric-key model), without considering other parties holding extra copies of the same encryption key. In this paper we study these schemes in both the symmetric-key and asymmetric-key models, and compare their efficiency in terms of message size and number of usages of the same encryption key to quantum state randomization schemes which use only classical keys.

1.2 Related Work

Quantum one-time pads were first proposed in [4, 5] for perfect security, then approximate security was considered in, e.g., [1, 2, 3]. All these schemes assume the sender and receiver share some secret classical string which is used only once to perform the encryption. We extend these models in the symmetric-key case by conditioning the encryption operation on a quantum key and considering security with multiple uses of the same key, and then in the asymmetric-key case by considering security with multiple users holding copies of the same encryption key.

The first scheme using quantum keys in an asymmetric-key model was proposed by Kawachi et al. [10], although they considered the restricted scenario of classical messages. Their scheme can encrypt a 1 bit classical message, and their security proof is computational, as it reduces the task of breaking the scheme to a graph automorphism problem. They extended their scheme to a multi-bit version [11], but without security proof. Hayashi et al. [9] then gave an information-theoretical security proof for [11]. The quantum asymmetric-key model we consider is a generalization and extension of that of [10, 11].

1.3 Main Contributions

The main result of this paper is that using quantum encryption keys has no advantage over classical keys with respect to the number of copies of the encryption key which can be safely created and to the size of the messages which can be encrypted, both in the symmetric and asymmetric-key models. Contrary to what was believed and motivated previous works with quantum keys, the intrinsic indistinguishability of quantum states does not allow more of these to be created and shared as encryption keys, than if these keys are purely classical.

To show this, we first find an upper bound on the quantum message size and on the number of copies of the encryption key which can be securely produced. We show that if t copies of the key are created and if the quantum messages encrypted are of dimension d, then they have to be such that $t \log d \lesssim \mathrm{H}(\mathcal{K})$ for the scheme to be secure, where $\mathrm{H}(\mathcal{K})$ is the entropy of the decryption key.

We then construct a quantum state randomization scheme and show that it meets this upper bound in both the symmetric and asymmetric-key models. The encryption keys this scheme uses are however all diagonal in the same bases, i.e., classical. This means that the scheme with classical keys is optimal in terms of message size and number of usages of the same key, and no scheme with quantum keys can perform better.

We also show how to extend quantum asymmetric-key encryption schemes for classical message (such as [11]) to encrypt quantum messages as well. To do this, we combine these schemes for classical messages with a standard quantum one-time pad, and prove that the resulting scheme is still secure.

1.4   Organization of the Paper

In Section 2 we develop the encryption models with quantum keys sketched in this introduction. We first redefine quantum state randomization schemes using quantum keys instead of classical keys in Section 2.1 and generalize the standard security definition for multiple usage of the same key in this symmetric-key model. In Section 2.2 we then show how to construct an asymmetric-key cryptosystem using such a quantum state randomization scheme with quantum keys and define its security. Section 2.3 contains a few notes about the special case of classical messages, which are relevant for the rest of the paper.

In Section 3 we find an upper bound on the message size and number of copies of the encryption key which can be created, both for the symmetric and asymmetric-key models.

In Section 4 we construct a quantum state randomization scheme which uses classical encryption keys, but which meets the optimality bounds for quantum keys from the previous section in both models. We give this construction in three steps. First in Section 4.1 we construct a scheme which can randomize classical messages only. Then in Section 4.2 we show how to combine this scheme for classical messages with a standard approximate quantum one-time pad to randomize any quantum state. And finally in Section 4.3 we calculate the key size of the scheme proposed and show that it corresponds to the bound found in Section 3.

We conclude in Section 5 with a brief summary and further comments about the results.

Technical proofs appear in Appendix A.

2   Encryption Model

2.1   Quantum Encryption Keys

Let us consider a setting in which we have two parties, a sender and a receiver, who wish to transmit a quantum state, σ, from one to the other in a secure way over an insecure channel. If they share a secret classical string, k, they can apply some completely positive, trace-preserving (CPTP) map $\mathcal{E}_k$ to the quantum message and send the cipher $\mathcal{E}_k(\sigma)$. If the key k was chosen with probability p_k, to any person who does not know this key the transmitted state is

$$\mathcal{R}(\sigma) = \sum_k p_k \mathcal{E}_k(\sigma), \qquad (4)$$

which will look random for "well chosen" maps $\mathcal{E}_k$. This is the most general from of quantum state randomization [6].

If instead the sender has a quantum state ρ_k, he can apply some CPTP map $\mathcal{E}$ to both the shared state and the quantum message, and send $\mathcal{E}(\rho_k \otimes \sigma)$. So for someone who does not know ρ_k the state sent is

$$\mathcal{R}(\sigma) = \sum_k p_k \mathcal{E}(\rho_k \otimes \sigma). \qquad (5)$$

It is clear that Eqs. (4) and (5) produce equivalent ciphers, because for every set of CPTP maps $\{\mathcal{E}_k\}_k$ there exists a map $\mathcal{E}$ and set of states $\{\rho_k\}_k$ such that for all messages σ, $\mathcal{E}_k(\sigma) = \mathcal{E}(\rho_k \otimes \sigma)$, and vice versa. The difference lies in the knowledge needed to perform the encryption. In the first case (Eq. (4)) the sender needs to know the secret key k to know which CPTP map $\mathcal{E}_k$ to apply. In the second case (Eq. (5)) the sender only needs to hold a copy of the encryption key ρ_k, he does not need to know what it is or what secret key k it corresponds to. This allows us to construct in Section 2.2 a quantum asymmetric-key cryptosystem in which copies of the same encryption key ρ_k can be used by many different users. In this section we focus on the symmetric-key model and define quantum state randomization (QSR) schemes with quantum encryption keys and their security in this model.

Definition 1. *Let $\mathcal{B}(\mathcal{H})$ denote the set of linear operators on $\mathcal{H}$.*

A quantum state randomization (QSR) scheme with quantum encryption keys consists of the following tuple,

$$\mathbb{T} = (P_\mathcal{K}, \{\rho_k\}_{k \in \mathcal{K}}, \mathcal{E}).$$

$\rho_k \in \mathcal{B}(\mathcal{H}_K)$ *are density operators on a Hilbert space $\mathcal{H}_K$. They are called* encryption keys *and are indexed by elements $k \in \mathcal{K}$ called* decryption keys.

$P_\mathcal{K}(\cdot)$ *is a probability distribution over the set of decryption keys $\mathcal{K}$, corresponding to the probability with which each en/decryption key-pair should be chosen.*

$\mathcal{E} : \mathcal{B}(\mathcal{H}_K \otimes \mathcal{H}_S) \to \mathcal{B}(\mathcal{H}_C)$, *is a completely positive, trace-preserving (CPTP) map from the set of linear operators on the joint system of encryption key and message Hilbert spaces, $\mathcal{H}_K$ and $\mathcal{H}_S$ respectively, to the set of linear operators on the cipher Hilbert space $\mathcal{H}_C$, and is called* encryption operator.

To encrypt a quantum message given by its density operator $\sigma \in \mathcal{B}(\mathcal{H}_S)$ with the encryption key ρ_k, the encryption operator is applied to the key and message, resulting in the cipher

$$\rho_{k,\sigma} := \mathcal{E}(\rho_k \otimes \sigma).$$

Definition 1 describes how to encrypt a quantum message, but for such a scheme to be useful, it must also be possible to decrypt the message for someone who knows which key k was used, i.e., it must be possible to invert the encryption operation.

Definition 2. *A QSR scheme given by the tuple $\mathbb{T} = (P_\mathcal{K}, \{\rho_k\}_{k \in \mathcal{K}}, \mathcal{E})$ is said to be* invertible *on the set $\mathcal{S} \subseteq \mathcal{B}(\mathcal{H}_S)$ if for every $k \in \mathcal{K}$ with $P_\mathcal{K}(k) > 0$ there exists a CPTP map $\mathcal{D}_k : \mathcal{B}(\mathcal{H}_C) \to \mathcal{B}(\mathcal{H}_S)$ such that for all density operators $\sigma \in \mathcal{S}$,*

$$\mathcal{D}_k \mathcal{E}(\rho_k \otimes \sigma) = \sigma.$$

Furthermore, a QSR scheme must – as its name says – randomize a quantum state. We define this in the same way as previous works on approximate quantum state randomization [1, 2, 3], by bounding the distance between the ciphers averaged over all possible choices of key and some state independent from the message. We however generalize this to encrypt t messages with the same key, because the asymmetric-key model we define Section 2.2 will need this. It is always possible to consider the case $t = 1$ in the symmetric-key model, if multiple uses of the same key are not desired.

We will use the trace norm as distance measure between two states, because it is directly related to the probability that an optimal measurement can distinguish between these two states, and is therefore meaningful in the context of eavesdropping. The trace norm of a matrix A is defined by $\|A\|_{\mathrm{tr}} := \mathrm{tr}\,|A| = \mathrm{tr}\,\sqrt{A^\dagger A}$, which is also equal to the sum of the singular values of A.

Definition 3. *A QSR scheme given by the tuple* $\mathbb{T} = (P_{\mathcal{K}}, \{\rho_k\}_{k \in \mathcal{K}}, \mathcal{E})$ *is said to be* (t, ϵ)*-randomizing on the set* $\mathcal{S} \subseteq \mathcal{B}(\mathcal{H}_S)$ *if there exists a density operator* $\tau \in \mathcal{B}\left(\mathcal{H}_C^{\otimes t}\right)$ *such that for all* t*-tuples of message density operators* $\omega = (\sigma_1, \ldots, \sigma_t) \in \mathcal{S}^{\times t}$

$$\|\mathcal{R}(\omega) - \tau\|_{tr} \leq \epsilon, \tag{6}$$

where $\mathcal{R}(\omega) = \sum_k P_{\mathcal{K}}(k)\rho_{k,\sigma_1} \otimes \cdots \otimes \rho_{k,\sigma_t}$ *and* $\rho_{k,\sigma_i} = \mathcal{E}(\rho_k \otimes \sigma_i)$.

2.2   Quantum Asymmetric-Key Cryptosystem

As announced in the previous section, the idea behind the quantum asymmetric-key cryptosystem model is that many different people hold a copy of some quantum state ρ_k which serves as encryption key, and anyone who wishes to send a message to the originator of the encryption keys uses a quantum state randomization scheme, as described in Definition 1. This is depicted in Section 1.

If the QSR scheme used to encrypt the messages is (t, ϵ)-randomizing and no more than t copies of the encryption key were released, an eavesdropper who intercepts the ciphers will not be able to distinguish them from some state independent from the messages, so not get any information about these messages. This is however not the only attack he may perform.

As we consider a scenario in which copies of the encryption key are shared between many different people, the adversary could hold one or many of them. If a total of t copies of the encryption key were produced and t_1 were used to encrypt messages $\omega = (\sigma_1, \ldots, \sigma_{t_1})$, in the worst case we have to assume that the adversary has the $t_2 := t - t_1$ remaining unused copies of the key. So his total state is

$$\rho_\omega^E := \sum_{k \in \mathcal{K}} P_{\mathcal{K}}(k)\rho_{k,\sigma_1} \otimes \cdots \otimes \rho_{k,\sigma_{t_1}} \otimes \rho_k^{\otimes t_2}, \tag{7}$$

where ρ_{k,σ_i} is the cipher of the message σ_i encrypted with the key ρ_k. This leads to the following security definition.

Definition 4. *We call a quantum asymmetric-key cryptosystem* (t, ϵ)*-indistinguishable on the set* $\mathcal{S} \subseteq \mathcal{B}(\mathcal{H}_S)$ *if for all* $t_1 \in \{0, 1, \ldots, t\}$, $t_2 := t - t_1$, *there exists a density operator* $\tau \in \mathcal{B}\left(\mathcal{H}_C^{\otimes t_1} \otimes \mathcal{H}_K^{\otimes t_2}\right)$ *such that for all* t_1*-tuples of message density operators* $\omega = (\sigma_1, \ldots, \sigma_{t_1}) \in \mathcal{S}^{\times t_1}$,

$$\left\|\rho_\omega^E - \tau\right\|_{tr} \leq \epsilon,$$

where ρ_ω^E *is the state the adversary obtains as defined in Eq. (7).*

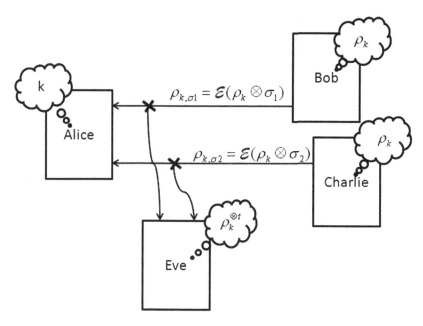

Fig. 1. *Quantum asymmetric-key cryptosystem model.* Bob and Charlie hold copies of Alice's encryption key ρ_k. To send her a message, they encrypt it with the key and a given QSR scheme, and send the resulting cipher to her. An eavesdropper, Eve, may intercept the ciphers as well as possess some copies of the encryption key herself.

Remark 1. Definition 4 is clearly more general than the security criteria of Definition 3 $((t, \epsilon)$-randomization) as this latter corresponds to the special case $t_1 = t$. However, for the scheme constructed in Section 4 the two are equivalent, and proving one proves the other. This is the case in particular if the encryption key is equal to the cipher of some specific message σ_0, i.e., $\rho_k = \rho_{k,\sigma_0} = \mathcal{E}(\rho_k \otimes \sigma_0)$, in which case holding an extra copy of the encryption key does not give more information about the decryption key than holding an extra cipher state.

2.3 Classical Messages

In the following sections we will also be interested in the special case of schemes which encrypt classical messages only. Classical messages can be represented by a set of mutually orthogonal quantum states, which we will take to be the basis states of the message Hilbert space and denote by $\{|s\rangle\}_{s \in \mathcal{S}}$. So these schemes must be invertible and randomizing on the set of basis states of the message Hilbert space.

When considering classical messages only, we will simplify the notation when possible and represent a message by a string s instead of by its density matrix $|s\rangle\langle s|$, e.g., the cipher of the message s encrypted with the key ρ_k is

$$\rho_{k,s} := \mathcal{E}\left(\rho_k \otimes |s\rangle\langle s|\right).$$

Remark 2. Definition 2 (invertibility) can be simplified when only classical messages are considered: a QSR scheme given by the tuple $\mathbb{T} = (P_\mathcal{K}, \{\rho_k\}_{k \in \mathcal{K}}, \mathcal{E})$ is invertible for the set of classical messages $\mathcal{S}$, if for every $k \in \mathcal{K}$ with $P_\mathcal{K}(k) > 0$ the ciphers $\{\rho_{k,s}\}_{s \in \mathcal{S}}$ are mutually orthogonal, where $\rho_{k,s} := \mathcal{E}(\rho_k \otimes |s\rangle\langle s|)$ for some orthonormal basis $\{|s\rangle\}_{s \in \mathcal{S}}$ of the message Hilbert space $\mathcal{H}_S$.

We will also use a different but equivalent definition to measure how well a scheme can randomize a message when dealing with classical messages. This new security criteria allows us to simplify some proofs.

Definition 5. *A QSR scheme given by the tuple* $\mathbb{T} = (P_\mathcal{K}, \{\rho_k\}_{k \in \mathcal{K}}, \mathcal{E})$ *is said to be* (t, ϵ)*-secure for the set of classical messages* $\mathcal{S}$ *if for all probability distributions* $P_{\mathcal{S}^t}(\cdot)$ *over the set of t-tuples of messages* $\mathcal{S}^{\times t}$,

$$\left\| \rho^{S^t C^t} - \rho^{S^t} \otimes \rho^{C^t} \right\|_{tr} \le \epsilon, \tag{8}$$

where $\rho^{S^t C^t}$ *is the state of the joint systems of t-fold message and cipher Hilbert spaces, and* ρ^{S^t} *and* ρ^{C^t} *are the result of tracing out the cipher respectively message systems. I.e.,*

$$\rho^{S^t C^t} = \sum_{s \in \mathcal{S}^{\times t}} P_{\mathcal{S}^t}(s) |s\rangle\langle s| \otimes \sum_{k \in \mathcal{K}} P_\mathcal{K}(k) \rho_{k,s_1} \otimes \cdots \otimes \rho_{k,s_t},$$

$$\rho^{S^t} = \sum_{s \in \mathcal{S}^{\times t}} P_{\mathcal{S}^t}(s) |s\rangle\langle s|,$$

$$\rho^{C^t} = \sum_{s \in \mathcal{S}^{\times t}} P_{\mathcal{S}^t}(s) \sum_{k \in \mathcal{K}} P_\mathcal{K}(k) \rho_{k,s_1} \otimes \cdots \otimes \rho_{k,s_t},$$

where $s = (s_1, \ldots, s_t)$.

This security definition can be interpreted the following way. No matter what the probability distribution on the secret messages is – let the adversary choose it – the message and cipher spaces are nearly in product form, i.e., the cipher gives next to no information about the message.

The following lemma proves that this new security definition is equivalent to the previous one (Definition 3) up to a constant factor.

Lemma 1. *If a QSR scheme is* (t, ϵ)*-randomizing for a set of classical messages* $\mathcal{S}$, *then it is* $(t, 2\epsilon)$*-secure for* $\mathcal{S}$. *If a QSR scheme is* (t, ϵ)*-secure for a set of classical messages* $\mathcal{S}$, *then it is* $(t, 2\epsilon)$*-randomizing for* $\mathcal{S}$.

Proof. Immediate after writing out the definitions explicitly, using the triangle inequality for one direction and considering the distribution on the message tuples $P_{\mathcal{S}^t}(s_1) = P_{\mathcal{S}^t}(s_2) = 1/2$ for any $s_1, s_2 \in \mathcal{S}^{\times t}$ for the converse. $\square$

3   Lower Bounds on the Key Size

It is intuitively clear that the more copies of the encryption key state ρ_k are created, the more information the adversary gets about the decryption key $k \in \mathcal{K}$

and the more insecure the scheme becomes. As it turns out, the number of copies of the encryption key which can be safely used is directly linked to the size of the decryption key, i.e., the cardinality of the decryption key set $\mathcal{K}$.

Let us assume a QSR scheme with quantum encryption keys is used to encrypt classical messages of size m. Then if t copies of the encryption key state are released and used, the size of the total message encrypted with the same decryption key k is tm. We prove in this section that the decryption key has to be of the same size as the total message to achieve information-theoretical security, i.e., $\log |\mathcal{K}| \gtrsim tm$. In Section 4 we then give a scheme which reaches this bound asymptotically.

Theorem 1. *If a QSR scheme given by the tuple $\mathbb{T} = (P_\mathcal{K}, \{\rho_k\}_{k \in \mathcal{K}}, \mathcal{E})$ is invertible for the set of classical messages $\mathcal{S}$, then when t messages $(s_1, \ldots, s_t)$ are chosen from $\mathcal{S}$ with (joint) probability distribution $P_{\mathcal{S}^t}(s_1, \ldots, s_t)$ and encrypted with the same key,*

$$\left\| \rho^{S^t C^t} - \rho^{S^t} \otimes \rho^{C^t} \right\|_{tr} \geq \frac{H(\mathcal{S}^t) - H(\mathcal{K}) - 2}{4t \log |S|}, \tag{9}$$

where $H(\cdot)$ is the Shannon entropy and $\rho^{S^t C^t}$ is the state of the t-fold message and cipher systems:

$$\rho^{S^t C^t} = \sum_{s \in \mathcal{S}^{\times t}} P_{\mathcal{S}^t}(s) |s\rangle\langle s| \otimes \sum_{k \in \mathcal{K}} P_\mathcal{K}(k) \rho_{k,s_1} \otimes \cdots \otimes \rho_{k,s_t},$$

$$\rho^{S^t} = \sum_{s \in \mathcal{S}^{\times t}} P_{\mathcal{S}^t}(s) |s\rangle\langle s|, \tag{10}$$

$$\rho^{C^t} = \sum_{s \in \mathcal{S}^{\times t}} P_{\mathcal{S}^t}(s) \sum_{k \in \mathcal{K}} P_\mathcal{K}(k) \rho_{k,s_1} \otimes \cdots \otimes \rho_{k,s_t},$$

where $s = (s_1, \ldots, s_t)$.

Proof in Appendix A.1.

Corollary 1. *For a QSR scheme to be (t, ϵ)-randomizing or (t, ϵ)-indistinguishable, it is necessary that*

$$H(\mathcal{K}) \geq (1 - 8\epsilon) t \log d - 2, \tag{11}$$

where d is the dimension of the message Hilbert space $\mathcal{H}_S$ and $H(\mathcal{K})$ is the entropy of the decryption key.

Proof in Appendix A.2.

Remark 3. Approximate quantum one-time pad schemes usually only consider the special case in which the cipher has the same dimension as the message [1, 3]. A more general scenario in which an ancilla is appended to the message is however also possible. It was proven in [6] that for perfect security such an extended scheme needs a key of the same size as in the restricted scenario, namely $2 \log d$. Corollary 1 for $t = 1$ proves the same for approximate security, namely roughly $\log d$ bits of key are necessary, just as when no ancilla is present.

4   Near-Optimal Scheme

To simplify the presentation of the QSR scheme, we first define it for classical messages in Section 4.1, show that it is invertible and find a bound on t, the number of copies of the encryption key which can be released, for it to be (t, ϵ)-randomizing for an exponentially small ϵ. In Section 4.2 we extend the scheme to encrypt any quantum message of a given size, and show again that it is invertible and randomizing. And finally in Section 4.3 we calculate the size of the key necessary to encrypt a message of a given length, and show that it is nearly asymptotically equal to the lower bound found in Section 3.

4.1   Classical Messages

Without loss of generality, let the message space be of dimension $\dim \mathcal{H}_S = 2^m$. The classical messages can then be represented by strings of length m, $\mathcal{S} := \{0, 1\}^m$. We now define a QSR scheme which uses encryption key states of dimension $\dim \mathcal{H}_K = 2^{m+n}$, where n is a security parameter, i.e., the scheme will be (t, ϵ)-randomizing for $\epsilon = 2^{-\Theta(n)}$.

We define the set of decryption keys to be the set of all $(m \times n)$ binary matrices,

$$\mathcal{K} := \{0, 1\}^{m \times n}. \tag{12}$$

This set has size $|\mathcal{K}| = 2^{mn}$ and each key is chosen with uniform probability.

For every decryption key $A \in \mathcal{K}$ the corresponding encryption key is defined as

$$\rho_A := \frac{1}{2^n} \sum_{x \in \{0,1\}^n} |Ax, x\rangle\langle Ax, x|, \tag{13}$$

where Ax is the multiplication of the matrix A with the vector x.

The encryption operator $\mathcal{E} : \mathcal{B}(\mathcal{H}_K \otimes \mathcal{H}_S) \to \mathcal{B}(\mathcal{H}_C)$ consists in applying the unitary

$$U := \sum_{\substack{x \in \{0,1\}^n \\ s, y \in \{0,1\}^m}} |y \oplus s, x\rangle\langle y, x|^K |s\rangle\langle s|^S$$

and tracing out the message system S, i.e.,

$$\rho_{A,s} := \operatorname{tr}_S \left(U \left(\rho_k^K \otimes |s\rangle\langle s|^S \right) U^\dagger \right).$$

This results in the cipher for the message s being

$$\rho_{A,s} = \frac{1}{2^n} \sum_{x \in \{0,1\}^n} |Ax \oplus s, x\rangle\langle Ax \oplus s, x|. \tag{14}$$

These states are mutually orthogonal for different messages s so by Remark 2 this scheme is invertible.

We now show that this scheme is (t, ϵ)-randomizing for $\epsilon = 2^{-\delta n + 1}$ and $t = (1 - \delta)n$, $0 < \delta < 1$.

Theorem 2. *For the QSR scheme defined above in Eqs. (12), (13) and (14) there exists a density operator $\tau \in \mathcal{B}(\mathcal{H}_C^{\otimes t})$ such that for all t-tuples of messages $s = (s_1, \ldots, s_t) \in \mathcal{S}^{\times t}$, if $t = (1 - \delta)n$, $0 < \delta < 1$, then*

$$\|\gamma_s - \tau\|_{tr} \leq 2^{-\delta n + 1},$$

where γ_s is the encryption of s with this scheme averaged over all possible keys, i.e., $\gamma_s = \sum_{A \in \mathcal{K}} P_{\mathcal{K}}(A) \rho_{A, s_1} \otimes \cdots \otimes \rho_{A, s_t}$.

Proof in Appendix A.3.

Corollary 2. *An asymmetric-key cryptosystem using this QSR scheme is (t, ϵ)-indistinguishable (Definition 4) for $\epsilon = 2^{-\delta n + 1}$ and $t = (1 - \delta)n$, $0 < \delta < 1$.*

Proof. Immediate from Theorem 2 by noticing that $\rho_{A,0} = \rho_A$. □

4.2 Quantum Messages

We will now extend the encryption scheme given above to encrypt any quantum state, not only classical ones. To do this we will show how to combine a QSR scheme with quantum keys which is (t, ϵ_1)-randomizing for classical messages (like the one from Section 4.1) with a QSR scheme with classical keys which is $(1, \epsilon_2)$-randomizing for quantum states (which is the case of any standard QSR scheme, e.g., [1, 2, 3, 4, 5, 6]) to produce a QSR scheme which is $(t, \epsilon_1 + t\epsilon_2)$-randomizing. The general idea is to choose a classical key for the second scheme at random, encrypt the quantum message with this scheme, then encrypt the classical key with the quantum encryption key of the first scheme, and send both ciphers.

Theorem 3. *Let a QSR scheme with quantum keys be given by the tuple $\mathbb{T}_1 = (P_{\mathcal{K}}, \{\rho_k\}_{k \in \mathcal{K}}, \mathcal{E})$, where $\mathcal{E} : \mathcal{B}(\mathcal{H}_K \otimes \mathcal{H}_S) \to \mathcal{B}(\mathcal{H}_C)$, and let a QSR scheme with classical keys be given by the tuple $\mathbb{T}_2 = (P_{\mathcal{S}}, \{\mathcal{F}_s\}_{s \in \mathcal{S}})$, where $\mathcal{F}_s : \mathcal{B}(\mathcal{H}_R) \to \mathcal{B}(\mathcal{H}_D)$. We combine the two to produce the QSR scheme with quantum encryption keys given by $\mathbb{T}_3 = (P_{\mathcal{K}}, \{\rho_k\}_{k \in \mathcal{K}}, \mathcal{G})$, where $\mathcal{G} : \mathcal{B}(\mathcal{H}_K \otimes \mathcal{H}_R) \to \mathcal{B}(\mathcal{H}_C \otimes \mathcal{H}_D)$ is defined by*

$$\mathcal{G}(\rho_k \otimes \sigma) := \sum_{s \in \mathcal{S}} P_{\mathcal{S}}(s) \mathcal{E}\left(\rho_k \otimes |s\rangle\langle s|\right) \otimes \mathcal{F}_s(\sigma). \qquad (15)$$

If $\mathbb{T}_1$ forms a quantum asymmetric-key cryptosystem which is invertible and (t, ϵ_1)-indistinguishable (respectively randomizing) for the basis states of $\mathcal{H}_S$ and $\mathbb{T}_2$ is an invertible and $(1, \epsilon_2)$-randomizing QSR scheme for any state on $\mathcal{H}_R$, then $\mathbb{T}_3$ forms an invertible and $(t, \epsilon_1 + t\epsilon_2)$-indistinguishable (respectively randomizing) cryptosystem for all density operator messages on $\mathcal{H}_R$.

Proof in Appendix A.4.

4.3 Key Size

To construct the QSR scheme for quantum messages as described in Section 4.2 we combine the scheme for classical messages from Section 4.1 and the approximate one-time pad scheme of Dickinson and Nayak [3].

The scheme from Section 4.1 is (t, ϵ_1)-randomizing for $t = (1 - \delta)n$ and $\epsilon_1 = 2^{-\delta n + 1}$, and uses a key with entropy $\mathrm{H}(\mathcal{K}) = nm = (t + \log \frac{1}{\epsilon_1} + 1)m$. The scheme of Dickinson and Nayak [3] is $(1, \epsilon_2)$-randomizing and uses a key with entropy $m = \log d + \log \frac{1}{\epsilon_2} + 4$ to encrypt a quantum state of dimension d. So by combining these our final scheme is $(t, \epsilon_1 + t\epsilon_2)$-randomizing and uses a key with entropy

$$\mathrm{H}(\mathcal{K}) = (t + \log \frac{1}{\epsilon_1} + 1)(\log d + \log \frac{1}{\epsilon_2} + 4)$$

to encrypt t states of dimension d. By choosing ϵ_1 and ϵ_2 to be polynomial in $\frac{1}{t}$ and $\frac{1}{\log d}$ respectively, the key has size $\mathrm{H}(\mathcal{K}) = t \log d + o(t \log d)$, which nearly reaches the asymptotic optimality found in Eq. (11), namely $\mathrm{H}(\mathcal{K}) \geq (1 - 8\epsilon)t \log d - 2$. Exponential security can be achieved at the cost of a slightly reduced asymptotic efficiency. For $\epsilon_1 = 2^{-\delta_1 t}$ and $\epsilon_2 = d^{-\delta_2}$ for some small $\delta_1, \delta_2 > 0$, the key has size $\mathrm{H}(\mathcal{K}) = (1 + \delta_1)(1 + \delta_2)t \log d + o(t \log d)$.

5 Consequence for Quantum Keys

The scheme presented in Section 4 uses the encryption keys

$$\rho_A = \frac{1}{2^n} \sum_{x \in \{0,1\}^n} |Ax, x\rangle\langle Ax, x|, \tag{16}$$

for some $(m \times n)$-matrix decryption key A. Although these keys are written as quantum states using the bra-ket notation to fit in the framework for QSR schemes with quantum keys developed in the previous sections, the states from Eq. (16) are all diagonal in the computational basis. So they are classical and could have been represented by a classical random variable $\mathcal{X}_A$ which takes the value (Ax, x) with probability 2^{-n}.

This scheme meets the optimality bound on the key size from Section 3. This bound tells us that for a given set of decryption keys $\mathcal{K}$, no matter how the encryption keys $\{\rho_k\}_{k \in \mathcal{K}}$ are constructed, the number of copies of the encryption keys which can be created, t, and the dimension of the messages which can be encrypted, d, have to be such that $t \log d \lesssim \mathrm{H}(\mathcal{K})$ for the scheme to be information-theoretically secure. But this bound is met by a scheme using classical keys, hence no scheme using quantum keys can perform better. So using quantum keys in a QSR scheme has no advantage with respect to the message size and number of usages of the same key over classical keys.

This result applies to both the symmetric-key and asymmetric-key models as the optimality was shown with respect to both (t, ϵ)-randomization (Definition 3) and (t, ϵ)-indistinguishability (Definition 4), the security definitions for the symmetric-key and asymmetric-key models respectively.

References

1. Hayden, P., Leung, D., Shor, P.W., Winter, A.: Randomizing quantum states: Constructions and applications. Communications in Mathematical Physics 250, 371–391 (2004)
2. Ambainis, A., Smith, A.: Small pseudo-random families of matrices: Derandomizing approximate quantum encryption. In: Jansen, K., Khanna, S., Rolim, J., Ron, D. (eds.) RANDOM 2004 and APPROX 2004. LNCS, vol. 3122, pp. 249–260. Springer, Heidelberg (2004)
3. Dickinson, P., Nayak, A.: Approximate randomization of quantum states with fewer bits of key. In: AIP Conference Proceedings, vol. 864, pp. 18–36 (2006)
4. Boykin, P.O., Roychowdhury, V.: Optimal encryption of quantum bits. Physical Review A 67, 42317 (2003)
5. Ambainis, A., Mosca, M., Tapp, A., de Wolf, R.: Private quantum channels. In: FOCS 2000: Proceedings of the 41st Annual Symposium on Foundations of Computer Science, Washington, DC, USA, vol. 547. IEEE Computer Society, Los Alamitos (2000)
6. Nayak, A., Sen, P.: Invertible quantum operations and perfect encryption of quantum states. Quantum Information and Computation 7, 103–110 (2007)
7. Nielsen, M.A., Chuang, I.L.: Quantum Computation and Quantum Information. Cambridge University Press, Cambridge (2000)
8. Harrow, A.W., Winter, A.: How many copies are needed for state discrimination? quant-ph/0606131 (2006)
9. Hayashi, M., Kawachi, A., Kobayashi, H.: Quantum measurements for hidden subgroup problems with optimal sample complexity. Quantum Information and Computation 8, 345–358 (2008)
10. Kawachi, A., Koshiba, T., Nishimura, H., Yamakami, T.: Computational indistinguishability between quantum states and its cryptographic application. In: Cramer, R. (ed.) EUROCRYPT 2005. LNCS, vol. 3494, pp. 268–284. Springer, Heidelberg (2005)
11. Kawachi, A., Koshiba, T., Nishimura, H., Yamakami, T.: Computational indistinguishability between quantum states and its cryptographic application. Full version of [10], quant-ph/0403069 (2006)
12. Alicki, R., Fannes, M.: Continuity of quantum conditional information. Journal of Physics A: Mathematical and General 37, L55–L57 (2004)

A   Proofs

A.1   Proof of Theorem 1 in Section 3 on Page 173

A theorem by Alicki and Fanes [12] tells us that for any two states ρ^{AB} and σ^{AB} on the joint system $\mathcal{H}_{AB} = \mathcal{H}_A \otimes \mathcal{H}_B$ with $\delta := \|\rho^{AB} - \sigma^{AB}\|_{\mathrm{tr}} \leq 1$ and $d_A := \dim \mathcal{H}_A$,

$$\left| \mathrm{S}\left(\rho^{AB}|\rho^B\right) - \mathrm{S}\left(\sigma^{AB}|\sigma^B\right) \right| \leq 4\delta \log d_A + 2h\left(\delta\right), \tag{17}$$

where $\mathrm{S}\left(\rho^{AB}|\rho^B\right) := \mathrm{S}\left(\rho^{AB}\right) - \mathrm{S}\left(\rho^B\right)$ is the conditional Von Neumann entropy and $h(p) := p \log \frac{1}{p} + (1-p) \log \frac{1}{1-p}$ is the binary entropy. $h(\delta) \leq 1$, so from Eq. (17) we get

$$\left\| \rho^{AB} - \sigma^{AB} \right\|_{\mathrm{tr}} \geq \frac{\left| \mathrm{S}\left(\rho^{AB}|\rho^B\right) - \mathrm{S}\left(\sigma^{AB}|\sigma^B\right) \right| - 2}{4 \log d_A}.$$

By applying this to the left-hand side of Eq. (9) we obtain

$$\left\| \rho^{S^t C^t} - \rho^{S^t} \otimes \rho^{C^t} \right\|_{\mathrm{tr}} \geq \frac{\mathrm{S}\left(\rho^{S^t}\right) + \mathrm{S}\left(\rho^{C^t}\right) - \mathrm{S}\left(\rho^{S^t C^t}\right) - 2}{4t \log |\mathcal{S}|}.$$

To prove this theorem it remains to show that

$$\mathrm{S}\left(\rho^{S^t}\right) + \mathrm{S}\left(\rho^{C^t}\right) - \mathrm{S}\left(\rho^{S^t C^t}\right) \geq \mathrm{H}\left(\mathcal{S}^t\right) - \mathrm{H}\left(\mathcal{K}\right).$$

For this we will need the two following bounds on the Von Neumann entropy (see e.g, [7]):

$$\mathrm{S}\left(\sum_{x \in \mathcal{X}} p_x \rho_x\right) \geq \sum_{x \in \mathcal{X}} p_x \, \mathrm{S}\left(\rho_x\right),$$

$$\mathrm{S}\left(\sum_{x \in \mathcal{X}} p_x \rho_x\right) \leq \mathrm{H}\left(\mathcal{X}\right) + \sum_{x \in \mathcal{X}} p_x \, \mathrm{S}\left(\rho_x\right).$$

Equality is obtained in the second equation if the states $\{\rho_x\}_{x \in \mathcal{X}}$ are all mutually orthogonal. By using these bounds and Eq. (10) we see that

$$\mathrm{S}\left(\rho^{S^t C^t}\right) = \mathrm{H}\left(\mathcal{S}^t\right) + \sum_{s \in \mathcal{S}^{\times t}} P_{\mathcal{S}^t}(s) \, \mathrm{S}\left(\sum_{k \in \mathcal{K}} P_{\mathcal{K}}(k) \rho_{k,s_1} \otimes \cdots \otimes \rho_{k,s_t}\right)$$

$$\leq \mathrm{H}\left(\mathcal{S}^t\right) + \mathrm{H}\left(\mathcal{K}\right) + \sum_{\substack{s \in \mathcal{S}^{\times t} \\ k \in \mathcal{K}}} P_{\mathcal{K}}(k) P_{\mathcal{S}^t}(s) \, \mathrm{S}\left(\rho_{k,s_1} \otimes \cdots \otimes \rho_{k,s_t}\right),$$

$$\mathrm{S}\left(\rho^{S^t}\right) = \mathrm{H}\left(\mathcal{S}^t\right),$$

$$\mathrm{S}\left(\rho^{C^t}\right) \geq \sum_{k \in \mathcal{K}} P_{\mathcal{K}}(k) \, \mathrm{S}\left(\sum_{s \in \mathcal{S}^{\times t}} P_{\mathcal{S}^t}(s) \rho_{k,s_1} \otimes \cdots \otimes \rho_{k,s_t}\right)$$

$$= \mathrm{H}\left(\mathcal{S}^t\right) + \sum_{\substack{s \in \mathcal{S}^{\times t} \\ k \in \mathcal{K}}} P_{\mathcal{K}}(k) P_{\mathcal{S}^t}(s) \, \mathrm{S}\left(\rho_{k,s_1} \otimes \cdots \otimes \rho_{k,s_t}\right).$$

We have equality in the last line because the scheme is invertible on $\mathcal{S}$, i.e., by Definition 2 and Remark 2 the states $\{\rho_{k,s_1} \otimes \cdots \otimes \rho_{k,s_t}\}_{s_1,\ldots,s_t \in \mathcal{S}}$ are mutually orthogonal. By putting this all together we conclude the proof. $\qquad \square$

A.2   Proof of Corollary 1 in Section 3 on Page 173

Definition 5 says that for a scheme to be (t, ϵ)-secure we need

$$\left\| \rho^{S^t C^t} - \rho^{S^t} \otimes \rho^{C^t} \right\|_{\mathrm{tr}} \leq \epsilon$$

for all probability distributions P_{S^t}. So for the uniform distribution we get from Theorem 1 that for a scheme to be (t, ϵ)-secure we need

$$\mathrm{H}\left(\mathcal{K}\right) \geq (1 - 4\epsilon)t \log |\mathcal{S}| - 2.$$

By Lemma 1 we then have the condition

$$H\left(\mathcal{K}\right) \geq (1 - 8\epsilon)t \log |\mathcal{S}| - 2$$

for the scheme to be (t, ϵ)-randomizing for the classical messages $\mathcal{S}$. And as classical messages are a subset of quantum messages – namely an orthonormal basis of the message Hilbert space – this bound extends to the case of quantum messages on a Hilbert space of dimension $d_S = |\mathcal{S}|$.

As (t, ϵ)-randomization is a special case of (t, ϵ)-indistinguishability, namely for $t_1 = t$, it is immediate that this lower bound also applies to (t, ϵ)-indistinguishability. $\square$

A.3   Proof of Theorem 2 in Section 4.1 on Page 175

The τ in question is the fully mixed state $\tau = \frac{1}{2^{t(m+n)}}\mathbb{I}$. By writing γ_s with the values of the ciphers from Eq. (14) we get

$$\gamma_s = \frac{1}{2^{mn}2^{tn}} \sum_{\substack{A \in \{0,1\}^{m \times n} \\ x_1,\ldots,x_t \in \{0,1\}^n}} |\ldots, Ax_i \oplus s_i, x_i, \ldots \rangle\langle \ldots, Ax_i \oplus s_i, x_i, \ldots|.$$

A unitary performing bit flips can take γ_s to γ_r for any $s, r \in \mathcal{S}^t$, so

$$\left\| \gamma_s - \frac{1}{2^{t(m+n)}}\mathbb{I} \right\|_{\mathrm{tr}} = \left\| \gamma_r - \frac{1}{2^{t(m+n)}}\mathbb{I} \right\|_{\mathrm{tr}},$$

and it is sufficient to evaluate

$$\left\| \gamma_0 - \frac{1}{2^{t(m+n)}}\mathbb{I} \right\|_{\mathrm{tr}} = \sum_{e \in \mathrm{EVec}(\gamma_0)} \left| w_e - \frac{1}{2^{t(n+m)}} \right|, \tag{18}$$

where e are the eigenvectors of γ_0 and w_e the corresponding eigenvalues.

So we need to calculate the eigenvalues of

$$\gamma_0 = \frac{1}{2^{mn}2^{tn}} \sum_{\substack{A \in \{0,1\}^{m \times n} \\ x_1,\ldots,x_t \in \{0,1\}^n}} |Ax_1, x_1, \ldots, Ax_t, x_t\rangle\langle Ax_1, x_1, \ldots, Ax_t, x_t|. \tag{19}$$

Let us fix $x_1, \ldots, x_t$. It is immediate from the linearity of Ax that if exactly d of the vectors $\{x_i\}_{i=1}^t$ are linearly independent, then

$$\sum_{A \in \{0,1\}^{m \times n}} |Ax_1, x_1, \ldots, Ax_t, x_t\rangle\langle Ax_1, x_1, \ldots, Ax_t, x_t|$$

uniformly spans a space of dimension 2^{dm}, and for different values of $x_1, \ldots, x_t$ these subspaces are all mutually orthogonal. Let D_t be the random variable representing the number of independent vectors amongst t binary vectors of length n, when chosen uniformly at random, and let $P_{D_t}(d) = \Pr[D_t = d]$ be the probability that exactly d of these vectors are linearly independent. The matrix given in Eq. (19) then has exactly $2^{tn} P_{D_t}(d) 2^{dm}$ eigenvectors with eigenvalue $\frac{1}{2^{dm} 2^{tn}}$, for $0 \le d \le t$. The remaining eigenvectors have eigenvalue 0.

So Eq. (18) becomes

$$\sum_{e \in \text{EVec}(\rho_0^E)} \left| w_e - \frac{1}{2^{t(m+n)}} \right| = 2 \sum_{d=0}^{t} 2^{tn} P_{D_t}(d) 2^{dm} \left(\frac{1}{2^{dm} 2^{tn}} - \frac{1}{2^{t(m+n)}} \right)$$

$$= 2 \sum_{d=0}^{t} P_{D_t}(d) \left(1 - 2^{-(t-d)m} \right)$$

$$\le 2 \sum_{d=0}^{t-1} P_{D_t}(d) = 2(1 - P_{D_t}(t))$$

$$\le 2^{t-n+1}.$$

For $t = (1-\delta)n$, $0 < \delta < 1$, we have for all $s \in \mathcal{S}^t$, $\|\gamma_s - \tau\|_{\text{tr}} \le 2^{-\delta n + 1}$.   □

A.4   Proof of Theorem 3 in Section 4.2 on Page 175

The invertibility of the scheme formed with $\mathbb{T}_3$ is immediate. To prove the indistinguishability we need to show that for all $t_1 \in \{0, 1, \ldots, t\}$, $t_2 := t - t_1$, there exists a density operator $\tau \in \mathcal{B}\left(\mathcal{H}_C^{\otimes t_1} \otimes \mathcal{H}_K^{\otimes t_2} \otimes \mathcal{H}_D^{\otimes t_1}\right)$ such that for all t_1-tuples of message density operators $\omega = (\sigma_1, \ldots, \sigma_{t_1}) \in \mathcal{B}(\mathcal{H}_R)^{\times t_1}$, $\|\rho_\omega^E - \tau\|_{\text{tr}} \le \epsilon$, where $\rho_\omega^E = \sum_{k \in \mathcal{K}} P_{\mathcal{K}}(k) \mathcal{G}(\rho_k \otimes \sigma_1) \otimes \cdots \otimes \mathcal{G}(\rho_k \otimes \sigma_{t_1}) \otimes \rho_k^{t_2}$.

Let us write $\gamma_s := \sum_{k \in \mathcal{K}} P_{\mathcal{K}}(k) \rho_{k,s_1} \otimes \cdots \otimes \rho_{k,s_{t_1}} \otimes \rho_k^{\otimes t_2}$, where $s = (s_1, \ldots, s_{t_1})$ and $\rho_{k,s_i} = \mathcal{E}(\rho_k \otimes |s_i\rangle\langle s_i|)$, and $\mu_\sigma := \sum_{s \in \mathcal{S}} P_{\mathcal{S}}(s) \mathcal{F}_s(\sigma)$. And let τ_1 and τ_2 be the two states such that $\|\gamma_s - \tau_1\|_{\text{tr}} \le \epsilon_1$ and $\|\mu_\sigma - \tau_2\|_{\text{tr}} \le \epsilon_2$ for all s and σ respectively. We define $\delta_s := \gamma_s - \tau_1$ and $\tau := \tau_1 \otimes \tau_2^{\otimes t_1}$. Then by the triangle inequality and changing the order of the registers

$$\|\rho_\omega^E - \tau\|_{\text{tr}} \le \left\| \sum_{s \in \mathcal{S}^{\times t_1}} P_{\mathcal{S}^t}(s) \delta_s \otimes \mathcal{F}_{s_1}(\sigma_1) \otimes \cdots \otimes \mathcal{F}_{s_{t_1}}(\sigma_{t_1}) \right\|_{\text{tr}}$$

$$+ \left\| \tau_1 \otimes \mu_{\sigma_1} \otimes \cdots \otimes \mu_{\sigma_{t_1}} - \tau \right\|_{\text{tr}}$$

$$\le \sum_{s \in \mathcal{S}^{\times t_1}} P_{\mathcal{S}^t}(s) \|\delta_s\|_{\text{tr}} + \sum_{i=1}^{t_1} \|\mu_{\sigma_i} - \tau_2\|_{\text{tr}}$$

$$\le \epsilon_1 + t_1 \epsilon_2.$$

As (t, ϵ)-randomization is a special case of (t, ϵ)-indistinguishability, namely for $t_1 = t$, it is immediate that $\mathbb{T}_3$ is also $(t, \epsilon_1 + t\epsilon_2)$-randomizing.   □

Secure PRNGs from Specialized Polynomial Maps over Any $\mathbb{F}_q$

Feng-Hao Liu[1], Chi-Jen Lu[2], and Bo-Yin Yang[2]

[1] Department of Computer Science, Brown University, Providence RI, USA
fenghao@cs.brown.edu
[2] Institute of Information Science, Academia Sinica, Taipei, Taiwan
{cjlu,byyang}@iis.sinica.edu.tw

Abstract. Berbain, Gilbert, and Patarin presented QUAD, a pseudo random number generator (PRNG) at Eurocrypt 2006. QUAD (as PRNG and stream cipher) may be proved secure based on an interesting hardness assumption about the one-wayness of multivariate quadratic polynomial systems over $\mathbb{F}_2$.

The original BGP proof only worked for $\mathbb{F}_2$ and left a gap to general $\mathbb{F}_q$. We show that the result can be generalized to any arbitrary finite field $\mathbb{F}_q$, and thus produces a stream cipher with alphabets in $\mathbb{F}_q$.

Further, we generalize the underlying hardness assumption to specialized systems in $\mathbb{F}_q$ (including $\mathbb{F}_2$) that can be evaluated more efficiently. Barring breakthroughs in the current state-of-the-art for system-solving, a rough implementation of a provably secure instance of our new PRNG is twice as fast and takes 1/10 the storage of an instance of QUAD with the same level of provable security.

Recent results on specialization on security are also examined. And we conclude that our ideas are consistent with these new developments and complement them. This gives a clue that we may build secure primitives based on specialized polynomial maps which are more efficient.

Keywords: sparse multivariate polynomial map, PRNG, hash function, provable security.

1 Introduction

Cryptographers have used multivariate polynomial maps for primitives since Matsumoto-Imai [26] but there is a dearth of results proving security based on plausible hardness assumptions. Berbain, Gilbert and Patarin presented a breakthrough in Eurocrypt 2006, when they proposed a PRNG/stream cipher that is provably secure provided that the class of multivariate quadratic polynomials is probabilistically one way:

Class $\mathcal{MQ}(q, n, m)$: For given q, n, m, the class $\mathcal{MQ}(q, n, m)$ consists of all systems of m quadratic polynomials in $\mathbb{F}_q$ with n variables. To choose a random system $\mathbf{S}$ from $\mathcal{MQ}(q, n, m)$, we write each polynomial $P_k(\mathbf{x})$ as

J. Buchmann and J. Ding (Eds.): PQCrypto 2008, LNCS 5299, pp. 181–202, 2008.

$\sum_{1 \le i \le j \le n} a_{ijk} x_i x_j + \sum_{1 \le i \le n} b_{ik} x_k + c_k$, where every a_{ijk}, b_{ik}, c_k is chosen uniformly in $\mathbb{F}_q$.

Solving $\mathbf{S}(\mathbf{x}) = \mathbf{b}$ for any $\mathcal{MQ}$ system S is known as the "multivariate quadratic" problem.

It is often claimed that the NP-completeness of this problem [19] is the basis for multivariate public-key cryptosystems. We could take instead P_i's to be polynomials of degree d instead of quadratic and get the class of "multivariate polynomial systems" $\mathcal{MP}(q, d, n, m)$. This contains $\mathcal{MQ}(q, n, m)$ as a subset, so solving arbitrary $\mathbf{S}(\mathbf{x}) = \mathbf{b}$ for any $\mathcal{MP}$ system S would be no easier. However, it is not easy to base a proof on worst-case hardness; the premise used in [7] is the following average-case hardness assumption:

Assumption $\mathcal{MQ}$: Given any k and prime power q, for parameters n, m satisfying $m/n = k + o(1)$, no probabilistic polynomial-time algorithm can solve (in poly(n)-time) any fixed $\varepsilon > 0$ proportion of systems $\mathbf{S}$ drawn from $\mathcal{MQ}(q, n, m)$, and a vector $\mathbf{b} = (b_1, b_2, \ldots, b_m)$ drawn from $\mathbf{S}(U_n)$, where U_n is uniform distribution over $(\mathbb{F}_q)^n$ such that $\mathbf{S}(\mathbf{x}) = \mathbf{b}$.

With this premise, [7, Theorem 4] proved the QUAD PRNG secure over $\mathbb{F}_2$. *However, a looseness factor in its security argument in the security proof means that provably secure QUAD instances over $\mathbb{F}_2$ are not yet of practical speed. It also does not work for fields larger than $\mathbb{F}_2$. A similar result over any $\mathbb{F}_q$ is non-trivial to prove, which we do here with different and more involved techniques. However, instances of QUAD with the same-size state over larger fields are significantly less secure [33].* To increase the difficulty of solving a system of nonlinear polynomial equations, we can plausibly change (a) the field size q, (b) the number of variables n, or (c) the degree d of the system (cf. [3,4,31]). Each costs time and space (for a reduction from the $\mathcal{MQ}$ problem in $\mathbb{F}_q$ case to $\mathbb{F}_2$ case, see [30]). Even with a hardware implementation, an increase in resource consumption is inevitable.

A logical next step is to combine all these approaches but find polynomials that are easier to evaluate. A natural candidate is sparsity in the chosen polynomials. To our survey, however, there are no prior positive results for provable security of specialized polynomial systems, and specifically sparse ones.

So the questions we are trying to answer are:

- *Can we prove a similar result to [7] allowing for more efficiently evaluated specialized systems?*
- *What do we know about how these specializations affect complexity of system-solving?*

1.1   Our New Ideas and Main Results

Instead of $\mathcal{MQ}$, we investigate a class $\mathcal{SMP}(q, d, n, m, (\eta_2, \ldots, \eta_d))$ of sparse polynomials systems with arbitrary affine parts and terms at other degrees with specified density. I.e., $\mathbf{S} = (P_1(\mathbf{x}), P_2(\mathbf{x}), \cdots, P_m(\mathbf{x})) \in \mathcal{SMP}(q, d, n, m, (\eta_2, \ldots, \eta_d))$ consists of m polynomials of degree d in the variables $\mathbf{x} = (x_1, x_2, \ldots, x_n)$; each P_i is a degree-d polynomial such that exactly $\eta_i = \eta_i(n)$

nonzero degree-i terms are present for each $i \geq 2$. The affine terms (coefficients) are totally randomly chosen. Also all the operations and coefficients are in $\mathbb{F}_q$.

To rephrase, the i-th polynomial we can be written as $P_i(\mathbf{x}) = \sum_{j=2}^{d} Q_j^{(i)}(\mathbf{x}) + \sum_{1 \leq j \leq n} a_{ij} x_j + c_i$ where each $Q_j^{(i)}(\mathbf{x})$ can be written in the form $\sum_{1 \leq \sigma(1) \leq \sigma(2) \leq \cdots \leq \sigma(j) \leq n} a_{(\sigma(1), \sigma(2), \ldots, \sigma(j))} x_{\sigma(1)} x_{\sigma(2)} \cdots x_{\sigma(j)}$, or the sum of η_j monomials with degree j. "A random system from $SMP(q, d, n, m, (\eta_2, \ldots, \eta_d))$" then has a probability distribution as follows: all a_{ij}, c_i are uniformly chosen from $\mathbb{F}_q$. To determine each $Q_j^{(i)}(\mathbf{x})$, we firstly uniformly choose η_j out of $\binom{n+j-1}{j}$ coefficients to be nonzero, then uniformly choose each of these nonzero coefficients from $\mathbb{F}_q^* := \mathbb{F}_q \setminus \{0\}$. All the others coefficients wil be zero.

We now propose a probabilistic one-wayness assumption to base a security theorem on.

Assumption SMP : For given q, d, and for $n, m, \eta_2, \ldots, \eta_d$ such that $m/n = k + o(1)$ and $\eta_i/n = k_i + o(1)$ (where $k, k_2, k_3, \ldots$ are constants) there is no probabilistic algorithm which can solve (in poly(n)-time) any fixed $\varepsilon > 0$ proportion of instances $\mathbf{S}(\mathbf{x})$ drawn from $SMP((q, d, n, m, (\eta_2, \ldots, \eta_d))$, and a vector $\mathbf{b} = (b_1, b_2, \ldots, b_m)$ drawn from $\mathbf{S}(U_n)$, where U_n is uniform distribution over $(\mathbb{F}_q)^n$ such that $\mathbf{S}(\mathbf{x}) = \mathbf{b}$.

In Secs. 2–3 Assumption SMP is shown to yield a secure PRNG (and hence a probably secure stream cipher), **for any** q. The key to this extension to general $\mathbb{F}_q$ involves a reconstruction over linear polynomials, which is a non-trivial generalization of the Goldreich-Levin hard core bit by Goldreich-Rubinfeld-Sudan [21].

We then check that SMP instances are hard to solve on average (i.e., not just worst case) via the known fastest generic (cf. Sec. 4 and Appendix B) and special-purpose algorithms. Finally we discuss their practical use. Preliminary implementations of our **SPELT** (Sparse Polynomials, Every Linear Term) can achieve 5541 and 11744 cycles per byte for a SMP-based *secure* stream cipher over $\mathbb{F}_{16}$ (quartic, 108 variables) and $\mathbb{F}_2$ (cubic, 208 variables) respectively. The former is at least twice as fast as any other stream ciphers provably secure at the same parameters (cf. Sec. 5.2).

There is another possible candidate for the one-wayness assumption, SRQ, proposed by Prof. Jintai Ding, that is worth studying. We put a brief description in the Appendix C, and address an interesting potential topic for the future work.

The authors would like to thank Prof. Jintai Ding for the proofreading, suggestions, and discussions. The full version of this work can be found at "http://eprint.iacr.org/2007/405."

1.2   Previous Work

There had been "provably secure" PRNGs based on discrete log [20], or on hardness of factorization (as in Blum, Blum, and Shub [10]) or a modification thereof [29], or MQ [7]. But the security proofs always require impractically high parameters for "provable security", which limit their utility. For example:

- The BBS stream generator at commonly used parameters is not provably secure [23, Sec. 6.1].

- With [29], the specified security level was 2^{70}, today's cryptographers usually aim for 2^{80} (3DES units).
- Similarly with QUAD there is a gap between the "recommended" instances and the provably secure instances (i.e., the tested instances were unprovable or unproven [33]).
- PRNGs based on decisional Diffie-Hellman assumption have almost no gap between the hardness of breaking the PRNG and solving the underlying intractable problem, but known primitives based on DDH and exponentiation in Z_p [22,16] are generally slower than those based on other assumptions.

The generic types of methods for solving polynomial systems — Faugère's $\mathbf{F_4}$-$\mathbf{F_5}$ and XL-derivatives — are not affected drastically by sparsity. In the former, sparsity is quickly lost and tests show that there is no substantial difference in timing when solving $\mathcal{SMP}$ instances. Recent versions of XL [33] speeds up proportionally to sparsity. We therefore surveyed the literature for recent results on solving or attacking specialized systems in crypto, listed below. **These results do not contradict our hardness assumption.**

- Aumasson-Meier (ICISC 2007) [1] shows that in some cases sparsity in primarily *underdefined* — *more variables than equations* — *systems* leads to improved attacks. Results are very intresting and takes more study but do not apply to overdetermined systems in general.
- Bard-Courtois-Jefferson [2] tests SAT solvers on uniformly sparse $\mathbb{F}_2$ equations, and gives numbers.
- Raddum-Samaev [27,28] attacks "clumped" systems (even though the title says "sparse"). Similarly the Courtois-Pieprzyk XSL attack [13] requires a lot of structures (i.e., "clumping").

2   PRNG Based on Specialized Polynomial Map in $\mathbb{F}_2$

This section both provides a recap of past results and extends them to specialized maps over $\mathbb{F}_2$. We will start with definitions and models, then give the key results on the provable security level.

Computational Distinguishability: Probability distributions D_1 and D_2 over a finite set Ω are **computationally distinguishable** with computing resources R and advantage ϵ if there exist a probabilistic algorithm A which on any input $x \in \Omega$ outputs answer 1 (accept) or 0 (reject) using computing resources at most R and satisfies $|\mathrm{Pr}_{x \in D_1} (A(x) = 1) - \mathrm{Pr}_{x \in D_2} (A(x) = 1)| > \epsilon$. The above probabilities are not only taken over x values distributed according to D_1 or D_2, but also over the random choices that are used by algorithm A. Algorithm A is called a distinguisher with advantage ϵ.

If no such algorithm exists, then we say that D_1 and D_2 are computationally indistinguishable with advantage ϵ. If R is not specified, we implicitly mean feasible computing resources (e.g., $< 2^{80}$ simple operations, and reasonable limits [usually polynomially many] in sampling from D_1 and D_2).

PRNG: Let $n < L$ be two integers and $K = \mathbb{F}_q$ be a finite field. The function $G : K^n \to K^L$ is said to be a Pseudorandom Number Generator (PRNG) if the probability distribution of the random variable $G(\mathbf{x})$, where the vector $\mathbf{x}$ is uniformly random in K^n, is computationally indistinguishable (with distinguisher resource R) from a uniformly random vector in K^L. *Usually $q = 2$ but it is not required.*

Linear polynomial maps: A linear polynomial map $R : (\mathbb{F}_q)^n \to (\mathbb{F}_q)$ means $R(\mathbf{x}) = \sum_{i=1}^n a_i x_i$, where $\mathbf{x} = (x_1, x_2, \ldots, x_n)$, and $x_1, x_2, \ldots, x_n$ are variables. If we give these variables values in $\mathbb{F}_q$, by setting $(x_1, x_2, \ldots, x_n) = (b_1, b_2, \ldots, b_n)$ for $b_i \in \mathbb{F}_q$, denoted as $\mathbf{b}$, then $R(\mathbf{b}) = \sum_{i=1}^n a_i b_i$ is an element in $\mathbb{F}_q$.

In the following sections, a "random" linear polynomial map (or form) has the coefficients a_i's randomly chosen from $\mathbb{F}_q$. Also, when we mention R or $R(\mathbf{x})$ refers to the function but when we write $R(\mathbf{b})$, that means the value of the function R with input vector $\mathbf{b}$.

Instance from $\mathcal{SMP}$ (or $\mathcal{MQ}$): If $\mathbf{S}$ is an instance drawn from $\mathcal{SMP}(q, d, n, m, (\eta_2, \ldots, \eta_d))$, then $\mathbf{S}(\mathbf{x}) = (P_1(\mathbf{x}), P_2(\mathbf{x}), \ldots, P_m(\mathbf{x}))$ ($\mathbf{x} = (x_1, x_2, \ldots, x_n)$ are variables) is a function that maps $(\mathbb{F}_q)^n \to (\mathbb{F}_q)^m$ and each $P_i(\mathbf{x})$ has the same probability distribution as that mentioned in section 1.2. For example, if $\mathbf{b} = (b_1, b_2, \ldots, b_n)$ is a vector in $(\mathbb{F}_q)^n$, then $\mathbf{S}(\mathbf{b}) = (P_1(\mathbf{b}), P_2(\mathbf{b}), \ldots, P_m(\mathbf{b}))$, a value in $(\mathbb{F}_q)^m$.

Note: Heretofore we will also say $\mathcal{SMP}(n, m)$ for short, if no confusion is likely to ensue.

Given any PRNG, there is a standard way to stretch it into an old-fashioned stream cipher (Prop. 1), i.e. stream cipher without IV and key setup. There are ways to set up an initial state securely, such as in Sec. 3.1. Thus we concentrate our efforts on building a PRNG from any $\mathcal{MQ}$ family of map from $\mathbb{F}_2^n \to \mathbb{F}_2^m$; in order, we need to

1. Show that if an instance $\mathbf{S}$ drawn from $\mathcal{MQ}$ is *not* a PRNG, then for a (secretly) given vector $\mathbf{b}$ we can predict, with the help of information from the value of $\mathbf{S}$, $\mathbf{S}(\mathbf{b})$, and any linear form R, the value of $R(\mathbf{b})$ with strictly larger than $1/2 + \epsilon$ probability; then
2. Use Goldreich-Levin theorem, which states that the value of any linear function R, $R(\mathbf{b})$ is a hardcore bit of any $\mathbb{F}_2^n \to \mathbb{F}_2^m$ one-way function $\mathbf{S}$, $\mathbf{S}(\mathbf{b})$, and R. I.e., *being able to guess with strictly larger than $1/2 + \epsilon$ probability $R(\mathbf{b})$ from $\mathbf{S}, \mathbf{S}(\mathbf{b})$, and R means that we can invert $\mathbf{S}(\mathbf{b})$ with non-negligible probability.*

2.1   From Distinguisher to Predictor

In fact, the following two results are valid for any $K = \mathbb{F}_q$. In [7], the proofs were covered only in the $\mathbb{F}_2$ case. However, the generalization is nontrivial but straitforward. Therefore, for simplicity, we put the generalized propositions here, though this section is for the $\mathbb{F}_2$ case.

Proposition 1 ([7]). *Take a stream cipher with* $\mathbf{Q} : K^n \to K^n$ *and* $\mathbf{P} : K^n \to K^r$ *as the update and output filter functions and random initial state* $\mathbf{x}_0$, *that is, starting from the initial state* $\mathbf{x}_0$, *at each step we update with* $\mathbf{x}_{i+1} = \mathbf{Q}(\mathbf{x}_i)$ *and output* $\mathbf{y}_i = \mathbf{P}(\mathbf{x}_i)$.

$$\mathbf{x}_0 \longrightarrow \mathbf{x}_1 = \mathbf{Q}(\mathbf{x}_0) \longrightarrow \mathbf{x}_2 = \mathbf{Q}(\mathbf{x}_1) \longrightarrow \mathbf{x}_3 = \mathbf{Q}(\mathbf{x}_2) \longrightarrow \cdots \qquad \textit{(state)}$$

$$\mathbf{y}_0 = \mathbf{P}(\mathbf{x}_0) \qquad \mathbf{y}_1 = \mathbf{P}(\mathbf{x}_1) \qquad \mathbf{y}_2 = \mathbf{P}(\mathbf{x}_2) \qquad \mathbf{y}_3 = \mathbf{P}(\mathbf{x}_3) \qquad \cdots \qquad \textit{(output)}$$

If we can distinguish between its first λ *blocks of output* $(\mathbf{y}_0, \mathbf{y}_1, \ldots, \mathbf{y}_{\lambda-1})$ *and a true random vector in* $K^{\lambda r}$ *with advantage* ϵ *in time* T, *then we can distinguish between the output of a true random vector in* K^{n+r} *and the output of* $\mathbf{S} = (\mathbf{P}, \mathbf{Q})$ *in time* $T + \lambda T_\mathbf{S}$ *with advantage* ϵ/λ. *[Standard Proof is in Appendix A.]*

Proposition 2 (an extention of [7]). *Let* $K = \mathbb{F}_q$. *Suppose there is an algorithm* A *that given a system* $\mathbf{S}(: K^n \to K^m)$ *chosen from* $\mathcal{SMP}(q, d, n, m, (\eta_2, \ldots, \eta_d))$ *distinguishing* $\mathbf{S}(U_n)$ *from a uniform random distribution* U_m, *(where* U_r *means uniform distribution over* K^r *for the* r,*) with advantage at least* ϵ *in time* T. *Then there is an algorithm* B *that, given (1) a system* $\mathbf{S} : K^n \to K^m$ *from* $\mathcal{SMP}(n, m)$, *(2) any* $K^n \to K$ *linear form* R, *and (3)* $\mathbf{y} = \mathbf{S}(\mathbf{b})$, *where* $\mathbf{b}$ *is an secret input value randomly chosen from* K^n, *predicts* $R(\mathbf{b})$ *with success probability at least* $(1 + \epsilon/2)/q$ *using at most* $T + 2T_\mathbf{S}$ *operations.*

Proof. Without loss of generality, we may suppose that A has probability at least ϵ higher to return 1 on an input distribution $(\mathbf{S}, \mathbf{S}(U_n))$ than on distribution $(\mathbf{S}, U_m)$. Define a recentered distinguisher

$$A'(\mathbf{S}, \mathbf{w}) := \begin{cases} A(\mathbf{S}, \mathbf{w}), & \text{probability } \frac{1}{2} \\ 1 - A(\mathbf{S}, \mathbf{u}), \ \mathbf{u} \in K^m \text{ uniform random}, & \text{probabilty } \frac{1}{2} \end{cases}$$

then A' returns 1 with probability $\frac{1 \pm \epsilon}{2}$ on input $(\mathbf{S}, \mathbf{S}(U_n))$ and with probability $\frac{1}{2}$ on input $(\mathbf{S}, U_m)$.

Now, given an input $\mathbf{S}$ and $\mathbf{y} \in K^m$, the algorithm B first randomly chooses a value $v \in K$ (representing a guess for $R(\mathbf{b})$), then randomly chooses a vector $\mathbf{u} \in K^m$, and form $\mathbf{S}' := \mathbf{S} + R\mathbf{u} : K^n \to K^m$. This is equal to S plus a random linear polynomial (see above for the meaning of random linear form) and is hence of $\mathcal{SMP}(n, m)$. Define algorithm B as following:

$$B(\mathbf{S}, \mathbf{y}, R) := \begin{cases} v, & \text{if } A'(\mathbf{S}', \mathbf{y} + v\mathbf{u}) = 1; \\ \text{uniformly pick an element from } K \backslash \{v\}, & \text{if } A'(\mathbf{S}', \mathbf{y} + v\mathbf{u}) = 0. \end{cases}$$

If $v = R(\mathbf{b})$, $\mathbf{y} + v\mathbf{u} = \mathbf{S}'(\mathbf{b})$, else $\mathbf{y} + v\mathbf{u}$ is equal to $\mathbf{S}'(\mathbf{b})$ plus a nonzero multiple of the random vector u, hence is equivalent to being uniformly random. The probability that $B := B(\mathbf{S}, \mathbf{S}(\mathbf{b}), R)$ is the correct guess is hence

$$\Pr(B = R(\mathbf{b})) = \Pr(B = v | v = R(\mathbf{b})) \Pr(v = R(\mathbf{b})) + \Pr(B = R(\mathbf{b}) | v \neq R(\mathbf{b})) \Pr(v \neq R(\mathbf{b}))$$

$$= \frac{1}{q}\left(\frac{1}{2} + \frac{\epsilon}{2}\right) + \left(\frac{q-1}{q}\right)\frac{1}{2}\left(\frac{1}{q-1}\right) = \frac{1}{q}\left(1 + \frac{\epsilon}{2}\right).$$

Note: *We see that the reasoning can work this way if and only if* $\mathbf{S}' = \mathbf{S} + R\mathbf{u}$ *have the same distribution as* $\mathbf{S}$*. Otherwise, we cannot guarentee the distinguisher* A' *will output the same distribution.*

2.2 Constructing a PRNG from $\mathcal{MQ}$ ($\mathbb{F}_2$ Case)

Proposition 3 ([25], [7]). *Suppose there is an algorithm B that given a system* $\mathbf{S}(: \mathbb{F}_2^n \to \mathbb{F}_2^m)$ *from* $\mathcal{MQ}(2, n, m)$*, a random n-bit to one-bit linear form R and the image $\mathbf{S}(\mathbf{b})$ of a randomly chosen unknown $\mathbf{b}$, predicts $R(\mathbf{b})$ with probability at least $\frac{1}{2} + \epsilon$ over all possible inputs $(\mathbf{S}, \mathbf{S}(\mathbf{b}), R)$ using time T, then there is an algorithm C that given $\mathbf{S}$ and the m-bit image $\mathbf{S}(\mathbf{b})$ of a randomly chosen n-bit vector $\mathbf{b}$ produces a preimage of $\mathbf{S}(\mathbf{b})$ with probability (over all $\mathbf{b}$ and $\mathbf{S}$) at least $\epsilon/2$ in time*

$$T' = \frac{8n^2}{\epsilon^2} \left(T + \log \left(\frac{8n}{\epsilon^2} \right) + \frac{8n}{\epsilon^2} T_{\mathbf{S}} \right)$$

Note: This is really the Goldreich-Levin theorem of which we omit the proof here. This essentially states that linear forms are hard-core of any one-way function. In fact, the tighter form [7, Proof of Theorem 3] (using a fast Walsh transform) can be simply followed word-for-word.

This above result (which only holds for $\mathbb{F}_2$) with Prop. 2 shows that any $\mathcal{MQ}$ family of maps induces PRNGs over $\mathbb{F}_2$. To get a useful stream cipher, we can combine Props. 1–3:

Proposition 4 ([25], [7]). *If $\mathbf{S} = (\mathbf{P}, \mathbf{Q})$ is an instance drawn from $\mathcal{MQ}(2, n, n + r)$, where $\mathbf{P} : \mathbb{F}_2^n \to \mathbb{F}_2^r$, $\mathbf{Q} : \mathbb{F}_2^n \to \mathbb{F}_2^n$ are the stream cipher as in Prop. 1, then if we can distinguish between λ output blocks of the stream cipher from truly random distribution in T time, we can find $\mathbf{b}$ from $\mathbf{S}(\mathbf{b})$, where $\mathbf{b}$ is a randomly chosen input, with probability at least $\frac{\epsilon}{8\lambda}$ in time*

$$T' = \frac{2^7 n^2 \lambda^2}{\epsilon^2} \left(T + (\lambda + 2) T_{\mathbf{S}} + \log \left(\frac{2^7 n \lambda^2}{\epsilon^2} \right) + 2 \right) + \frac{2^7 n \lambda^2}{\epsilon^2} T_{\mathbf{S}} \qquad (1)$$

Note: Roughly this means that if we let $r = n$, want to establish a safety level of 2^{80} multiplications, want $L = \lambda r = 2^{40}$ bits between key refreshes, and can accept $\epsilon = 10^{-2}$, then $T' \lesssim 2^{230}/n$. All we need now is to find a map from $\mathbb{F}_2^n \to \mathbb{F}_2^{2n}$ which takes this amount of time to invert.

As we see below, unless equation-solving improves greatly for sparse systems, this implies that a handful of cubic terms added to a QUAD system with $n = r = 208$, $q = 2$ can be deemed secure to 2^{80}. There is no sense in going any lower than that, because solving a system with n bit-variables can never take much more effort than 2^n times whatever time it takes to evaluate one equation.

3 PRNG Based on $\mathcal{SMP}$ in $\mathbb{F}_q$

In Proposition 3, [7] transformed the problem into a variation of Goldreich-Levin theorem (in $\mathbb{F}_2$). *The transformation still works in $\mathbb{F}_q$; however, Goldreich-Levin* *theorm gets stuck in this place.* Here we show a way to extend the main results to $\mathbb{F}_q$, by using a generalization of the Goldreich-Levin hard-core bit theorem.

Proposition 5 ([25] and contribution of this paper). *Let $K = \mathbb{F}_q$. Suppose there is an algorithm B that given a system $\mathbf{S}(\colon K^n \to K^m)$ from $\mathcal{SMP}(n, m)$, a random $K^n \to K$ linear form R and the image $\mathbf{S}(\mathbf{b})$ of a randomly chosen unknown $\mathbf{b}$, predicts $R(\mathbf{b})$ with probability at least $\frac{1}{q} + \epsilon$ over all possible inputs $(\mathbf{S}, \mathbf{S}(\mathbf{b}), R)$ using time T, then there is an algorithm C that given $\mathbf{S}$ and the m-bit image $\mathbf{S}(\mathbf{b})$ of a randomly chosen vector $\mathbf{b} \in K^n$ produces a preimage of $\mathbf{S}(\mathbf{b})$ with probability (over all $\mathbf{b}$ and $\mathbf{S}$) at least $\epsilon/2$ in time*

$$T' \leq 2^{10} \left(\frac{nq}{\epsilon^5}\right) \log^2 \left(\frac{n}{\epsilon}\right) T + \left(1 - \frac{1}{q}\right)^2 \epsilon^{-2} T_{\mathbf{S}}$$

Remark [intuition of why argument in $\mathbb{F}_2$ cannot be applied in $\mathbb{F}_q$]: If we know that one out of two exclusive possibilities takes place with probability strictly larger than 50%, then the other one must happen strictly less often 50%. If we know that one of q possibilities takes place with probability strictly greater than $1/q$, we cannot be sure that another possibility does not occur with even higher possibility. Therefore, we can only treat this as a case of learning a linear functional with queries to a highly noisy oracle. **Due to this difference, the order of ϵ in T'/T is as high as ϵ^{-5} in Prop. 5, but only ϵ^{-2} in Prop. 3.**

Proposition 6 ([25] and contribution or this paper). *If $\mathbf{S} = (\mathbf{P}, \mathbf{Q})$ is an instance drawn from a $\mathcal{SMP}(n, n+r)$, where $\mathbf{P} : \mathbb{F}_q^n \to \mathbb{F}_q^r$, $\mathbf{Q} : \mathbb{F}_q^n \to \mathbb{F}_q^n$ are the stream cipher as in Prop. 1, then if we can distinguish between λ output blocks of the stream cipher and uniform distribution in T time, we can invert $\mathbf{S}(\mathbf{b})$ with probability at least $\frac{\epsilon}{4q\lambda}$ in time*

$$T' = 2^{15} \frac{nq^6 \lambda^5}{\epsilon^5} \log^2 \left(\frac{2qn\lambda}{\epsilon}\right) (T + (\lambda + 2)T_{\mathbf{S}}) + \left(1 - \frac{1}{q}\right)^2 \frac{4q^2\lambda^2}{\epsilon^2} T_{\mathbf{S}} \quad (2)$$

This is a straightforward combination of Props. 1, 2, and 5. In the remainder of this section, we give a proof to Prop. 5 by a variation of the procedure used by Goldreich-Rubinfeld-Sudan [21, Secs. 2 and 4], to give it concrete values that we can derive security proofs from.

3.1   Conversion to a Modern (IV-Dependent Stream) Cipher

This paper mostly deals with the security of PRNGs, which are essentially old-fashioned stream ciphers. If we have a secure PRNG $\mathbf{S}' = (\mathbf{s}_0, \mathbf{s}_1)$, where both $\mathbf{s}_0, \mathbf{s}_1$ are maps from $K^n \to K^n$ — note that $\mathbf{S}'$ can be identical to $\mathbf{S}$ — then the following is a standard way to derive the initial state $\mathbf{x}_0 \in K^n$ from the bitstream (key) $\mathbf{c} = (c_1, c_2, \ldots, c_{KL}) \in \{0, 1\}^{KL}$ and an initial $\mathbf{u} \in K^n$, where KL is the length of the key:

$$\mathbf{x}_0 := \mathbf{s}_{c_{KL}}(\mathbf{s}_{c_{KL-1}}(\cdots (\mathbf{s}_{c_2}(\mathbf{s}_{c_1}(\mathbf{u})))\cdots)).$$

This is known as the tree-based construction. From an old-fashioned provably secure stream cipher (i.e., the key is the initial state), the above construction achieves security in the resulting IV-dependent stream cipher, at the cost of some additional looseness in the security proof. A recent example of this is [6].

Thus, all our work really applies to the modern type of stream ciphers which require an IV-dependent setup, except that the security parameters may be slightly different.

3.2   Hardcore Predicate and Learning Polynomials

Let $\mathbf{x} = (x_1, x_2, \ldots, x_n)$, $\mathbf{b} = (b_1, b_2, \ldots, b_n)$, and x_i, b_i are elements in a finite field $K = \mathbb{F}_q$. Given an arbitrary strong one way function $h(\mathbf{x})$, then $F(\mathbf{x}, \mathbf{b}) = (h(\mathbf{x}), \mathbf{b})$ is also a one way function. Claim $\mathbf{x} \cdot \mathbf{b}$ is the hard-core bit of $F(\mathbf{x}, \mathbf{b})$, where $\mathbf{x} \cdot \mathbf{b}$ means their inner product.

Supposed we have a predictor P which predicts its hardcore $\mathbf{x} \cdot \mathbf{b}$ given $(h(\mathbf{x}), \mathbf{b})$ with probability more than $\frac{1}{q} + \epsilon$, then we can write in the math form:

$$\Pr_{\mathbf{b}, \mathbf{x}} \left[P(h(\mathbf{x}), \mathbf{b}) = \mathbf{x} \cdot \mathbf{b} \right] > \frac{1}{q} + \epsilon.$$

By Markov inequality, we know there must be more than $\epsilon/2$ fraction of x such that $\Pr_{\mathbf{b}}[P(h(\mathbf{x}), \mathbf{b}) = \mathbf{x} \cdot \mathbf{b}] > \frac{1}{q} + \frac{\epsilon}{2}$. For this fraction of x, we are trying to find the inverse of $h(\mathbf{x})$ ($F(\mathbf{x})$ as well) through the predictor. Also $\mathbf{x} \cdot \mathbf{b}$ can be written as $\sum b_i x_i$, then

$$\Pr_{\mathbf{b}} \left[P(h(\mathbf{x}), \mathbf{b}) = \sum b_i x_i \right] > \frac{1}{q} + \frac{\epsilon}{2}.$$

This means that, *if we can find a polynomial which almost matches an arbitrary function P, a predictor function, then we can eventually invert $\mathbf{x}$ from $F(\mathbf{x})$ a non-negligible portion of the time.* Now we try to reconstruct such linear polynomials through the access of the predictor, largely following the footsteps of [21].

3.3   Intuition of Reconstructing Linear Polynomials

Now we are given some oracle accesses to a function $f : K^n \to K$, where K is a finite field and $|K| = q$. We need to find all linear polynomials which match f with at least $\frac{1}{q} + \epsilon$ fraction of inputs x. Let $p(x_1, x_2, \ldots, x_n) = \sum_1^n p_i x_i$, and i-th prefix of p is $\sum_1^i p_j x_j$. The algorithm runs n rounds, and in the i-th round, it extends all possible candidates from the $(i-1)$-th round with all elements in K and screens them, filtering out most bad prefixes. The pseudocode of the algorithm is presented in Algorithm 2. Since we want the algorithm to be efficient, we must efficiently screen possible prefixes from all extensions. We now introduce a screening algorithm to be called TestPrefix.

Algorithm 1. TestPrefix(f,ϵ,n,$(c_1, c_2 \ldots, c_i)$)[21]

Repeat $\text{poly}_1(\frac{n}{\epsilon})$ times:
Pick $s = s_{i+1}, \ldots, s_n \in_R \text{GF}(q)$
Let $t = \text{poly}_2\left(\frac{n}{\epsilon}\right)$
for $k = 1$ to t **do**
    Pick $r = r_1, r_2 \ldots, r_i \in_R \text{GF}(q)$
    $\sigma^{(k)} = f(r, s) - \sum_{j=1}^{i} c_j r_j$
end for
If there is $\sigma^{(k)} = \sigma$ for at least $\frac{1}{q} + \frac{\epsilon}{3}$ fraction of the k's then ouput accept and halt
endRepeat
If all iterations were completed without accepting, then reject

---

Algorithm 2. Find All Polynomials(f, ϵ)[21]

---

set a candidate queue Q[i] which stores all the candidates $(c_1, c_2, c_3, \ldots, c_i)$ in the i-th round
for $i = 1$ to n **do**
    Pick all elements in Q[i]
    TestPrefix(f,ϵ,n,$(c_1, c_2 \ldots, c_i, \alpha)$) for all $\alpha \in \text{F}$
    If TestPrefix accepts, then push $(c_1, c_2 \ldots, c_i, \alpha)$ into Q[$i+1$] i.e. it is a candidate
    in the $(i+1)$-th round
end for

Supposed we are testing the i-th prefix $(c_1, c_2, \ldots, c_i)$, we are going to evaluate the quantity of:

$$P_s(\sigma) := \Pr_{r_1, r_2 \ldots, r_i \in K} \left[f(r, s) = \sum_{j=1}^{i} c_j r_j + \sigma \right]$$

where $r = (r_1, r_2, \ldots, r_i)$. The value of σ can be thought as a guess of $\sum_{i+1}^{n} p_j s_j$. For every s, we can estimate the probability by a sample of several r's, and the error rate can be controlled by the times of sampling. If such s makes the probability significantly larger than $1/q$, then we accept. If no such s exists, we reject. The detailed algorithm is stated in the Algorithm 1: TestPrefix.

If a candidate $(c_1, c_2, \ldots, c_i)$ passes through the Algorithm 1 for at least one suffix s, there is a σ such that the estimate of $P_s(\sigma)$ is greater than $\frac{1}{q} + \frac{\epsilon}{3}$. For a correct candidate $(c_1, c_2, \ldots, c_i)$, i.e. $(c_1, c_2, \ldots, c_i)$ is the prefix of $p = (p_1, p_2, \ldots, p_n)$ which matches f for at least $\frac{1}{q} + \epsilon$, and an arbitrary $\sigma = \sum_{i+1}^{n} p_j s_j$, it satisfies that $E_s[P_s(\sigma)] \geq \frac{1}{q} + \epsilon$. By Markov's inequality, for at least $\epsilon/2$ fraction of s and some corresponding σ, it holds that $P_s(\sigma) \geq \frac{1}{q} + \frac{\epsilon}{2}$. In Algorithm 1, we set $\frac{1}{q} + \frac{\epsilon}{3}$ as the passing criteria; thus the correct candidate will pass though the Algorithm 1 with great probability. However, [21, Sec. 4] shows that the total passing number of candidates in each round is limited. In fact, only a small number of candidates will pass the test. This maximum (also given by [21, Sec. 4]) number of prefixes that pass the test is $\leq (1 - \frac{1}{q})^2 \epsilon^{-2}$.

3.4   Giving Concrete Values to "Order of Polynomially Many"

Since there are $\epsilon/2$ fraction of suffix s such that $P_s(\sigma) \geq \frac{1}{q} + \frac{\epsilon}{2}$, we can randomly choose the suffix polynomially many times (k_1 times) to ensure that we would select such s with high probability. Also, for such s, if we choose polynomially many times (k_2 times) of r, there would be high probability that we would find some α for at least $\frac{1}{q} + \frac{\epsilon}{3}$ fraction. We are estimating how the polynomially many should be as the following:

$$\Pr[\text{ TestPrefix fails }] \leq$$

$$\Pr[\text{no such } s \text{ is chosen }] + \Pr\left[\text{ no single element exists more than } \frac{1}{q} + \frac{\epsilon}{3} \text{ fraction}\right]$$

$$\Pr[\text{ no such } s \text{ is chosen}] \leq (1 - \epsilon/2)^{k_1} \leq e^{-\frac{k_1 \epsilon}{2}} \leq \frac{1}{2} \frac{\epsilon}{\left(1 - \frac{1}{q}\right)^2 \epsilon^{-2} nq}$$

So, we take k_1 as $O(\frac{1}{\epsilon} \log(\frac{n}{\epsilon})) \approx 3\frac{1}{\epsilon} \log(\frac{n}{\epsilon})$. On the other hand, we want to estimate the probability of there are no σ's with fraction at least $\frac{1}{q} + \frac{\epsilon}{3}$. For a correct suffix s, we know for uniform r, we get that σ with probability more than $\frac{1}{q} + \frac{\epsilon}{2}$. Let X_i be the random variable with value 1 if the i-th trial of r gets the correct σ, 0 otherwise. Then we have $\Pr[X_i = 1] \geq \frac{1}{q} + \frac{\epsilon}{2}$. Suppose we do k_2 trials:

$$\Pr\left[\text{no single element exists more than } \frac{1}{q} + \frac{\epsilon}{3} \text{ fraction}\right] \leq \Pr\left[\sum_1^{k_2} X_i < (\frac{1}{q} + \frac{\epsilon}{3})k_2\right]$$

$$\leq \Pr\left[\left|\frac{\sum_{i=1}^{k_2} X_i}{k_2} - \left(\frac{1}{q} + \frac{\epsilon}{2}\right)\right| \geq \frac{\epsilon}{6}\right],$$

since these X_i's are independent, then by Chernoff's bound we have

$$\Pr\left[\left|\frac{\sum_{i=1}^{k_2} X_i}{t} - \left(\frac{1}{q} + \frac{\epsilon}{2}\right)\right| \geq \frac{\epsilon}{6}\right] \leq 2e^{-\frac{k_2 \epsilon^2}{2 \times 36}} \leq \frac{1}{2} \frac{\epsilon}{\left(1 - \frac{1}{q}\right)^2 \epsilon^{-2} nq},$$

$k_2 = O(\frac{\log(n/\epsilon)}{\epsilon^2}) \approx 216 \frac{\log(n/\epsilon)}{\epsilon^2}$ is sufficient to make the inequality hold. Thus, we have

$$\Pr[\text{ TestPrefix fails }] \leq \frac{\epsilon}{\left(1 - \frac{1}{q}\right)^2 \epsilon^{-2} nq}.$$

Also, $\Pr[\text{ Algorithm 2 fails }] \leq \Pr[\text{ one TestPrefix fails }] \leq \sum_{\text{all TestPrefix run}} \Pr[\text{ TestPrefix fails }]$

$$\leq \left(\left(1 - \frac{1}{q}\right)^2 \epsilon^{-2} nq\right) \frac{\epsilon}{\left(1 - \frac{1}{q}\right)^2 \epsilon^{-2} nq} = \epsilon$$

Therefore, the algorithm will work with high probability. The worst case running time of algorithm 2 should be: $k_1 k_2 (1 - \frac{1}{q})^2 \frac{1}{\epsilon^2} nq = O(\frac{n}{\epsilon^5} \log^2(\frac{n}{\epsilon})) \lesssim 2^{10} \left(\frac{nq}{\epsilon^5}\right) \log^2(\frac{n}{\epsilon})$.

Note: $\left(1 - \frac{1}{q}\right)^2 \epsilon^{-2}$ is the maximum number of candidates which pass in each round.

4   On $\mathcal{SMP}$ under Generic Solvers

To verify that $\mathcal{SMP}$ represent one way property, we need to show that

1. Generic system-solvers do not run substantially faster on them; and
2. There are no specialized solvers that can take advantage of the sparsity.

Here "generic" means the ability to handle any multivariate polynomial system with n variables and m equations in $\mathbb{F}_q$. There are two well-known types of generic methods for solving polynomial systems, both related to the original Buchberger's algorithm. One is Faugère's $\mathbf{F_4}$-$\mathbf{F_5}$ and the other is XL-derivatives. In the former, sparsity is quickly lost and tests show that there are little difference in timing when solving $\mathcal{SMP}$ instances. With recent versions of XL [33], the sparsity results in a proportional decrease in complexity. The effect of sparsity on such generic methods should be predictable and not very drastic, as shown by some testing (cf. Sec. 4.1). We briefly describe what is known about XL and $\mathbf{F_4}$-$\mathbf{F_5}$ in Appendix B.

4.1   Testing the One-Wayness with Generic Solvers

We conducted numerous tests on $\mathcal{SMP}$ maps at various degrees and sparsity over the fields $\mathbb{F}_2$, $\mathbb{F}_{16}$, and $\mathbb{F}_{256}$. For example, Table 1 lists our tests in solving random $\mathcal{MQ}(256, n, m)$ instances where each polynomial only has n quadratic terms [we call these instances $\mathcal{SMQ}(256, n, m, n)$] with $\mathbf{F_4}$ over GF(256). It takes almost the same time as solving an $\mathcal{MQ}$ instance of the same size.

For XL variants that use sparse solvers as the last step [33] test results (one of which is shown in Table 2) confirms the natural guess: For $\mathcal{SMP}$ instances where the number of non-linear terms is not overly small, the solution degree of XL is unchanged, and the speed naturally goes down as the number of terms, nearly in direct proportion (in Tab. 2, should be close to $n/4$).

Table 1. $\mathcal{SMQ}(256, n, m, n)$ timing (sec): MAGMA 2.12, 2GB RAM, Athlon64x2 2.2GHz

$m - n$	D_{XL}	D_{reg}	$n = 9$	$n = 10$	$n = 11$	$n = 12$	$n = 13$
0	2^m	m	6.03	46.69	350.38	3322.21	sigmem
1	m	$\lceil \frac{m+1}{2} \rceil$	1.19	8.91	53.64	413.34	2535.32
2	$\lceil \frac{m+1}{2} \rceil$	$\lceil \frac{m+2-\sqrt{m+2}}{2} \rceil$	0.31	2.20	12.40	88.09	436.10

Table 2. XL/Wiedemann timing (sec) on Core2Quad 2.4GHz, icc, 4-thread OpenMP, 8GB RAM

n	7	8	9	10	11	12	13
D	5	6	6	7	7	8	8
$\mathcal{SMQ}(256, n, n+2, n)$	$9.34 \cdot 10^{-2}$	$1.17 \cdot 10^0$	$4.04 \cdot 10^0$	$6.02 \cdot 10^1$	$1.51 \cdot 10^2$	$2.34 \cdot 10^3$	$5.97 \cdot 10^3$
$\mathcal{MQ}(256, n, n+2)$	$2.06 \cdot 10^{-1}$	$2.92 \cdot 10^0$	$1.10 \cdot 10$	$1.81 \cdot 10^2$	$4.94 \cdot 10^2$	$8.20 \cdot 10^3$	$2,22 \cdot 10^4$
ratio	2.20	2.49	2.73	3.00	3.27	3.50	3.72

For $\mathbb{F}_2$, there are many special optimizations made for $\mathbf{F_4}$ in MAGMA, so we ran tests at various densities of quadratic terms in version 2.12-20 and 2.13-8. Typical results are given in Fig. 1. Most of the time the data points are close to each other. In some tests they overlap each other so closely that no difference in the timing is seen in a diagram.

4.2   A Brief Discussion on Specialization and Security

Since generic system-solvers show no unexpected improvement on our specializations, it remains for us to check that there are no other big improvements in solving specialized systems for. We list below what we know of recent new attempts on solving or attacking specialized systems in crypto, and show that *our results are consistent with these new results and somewhat complements them.*

- Aumasson-Meier [1] presented several ideas to attack primitives built on sparse polynomials systems, which we sketch separately in Sec. 4.3 below.
- Raddum-Samaev [27,28] attacks what they term "sparse" systems, where each equation depend on a small number of variables. Essentially, the authors state that for systems of equations in n bit variables such that each equation depends on only k variables, we can solve the system in time roughly proportional to $2^{(1-\frac{1}{k})n}$ using a relatively small memory footprint. Since XL for cubics and higher degrees over $\mathbb{F}_2$ is more time-consuming than brute-force, this is fairly impressive. However, the "sparsity" defined by the authors is closer to "input locality" and very different from what people usually denote with this term. The attack is hence not applicable to $\mathcal{SMP}$-based stream ciphers.

    In a similar vein is the purported XSL attack on AES [13]. While the S was supposed to stand for Sparse, it really requires Structure – i.e., each equation depending on very few variables. So, whether that attack actually works or not, it does not apply to $\mathcal{SMP}$-based systems.
- Bard-Courtois-Jefferson [2] use SAT solvers on uniformly sparse $\mathbb{F}_2$ equations and give experimental numbers. According to the authors, the methods takes up much less memory than $\mathbf{F_4}$ or derivatives, but is slower than these traditional methods when they have enough memory.

    Some numbers for *very* overdefined and *very* sparse systems shows that converting to a conjunctive normal form and then running a SAT solver can have good results. This seems to be a very intriguing approach, but so far there are no theoretical analysis especially for when the number of equations is a few times the number of variables, which is the case for $\mathcal{SMP}$ constructions.

4.3 Solutions and Collisions in Sparse Polynomial Systems

Aumasson-Meier recent published [1] some quite interesting ideas on finding solutions or collisions for primitives using sparse polynomial systems (e.g., hashes proposed in [15]).

They showed that which implies that using sparse polynomials systems of uniform density *(in every degree)* for Merkle-Damgård compression will not be universally collision-free. Some *underdefined* systems that are sparse in the higher degrees can be solved with lower complexity. Their results do not apply to overdetermined systems in general. We summarize relevant results below.

1. Overdetermined higher-degree maps that are sparse of uniform density, or at least sparse in the linear terms, is shown to have high probability of trivial collisions and near-collisions.

   It seems that everyone agrees, that linear terms should be totally random when constructing sparse polynomial systems for symmetric primitives.

2. Suppose we have an *underdetermined* higher-degree map sparse in the non-affine part, i.e.,

$$\mathbf{P} : \mathbb{F}_2^{n+r} \to \mathbb{F}_2^n, \ \mathbf{P(x)} = \mathbf{b} + M\mathbf{x} + \mathbf{Q(x)}$$

   where $\mathbf{Q}$ has only quadratic or higher terms and is sparse. Aumasson-Meier suggests that we can find $\mathbf{P}^{-1}(\mathbf{y})$ as follows: find a basis for the kernel space of the augmented matrix $[M; \mathbf{b} + \mathbf{y}]$. Collect these basis vectors in a $(n + r + 1) \times (r + 1)$ matrix M' as a linear code. For an arbitrary $\mathbf{w} \in \mathbb{F}_2^{r+1}$, the codeword $\bar{\mathbf{x}} = M'\mathbf{w}$ will represent a solution to $\mathbf{y} = M\mathbf{x} + \mathbf{b}$ if its last component is 1. Use known methods to find relatively low-weight codewords for the code M' and substitute into $\mathbf{Q(x)}$, expecting it to vanish with non-negligible probability.

   Aumasson-Meier proposes to apply this for collisions in Merkle-Damgård hashes with cubic compressor functions. It *does not work* for fields other than $\mathbb{F}_2$ or *overdetermined* systems. Its exact complexity is unknown and requires some further work.

3. Conversely, it has been suggested if we have an *overdetermined* higher-degree map

$$\mathbf{P} : \mathbb{F}_2^n \to \mathbb{F}_2^{n+r}, \ \mathbf{P(x)} = \mathbf{b} + M\mathbf{x} + \mathbf{Q(x)}$$

   where $\mathbf{Q}$ has only quadratic or higher terms and is *extremely* sparse, we can consider $\mathbf{P(x)} = \mathbf{y}$ as $M\mathbf{x} = (\mathbf{y} + \mathbf{b}) + \mathbf{perturbation}$, and use known methods for decoding attacks, i.e., solving overdetermined linear equations with perturbation. However, $\mathcal{SMP}$ maps with a moderate number of quadratic terms will be intractable.

We note that other specialized polynomials can be constructed that are also easier to evaluate such as the SRQ construction (cf. Appendix C) which also can carry through the same arguments as $\mathcal{SMP}$, so our process is more general than it looks.

5   Summary of Uses for Specialized Polynomial Systems

All information seems to point to the conclusion that we always use totally random linear terms, no matter what else we do. With that taken into account, specialized random systems (such as $\mathcal{SMP}$) represent improvements over generic systems in terms of storage and (likely) speed.

5.1   The Secure Stream Ciphers SPELT

We build a stream cipher called $\text{SPELT}(q, d, n, r, (\eta_2, \ldots, \eta_d))$, which resembles the construction in section 2:

We specify a prime power q (usually a power of 2), positive integers n and r, a degree d. We have "update function" $\mathbf{Q}_i = (Q_{i,1}, Q_{i,2}, \ldots, Q_{i,n}) : \mathbb{F}_q^n \to \mathbb{F}_q^n$ and "output filter" $\mathbf{P}_i = (P_{i,1}, P_{i,2}, \ldots, P_{i,r}) : \mathbb{F}_q^n \to \mathbb{F}_q^r$, for $i \in \{0, 1\}$. We still do $\mathbf{y}_n = \mathbf{P}(\mathbf{x}_n)$ [output]; $\mathbf{x}_{n+1} = \mathbf{Q}(\mathbf{x}_n)$ [transition], iterated according to the initial vector. To repeat, every polynomial here is of degree d. Affine (constant and linear) term or coefficient are still uniformly random. But terms of each degree are selected according to different densities of terms, such that **the degree-i terms are sparse to the point of having only η_i terms.** *The difference between Eq. 1 and Eq. 2, which governs the maximum provable security levels we can get, affects our parameter choices quite a bit, as seen below.*

By Eq. 2, if $L = \lambda n \lg q$ is the desired keystream length, the looseness factor T'/T is roughly

$$\frac{2^{15} q^6 (L/\epsilon)^5}{n^4 \lg^5 q} \lg^2 \left(\frac{2qL}{\epsilon \lg q} \right)$$

If we let $q = 16$, $r = n$, want a safety level of $T = 2^{80}$ multiplications, $L = 2^{40}$ bits between key refreshes, and can accept $\epsilon = 10^{-2}$, then $T' \lesssim 2^{354}/n^4$. We propose the following instances:

- SPELT using $q = 16$, $d = 3$ (cubics), $n = r = 160$, 20 quadratic and 15 cubic terms per equation. Projected XL degree is 54, storage requirement is 2^{184} bytes. T' is about 2^{346} multiplications, which guarantees $\gtrsim 2^{88}$ multiplications security. This runs at 6875 cycles/byte.
- SPELT using $d = 4$ (quartics), $n = r = 108$, 20 quadratic, 15 cubic, and 10 quartic terms per equation. Projected XL degree is 65, storage requirement is 2^{174} bytes. T' is about 2^{339} multiplications guaranteeing $\gtrsim 2^{81}$ multiplications security at a preliminary 5541 cycles/byte.
- SPELT using $q = 2$, $n = r = 208$, $d = 3$ (cubics), with 20 cubic terms each equation. Preliminary tests achieve 11744 cycles/byte. The expected complexity for solving 208 variables and 416 equations is $\sim 2^{224}$ (by brute-force trials, which is much faster than XL here), which translates to a 2^{82} proven security level.

5.2   Comparisons: A Case for SPELT

All modern-day microprocessor are capable of doing 64-bit arithmetic at least, and there is a natural way to implement QUAD that runs very fast over $\mathbb{F}_2$, limited only by the ability to stream data. However, as number of variables goes up, the storage needed for QUAD goes up cubically, and for parameter choices that are secure, the dataset overflows even the massive caches of an Intel Core 2. That is what slows down QUAD(2, 320, 320) — tests on a borrowed ia64 server shows that it is almost exactly the same speed as the SPELT(2, 3, 208, 208, [480, 20]). Looking at the numbers, it seems that the idea of specializd polynomials is a good complement to the approach of using polynomial maps for symmetric primitives introduced by Berbain-Gilbert-Patarin.

Table 3. Point-by-Point, SPELT vs. QUAD on a K8 or C2

Stream Cipher	Block	Storage	Cycles/Byte	Security Level
SPELT (2,3,208,208,[480,20])	208b	0.43 MB	11744	2^{82} Proven
SPELT (16,4,108,108,[20,15,10])	864b	48 kB	5541	2^{80} Proven
QUAD (2,320,320)	320b	3.92 MB	13646	2^{82} Proven
QUAD (2,160,160)	160b	0.98 MB	2081	2^{140} Best Attack
SPELT (16,4,32,32,[10,8,5])	128b	8.6 kB	1244	2^{152} Best Attack

We hasten to add that our programming is quite primitive, and may not match the more polished implementations (e.g., [5]). We are still working to improve our programming and parameter choices. Also, in hardware implementations, the power of sparsity should be even more pronounced.

5.3   For Possible Use in Hash Functions

In [8] Billet *et al* proposes to use two-staged constructions with a random 192-bit to 464-bit expanding quadratic map followed by a 464-bit to 384-bit quadratic contraction. They show that in general a PRNG followed by a one-way compression function is a one-way function.

In [15] the same construction is proposed but with SRQ quadratics (see Appendix C) and no proof. Now we see that the abovementioned results from [8] and Prop. 6, which justify the design up to a point. This is an area that still takes some study, and perhaps require extra ideas, such as having a hybrid construction with a sparse polynomial expansion stage and a different kind of contraction stage.

References

1. Aumasson, J.-P., Meier, W.: Analysis of multivariate hash functions. In: Nam, K.-H., Rhee, G. (eds.) ICISC 2007. LNCS, vol. 4817, pp. 309–323. Springer, Heidelberg (2007)

2. Bard, G.V., Courtois, N.T., Jefferson, C.: Efficient methods for conversion and solution of sparse systems of low-degree multivariate polynomials over gf(2) via sat-solvers. Cryptology ePrint Archive, Report 2007/024 (2007), http://eprint.iacr.org/
3. Bardet, M., Faugère, J.-C., Salvy, B.: On the complexity of Gröbner basis computation of semi-regular overdetermined algebraic equations. In: Proceedings of the International Conference on Polynomial System Solving, pp. 71–74 (2004) (Previously INRIA report RR-5049)
4. Bardet, M., Faugère, J.-C., Salvy, B., Yang, B.-Y.: Asymptotic expansion of the degree of regularity for semi-regular systems of equations. In: Gianni, P. (ed.) MEGA 2005 Sardinia (Italy) (2005)
5. Berbain, C., Billet, O., Gilbert, H.: Efficient implementations of multivariate quadratic systems. In: Biham, E., Youssef, A.M. (eds.) SAC 2006. LNCS, vol. 4356, pp. 174–187. Springer, Heidelberg (2007)
6. Berbain, C., Gilbert, H.: On the security of IV dependent stream ciphers. In: Biryukov, A. (ed.) FSE 2007. LNCS, vol. 4593, pp. 254–273. Springer, Heidelberg (2007)
7. Berbain, C., Gilbert, H., Patarin, J.: QUAD: A practical stream cipher with provable security. In: Vaudenay, S. (ed.) EUROCRYPT 2006. LNCS, vol. 4004, pp. 109–128. Springer, Heidelberg (2006)
8. Billet, O., Robshaw, M.J.B., Peyrin, T.: On building hash functions from multivariate quadratic equations. In: Pieprzyk, J., Ghodosi, H., Dawson, E. (eds.) ACISP 2007. LNCS, vol. 4586, pp. 82–95. Springer, Heidelberg (2007)
9. Biryukov, A. (ed.): FSE 2007. LNCS, vol. 4593. Springer, Heidelberg (2007)
10. Blum, L., Blum, M., Shub, M.: Comparison of two pseudo-random number generators. In: Rivest, R.L., Sherman, A., Chaum, D. (eds.) CRYPTO 1982, pp. 61–78. Plenum Press, New York (1983)
11. Buchberger, B.: Ein Algorithmus zum Auffinden der Basiselemente des Restklassenringes nach einem nulldimensionalen Polynomideal. PhD thesis, Innsbruck (1965)
12. Courtois, N.T., Klimov, A., Patarin, J., Shamir, A.: Efficient algorithms for solving overdefined systems of multivariate polynomial equations. In: Preneel, B. (ed.) EUROCRYPT 2000. LNCS, vol. 1807, pp. 392–407. Springer, Heidelberg (2000), http://www.minrank.org/xlfull.pdf
13. Courtois, N.T., Pieprzyk, J.: Cryptanalysis of block ciphers with overdefined systems of equations. In: Zheng, Y. (ed.) ASIACRYPT 2002. LNCS, vol. 2501, pp. 267–287. Springer, Heidelberg (2002)
14. Diem, C.: The XL-algorithm and a conjecture from commutative algebra. In: Lee, P.J. (ed.) ASIACRYPT 2004. LNCS, vol. 3329. Springer, Heidelberg (2004)
15. Ding, J., Yang, B.-Y.: Multivariate polynomials for hashing. In: Inscrypt. LNCS. Springer, Heidelberg (2007), http://eprint.iacr.org/2007/137
16. Farashahi, R.R., Schoenmakers, B., Sidorenko, A.: Efficient pseudorandom generators based on the ddh assumption. In: Public Key Cryptography, pp. 426–441 (2007)
17. Faugère, J.-C.: A new efficient algorithm for computing Gröbner bases (F_4). Journal of Pure and Applied Algebra 139, 61–88 (1999)
18. Faugère, J.-C.: A new efficient algorithm for computing Gröbner bases without reduction to zero (F_5). In: International Symposium on Symbolic and Algebraic Computation — ISSAC 2002, pp. 75–83. ACM Press, New York (2002)
19. Garey, M.R., Johnson, D.S.: Computers and Intractability — A Guide to the Theory of NP-Completeness. W.H. Freeman and Company, New York (1979)
20. Gennaro, R.: An improved pseudo-random generator based on the discrete logarithm problem. Journal of Cryptology 18, 91–110 (2000)

21. Goldreich, O., Rubinfeld, R., Sudan, M.: Learning polynomials with queries: The highly noisy case. SIAM Journal on Discrete Mathematics 13(4), 535–570 (2000)
22. Jiang, S.: Efficient primitives from exponentiation in zp. In: Batten, L.M., Safavi-Naini, R. (eds.) ACISP 2006. LNCS, vol. 4058, pp. 259–270. Springer, Heidelberg (2006)
23. Koblitz, N., Menezes, A.: Another look at provable security (part 2). In: Barua, R., Lange, T. (eds.) INDOCRYPT 2006. LNCS, vol. 4329, pp. 148–175. Springer, Heidelberg (2006)
24. Lazard, D.: Gröbner-bases, Gaussian elimination and resolution of systems of algebraic equations. In: van Hulzen, J.A. (ed.) ISSAC 1983 and EUROCAL 1983. LNCS, vol. 162, pp. 146–156. Springer, Heidelberg (1983)
25. Levin, L., Goldreich, O.: A hard-core predicate for all one-way functions. In: Johnson, D.S. (ed.) 21st ACM Symposium on the Theory of Computing — STOC 1989, pp. 25–32. ACM Press, New York (1989)
26. Matsumoto, T., Imai, H.: Public quadratic polynomial-tuples for efficient signature verification and message-encryption. In: Günther, C.G. (ed.) EUROCRYPT 1988. LNCS, vol. 330, pp. 419–545. Springer, Heidelberg (1988)
27. Raddum, H., Semaev, I.: New technique for solving sparse equation systems. Cryptology ePrint Archive, Report 2006/475 (2006), http://eprint.iacr.org/
28. Semaev, I.: On solving sparse algebraic equations over finite fields (part ii). Cryptology ePrint Archive, Report 2007/280 (2007), http://eprint.iacr.org/
29. Steinfeld, R., Pieprzyk, J., Wang, H.: On the provable security of an efficient rsa-based pseudorandom generator. In: Lai, X., Chen, K. (eds.) ASIACRYPT 2006. LNCS, vol. 4284, pp. 194–209. Springer, Heidelberg (2006)
30. Wolf, C.: Multivariate Quadratic Polynomials in Public Key Cryptography. PhD thesis, Katholieke Universiteit Leuven (2005), http://eprint.iacr.org/2005/393
31. Yang, B.-Y., Chen, J.-M.: All in the XL family: Theory and practice. In: Park, C.-s., Chee, S. (eds.) ICISC 2004. LNCS, vol. 3506, pp. 67–86. Springer, Heidelberg (2005)
32. Yang, B.-Y., Chen, J.-M.: Theoretical analysis of XL over small fields. In: Wang, H., Pieprzyk, J., Varadharajan, V. (eds.) ACISP 2004. LNCS, vol. 3108, pp. 277–288. Springer, Heidelberg (2004)
33. Yang, B.-Y., Chen, O.C.-H., Bernstein, D.J., Chen, J.-M.: Analysis of QUAD. In: Biryukov [9], pp. 290–307

A   Proof of Prop. 1

Proof. We introduce hybrid probability distributions $D_i(\mathbf{S})$ over K^L ($L := \lambda r$): For $0 \le i \le \lambda$ respectively associate with the random variables

$$t^i(\mathbf{S}, \mathbf{x}) := \big(\mathbf{w}_1, \mathbf{w}_2, \ldots, \mathbf{w}_i, \mathbf{P}(\mathbf{x}), \mathbf{P}(\mathbf{Q}(\mathbf{x})), \ldots, \mathbf{P}(\mathbf{Q}^{\lambda-i-1}(\mathbf{x})))$$

where the $\mathbf{w}_j$ and $\mathbf{x}$ are random independent uniformly distributed vectors in K^n and we use the notational conventions that $(\mathbf{w}_1, \mathbf{w}_2, \ldots, \mathbf{w}_i)$ is the null string if $i = 0$, and that

$$\big(\mathbf{P}(\mathbf{x}), \mathbf{P}(\mathbf{Q}(\mathbf{x})), \ldots, \mathbf{P}(\mathbf{Q}^{\lambda-i-1}(\mathbf{x})))$$

is the null string if $i = \lambda$. Consequently $D_0(\mathbf{S})$ is the distribution of the L-unit keystream and $D_\lambda(\mathbf{S})$ is the uniform distribution over K^L. We denote by $p_i(\mathbf{S})$

the probability that A accepts a random L-long sequence distributed according to $D_i(\mathbf{S})$, and p_i the mean value of $p_i(\mathbf{S})$ over the space of sparse polynomial systems $\mathbf{S}$. We have supposed that algorithm A distinguishes between $D_0(\mathbf{S})$ and $D_\lambda(\mathbf{S})$ with advantage , in other words that $|p_0 - p_\lambda| \geq \epsilon$.

Algorithm B works thus: on input $(\mathbf{x}_1, \mathbf{x}_2) \in K^{n+r}$ with $\mathbf{x}_1 \in K^r$, $\mathbf{x}_2 \in K^n$, it selects randomly an i such that $0 \leq i \leq \lambda - 1$ and constructs the L-long vector

$$t(\mathbf{S}, \mathbf{x}_1, \mathbf{x}_2) := (\mathbf{w}_1, \mathbf{w}_2, \ldots, \mathbf{w}_i, \mathbf{x}_1, \mathbf{P}(\mathbf{x}_2), \mathbf{P}(\mathbf{Q}(\mathbf{x}_2)), \ldots, \mathbf{P}(\mathbf{Q}^{\lambda-i-1}(\mathbf{x}_2))).$$

If $(\mathbf{x}_1, \mathbf{x}_2)$ is distributed accordingly to the output distribution of $\mathbf{S}$, i.e. $(\mathbf{x}_1, \mathbf{x}_2) = \mathbf{S}(\mathbf{x}) = (\mathbf{P}(\mathbf{x}), \mathbf{Q}(\mathbf{x}))$ for a uniformly distributed value of $\mathbf{x}$, then

$$t(\mathbf{S}, \mathbf{x}_1, \mathbf{x}_2) := (\mathbf{w}_1, \mathbf{w}_2, \ldots, \mathbf{w}_i, \mathbf{P}(\mathbf{x}), \mathbf{P}(\mathbf{Q}(\mathbf{x})), \ldots, \mathbf{P}(\mathbf{Q}^{\lambda-i-1}(\mathbf{x})))$$

is distributed according to $D_i(\mathbf{S})$. Now if $(\mathbf{x}_1, \mathbf{x}_2)$ is distributed according to the uniform distribution, then

$$t(\mathbf{S}, \mathbf{x}_1, \mathbf{x}_2) = (\mathbf{w}_1, \mathbf{w}_2, \ldots, \mathbf{w}_i, \mathbf{x}_1, \mathbf{P}(\mathbf{x}_2), \mathbf{P}(\mathbf{Q}(\mathbf{x}_2)), \ldots, \mathbf{P}(\mathbf{Q}^{\lambda-i-2}(\mathbf{x}_2)))$$

which is distributed according to $D_{i+1}(\mathbf{S})$. To distinguish between the output of $\mathbf{S}$ from uniform, algorithm B calls A with inputs $(\mathbf{S}, t(\mathbf{S}, \mathbf{x}_1, \mathbf{x}_2))$ and returns that same return value. Hence

$$\left| \Pr_{\mathbf{S}, \mathbf{x}}(B(\mathbf{S}, \mathbf{S}(\mathbf{x})) = 1 - \Pr_{\mathbf{S}, \mathbf{x}}(B(\mathbf{S}, \mathbf{S}(\mathbf{x}_1, \mathbf{x}_2)) = 1 \right|$$

$$= \left| \frac{1}{\lambda} \sum_{i=0}^{\lambda-1} p_i - \frac{1}{\lambda} \sum_{i=0}^{\lambda-1} p_i \right| = \frac{1}{\lambda} |p_0 - p_\lambda| \geq \frac{\epsilon}{\lambda}.$$

B   XL and $\mathbf{F}_4$-$\mathbf{F}_5$ Families for System-Solving

The XL and $\mathbf{F}_4$-$\mathbf{F}_5$ families of algorithms are spiritual descendants of Lazard's idea [24]: run an elimination on an extended Macaulay matrix (i.e., extending the resultant concept to many variables) as an improvement to Buchberger's algorithm for computing Gröbner bases [11].

Since we cannot discuss these methods in detail, we try to describe them briefly along with their projected complexities. Again, suppose we have the system $P_1(\mathbf{x}) = P_2(\mathbf{x}) = \cdots = P_m(\mathbf{x}) = 0$, where P_i is a degree-d_i polynomial in $\mathbf{x} = (x_1, \ldots, x_n)$, coefficients and variables in $K = \mathbb{F}_q$.

Method XL [12]: Fix a degree $D(\geq \max P_i)$. The set of degree-D-or-lower monomials is denoted $\mathcal{T} = \mathcal{T}^{(D)}$. $|\mathcal{T}^{(D)}|$ is the number of degree $\leq D$ monomials and will be denoted $T = T^{(D)}$. We now take each equation $P_i = 0$ and multiply it by every monomial up to $D - d_i$ to get an equation that is at most degree D. Collect all such equations in the set $\mathcal{R} = \mathcal{R}^{(D)} := \bigcup_{i=1}^m \{(uP_i = 0) : u \in \mathcal{T}^{(D-d_i)}\}$. We treat every monomial in $\mathcal{T}$ as independent and try to solve $\mathcal{R}$ as a linear system of equations.

The critical parameter is the difference between $I = \dim(\mathrm{span}\mathcal{R})$, the rank of the space of equations $\mathcal{R}$, and T. If $T - I = 0$, the original system cannot be satisfied;

if $T - I = 1$, then we should find a unique solution (with very high probability). Also, if $T - I < \min(D, q - 1)$, we can reduce to a univariate equation [12]. We would like to predict D_0, the smallest D enabling resolution.

Note: For any pair of indices $i, j \leq m$, among linear combinations of the multiples of $P_j = 0$ will be $P_i P_j = 0$, and among linear combinations of the multiples of $P_i = 0$ will be $P_i P_j = 0$ — i.e., one dependency in span$\mathcal{R}$. In $\mathbb{F}_q$, $(P_i)^q = P_i$ which generates a similar type of dependency.

Proposition 7 ([32]). *Denote by $[u]s$ the coefficient of the monomial u in the expansion of s, then:*

1. $T = [t^D] \dfrac{(1 - t^q)^n}{(1 - t)^{n+1}}$ *which reduces to* $\binom{n+D}{D}$ *when* $q > D$, *and* $\sum_{j=0}^{D} \binom{n}{j}$ *when* $q = 2$.

2. *If the system is regular up to degree D, i.e., if **the relations $\mathcal{R}^{(D)}$ has no other dependencies than the obvious ones generated by $P_i P_j = P_j P_i$ and $P_i^q = P_i$**, then*

$$T - I = [t^D]\, G(t), \text{ where } G(t) := G(t; n; d_1, d_2, \ldots, d_m) = \frac{(1 - t^q)^n}{(1 - t)^{n+1}} \prod_{j=1}^{m} \left(\frac{1 - t^{d_j}}{1 - t^{q\, d_j}} \right).$$

$$(3)$$

3. *For overdefined systems, Eq. 3 cannot hold when $D > D_{XL} = \min\{D : [t^D] G(t) \leq 0\}$. If Eq. 3 holds up for every $D < D_{XL}$ and resolves at D_{XL}, we say that the system is **q-semiregular**. It is generally believed [3,14] that **for random systems it is overwhelmingly likely that $D_0 = D_{XL}$, and indeed the system is not q-semiregular with very small probability.***

4. *When it resolves, XL takes $C_{XL} \lesssim (c_0 + c_1 \lg T)\, \tau\, T^2$ multiplications in $\mathbb{F}_q$, using a sparse solver like Wiedemann [31]. Here τ is the average number of terms per equation.*

We cannot describe methods $\mathbf{F_4}$-$\mathbf{F_5}$ [17,18], which are just too sophisticated and complex to present here. Instead, we simply sketch a result that yields their complexities:

Proposition 8. *[3] For q-semiregular systems, $\mathbf{F_4}$ or $\mathbf{F_5}$ operates at the degree*

$$D = D_{reg} := \min \left\{ D : [t^D] \left(\frac{(1 - t^q)^n}{(1 - t)^n} \prod_{j=1}^{m} \left(\frac{1 - t^{d_j}}{1 - t^{q\, d_j}} \right) \right) < 0 \right\},$$

and take $\lesssim (c_0' + c_1' \lg \bar{T})\bar{T}^{\omega}$ multiplications, where $\bar{T} = [t^{D_{reg}}]\, ((1 - t^q)^n (1 - t)^{-n})$ counts the monomials of degree exactly D_{reg}, and $2 < \omega \leq 3$ is the order of matrix multiplication used.

We do not know what works best under various resource limitations. We take the position of [33], e.g., XL with a sparse solver represents the best way to solve large and more or less random overdetermined systems when *the size of main memory space* is the critical restraint.

C   SRQ, a Potential Candidate for One Way Function

An SRQ (Sparse Rotated Quadratics) instance is an $\mathcal{MQ}$ system specialized so that it is non-sparse but can be computed with fewer computations than normal quadratics.

Problem SRQ(q, n, m, h)**:** In $\mathbb{F}_q$, solve $P_1(\mathbf{x}) = P_2(\mathbf{x}) = \cdots = P_m(\mathbf{x}) = 0$. The P_i are quadratics formed from "sequence of rotations", that is Start with $P_0 = x_1 x_2 + x_3 x_4 + \cdots + x_{n-1} x_n$ (where n is even), and obtain successive P_j by performing sparse affine maps on $\mathbf{x}$. I.e., $\mathbf{x}^{(0)} := \mathbf{x}$, $\mathbf{x}^{(i)} := M^{(i)} \mathbf{x}^{(i-1)} + \mathbf{b}^{(i)}$, $y_i := P_i(\mathbf{x}) := P_0(\mathbf{x}^{(i)}) + c_i$, $\forall i$. Matrices $M^{(i)}$ are randomly chosen, invertible and sparse with h entries per row.

The idea behind SRQ is that any quadratic map can be written as $f \circ L$, where f is a standard form and L is an invertible linear map. Now we will choose L to be sparse. A standard form for characteristic 2 fields is the "rank form" which for full-rank quadratics is

$$P_0(\mathbf{x}) = x_1 x_2 + x_3 x_4 + \cdots x_{n-1} x_n.$$

Clearly, by taking a random $\mathbf{c}$ and b, we can give $P_0(\mathbf{x} + \mathbf{c}) + b$ *any* random affine part. Since each $\mathbf{x}^{(i)}$ is related to $\mathbf{x} = \mathbf{x}^{(0)}$ by an invertible affine map, this holds for every component P_i. This means that results pertaining to sparsity of the linear terms such as [1] (cf. Sec. 4.3) never apply, and hence it is plausible for SRQ to form a one way function class.

In Fig. 1, the samples labelled "sparse non-random" are SRQ tests. It seem as if their behavior under MAGMA's $\mathbf{F}_4$ is no different than normal quadratics.

In this SRQ construction, even if $h = 3$ (the rotation matrices $M^{(i)}$ have only three entries per row), the number of cross-terms in each equations still quickly increases to have as many terms as totally random ones, so point 2 in Sec. 4.3 does not apply here. Indeed, since a quadratic over $\mathbb{F}_2$ of rank $2k$ has bias 2^{-k-1}, the SRQ form acts exactly like a random quadratic under point 3 in Sec. 4.3.

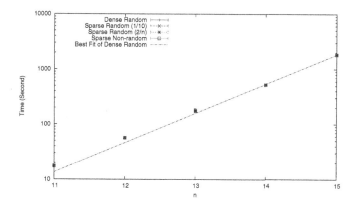

Fig. 1. "Sparsely $2n \to 3n$ $\mathbb{F}_2$ quadratics" in MAGMA

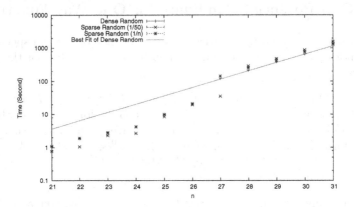

Fig. 2. "Sparsely $n \to 2n$ $\mathbb{F}_2$ quadratics" in MAGMA

MXL2: Solving Polynomial Equations over GF(2) Using an Improved Mutant Strategy

Mohamed Saied Emam Mohamed[1], Wael Said Abd Elmageed Mohamed[1],
Jintai Ding[2], and Johannes Buchmann[1]

[1] TU Darmstadt, FB Informatik,
Hochschulstrasse 10, 64289 Darmstadt, Germany
{mohamed,wael,buchmann}@cdc.informatik.tu-darmstadt.de
[2] Department of Mathematical Sciences, University of Cincinnati,
Cincinnati OH 45220, USA
jintai.ding@uc.edu

Abstract. MutantXL is an algorithm for solving systems of polynomial equations that was proposed at SCC 2008. This paper proposes two substantial improvements to this algorithm over GF(2) that result in significantly reduced memory usage. We present experimental results comparing *MXL2* to the XL algorithm, the MutantXL algorithm and Magma's implementation of F_4. For this comparison we have chosen small, randomly generated instances of the MQ problem and quadratic systems derived from HFE instances. In both cases, the largest matrices produced by *MXL2* are substantially smaller than the ones produced by MutantXL and XL. Moreover, for a significant number of cases we even see a reduction of the size of the largest matrix when we compare *MXL2* against Magma's F_4 implementation.

1 Introduction

Solving systems of multivariate quadratic equations is an important problem in cryptology. The problem of solving such systems over finite fields is called the Multivariate Quadratic (MQ) problem. In the last two decades, several cryptosystems based on the MQ problem have been proposed as in [1,2,3,4,5]. For generic instances it is proven that the MQ problem is NP-complete [6]. However for some cryptographic schemes the problem of solving the corresponding MQ system has been demonstrated to be easier, allowing these schemes to be broken. Therefore it is very important to develop efficient algorithms to solve MQ systems.

Recently, MutantXL [7] and MutantF4 [8] were proposed at SCC 2008, two algorithms based on Ding's mutant concept. Roughly speaking, in algorithms that operate on linearized representations of the polynomial system by increasing degree – such as F_4 and XL – this concept proposes to maximize the effect of lower-degree polynomials occurring during the computation. In this paper, we present MutantXL2 (*MXL2*) – a new algorithm based on MutantXL that oftentimes allows to solve systems with significantly smaller matrix sizes than

J. Buchmann and J. Ding (Eds.): PQCrypto 2008, LNCS 5299, pp. 203–215, 2008.

XL and MutantXL. Moreover, experimental results for both HFE systems and random systems demonstrate that for a significant number of cases we even get a reduction of the size of the largest matrix when comparing *MXL2* against Magma's F_4 implementation.

The paper is organized as follows. In Section 2 the key ideas of the *MXL2* algorithm and the required definitions are presented. A formal description and explanations of the algorithm are in Section 3. Section 4 contains the experimental results. In Section 5 we conclude our paper.

2   Improvements to the Mutant Strategy

In this section we present the key ideas of the *MXL2* algorithm and explain their importance for solving systems of multivariate quadratic polynomial equations more efficiently. Throughout the paper we will use the following notations: Let $X := \{x_1, \ldots, x_n\}$ be a set of variables, upon which we impose the following order: $x_1 < x_2 < \ldots < x_n$. Let

$$R = \mathbb{F}_2[x_1, \ldots, x_n]/(x_1^2 - x_1, \ldots, x_n^2 - x_n)$$

be the ring of polynomial functions over $\mathbb{F}_2$ in X with the monomials of R ordered by the graded lexicographical order $<_{glex}$. By an abuse of notation, we call the elements of R polynomials throughout this paper. Let $P = (p_1, \ldots, p_m) \in R^m$ be a sequence of m quadratic polynomials in R. Throughout the operation of the algorithms described in this paper, a degree bound D will be used. This degree bound denotes the maximum degree of the polynomials contained in P. Note that the contents of P will be changed throughout the operation of the algorithm.

Some algorithms for solving the system

$$p_j(x_1, \ldots, x_n) = 0, 1 \leq j \leq m \tag{1}$$

such as XL and MutantXL are based on finding new elements in the ideal generated by the polynomials of P that correspond to equations that are easy to solve, i.e. univariate or linear polynomials. The MutantXL algorithm is an application of the mutant concept to the XL algorithm. The following definitions explain the term *mutant*:

Definition 1. *Let $g \in R$ be a polynomial in the ideal generated by the elements of P. Naturally, it can be written as*

$$g = \sum_{p \in P} g_p p \tag{2}$$

where $g_p \in R$, $p \in P$. The level of this representation is defined to be

$$\max\{\deg(g_p p) \ : \ p \in P\}.$$

Note that this level depends on P. The level *of the polynomial g is defined to be the minimum level of all of its representations.*

Definition 2. *Let $g \in R$ be a polynomial in the ideal generated by the elements of P. The polynomial g is called a* mutant *with respect to P if its degree is less than its level.*

Next, we explain the meaning of mutants. When a mutant is written as a linear combination (2), then one of the polynomials $g_p p$ has a degree exceeding the degree of the mutant. This means that a mutant of degree d cannot be found as a linear combination of polynomials of the form mp where m is a monomial, $p \in P$ and the degree of mp is at most d. However, such mutants could help in solving the system (1) if we can find them efficiently.

Given a degree bound D, the MutantXL algorithm extends the system of polynomial equations (1) by multiplying the polynomials on the left-hand side by all monomials up to degree $D - \deg(p_i)$. Then the system is linearized by considering the monomials as new variables and applying Gaussian elimination on the resulting linear system. MutantXL searches for univariate equations, if no such equations exist, it searches for mutants, that are new polynomials of degree $< D$. If mutants are found, they are multiplied by all monomials such that the produced polynomials have degree $\leq D$. Using this strategy, MutantXL achieves to enlarge the system without incrementing D.

In many experiments with MutantXL on some HFE systems and some randomly generated multivariate quadratic systems, we noticed that there are two problems. The first occurs when the number of lower degree mutants is very large, we observed this produces many reductions to zero. A second problem occurs when an iteration does not produce mutants at all or produces only an insufficient number of mutants to solve the system at lower degree D. In this case MutantXL behaves like XL.

Our proposed improvements handle both problems, while using the same linearization strategy as the original MutantXL. This allows us to compute the solution with fewer polynomials. To handle the first problem, we need the following notation.

Let $S_k : \{ m \in R : deg(m) \leq k\}$ be the set of all monomials of R that have degree less than or equal to k. Combinatorially, the number of elements of this set can be computed as

$$|S_k| = \sum_{\ell=1}^{k} \binom{n}{\ell}, 1 \leq k \leq n \tag{3}$$

where n is the number of variables.

The *MXL2* algorithm as well as MutantXL are based on the mutant concept, however *MXL2* introduces a heuristic strategy of only choosing the minimum number of mutants, which will be called *necessary mutants*. Let k be the degree of the lowest-degree mutant occuring and the number of the linearly independent elements of degree $\leq k+1$ in P be $Q(k+1)$. Then the smallest number of mutants that are needed to generate $|S_{k+1}|$ linearly independent equations of degree $\leq$ $k + 1$ is

$$\lceil(|S_{k+1}| - Q(k + 1))/n\rceil, \tag{4}$$

where S_{k+1} is as in (3) and n is the number of variables. Therefore by multiplying only the necessary number of mutants, the system can potentially be solved by a smaller number of polynomials and a minimum number of multiplication. This handles the first problem. In the following we explain how *MXL2* solves the second problem.

Suppose we have a system with not enough mutants. In this case we noticed that in the process of space enlargement, MutantXL multiply all original polynomials by all monomials of degree $D - 2$. In most cases only a small number of extended polynomials that are produced are needed to solve the system. Moreover the system will be solved only when some of these elements are reduced to lower degree elements. To be more precise, the degree of the extended polynomials is decreased only if the higher degree terms are eliminated. We have found that by using a partitioned enlargement strategy and a successive multiplication of polynomials with variables method, while excluding redundant products, we can solve the system with a smaller number of equations. To discuss this idea in details we first need to define the following:

Definition 3. *The leading variable of a polynomial p in R is x, if x is the smallest variable, according to the order defined on the variables, in the leading term of p. It can be written as*

$$LV(p) = x \tag{5}$$

Definition 4. *Let $P_k = \{p \in P: deg(p) = k\}$ and $x \in X$. We define P_k^x as follows*

$$P_k^x = \{p \in P_k : LV(p) = x\} \tag{6}$$

In the process of space enlargement, *MXL2* deals with the polynomials of P_D differently. Let P_D be divided into a set of subsets depending on the leading variable of each polynomial in it. In other words, $P_D = \bigcup_{x \in X} P_D^x$, where X is the set of variables as defined previously and P_D^x as in (6). *MXL2* enlarges P by increments D and multiplies the elements of P_D as follows: Let x be the largest variable, according to the order defined on the variables, that has $P_D^x \neq \emptyset$. *MXL2* successively multiplies each polynomial of P_D^x by variables such that each variable is multiplied only once. This process is repeated for the next smaller variable x with $P_D^x \neq \emptyset$ until the solution is obtained, otherwise the system enlarges to the next D. Therefore *MXL2* may solve the system by enlarging only subsets of P_D, while MutantXL solves the system by enlarging all the elements of P_D. *MXL2* handles the second problem by using this partitioned enlargement strategy.

In the next section we describe *MXL2*. In section 4 we present examples that show that *MXL2* completely beats the first version of MutantXL and beats in most cases Magma's implementation of F_4 for only the memory efficiency.

3   *MXL2* Algorithm

In this Section we explain the *MXL2* algorithm. We use the notation of the previous section. So P is a finite set of polynomials in R. For simplicity, we assume that the system (1) is quadratic and has a unique solution.

We use a graded lexicographical ordering in the process of linearization and during the Gaussian elimination. *MXL2* creates a *multiplication history* one dimension array to store each previous variable multiplier of each polynomial and for the originals the previous multiplier is 1. The set of solutions of the system is defined as $\{x = b : x \text{ is variable and } b \in \{0,1\}\}$. The description of the algorithm is as follows.

- *Initialization* Use Gaussian elimination to make P linearly independent. Set the set of *root polynomials* to $\emptyset$, the *total degree bound* D to 2, the *elimination degree* to D, *system extended* to false, *mutants* to $\emptyset$, and *multiplication history* to a one dimension array with number of elements as P and initialize these elements by ones (Algorithm 1 lines 16 – 21).
- *Gauss* Use linearization to transform the set of all polynomials in P of degree $\leq$ *elimination degree* into reduced row echelon form (Algorithm 1 lines 23 and 24).
- *Extract Roots* copy all new polynomials of degree ≤ 2 to the root polynomials set (Algorithm 1 line 25).
- If there are univariate polynomials in the *roots*, then determine the values of the corresponding variables, and remove the solved variables from the variable set. If this solves the system return the solution and terminate. Otherwise, substitute the values for the variables in the *roots*, set P to the *roots*, set *elimination degree* to the maximum degree of the *roots*, reset the *multiplication history* to an array of number of elements as P and initialize these elements to ones, and go back to *Gauss* (Algorithm 1 lines 26 – 32).
- *Extract Mutants* copy all new polynomials of degree $<$ D from $\{P\}$ to *mutants* (Algorithm 1 line 34).
- If there are mutants found, then extend the *multiplication history* by an array of the number of elements of the same length as the new polynomials initialized by ones, multiply the necessary number of mutants having the minimum degree, as stated in Section 2, by all variables, set the *multiplication history* for each new polynomial by its variable multiplier, include the resulting polynomials in P, set the *elimination degree* to that minimum degree + 1, and remove all multiplied mutants from *mutants* (Algorithm 2 lines 9 – 20).
- Otherwise, if *system extended* is false; then increment D by 1, set x to the largest leading variable under the variable order satisfies that $P_{D-1}^x \neq \emptyset$, set *system extended* to true; multiply each polynomial p in P_{D-1}^x by all unsolved variables $<$ the variable stored in the *multiplication history* of p, include the resulting polynomials in P, set x to the next smaller leading variable satisfies that $P_{D-1}^x \neq \emptyset$, if there is no such variable, then set *system extended* to false, *elimination degree* to D, and go back to *Gauss* (Algorithm 2 lines 22 – 39).

To give a more formal description of *MXL2* algorithm and its sub-algorithms, firstly we need to define the following subroutines:

Solve(*Roots*, X): if there are univariate equations in the *roots*, then solve them and return the solutions.
Substitute(*Solution*, *roots*): use all the solutions found to simplify the *roots*.
Reset(*history*, n): reset history to an array with number of elements equal to n and initialized by ones.
Extend(*history*, n): append to history an array with number of elements equal to n and initialized by ones.
SelectNecessary(M, D, k, n): compute the necessary number of mutants with degree k as in equation (4), let the mutants be ordered depending on their leading terms, then return the necessary mutants by ascending order.
Xpartition(P, x): return $\{p \in P : LV(p) = x\}$.
LargestLeading(P): return $\max\{y : y = LV(p), p \in P, y \in X\}$.
NextSmallerLeading(P, x): return $\max\{y: y = LV(p), p \in P, y \in X$ and $y < x\}$.

Algorithm1. *MXL2*

1. **Inputs**
2. F: set of quadratic polynomials.
3. D: highest system degree starts by 2.
4. X: set of variables.
5. **Output**
6.   *Solution*: solution of F=0.
7. **Variables**
8. RP: set of all regular polynomials produced during the process.
9. M: set of mutants.
10.   *roots*: set of all polynomials of degree ≤ 2
11. x: variable
12.   *ed*: elimination degree
13.   *history*: array of length $\#RP$ to store previous variable multiplier
14.   *extended*: a flag to enlarge the system
15. **Begin**
16. $RP \leftarrow F$
17. $M \leftarrow \varnothing$
18. *Solution* $\leftarrow \varnothing$
19. *ed* $\leftarrow 2$
20. *history* $\leftarrow [1, \ldots, 1]$
21. *extended* $\leftarrow$ false
22. **repeat**
23.   Linearize RP using graded lex order
24.   Gauss(Extract($RP, ed, \leq$), *history*)
25.   *roots* $\leftarrow$ *roots* $\cup$ Extract($RP, 2, \leq$)
26.   *Solution* $\leftarrow$ *Solution* $\cup$ Solve(*roots*, X)
27.   **if** there are solutions **then**

28. $roots \leftarrow$ Substitute($Solution, roots$)
29. $RP \leftarrow roots$
30. $history \leftarrow$ Reset($history, \#roots$)
31. $M \leftarrow \emptyset$
32. $ed \leftarrow D \leftarrow \max\{deg(p) : p \in roots\}$
33.   **else**
34. $M \leftarrow M \cup$ Extract($RP, D - 1, \leq$)
35. $RP \leftarrow RP \cup$ Enlarge($RP, M, X, D, x, history, extended, ed$)
36.   **end if**
37. **until** $roots = \varnothing$
38. **End**

Algorithm2: Enlarge($RP, M, X, D, x, history, extended, ed$)

1. *history, extended, ed*: may be changed during the process.
2. **Variable**
3. NP: set of new polynomials.
4. NM: necessary mutants
5. Q: set of degree D-1 polynomials have leading variable x
6. k: minimum degree of the mutants
7. **Begin**
8. $NP \leftarrow \emptyset$
9. **if** $M \neq \emptyset$ **then**
10. $k \leftarrow \min\{deg(p) \in M\}$
11. $NM \leftarrow$ SelectNecessary($M, D, k, \#X$)
12.   Extend($history, \#X \cdot \#NM$)
13.   **for all** $p \in NM$ **do**
14.   **for all** y in X **do**
15. $NP \leftarrow NP \cup \{y \cdot p\}$
16. $history[y \cdot p] = y$
17.   **end for**
18.   **end for**
19. $M \leftarrow M \setminus SM$
20. $ed \leftarrow k + 1$
21. **else**
22.   **if** not *extended* **then**
23. $D \leftarrow D + 1$
24. $x \leftarrow$ LargestLeading(Extract($RP, D - 1, =$))
25. $extended \leftarrow$ true
26.   **end if**
27. $Q \leftarrow$ XPartition(Extract($RP, D - 1, =$), x)
28.   Extend($history, \#X \cdot \#Q$)
29.   **for all** $p \in Q$ **do**
30.   **for all** $y \in X: y < history[p]$ **do**
31. $NP \leftarrow NP \cup \{y \cdot p\}$
32. $history[y \cdot p] \leftarrow y$

33.   **end for**
34.   **end for**
35. $x \leftarrow$ NextSmallerLeading(Extract$(RP, D - 1, =), x$)
36.   **if** x is undefined **then**
37.   *extend* $\leftarrow$ false
38.   **end if**
39. $ed \leftarrow D$
40. **end if**
41. Return NP
42. **End**

Algorithm3: Extract$(P, degree, operation)$

1. P: set of polynomials
2. SP: set of selected polynomials
3. *operation*: conditional operations belongs to $\{<, \leq, >, \geq, =\}$
4. **Begin**
5. **for all** $p \in P$ **do**
6.   **if** $\deg(p)$ *operation degree* **then**
7. $SP \leftarrow SP \cup \{p\}$
8.   **end if**
9. **end for**
10. **End**

We show that the system is partially enlarged, so *MXL2* leads to the original MutantXL if the system is solved with the last partition enlarged. Whereas *MXL2* outperforms the original MutantXL if it solves the system by earlier partition enlarged. This will be clarified experimentally in the next section.

4   Experimental Results

In this section, we present the experimental results for our implementation of the *MXL2* algorithm. We compare *MXL2* with the original MutantXL, Magma's implementation of F_4, and the XL algorithm for some random systems (5-24 equations in 5-24 variables). The results can be found in Table 1. Moreover, we have another comparison for *MXL2*, original MutantXL, and Magma for some HFE systems (25-55 equations in 25-55 variables) in order to clarify that mutant strategy has the ability to be helpful with different types of systems. See the results in Table 2. For XL and MutantXL, all monomials up to the degree bound D are computed and accounted for as columns in the matrix, even if they did not appear in any polynomial. For *MXL2* on the other hand, we omitted columns that only contained zeros.

Random systems were taken from [9], HFE systems (30-55 equations in 30-55 variables) were generated with code contained in [10], and one HFE system (25 equations in 25 variables) was taken from the Hotaru distribution [11]. The results for F_4 were obtained using Magma version 2.13-10; the parameter

Table 1. Random Comparison

# Var # Eq	XL	MutantXL	Magma	MXL2
5	30×26	30×26	30×26	**20×25**
6*	42×42	47×42	46×40	**33×38**
7*	203×99	154×64	154×64	**63×64**
8*	296×163	136×93	131×88	**96×93**
9	414×256	414×256	480×226	**151×149**
10	560×386	560×386	624×3396	**228×281**
11	737×562	737×562	804×503	**408×423**
12	948×794	948×794	1005×704	**519×610**
13	1196×1093	1196×1093	1251×980	**1096×927**
14*	6475×3473	1771×1471	1538×1336	**1191×1185**
15*	8520×4944	2786×2941	2639×1535	**1946×1758**
16	11016×6885	11016×6885	9993×4034	**2840×2861**
17	14025×9402	14025×9402	12382×5784	**3740×4184**
18	17613×12616	17613×12616	15187×8120	**6508×7043**
19	21850×16664	21850×16664	18441×11041	**9185×11212**
20	26810×21700	26810×21700	22441×14979	**14302×12384**
21*	153405×82160	31641×27896	26860×19756	**14365×20945**
22*	194579×110056	92831×35443	63621×21855	**35463×25342**
23*	244145×145499	76558×44552	41866×29010	**39263×36343**
24*	no sol. obtained	298477×190051	207150×78637	**75825×69708**

`HFE:=true` was used to solve HFE systems. The MXL2 algorithm has been implemented in C/C++ based on the latest version of M4RI package [12]. For each example, we give the number of equations (#Eq), number of variables (#Var), the degree of the hidden univariate high-degree polynomial for HFE (HUD) and the size of the largest linear system to which Gauss is applied. The '*' in the first column for random systems means that, there are some mutants in this system.

In all experiments, the highest degree of the polynomials generated by MutantXL and MXL2 is equal to the highest degree of the S-polynomial in Magma. In MXL2 implementation, we use only one matrix from starting to the end of the process by enlarging and extending the initial matrix, the largest matrix is the accumulative of all polynomials that are held in the memory. unfortunately, in Magma we can not know the total accumulative matrices size because it is not an open source.

In Table 1, we see that in practice MXL2 is an improvement for memory efficiency over the original MutantXL. For systems for which mutants are produced during the computation, MutantXL is better than XL. If no mutants occur, MutantXL behaves identically to XL. Comparing XL, MutantXL, and MXL2; MXL2 is the most efficient even if there are no mutants. In almost all cases MXL2 has the smallest number of columns as well as a smaller number of rows compared to the F_4 implementation contained in Magma. We can see easily that 70% of the cases MXL2 is better, 5% is equal, and 25% is worse.

Table 2. HFE Comparison

# Var # Eq	HUD	Magma	MutantXL	MXL2
25	96	12495×15276	14219×15276	**11926×15276**
30	64	23832×31931	26922×31931	**19174×31931**
35	48	27644×59536	31255×59536	**30030×59536**
40	33	45210×102091	49620×102091	**46693×102091**
45	24	43575×164221	57734×164221	**45480×164221**
50	40	75012×251176	85025×251176	**67826×251176**
55	48	104068×368831	119515×368831	**60116×368831**

Table 3. Time Comparison

System	MutantXL	MXL2
RND5	0.004	0.001
RND6	0.001	0.004
RND7	0.004	0.008
RND8	0.004	0.001
RND9	0.016	0.012
RND10	0.024	0.016
RND11	0.044	0.024
RND12	0.072	0.040
RND13	0.112	0.084
RND14	0.252	0.184
RND15	0.372	0.256
RND16	13.629	1.636
RND17	28.342	2.420
RND18	92.078	9.561
RND19	178.971	20.057
RND20	346.062	70.001
RND21	699.108	126.576
RND22	1182.410	498.839
RND23	1636.000	854.753
RND24	23370.001	12384.700

In Table 2, we also present HFE systems comparison. In all these seven examples for all the three algorithms (Magma's F_4, MutantXL, and MXL2), all the monomials up to degree bound D appear in Magma, MutantXL, and MXL2. therefore, the number of columns are equal in all the three algorithms. It is clear that MXL2 has a smaller number of rows in four cases of seven. In all cases MXL2 outperforms MutantXL.

A time comparison in seconds for random systems between MutantXL and MXL2 can be found in Table 3. We use in this comparison a Sun Fire X2200 M2 server with 2 dual core Opteron 2218 CPU running at 2.6GHz and 8GB of RAM. We did not make such a comparison between Magma and MXL2 for HFE instances. This is due to the following reasons: we use a special Magma

Table 4. Strategy Comparison

# Var # Eq	Method1	Method2	Method3	Method4
5	30×26	30×26	25×25	**20×25**
6	47×42	47×42	33×38	**33×38**
7	154×64	63×64	154×64	**63×64**
8	136×93	96×93	136×93	**96×93**
9	414×239	414×239	232×149	**151×149**
10	560×367	560×367	318×281	**228×281**
11	737×541	737×541	408×423	**408×423**
12	948×771	948×771	519×610	**519×610**
13	1196×1068	1196×1068	1616×967	**1096×927**
14	1771×1444	1484×1444	1485×1185	**1191×1185**
15	2786×1921	1946×1921	2681×1807	**1946×1758**
16	11016×5592	10681×5592	6552×2861	**2840×2861**
17	14025×7919	13601×7919	4862×4184	**3740×4184**
18	17613×10930	17086×10930	6508×7043	**6508×7043**
19	21850×14762	21205×14762	9185×11212	**9185×11212**
20	26810×19554	26031×19554	14302×12384	**14302×12384**
21	31641×25447	31641×25447	14428×20945	**14365×20945**
22	92831×34624	38116×32665	56385×28195	**35463×25342**
23	76558×43650	45541×43650	39263×36343	**39263×36343**
24	298477×190051	297810×190051	75825×69708	**75825×69708**

implementation for HFE systems by using the HFE:=true parameter, the *MXL2* implementation is based on M4RI package which is not in its optimal speed as claimed by M4RI contributors and the *MXL2* implementation itself is not optimal at this point. From Table 3, it is clear that the *MXL2* has a good performance for speed compared to MutantXL.

In order to shed light on which strategy (necessary mutants or partitioned enlargement) worked more than the other in which case, we make another comparison for random systems. In this comparison, we have 4 methods that cover all possibilities to use the two strategies. Method1 is for multiplying all lower degree mutants that are extracted at certain level, non of the two strategies are used. Method2 is for multiplying only our claimed necessary number of mutants, necessary mutant strategy. We use Method3 for partitioned enlargement strategy, multiplications are for all lower degree mutants. For both the two strategies which is *MXL2* too, we use Metod4. See Table 4.

In Table 4, comparing Method1 and Method2, we see that practically the necessary mutant strategy sometimes has an effect in the cases which have a large enough number of hidden mutants (cases 7, 8, 14, 15, 22 and 23). In a case that has less mutants (cases 6, 21 and 24) or no mutants at all (cases 5, 9, 10-13, and 16-20), the total number of rows is the same as in Method1. Furthermore, in case 22 because of not all mutants were multiplied, the number of columns is decreased. By comparing Method1 and Method3, most of the cases in the partitioned enlargement strategy have a smaller number of rows except for case

13 which is worst because Method3 extracts mutants earlier than Method1, so it multiplies all these mutants while MutantXL solves and ends before multiplying them. In a case that is solved with the last partition, the two methods are identical (case 7 and 8).

Indeed, using both the two strategies as in Method4 is the best choice. In all cases the number of rows in this method is less than or equal the minimum number of rows for both Method2 and Method3,

$$\#rows \ in \ Method4 \leq min(\#rows \ in \ Method2, \#rows \ in \ Method3)$$

In some cases (13, 15 and 22) using both the two strategies leads to a smaller number of columns.

5   Conclusion

Experimentally, we can conclude that the $MXL2$ algorithm is an efficient improvement over the original MutantXL in case of GF(2). Not only can $MXL2$ solve multivariate systems at a lower degree than the usual XL but also can solve these systems using a smaller number of polynomials than the original MutantXL, since we produce all possible new equations without enlarging the number of the monomials. Therefore the size of the matrix constructed by $MXL2$ is much smaller than the matrix constructed by the original MutantXL. We did not claim that we are absolutely better than F_4 but we are going in this direction. We apply the mutant strategy into two different systems, namely random and HFE. We believe that mutant strategy is a general approach that can improve most of multivariate polynomial solving algorithms.

In the future we will study how to build $MXL2$ using a sparse matrix representation instead of the dense one to optimize our implementation. We also need to enhance the mutant selection strategy to reduce the number of redundant polynomials, study the theoretical aspects of the algorithm, apply the algorithm to other systems of equations, generalize it to other finite fields and deal with systems of equations that have multiple solutions.

Acknowledgment

We would like to thank Ralf-Philipp Weinmann for several helpful discussions and comments on earlier drafts of this paper.

References

1. Matsumoto, T., Imai, H.: Public Quadratic Polynomial-Tuples for Efficient Signature-Verification and Message-Encryption. In: Günther, C.G. (ed.) EURO-CRYPT 1988. LNCS, vol. 330, pp. 419–453. Springer, Heidelberg (1988)
2. Patarin, J.: Hidden Fields Equations (HFE) and Isomorphisms of Polynomials (IP): two new families of Asymmetric Algorithms. In: Maurer, U.M. (ed.) EUROCRYPT 1996. LNCS, vol. 1070, pp. 33–48. Springer, Heidelberg (1996)

3. Patarin, J., Goubin, L., Courtois, N.: C^{*}_{-+} and HM: Variations Around Two Schemes of T. Matsumoto and H. Imai. In: Ohta, K., Pei, D. (eds.) ASIACRYPT 1998. LNCS, vol. 1514, pp. 35–50. Springer, Heidelberg (1998)
4. Moh, T.: A Public Key System With Signature And Master Key Functions. Communications in Algebra 27, 2207–2222 (1999)
5. Ding, J.: A New Variant of the Matsumoto-Imai Cryptosystem through Perturbation. In: Bao, F., Deng, R., Zhou, J. (eds.) PKC 2004. LNCS, vol. 2947, pp. 305–318. Springer, Heidelberg (2004)
6. Courtois, N.T., Klimov, A., Patarin, J., Shamir, A.: Efficient Algorithms for Solving Overdefined Systems of Multivariate Polynomial Equations. In: Preneel, B. (ed.) EUROCRYPT 2000. LNCS, vol. 1807, pp. 392–407. Springer, Heidelberg (2000)
7. Ding, J., Buchmann, J., Mohamed, M.S.E., Moahmed, W.S.A., Weinmann, R.P.: MutantXL. In: Proceedings of the 1st international conference on Symbolic Computation and Cryptography (SCC 2008), Beijing, China, LMIB, pp. 16–22 (2008), http://www.cdc.informatik.tu-darmstadt.de/reports/reports/MutantXL_Algorithm.pdf
8. Ding, J., Cabarcas, D., Schmidt, D., Buchmann, J., Tohaneanu, S.: Mutant Gröbner Basis Algorithm. In: Proceedings of the 1st international conference on Symbolic Computation and Cryptography (SCC 2008), Beijing, China, LMIB, pp. 23–32 (2008)
9. Courtois, N.T.: Experimental Algebraic Cryptanalysis of Block Ciphers (2007), http://www.cryptosystem.net/aes/toyciphers.html
10. Segers, A.: Algebraic Attacks from a Gröbner Basis Perspective. Master's thesis, Department of Mathematics and Computing Science, TECHNISCHE UNIVERSITEIT EINDHOVEN, Eindhoven (2004)
11. Shigeo, M.: Hotaru (2005), http://cvs.sourceforge.jp/cgi-bin/viewcvs.cgi/hotaru/hotaru/hfe25-96?view=markup
12. Albrecht, M., Bard, G.: M4RI – Linear Algebra over GF(2) (2008), http://m4ri.sagemath.org/index.html

Side Channels in the McEliece PKC

Falko Strenzke[1], Erik Tews[2], H. Gregor Molter[3], Raphael Overbeck[4],
and Abdulhadi Shoufan[3]

[1] FlexSecure GmbH, Germany*
strenzke@flexsecure.de
[2] Cryptography and Computeralgebra, Department of Computer Science,
Technische Universität Darmstadt, Germany
e_tews@cdc.informatik.tu-darmstadt.de
[3] Integrated Circuits and Systems Lab, Department of Computer Science,
Technische Universität Darmstadt, Germany
{molter,shoufan}@iss.tu-darmstadt.de
[4] Ecole Polytechnique Fédérale de Lausanne, Switzerland
raphael.overbeck@epfl.ch

Abstract. The McEliece public key cryptosystem (PKC) is regarded
as secure in the presence of quantum computers because no efficient
quantum algorithm is known for the underlying problems, which this
cryptosystem is built upon. As we show in this paper, a straightforward implementation of this system may feature several side channels.
Specifically, we present a Timing Attack which was executed successfully
against a software implementation of the McEliece PKC. Furthermore,
the critical system components for key generation and decryption are
inspected to identify channels enabling power and cache attacks. Implementation aspects are proposed as countermeasures to face these attacks.

Keywords: side channel attack, timing attack, post quantum cryptography.

1   Introduction

Current cryptographic systems depend on complex mathematical problems such
as the factorization of large prime numbers and the calculation of discrete logarithms [1,2,3,4]. These systems are known to be vulnerable against certain algorithms which could be implemented efficiently on quantum computers [5,6,7].
New classes of cryptographic schemes will be needed to guarantee system and
network security also in the presence of quantum computers. Examples for
theses classes are the hash-based cryptography, such as the Merkle signature
scheme [8,9], and code-based cryptography such as McEliece PKC [10,11].

The McEliece PKC is based on Goppa codes. The strongest known attack
is based on solving the NP-hard decoding problem, and no quantum algorithm
has been proposed which increases the efficiency of this attack [12]. So, although

---

* A part of the work of F. Strenzke was done at[2].

J. Buchmann and J. Ding (Eds.): PQCrypto 2008, LNCS 5299, pp. 216–229, 2008.
© Springer-Verlag Berlin Heidelberg 2008

well-studied regarding its security against algorithm attacks, to the best of our knowledge, the McEliece PKC has never been analyzed with respect to side channel attacks. Side channel attacks target a cryptographic system taking advantage of its implementation [13,14,15,16]. Algorithm execution is associated with measurable quantities such as power consumption and execution time. The amounts of these quantities depend on the data processed by the algorithm. If the processed data is secret such as a private key, then the measured quantities may disclose the secret totally or partially. To prevent side channel attacks, countermeasures must be included during the implementation of the algorithm.

Our contribution

This paper addresses side channel attacks on the McEliece PKC and corresponding countermeasures. It is constructed as follows. Section 2 presents as preliminaries the Goppa code and the McEliece PKC in brief. Section 3 details a timing attack on the degree of error locator polynomial, which is used in the error correction step in the decryption algorithm. A theoretical justification for this attack is presented as well as experimental results of the execution of the attack against a software implementation. Also, countermeasures are addressed. Section 4 outlines two other side channel attacks and related countermeasures: a power attack on the construction of the parity check matrix during key generation and a cache attack on the permutation of code words during decryption. Section 5 concludes the paper.

2 Preliminaries

In this section we assume that the reader is familiar with the basics of error correction codes. We use the notation given e.g. in [17].

2.1 Goppa Codes

Goppa codes [18] are a class of linear error correcting codes. The McEliece PKC makes use of irreducible binary Goppa codes, so we will restrict ourselves to this subclass.

Definition 1. *Let the polynomial*

$$g(Y) = \sum_{i=0}^{t} g_i Y^i \in \mathbb{F}_{2^m}[Y] \tag{1}$$

be monic and irreducible over $\mathbb{F}_{2^m}[Y]$*, and let* m*,* t *be positive integers. Then* $g(Y)$ *is called a* Goppa polynomial *(for an irreducible binary Goppa code).*
  Then an irreducible binary Goppa code is defined as

$$\mathcal{G}(\mathbb{F}_{2^m}, g(Y)) = \{c \in \mathbb{F}_2^n | S_c(Y) := \sum_{i=0}^{n-1} \frac{c_i}{Y - \gamma_i} = 0 \bmod g(Y)\} \tag{2}$$

where $n = 2^m$, $S_c(Y)$ is the syndrome of c, the γ_i, $i = 0, \ldots, n-1$ are pairwise distinct elements of $\mathbb{F}_{2^m}$, and c_i are the entries of the vector c.

The code defined in such way has length n, dimension $k = n - mt$ and can correct up to t errors. The canonical check matrix H for $\mathcal{G}(\mathbb{F}_{2^m}, g(Y))$ can be computed from the syndrome equation and is given in Appendix A.

2.2   The McEliece PKC

The McEliece PKC is named after its inventor [10]. It is a public key encryption scheme based on general coding theory. In the following, we will give a brief description of the individual algorithms for key generation, encryption and decryption, without presenting the mathematical foundations behind the scheme or the consideration of its security. For these considerations, the reader is referred to [19].

Here, we describe the PKC without any CCA2-conversion, as it was originally designed. Without such a conversion, the scheme will be vulnerable against adaptive chosen-ciphertext attacks [19]. However, a suitable conversion, like the Korbara-Imai-Conversion [11], will solve this problem. In Section 3.2 we show that the usage of a CCA2-conversion does not prevent the side channel attack described in Section 3.1.

Parameters of the McEliece PKC. The security parameters $m \in \mathbb{N}$ and $t \in \mathbb{N}$ with $t \ll 2^m$ have to be chosen in order to set up a McEliece PKC. An example for secure values would be $m = 11$, $t = 50$. These values can be derived from the considerations given in [19] or [20]. In addition, $\mathbb{F}_{2^m}$ and the γ_i are public parameters.

Key Generation

The private key. The secret key consists of two parts. The first part of the secret key in the McEliece PKC is a Goppa polynomial $g(Y)$ of degree t over $\mathbb{F}_{2^m}$ according to definition 1, with random coefficients. The second part of the private key is a randomly created $n \times n$ permutation matrix $\mathbf{P}$.

The public key. The public key is generated from the secret key as follows. First, compute $\mathbf{H}$ on the basis of $g(Y)$. Then take $\mathbf{G}^{\mathrm{pub}} = [\mathbb{I}_k \mid \mathbf{R}]$ as the generator in systematic form corresponding to the parity check matrix $\mathbf{H}\mathbf{P}^{\top}$ (refer to Appendix A for the creation of the parity check matrix and the generator of a Goppa code).

Encryption. Assume Alice wants to encrypt a message $v \in \mathbb{F}_2^k$. Firstly, she has to create a random binary vector e of length n and Hamming weight $\mathrm{wt}(e) = t$. Then she computes the ciphertext $z = v\mathbf{G}^{\mathrm{pub}} \oplus e$.

Decryption. In order to decrypt the ciphertext, Bob computes $z\mathbf{P}$. Then he applies error correction by executing an error correction algorithm, such as the Patterson Algorithm described in Section 2.3, to determine $e\mathbf{P}$. Afterwards, he recovers the message v as the first k bits of $z \oplus e\mathbf{P}\mathbf{P}^{-1}$.

2.3   Error Correction for Irreducible Binary Goppa Codes

In the following we briefly describe how error correction can be performed with binary irreducible Goppa codes. The *error correction* of Goppa codes makes use of the so called error locator polynomial

$$\sigma_e(X) = \prod_{j \in \mathcal{T}_e} (X - \gamma_j) \in \mathbb{F}_{2^m}[X], \tag{3}$$

where $\mathcal{T}_e = \{i | e_i = 1\}$ and e is the error vector of the distorted code word to be decoded. Once the error locator polynomial is known, the error vector e is determined as

$$e = (\sigma_e(\gamma_0), \sigma_e(\gamma_1), \cdots, \sigma_e(\gamma_{n-1})) \oplus (1, 1, \cdots, 1). \tag{4}$$

The *Patterson Algorithm* is an efficient algorithm for the determination of the error locator polynomial. It can be found in detail in [19]. We will restrict our description to those features that are necessary to understand the attack we are going to present. Also, we do not provide derivations for most of the equations we specify in the following.

The Patterson Algorithm actually does not determine $\sigma_e(X)$ as defined in Equation 3, but computes $\bar{\sigma}_e(X) = \sigma_e(X) \bmod g(X)$, where $\bar{\sigma}_e(X) = \sigma_e(X)$ if wt $(e) \leqslant t$.

The algorithm uses the fact that the error locator polynomial can be written as

$$\bar{\sigma}_e(X) = \alpha^2(X) + X\beta^2(X). \tag{5}$$

Defining $\tau(X) = \sqrt{S_z^{-1}(X) + X} \bmod g(X)$, with $S_z(X)$ being the syndrome of the distorted code word z, the following equation holds:

$$\beta(X)\tau(X) = \alpha(X) \bmod g(X) \tag{6}$$

Then, assuming that no more than t errors occurred, Equation 6 can be solved by applying the Euclidean algorithm with a breaking condition concerning the degree of the remainder [19]. Specifically, the remainder in the last step is taken as $\alpha(X)$ and the breaking condition is deg $(\alpha(X)) \leqslant \lfloor \frac{t}{2} \rfloor$. It can be shown that then, deg $(\beta(X)) \leqslant \lfloor \frac{t-1}{2} \rfloor$.

From this, it follows that the polynomial $\bar{\sigma}_e(X)$ defined over Equation 5 will be of degree $\leqslant t$. In the case that the number of errors is no larger than t, from Equation 3 it follows that deg $(\bar{\sigma}_e(X)) =$ wt (e) since then $\bar{\sigma}_e(X) = \sigma_e(X)$

For the case of more than t errors, we give the following remark.

Remark 1. If wt $(e) > t$, then the deg $(\bar{\sigma}_e(X)) = t$ with probability $1 - 2^{-m}$.

This remark can be justified easily: Since the $\sigma_e(X)$ computed via Equation 3 would yield deg $(\sigma_e(X)) =$ wt (e), we find that the calculation mod $g(X)$ in Equation 6 leads to polynomials $\bar{\sigma}_e(X)$ of degree t with coefficients that we can assume to be almost randomly distributed, where the leading coefficient is not necessarily non zero. But clearly, for random coefficients out of $\mathbb{F}_{2^m}$, the probability that the leading coefficient is not zero is $1 - 2^{-m}$, which is amounts to 0.9995 for $m = 11$. Furthermore, experimental results confirm the claim of the remark.

3   Attack on the Degree of the Error Locator Polynomial

The dependence of the degree of the error locator polynomial $\bar{\sigma}_e(X)$ on the number of errors in the decoding algorithm, which we examined in Section 2.3, can be used as a basis of a chosen-ciphertext side channel attack. We will describe it as a pure timing attack, though it clearly could be supported by incorporating analysis of the respective power traces.

3.1   The Timing Attack

When computing the error vector according to Equation 4, the error locator polynomial is evaluated 2^m times. Clearly, in a naive implementation, the time taken by the evaluation will increase with the degree of $\bar{\sigma}_e(X)$.

The scenario for our attack is as follows: Alice encrypts a plaintext v to a ciphertext $z = v\mathbf{G}^{\mathrm{pub}} \oplus e$ according to the algorithm described in Section 2.2. Eve receives a copy of z, and mounts the side channel attack by submitting manipulated ciphertexts z_i to Bob, who applies the decryption algorithm according to Section 2.2 to every single one of them. It is assumed that the decryption algorithm makes use of the Patterson Algorithm. Eve is able to measure the execution time of each decryption. In order to achieve a simple model, let us further assume that the only cause of timing differences is the evaluation of the error locator polynomial $\sigma_e(X)$ in the Patterson Algorithm according to Equation 4.

The attack is described in algorithm 1. Here, sparse_vec (i) denotes the vector with zeros as entries except for the i-th position having value 1, and the first position being indexed by 0. The key idea is to flip the bit at position i in z, resulting in z_i, and then to find out whether the i-th position of e was zero or one. This in turn can be derived from the running time of the decryption algorithm on input z_i, since $\bar{\sigma}_e(X)$ will be of degree $t-1$ if $e_i = 1$, and of degree t otherwise.

3.2   The Timing Attack in the Presence of a CCA2-Conversion

A conversion like Pointcheval's [21] or Korbara and Imai's [11] makes sure that ciphertexts manipulated in the way described in algorithm 1 will not be decrypted, i.e. no plaintext will be output by the decryption device. This is ensured by a respective check performed after the error vector e has been determined via the Patterson Algorithm.

However, the possibility of our side channel attack is not affected by this fact, since in the presence of the conversion the attacker will still find a substring of the ciphertext which actually is equivalent to $z = v\mathbf{G}^{\mathrm{pub}} \oplus e$ and choose this as the target of his manipulations. Furthermore, the Patterson Algorithm will run

---

Algorithm 1. Timing Attack against the evaluation of $\sigma_e(X)$

Require: ciphertext z, and the parameter t, of the McEliece PKC.
Ensure: a guess e' of the error vector e used by Alice to encrypt z.
1: **for** $i = 0$ to $n - 1$ **do**
2:     Compute $z_i = z \oplus$ sparse_vec (i).
3:     Take the time u_i as the mean of N measured decryption times where z_i is used
       as the input to the decryption device.
4: **end for**
5: Put the t smallest timings u_i into the set M.
6: **return**   the vector e' with entries $e_i' = 1$ when $u_i \in M$ and all other entries as
   zeros.

---

through all its steps regardless of whether the ciphertext has been manipulated
or not. Only afterwards the algorithm will detect the manipulation and refuse
decryption.

3.3   Implementation of the Attack

We realized the attack against a software implementation of McEliece. Specifically, our target was the implementation of the scheme in the FlexiProvider[1],
which is a Java Cryptographic Extension (JCE) Provider. The implementation
uses the Patterson Algorithm in the decoding step of the decryption phase. For
simplicity, we did not include any CCA2-Conversion.

We executed the attack on an AMD Opteron 2218 CPU running at 2.6 GHz
under Linux 2.6.20 and Java 6 from Sun. A single attack with $N = 2$ took
less than 2 minutes, which makes it very effective and useable in a real world
scenario. Even a remote attack against a TLS server using McEliece seems to be
possible.

The security parameters we used for the attack are $m = 11$ and $t = 50$. The
attack algorithm was realized just as depicted in algorithm 1. With the choice of
$N = 2$ we recovered all positions of e correctly in half of the executed attacks.
The exact results can be found in Appendix C.

3.4   Proposed Countermeasure

The reason for the comparatively high efficiency of the attack is that the error
locator polynomial is evaluated 2^m times in the Patterson Algorithm. For the
security parameter $m = 11$, as in our example, these are 2048 evaluations. This
means that even a small difference in a single evaluation will be inflated to
considerable size.

In order to avoid the differences in the decryption time arising from the different degrees of $\bar{\sigma}_e(X)$, it is a straightforward countermeasure to simply raise
its degree artificially in the case that it is found to be lower than t. Note that
furthermore all coefficients in the polynomial of degree t have to be non zero in
order to avoid timing differences.

---

[1] http://www.flexiprovider.de/

3.5   Improvements of the Attack

The simple version of the timing attack provided in algorithm 1 already enabled successful attacks under idealized conditions. For real life scenarios, two improvements of the attack are feasible.

- Once the attacker has found one position j with $e_j = 1$, he can apply an improved version of the attack. Specifically, he can then create the manipulated ciphertexts

$$z'_i = z_i \oplus \text{sparse\_vec}\,(j)$$

  for all $i \neq j$ and use them as input for the decryption device. As a result, each z'_i will contain either t or $t-2$ errors. Where in algorithm 1 the attacker had to distinguish between timings resulting from degrees of $\bar{\sigma}_e(X)$ differing by 1, this difference in degrees is now 2, resulting in an even higher difference in the timings.
- In the attack given in Algorithm 1, it is already provided that the attacker takes the average time of multiple decryptions of the same ciphertext in order to decrease noise. Still, certain deterministic timing differences could arise in the algorithm, causing certain timings u_p and u_q to differ considerably, even though $e_p = e_q$.

  However, once the attacker knows a number of error and non-error positions, he can modify z_i in a way such that the number of errors remains constant. Each of these ciphertexts will contain the same number of errors with respect to the Goppa code as z_i, but will cause the Patterson Algorithm to start with a different syndrome. Thus, if the attacker averages over the corresponding execution times, he can eliminate the possible timing differences arising from certain syndromes.

4   Other Side Channels

The McEliece system contains several other operations, which enable side channel attacks, if these operations are implemented in a straightforward manner, i.e. one-to-one according to the algorithm specification. In this section, two of these critical operations are presented: the setup of the parity check matrix $\mathbf{H}$ during key generation and the calculation of the matrix $z\mathbf{P}$ during decryption. The first one presents a potential side channel for power attacks [14], the second one for cache attacks [22].

4.1   Generation of Parity Check Matrix

The parity check matrix $\mathbf{H}$ is generated by applying complex matrix operations over $\mathbb{F}_{2^m}$ based on the secret polynomial $g(Y)$. According to [19] an element of the check matrix $\mathbf{H}$ can be written as

$$h_{i,j} = g(\gamma_{j-1})^{-1} \sum_{s=t-i+1}^{t} g_s \gamma_{j-1}^{s-t+i-1}, \tag{7}$$

where $i = 1, \ldots, t$ and $j = 1, \ldots, n$ (see Appendix A).

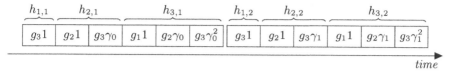

The figure shows a sequence of boxes labeled with braces above:

$h_{1,1}$ | $h_{2,1}$ | $h_{3,1}$ | $h_{1,2}$ | $h_{2,2}$ | $h_{3,2}$

| $g_3 1$ | $g_2 1$ | $g_3 \gamma_0$ | $g_1 1$ | $g_2 \gamma_0$ | $g_3 \gamma_0^2$ | $g_3 1$ | $g_2 1$ | $g_3 \gamma_1$ | $g_1 1$ | $g_2 \gamma_1$ | $g_3 \gamma_1^2$ |

time

Fig. 1. Execution Order: Polynomial Multiplication

Inspecting this relation, two operations may be critical for power attacks [16]. These are the polynomial evaluation for the field elements $g(\gamma_j)$ and the multiplication of the polynomial coefficients with the powers of the field elements $g_s \gamma_{j-1}^{s-t+i-1}$.

Polynomial multiplication. Figure 1 shows schematically the multiplication steps executed to calculate the first and second column of **H**. Here, we use $t = 3$ for simplicity. Remember that **H** has t rows and n columns.

From this figure it is evident that the multiplication steps and, thus, their power traces reveal high regularity. An exact application of the above relation results in multipliying g_3 by 1 once for each column of **H**. Obviously, the power trace of these products may be used to indicate the start of the processing of a new column, which is essential for power attacks. Furthermore, it is highly probable that the power traces of $g_2 \gamma_0$ and $g_2 \gamma_1$ can be used to estimate the secret coefficient g_2 as the γ_i are public.

To complicate this attack, the multiplications $g_s \gamma_{j-1}$ must be performed in a manner, which does not leak information on g_s. This can be achieved (at least partially) by masking. Each g_s is multiplied by a random value $r_i \in \mathbb{F}_{2^m}$ before multiplying it by the field element γ_{j-1}. The de-masking using r_i^{-1} is performed after calculating the sum:

$$h_{i,j} = g(\gamma_{j-1})^{-1} r_i^{-1} \left(\sum_{s=t-i+1}^{t} (r_i g_s) \gamma_{j-1}^{s-t+i-1} \right). \tag{8}$$

In the above equation, the parentheses denote in which order the evaluation shall be performed.

This masking will be even more profitable if it is combined with a randomization of the order of term estimations. By this means the association of power traces with time is blurred considerably.

Polynomial evaluation. This operation is highly time-consuming and is performed in a pre-estimation phase, as a rule. The description in this section relates to this pre-estimation. Referring to the definition of the generator polynomial $g(Y)$, its evaluation for a field element γ_j can be written as $\sum_{i=0}^{t} g_i \gamma_j^i$. This means that polynomial evaluation amounts to multiplication over $\mathbb{F}_{2^m}$ with highly regular patterns, which again presents a possible side channel for power attacks. Fig. 2 depicts the chronological sequence of evaluating a polynomial of degree $t = 3$ for two field elements in a straightforward implementation. Similar to the case presented previously, countermeasures of masking and randomization should be employed.

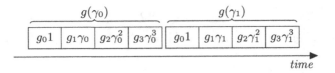

$$g(\gamma_0) \qquad\qquad g(\gamma_1)$$

$g_0 1$	$g_1\gamma_0$	$g_2\gamma_0^2$	$g_3\gamma_0^3$	$g_0 1$	$g_1\gamma_1$	$g_2\gamma_1^2$	$g_3\gamma_1^3$

time

Fig. 2. Execution Order: Polynomial Evaluation

Using polynomial evaluation as power side channels is also possible in the decryption phase when the error vector is determined according to Equation 4.

4.2   Estimation of the Matrix $z\mathbf{P}$

Presenting a possible power analysis attack scenario in Section 4.1, we will now focus upon a possible cache attack [22] scenario. Cache attacks, a specific type of so called microarchitectural attacks, have already been successfully mounted against software implementations [23].

The decryption of a ciphertext may also leak the other private key part, the permutation matrix $\mathbf{P}$. We assume that the permutation matrix itself is not stored directly as a matrix in the memory; it is rather implemented as some lookup-table for the rows and columns to save memory. This lookup-table is used in the decryption phase to compute $z\mathbf{P}$ and $e\mathbf{P}$.

In a straightforward implementation one may calculate these permutations by the following algorithm:

Algorithm 2. Permutation of $z' = z\mathbf{P}$

Require: Private permutation matrix $\mathbf{P}$ lookup-table $t^{\mathbf{P}}$ and ciphertext vector $z \in \mathbb{F}_2^n$.
Ensure: The permutation $z' = z\mathbf{P}$.
 1: **for** $i = 1$ to n **do**
 2:     Lookup $j = t_i^{\mathbf{P}}$.
 3:     Set $z_i' = z_j$.
 4: **end for**
 5: **return** permutated vector z'.

The code in algorithm 2 will create memory access on addresses depending on the secret permutation $\mathbf{P}$. An attacker can use this to gain information about $\mathbf{P}$. Let us assume a scenario where the attacker has access to the system running the decryption process, and where the CPU of the computer supports simultaneous multithreading. The attacker executes a spy process parallel to the process of the decryption application. Let us further assume that the attacker knows the position of z in the main memory. Ideally, between any two iterations of the loop in algorithm 2, the spy process erases the content of z from the CPU cache and fills the respective cache blocks with some data of his own. It also regularly performs memory access to this data, measuring the execution time for this access.

From these timings, gathered while the decryption process was running in parallel, the attacker will be able to judge with certain precision which part of z was accessed during which iteration. Specifically, assume that for a certain iteration the time taken by the memory access of the spy process to a certain date indicates a cache miss. Then the attacker knows that the decryptions process accessed just that part of z, which was stored in the same cache block. Note that the rule relating main memory addresses to cache blocks is system dependent and thus known to the attacker.

Due to the fact that in general the size of a cache block will be larger than one entry z_i, usually the attacker will not be able to get the exact index of the entry of z which has been accessed. Instead he will find out that for example an entry between z_0 and z_{31} must have been accessed. If the memory location of z differs in different executions and does not always have the same offset from the beginning of a cache block, the attacker might be able to narrow the access down to a single entry of z.

In a weaker scenario, where the system running the decryption process does not support simultaneous multithreading, the attacker will not be able to peek into the decryption routine at every iteration, but with some probability the operating system will perform a context switch, interrupting algorithm 2 and continuing the spy process. In such a scenario the attack would be much harder, but still not impossible, assuming the attacker can repeat the measurement often enough.

Countermeasures. A possible contermeasure is to modify algorithm 2 to an algorithm whose memory access doesn't depend on the content of $t^{\mathbf{P}}$. We have implemented algorithm 3, which satisfies this requirement. It has constant running time, performs no jumps depending on secret input, and does only access memory addresses depending on public input. Therefore, it should be secure against timing-, cache-, and branch prediction attacks [24]. Unfortunatly, this increases the running time from $O(2^m)$ to $O((2^m)^2)$. Here, the operators $\sim$, $\&$, $>>$, $\& =$, $|$, and $-$ are used as they are used in the C programming language.

The idea behind algorithm 3 is the following: As in algorithm 2, $t_i^{\mathbf{P}}$ is read in line 2. Algorithm 2 would now read z_j and write it to z_i'. The write to z_i' is not critical, because i is public, but j depends on $\mathbf{P}$ and a read of z_j would reveal information about j and therefore about $\mathbf{P}$.

Algorithm 3 uses the following countermeasure. In line 3, z_i' is initialized with 0. In line 4, a new loop is started, where k runs from 0 to $n-1$. In every iteration, z_i' is read to l and z_k is read to m. Now, we have to distinguish between two cases:

1. $j = k$: In this case, we want to write $m = z_k = z_j$ to z_i', as in algorithm 2.
2. $j \neq k$: In this case, we don't want to modify z_i'. But to create the same memory access as in case 1, we assign $l = z_i'$ to z_i', and therefore leave z_i' unchanged.

In order to do this without an if-then-else statement, the following trick is used by algorithm 3: The XOR-difference s between j and k is computed in

---

Algorithm 3. secure permutation of $z' = z\mathbf{P}$

Require: Private permutation matrix $\mathbf{P}$ lookup-table $t^{\mathbf{P}}$ and ciphertext vector $z \in \mathbb{F}_2^n$
Ensure: The permutation $z' = z\mathbf{P}$

1: **for** $i = 0$ to $n - 1$ **do**
2:    $j = t_i^{\mathbf{P}}$
3:    $z_i' = 0$
4:    **for** $k = 0$ to $n - 1$ **do**
5:       $l = z_i'$
6:       $m = z_k$
7:       $s = j \oplus k$
8:       $s \mathrel{|}= s >> 1$
9:       $s \mathrel{|}= s >> 2$
10:       $s \mathrel{|}= s >> 4$
11:       $s \mathrel{|}= s >> 8$
12:       $s \mathrel{|}= s >> 16$
13:       $s \mathrel{\&}= 1$
14:       $s = \sim (s - 1)$
15:       $z_i' = (s \& l) | ((\sim s) \& m)$
16:    **end for**
17: **end for**
18: **return** z'

---

line 7. If the difference is 0, $j = k$ and we are in case 1. If the difference is not 0, then we are in case 2.

Lines 8 to 14 now make sure, that if s is not 0, all bits in s will be set to 1. Now, the expression $(s \& l) | ((\sim s) \& m)$ will evaluate to l, and l will be written to z_i' in line 15.

If s was 0 after line 7, s will still be 0 after line 14. Now the expression $(s \& l) | ((\sim s) \& m)$ will evaluate to m, and m will be written to z_i' in line 15.

5   Conclusion

In this paper we have shown that the McEliece PKC like most known public key cryptosystems, bears a high risk of leaking secret information through side channels if the implementation does not feature appropriate countermeasures. We have detailed a timing attack, which was also implemented and executed against an existing software implementation of the cryptosystem. Our results show the high vulnerability of an implementation without countermeasures.

Furthermore, we presented a feasible power attack against the key generation phase, where certain operations involve the same secret value repeatedly. In general, key generation is a more difficult target for a side channel attack than decryption, because in contrast to that operation the attacker can only perform one measurement. But our considerations show, that without countermeasures, an implementation of the key generation might be vulnerable to a sophisticated power attack.

The cache attack designed to reveal the permutation that is part of the secret key, again benefits from the fact that the number of measurements the attacker may perform is in principle without any restraint. Thus the proposed secure algorithm seems to be an important countermeasure for software implementations intended for use in a multi user operating system.

Clearly, other parts of the cryptosystem require to be inspected with the same accuracy. This is especially true for the decryption phase, where the secret Goppa polynomial is employed in different operations.

The McEliece PKC, though existing for 30 years, has not experienced wide use so far. But since it is one of the candidates for post quantum public key cryptosystems, it might become practically relevant in the near future. With our work, besides the specific problems and solutions we present, we want to demonstrate that with the experience gathered in recent work exposing the vulnerabilities of other cryptosystems, it is possible to identify the potential side channels in a cryptosystem before it becomes commonly adopted.

References

1. Diffie, W., Hellman, M.: New directions in cryptography. IEEE Transactions on Information Theory 22(6), 644–654 (1976)
2. Rivest, R.L., Shamir, A., Adleman, L.: A method for obtaining digital signatures and public-key cryptosystems. Communications of the ACM 21(2), 120–126 (1978)
3. Miller, V.S.: Use of Elliptic Curves in Cryptography. In: Williams, H.C. (ed.) CRYPTO 1985. LNCS, vol. 218, pp. 417–426. Springer, Heidelberg (1986)
4. ElGamal, T.: A Public Key Cryptosystem and A Signature Based on Discrete Logarims. IEEE Transactions on Information Theory (1985)
5. Shor, P.W.: Algorithms for quantum computation: discrete logarithms and factoring. In: Proceedings, 35-th Annual Symposium on Foundation of Computer Science (1994)
6. Shor, P.W.: Polynomial time algorithms for prime factorization and discrete logarithms on a quantum computer. SIAM Journal on Computing 26(5), 1484–1509 (1997)
7. Proos, J., Zalka, C.: Shor's discrete logarithm quantum algorithm for elliptic curves, Technical Report quant-ph/0301141, arXiv (2006)
8. Merkle, R.: A Certified Digital Signature. In: Proceedings of the 9th Annual International Cryptology Conference on Advances in Cryptology, pp. 218–238 (1989)
9. Buchmann, J., Garcia, L., Dahmen, E., Doering, M., Klintsevich, E.: CMSS-An Improved Merkle Signature Scheme. In: 7th International Conference on Cryptology in India-Indocrypt, vol. 6, pp. 349–363 (2006)
10. McEliece, R.J.: A public key cryptosystem based on algebraic coding theory. DSN progress report 42-44, 114–116 (1978)
11. Korbara, K., Imai, H.: Semantically secure McEliece public-key cryptosystems - conversions for McEliece PKC. In: Kim, K.-c. (ed.) PKC 2001. LNCS, vol. 1992. Springer, Heidelberg (2001)
12. Menezes, A., van Oorschot, P., Vanstone, S.: Handbook of Applied Cryptography. CRC Press, Boca Raton (1996)
13. Kocher, P.: Timing Attacks on Implementations of Diffie-Hellman, RSA, DSS, and Other Systems. In: Proceedings of the 16th Annual International Cryptology Conference on Advances in Cryptology, pp. 104–113 (1996)

14. Kocher, P.: Differential Power Analysis. In: Wiener, M. (ed.) CRYPTO 1999. LNCS, vol. 1666, pp. 388–397. Springer, Heidelberg (1999)
15. Tsunoo, Y., Tsujihara, E., Minematsu, K., Miyauchi, H.: Cryptanalysis of Block Ciphers Implemented on Computers with Cache. In: International Symposium on Information Theory and Applications, pp. 803–806 (2002)
16. Schindler, W., Lemke, K., Paar, C.: A Stochastic Model for Differential Side Channel Cryptanalysis. In: Rao, J.R., Sunar, B. (eds.) CHES 2005. LNCS, vol. 3659, pp. 30–46. Springer, Heidelberg (2005)
17. MacWilliams, F.J., Sloane, N.J.A.: The theory of error correcting codes. North-Holland, Amsterdam (1997)
18. Goppa, V.D.: A new class of linear correcting codes. Problems of Information Transmission 6, 207–212 (1970)
19. Engelbert, D., Overbeck, R., Schmidt, A.: A Summary of McEliece-Type Cryptosystems and their Security. Journal of Mathematical Cryptology (2006) (accepted for publication)
20. Canteaut, A., Chabaud, F.: A new algorithm for finding minimum-weight words in a linear code: application to primitive narrow-sense BCH-codes of length 511. IEEE Transactions on Information Theory 44(1), 367–378 (1998)
21. Pointcheval, D.: Chosen-chipertext security for any one-way cryptosystem. In: Imai, H., Zheng, Y. (eds.) PKC 2000. LNCS, vol. 1751, pp. 129–146. Springer, Heidelberg (2000)
22. Percival, C.: Cache missing for fun and profit, http://www.daemonology.net/papers/htt.pdf
23. Schindler, W., Acıiçmez, O.: A Vulnerability in RSA Implementations due to Instruction Cache Analysis and its Demonstration on OpenSSL. In: Malkin, T. (ed.) CT-RSA 2008. LNCS, vol. 4964, Springer, Heidelberg (2008)
24. Acıiçmez, O., Seifert, J.P., Koç, Ç.: Predicting secret keys via branch prediction. In: Abe, M. (ed.) CT-RSA 2007. LNCS, vol. 4377. Springer, Heidelberg (2007)

A Parity Check Matrix and Generator of an Irreducible Binary Goppa Code

The parity check matrix $\mathbf{H}$ of a Goppa code determined by the Goppa polynomial g can be determined as follows. $\mathbf{H} = \mathbf{XYZ}$, where

$$\mathbf{X} = \begin{bmatrix} g_t & 0 & 0 & \cdots & 0 \\ g_{t-1} & g_t & 0 & \cdots & 0 \\ \vdots & \vdots & \vdots & \ddots & \vdots \\ g_1 & g_2 & g_3 & \cdots & g_t \end{bmatrix}, \mathbf{Y} = \begin{bmatrix} 1 & 1 & \cdots & 1 \\ \gamma_0 & \gamma_1 & \cdots & \gamma_{n-1} \\ \vdots & \vdots & \ddots & \vdots \\ \gamma_0^{t-1} & \gamma_1^{t-1} & \cdots & \gamma_{n-1}^{t-1} \end{bmatrix},$$

$$\mathbf{Z} = \mathrm{diag}\left(\frac{1}{g(\gamma_0)}, \frac{1}{g(\gamma_1)}, \ldots, \frac{1}{g(\gamma_{n-1})}\right).$$

Here $\mathrm{diag}(\ldots)$ denotes the diagonal matrix with entries specified in the argument. $\mathbf{H}$ is $t \times n$ matrix with entries in the field $\mathbb{F}_{2^m}$.

As for any error correcting code, the parity check matrix allows for the computation of the syndrome of a distorted code word:

$$S_{\mathbf{z}}(Y) = \mathbf{z}\mathbf{H}^\top \left(Y^{t-1}, \cdots, Y, 1\right)^\top.$$

The multiplication with $\left(Y^{t-1}, \cdots, Y, 1\right)^{\top}$ is used to turn the coefficient vector into a polynomial in $\mathbb{F}_{2^{mt}}$.

The generator of the code is constructed from the parity check matrix in the following way:

Transform the $t \times n$ matrix $\mathbf{H}$ over $\mathbb{F}_{2^m}$ into an $mt \times n$ matrix $\mathbf{H}_2$ over $\mathbb{F}_2$ by expanding the rows. Then, find an invertible matrix $\mathbf{S}$ such that

$$\mathbf{S} \cdot \mathbf{H}_2 = \left[\mathbb{I}_{mt} \mid \mathbf{R}^{\top}\right],$$

i.e., bring H into a systematic form using the Gauss algorithm. Here, $\mathbb{I}_x$ is the $x \times x$ identity matrix. Now take $\mathbf{G} = [\mathbb{I}_k \mid \mathbf{R}]$ as the public key. $\mathbf{G}$ is a $k \times n$ matrix over $\mathbb{F}_2$, where $k = n - mt$.

B The Extended Euclidean Algorithm (XGCD)

The extended Euclidean algorithm can be used to compute the greatest common divisor (gcd) of two polynomials [17].

In order to compute the gcd of two polynomials $r_{-1}(Y)$ and $r_0(Y)$ with $\deg(r_0)(Y) \leqslant \deg(r_{-1}(Y))$, we make repeated divisions to find the following sequence of equations:

$$\begin{aligned} r_{-1}(Y) &= q_1(Y)r_0(Y) + r_1(Y), & \deg(r_1) &< \deg(r_0), \\ r_0(Y) &= q_2(Y)r_1(Y) + r_2(Y), & \deg(r_2) &< \deg(r_1), \end{aligned}$$

$$\cdots$$

$$\begin{aligned} r_{i-2}(Y) &= q_i(Y)r_{i-1}(Y) + r_j(Y), & \deg(r_i) &< \deg(r_{i-1}), \\ r_{i-1}(Y) &= q_{i+1}(Y)r_i(Y) \end{aligned}$$

Then $r_i(Y)$ is the gcd of $r_{-1}(Y)$ and $r_0(Y)$.

C Experimental Results for the Timing Attack

Here, we show the experimentally determined probabilities (see Section 3.3) for the respective amounts of correctly guessed error positions.

	$N = 1$	$N = 2$
$\text{Prob}\,(\text{wt}\,(e' \oplus e) \leqslant 0)$	0%	48%
$\text{Prob}\,(\text{wt}\,(e' \oplus e) \leqslant 2)$	0%	77%
$\text{Prob}\,(\text{wt}\,(e' \oplus e) \leqslant 4)$	0%	96%
$\text{Prob}\,(\text{wt}\,(e' \oplus e) \leqslant 6)$	4%	99%
$\text{Prob}\,(\text{wt}\,(e' \oplus e) \leqslant 8)$	9%	99%
$\text{Prob}\,(\text{wt}\,(e' \oplus e) \leqslant 10)$	16%	100%
$\text{Prob}\,(\text{wt}\,(e' \oplus e) \leqslant 12)$	22%	100%
$\text{Prob}\,(\text{wt}\,(e' \oplus e) \leqslant 14)$	32%	100%
$\text{Prob}\,(\text{wt}\,(e' \oplus e) \leqslant 16)$	46%	100%
$\text{Prob}\,(\text{wt}\,(e' \oplus e) \leqslant 18)$	60%	100%
$\text{Prob}\,(\text{wt}\,(e' \oplus e) \leqslant 20)$	74%	100%
$\text{Prob}\,(\text{wt}\,(e' \oplus e) \leqslant 22)$	83%	100%
$\text{Prob}\,(\text{wt}\,(e' \oplus e) \leqslant 24)$	89%	100%

Author Index

Lecture Notes in Computer Science

Sublibrary 4: Security and Cryptology

For information about Vols. 1– 4176
please contact your bookseller or Springer

Vol. 4833: K. Kurosawa (Ed.), Advances in Cryptology – ASIACRYPT 2007. XIV, 583 pages. 2007.

Vol. 4817: K.-H. Nam, G. Rhee (Eds.), Information Security and Cryptology - ICISC 2007. XIII, 367 pages. 2007.

Vol. 4812: P. McDaniel, S.K. Gupta (Eds.), Information Systems Security. XIII, 322 pages. 2007.

Vol. 4784: W. Susilo, J.K. Liu, Y. Mu (Eds.), Provable Security. X, 237 pages. 2007.

Vol. 4779: J.A. Garay, A.K. Lenstra, M. Mambo, R. Peralta (Eds.), Information Security. XIII, 437 pages. 2007.

Vol. 4776: N. Borisov, P. Golle (Eds.), Privacy Enhancing Technologies. X, 273 pages. 2007.

Vol. 4752: A. Miyaji, H. Kikuchi, K. Rannenberg (Eds.), Advances in Information and Computer Security. XIII, 460 pages. 2007.

Vol. 4734: J. Biskup, J. López (Eds.), Computer Security – ESORICS 2007. XIV, 628 pages. 2007.

Vol. 4727: P. Paillier, I. Verbauwhede (Eds.), Cryptographic Hardware and Embedded Systems - CHES 2007. XIV, 468 pages. 2007.

Vol. 4691: T. Dimitrakos, F. Martinelli, P.Y.A. Ryan, S. Schneider (Eds.), Formal Aspects in Security and Trust. VIII, 285 pages. 2007.

Vol. 4677: A. Aldini, R. Gorrieri (Eds.), Foundations of Security Analysis and Design IV. VII, 325 pages. 2007.

Vol. 4657: C. Lambrinoudakis, G. Pernul, A.M. Tjoa (Eds.), Trust, Privacy and Security in Digital Business. XIII, 291 pages. 2007.

Vol. 4637: C. Kruegel, R. Lippmann, A. Clark (Eds.), Recent Advances in Intrusion Detection. XII, 337 pages. 2007.

Vol. 4631: B. Christianson, B. Crispo, J.A. Malcolm, M. Roe (Eds.), Security Protocols. IX, 347 pages. 2007.

Vol. 4622: A. Menezes (Ed.), Advances in Cryptology - CRYPTO 2007. XIV, 631 pages. 2007.

Vol. 4593: A. Biryukov (Ed.), Fast Software Encryption. XI, 467 pages. 2007.

Vol. 4586: J. Pieprzyk, H. Ghodosi, E. Dawson (Eds.), Information Security and Privacy. XIV, 476 pages. 2007.

Vol. 4582: J. López, P. Samarati, J.L. Ferrer (Eds.), Public Key Infrastructure. XI, 375 pages. 2007.

Vol. 4579: B.M. Hämmerli, R. Sommer (Eds.), Detection of Intrusions and Malware, and Vulnerability Assessment. X, 251 pages. 2007.

Vol. 4575: T. Takagi, T. Okamoto, E. Okamoto, T. Okamoto (Eds.), Pairing-Based Cryptography – Pairing 2007. XI, 408 pages. 2007.

Vol. 4567: T. Furon, F. Cayre, G. Doërr, P. Bas (Eds.), Information Hiding. XI, 393 pages. 2008.

Vol. 4521: J. Katz, M. Yung (Eds.), Applied Cryptography and Network Security. XIII, 498 pages. 2007.

Vol. 4515: M. Naor (Ed.), Advances in Cryptology - EUROCRYPT 2007. XIII, 591 pages. 2007.

Vol. 4499: Y.Q. Shi (Ed.), Transactions on Data Hiding and Multimedia Security II. IX, 117 pages. 2007.

Vol. 4464: E. Dawson, D.S. Wong (Eds.), Information Security Practice and Experience. XIII, 361 pages. 2007.

Vol. 4462: D. Sauveron, K. Markantonakis, A. Bilas, J.-J. Quisquater (Eds.), Information Security Theory and Practices. XII, 255 pages. 2007.

Vol. 4450: T. Okamoto, X. Wang (Eds.), Public Key Cryptography – PKC 2007. XIII, 491 pages. 2007.

Vol. 4437: J.L. Camenisch, C.S. Collberg, N.F. Johnson, P. Sallee (Eds.), Information Hiding. VIII, 389 pages. 2007.

Vol. 4392: S.P. Vadhan (Ed.), Theory of Cryptography. XI, 595 pages. 2007.

Vol. 4377: M. Abe (Ed.), Topics in Cryptology – CT-RSA 2007. XI, 403 pages. 2006.

Vol. 4356: E. Biham, A.M. Youssef (Eds.), Selected Areas in Cryptography. XI, 395 pages. 2007.

Vol. 4341: P.Q. Nguyên (Ed.), Progress in Cryptology - VIETCRYPT 2006. XI, 385 pages. 2006.

Vol. 4332: A. Bagchi, V. Atluri (Eds.), Information Systems Security. XV, 382 pages. 2006.

Vol. 4329: R. Barua, T. Lange (Eds.), Progress in Cryptology - INDOCRYPT 2006. X, 454 pages. 2006.

Vol. 4318: H. Lipmaa, M. Yung, D. Lin (Eds.), Information Security and Cryptology. XI, 305 pages. 2006.

Vol. 4307: P. Ning, S. Qing, N. Li (Eds.), Information and Communications Security. XIV, 558 pages. 2006.

Vol. 4301: D. Pointcheval, Y. Mu, K. Chen (Eds.), Cryptology and Network Security. XIII, 381 pages. 2006.

Vol. 4300: Y.Q. Shi (Ed.), Transactions on Data Hiding and Multimedia Security I. IX, 139 pages. 2006.

Vol. 4298: J.K. Lee, O. Yi, M. Yung (Eds.), Information Security Applications. XIV, 406 pages. 2007.

Vol. 4296: M.S. Rhee, B. Lee (Eds.), Information Security and Cryptology – ICISC 2006. XIII, 358 pages. 2006.

Vol. 4284: X. Lai, K. Chen (Eds.), Advances in Cryptology – ASIACRYPT 2006. XIV, 468 pages. 2006.

Vol. 4283: Y.Q. Shi, B. Jeon (Eds.), Digital Watermarking. XII, 474 pages. 2006.

Vol. 4266: H. Yoshiura, K. Sakurai, K. Rannenberg, Y. Murayama, S.-i. Kawamura (Eds.), Advances in Information and Computer Security. XIII, 438 pages. 2006.

Vol. 4258: G. Danezis, P. Golle (Eds.), Privacy Enhancing Technologies. VIII, 431 pages. 2006.

Vol. 4249: L. Goubin, M. Matsui (Eds.), Cryptographic Hardware and Embedded Systems - CHES 2006. XII, 462 pages. 2006.

Vol. 4237: H. Leitold, E.P. Markatos (Eds.), Communications and Multimedia Security. XII, 253 pages. 2006.

Vol. 4236: L. Breveglieri, I. Koren, D. Naccache, J.-P. Seifert (Eds.), Fault Diagnosis and Tolerance in Cryptography. XIII, 253 pages. 2006.

Vol. 4219: D. Zamboni, C. Krügel (Eds.), Recent Advances in Intrusion Detection. XII, 331 pages. 2006.

Vol. 4189: D. Gollmann, J. Meier, A. Sabelfeld (Eds.), Computer Security – ESORICS 2006. XI, 548 pages. 2006.